M000035501

PEARSON BACCALAUREATE

English: A
Literature

JAN ADKINS • CONRAD HUGHES

Supporting every learner across the IB continuum

Pearson Education Limited is a company incorporated in England and Wales, having its registered office at Edinburgh Gate, Harlow, Essex, CM20 2JE. Registered company number: 872828.

www.pearsonglobalschools.com

Text © Pearson Education Limited 2011

First published 2011

20 19 18 17 16 15
IMP 10 9 8 7 6 5 4 3

ISBN 978 0 435032 62 3

Edited by Chris McNab/Editorial assistant Judith John
Designed by Tony Richardson
Typeset by TechType
Original illustrations © Pearson Education Limited 2011
Illustrated by TechType
Cover design by Tony Richardson
Printed in Slovakia by Neografia

Acknowledgements and dedications

We would like to thank several students whose essays were used in the Commentary and Comparative Essay chapters: Hannah Couture, Erica Edmondson, Will Keyes, Maggie Tobin, and Kelly Vasbinder. Conrad Hughes would also like to dedicate this book to Estelle, Melchior and Héloise.

The authors and publisher would like to thank the following individuals and organizations for permission to reproduce photographs:

(Key: b-bottom; c-centre; l-left; r-right; t-top)

Alamy Images: vl, vr, 40bl, 41t, 43br, 44tl, 88 (essay), 88 (manifesto), 89tr, 89cl, 90cl, 93cr, vicr, 100c, 100r, 122cr, 127cl, 132tr, 163l, 163r, 165bl, 186tr, 190b, 196b, 247tr, 248tl, 254b, 264br, 266tl, 267tl, 268tr, 270tl; **Corbis:** 94l, 183br, 186tc; **Fotolia.com:** 62cl, 88 (newspapers), 88 (sign), 90tl, vitr, 100l, 114br, 148tr, 148br, 163c, 169cr, 170tc (scales), 170tr, 170bc, 171tr, 180bl, 188bl, 211l, 228 (rice field), 229b, 244l, 261tr; **Getty Images:** 44tr, 186tl, 192bl; **Glow Images:** 94r, 96tl, 96cl, 96bl; **iStockphoto:** 191cr, 228 (market); **Pearson Education Ltd:** 3tl, 3tr, 3bl, 3br, 4b, 16c, 17br, 22t, 79tr, 262tl, 264bl; **Shutterstock.com:** 39b, 41b, 42tl, 42cr, 42bl, 61br, 82bl, 85tr, 121tl, 175t, 196t, 211r, 228 (beach), 228 (cafe shop), 228 (cow), 228 (mosque), 228 (new york), 230b, 237tr, 244r

All other images © Pearson Education Limited

Every effort has been made to trace the copyright holders and we apologize in advance for any unintentional omissions. We would be pleased to insert the appropriate acknowledgment in any subsequent edition of this publication.

The assessment statements, assessment information and past examination questions have been reproduced from IBO documents and past examination papers. Our thanks go to the International Baccalaureate Organization for permission to reproduce its intellectual copyright.

The publisher and authors would also like to thank the following for permission to use © material:

Extract from *The Invisible Man* by Ralph Ellison. Published by Penguin / Random House US; Extract from *The Sorrow of War* by Bao Ninh. Published by Pantheon Books; Extract from *Things Fall Apart* by Chinua Achebe. Published by Heinemann; Extract from *The Old Gringo* by Carlos Fuentessions. Published by Farrar Strauss Giroux (1985); Extract from *The Pickup* by Nadine Gordimer. Reproduced by permission of Bloomsbury Publishing; Extract from *Accident: A Day's News* by Christa Wolf. Published by Farrar Strauss Giroux (1989); Bapsi Sidhwa, extract from *Cracking India* (Minneapolis: Milkweed Editions, 1992). Copyright © 1992 by Bapsi Sidhwa. Reprinted with permission from Milkweed Editions (www.milkweed.org); Extract from *Purple Hibiscus* by Chimamanda Ngozi Adichie. Copyright Chimamanda Ngozi Adichie, 2003. Reprinted by permission of

HarperCollins Publishers Ltd; Extract from *Oryx and Crake* by Margaret Atwood, copyright O. W. Toad 2003. Reproduced by permission of Bloomsbury Publishing; Extract from *Their Eyes Were Watching God* by Zora Neale Hurston. Reproduced with permission of Little Brown Publishers. Copyright 1937 by Harper & Row, Publishers, Inc., renewed copyright 1965 by John C. Hurston and Joel Hurston. Reprinted by permission of HarperCollins Publishers; From *The Wars* by Timothy Findley. Copyright Timothy Findley, 1977. Reprinted by permission of Penguin Group (Canada); Extract from *Fiela's Child* by Dalene Matthee. Published by Penguin / University of Chicago Press; Extract from *July's People* by Nadine Gordimer. Published by Jonathan Cape Ltd. (Random House) / A P Watt; Extract from *Monkey Bridge* by Lan Cao. Published by Penguin Putnam Inc; Open market edition (19 Nov 2001); Extract from *As I Lay Dying* by William Faulkner. Reproduced with permission of Curtis Brown Group Ltd, London on behalf of The Estate of William Faulkner, Copyright William Faulkner 1930. Reprinted by permission of Random House Inc; Extract from 'Roselily' by Alice Walker; Extract from 'The Handsomest Drowned Man in the World' by Gabriel Garcia Marquez. Published by Lectorum Publications Inc; Extract from 'Short Cuts' by Raymond Carver, published by The Harvill Press. Reprinted by permission of The Random House Group Ltd; Extract from *The Empty Space* by Peter Brook. Copyright © 1968 by Peter Brook. All rights reserved. Reprinted with permission of Scribner, a division of Simon & Schuster, Inc; Text of Act 1 of *A Doll's House* by Henrik Ibsen (trans. James McFarlane); Extract from *'Master Harold'... and the boys* by Athol Fugard, 1982. Published by Samuel French Trade; Extract from Act 1 of *The Visit* by Friedrich Durrenmatt's play (trans. by Patrick Bowles), 1956. Published by Jonathan Cape Ltd. (Random House); Poem 'Planetarium' by Adrienne Rich, (1968). Published by W.W. Norton & Co; Extract from 'Poetry: The Unsayable Said' by Donald Hall, 1993 (http://www.negotiationlawblog.com/uploads/file/The%20Unsayable%20Said%20Hall.pdf). Published by Copper Canyon Press; Poem 'Poetry' by Marianne Moore, (1924). Published by Faber & Faber; Extract from 'Blood' (1986) from *19 Varieties of Gazelle: Poems of the Middle East* by Naomi Shihab Nye. Published by Greenwillow Books (Harper Collins); Poem 'My Son, My Executioner' by Donald Hall, (1955). Published by Houghton Mifflin; Poem 'The Writer' from *Collected Poems 1943-2004* copyright © 2004 by Richard Wilbur, reprinted by permission of Houghton Mifflin Harcourt Publishing Company; Poem 'Digging' by Seamus Heaney, (1980). Published by Faber & Faber; Poem 'Cinderella' by Anne Sexton, (1970). Published by Houghton Mifflin; Poem 'Those Winter Sundays'. Copyright 1966 by Robert Hayden, from *Collected Poems of Robert Hayden* by Robert Hayden, edited by Frederick Glaysher. Used by Permission of Liveright Publishing Corporation; Poem 'My Papa's Waltz' by Theodore Roethke (1948). Published by Doubleday / Random House US; Poem 'Buffalo Bill's' by E.E. Cummings. Copyright 1923, 1951, 1991 by the Trustees for the E.E. Cummings Trust. Copyright 1976 by George James Firmage, from *Complete Poems:1904–1962* by E.E. Cummings, edited by George J. Firmage. Used by permission of Liveright Publishing Corporation; Poem 'How Everything Happens' by May Swenson (1967). Published by Houghton Mifflin; Poem 'In the Rear-View Mirror' from *Below the Surface*. Copyright 1999 by Robert B. Shaw. Used by permission of Copper Beech Press, P.O. Box 2578, Providence, RI 02906, USA; Poem 'A Lesson for this Sunday' by Derek Walcott (1962). Published by Farrar, Straus & Giroux; Poem 'Night Crossing' by Sylvia Kantaris (1989). Published by Bloodaxe Books; Poem 'Water' by Robert Lowell (d. 1977). Published by Farrar, Straus & Giroux; Poem 'Curiosity' by Alastair Reid (1978). Reproduced by permission of Birlinn Ltd; Poem 'Patchwork' by Eavan Boland, (2007). Published by W.W. Norton & Co; Albert Camus' essay 'The Myth of Sisyphus' (1942): http://www.sccs.swarthmore.edu/users/00/pwillen1/lit/msysip.htm. Published by Penguin; Extract from 'Strike Against War' by Helen Keller, (1916) http://famousquotes.me.uk/speeches/Helen-Keller/index.htm. Published by Dodo Press; Extract from *If This is a Man* by Primo Levi (1979). Reproduced by permission of Random House Group; Extract from 'Letter from a Birmingham Jail' by Martin Luther King Jr., (1963) http://www.africa.upenn.edu/Articles_Gen/Letter_Birmingham.html; Extract from 'Shooting an Elephant' by George Orwell, (1936) http://www.online-literature.com/orwell/887/. Published by Penguin; Extract from 'Tragedy and the Common Man' an Essay by Arthur Miller, 1949. Published by Methuen Drama; Extract from 'I have a Dream' by Martin Luther King Jr., http://www.dadalos.org/deutsch/vorbilder/vorbilder/mlk/dream.htm; Extract from 'We Will Fight Them on the Beaches' by Winston Churchill, http://history.hanover.edu/courses/excerpts/111chur.html; Extract from Barack Obama's Inaugural Address; Extract from *The Feminine Mystique* by Betty Friedan, published by Victor Gollancz, an imprint of The Orion Publishing Group. Reprinted by permission of The Orion Publishing Group, London; Poem 'Two Sisters of Persephone' by Sylvia Plath, (1956). Published by Faber & Faber; Poem 'Child and Insect' by Robert Druce, (1980). Published by Brockhampton Press (Hodder Headline); Poem 'Night Crossing' by Sylvia Kantaris, (1989). Published by Bloodaxe Books; Poem 'The Sleeping Zemis' from *Turn Thanks: Poems*. Copyright 1999 by Lorna Goodison. Used with permission of the poet and the University of Illinois Press; Extract from *Beloved* by Toni Morrison, (1987). Published by Everyman Press; HL paper 1, 1996 exam, from Peter Carey's *Oscar and Lucinda* (1988). Published by Harper Perennial US / Faber & Faber; Poem 'Penelope' by Carol Ann Duffy, (2001); Poem 'Pomegranates' from *The Bad Poetry Collection* by Conrad Hughes; Poem 'The Mowed Hollow' from *Conscious and Verbal* by Les Murray, (1999). Published by Farrar, Straus & Giroux; Extract from 'Deadly Identities' by Amin Maalouf, (1998). Published by Vintage Classics (Random House); Poem 'The Road Not Taken' from *The Poetry of Robert Frost* edited by Edward Connery Latham, published by Jonathan Cape. Reprinted by permission of The Random House Group Ltd; Poem 'Waiting for the Barbarians' by C.P. Cavafy, translated by Edmund Keeley. Copyright © 1975 by Edmund Keeley and Philip Sherrard. Reprinted by permission of Princeton University Press.; Extract from *The Narrow Road to the Deep North and Other Travel Sketches* by Matsuo Basho (Translated by Nobuyuki Yuasa), (1966) http://www.cddc.vt.edu/bps/gateway/passages/basho-oku.htm. Published by Penguin Classics; Extract from 'Song of Lawino' by Okot p'Bitek, (1966) http://danielruhweza.blogspot.com/2011/02/excerpt-from-song-of-lawino.html. Published by East African Educational Publishers Ltd; *Theory of Knowledge* by Ernst Cassirer. Reproduced by permission of Yale University Press.

CONTENTS

INTRODUCTION

What is literature?

Literature is at the heart of human expression. It is an art form that deals with the human condition in four different genres: poetry, fiction, prose non-fiction (or 'prose other than fiction') and drama.

The oldest forms of literature are non-fictional inventories and descriptions of events, battles and settlements, such as the fascinating depiction of battle ordained on the Narmer Palette and poems such as the Sumerian epic *Gilgamesh*. These date back about 5,000 years.

If we are to consider the oral tradition, story-telling goes back even further – myths and legends seem to have been in existence as long as human beings have had a conscious recollection and understanding of the world.

Poetry became the dominant form of literature in the Middle East and Mediterranean from about 700 BC, with famous poets being Sappho and Homer. The tradition of epic poetry continued into the Roman and medieval periods with the works of Virgil and Dante.

 Ancient classics

Homer is considered the most important epic poet of ancient Greece. His two masterpieces, *The Iliad* and *The Odyssey*, respectively describing a period of the Trojan War and Odysseus' trip back from Troy to Ithaca, remain central literary archetypes in Western literature. Virgil, the famous Latin poet who wrote under Augustus, tells the story of Aeneas, a Trojan who finds his way back from Troy to Italy in his Latin masterpiece *The Aeneid*.

Story-telling goes back as far as we can trace our history. On the left we see the Narmer Palette – an Egyptian pictorial tablet dating back to the 31st century BC – and on the right Lascaux cave paintings from France, estimated at 17,300 years old.

Theatre as an established and popular art form became prominent in ancient Greece, particularly around 500 BC, when the famous Attic poets Aeschylus, Euripides and Sophocles wrote tragedies for the festival of Dionysus in Athens, along with figures such as Aristophanes, who wrote comedies. Drama was a prominent form of literary expression throughout the Middle Ages too, with the so-called 'morality plays' reflecting on ethical dilemmas and spiritual conduct. The explosion of popular theatre in the Renaissance (14th–17th centuries) put Shakespeare at the forefront of drama, and to this day his plays are considered unsurpassed works of extraordinary genius.

There is some debate over what stands as history's first novel. Some say it is La Fayette's *La Princesse de Clèves*, others cite Cervantes' *Don Quixote,* while English critics often point to Daniel Defoe's *Moll Flanders*. The debate is in part due to the difficulty of defining the exact parameters of the novel, as here we have a form that is not as simple to delineate as poetry or drama. In any case, it was after the invention of the printing press in the 15th century that it became possible to circulate extended pieces of prose for wider readership, and this in part is what led to the development of this genre.

Some would argue that the Golden Age of the novel was the 19th century, where the art form was brought to a high point of elaborate literary expression by such masters as Dostoevsky, Tolstoy, Goethe, Balzac, Stendhal, Eliot, Austen, Dickens, Hardy and Melville. The 20th century brought a new type of style with it – more concentrated and immediate, with groundbreaking examples being Kafka's *The Trial*, Camus' *The Outsider*, Fitzgerald's *The Great Gatsby* and Golding's *Lord of the Flies.*

Shakespeare's so-called 'Major Tragedies' are *Othello, King Lear, Macbeth, Hamlet* and *Antony and Cleopatra.*

In essence, the study of literature is a voyage into the minds of great men and women, an exploration of the inner eye of the psyche and possibly the most complex and nuanced of all art forms. To read a fine work of literature is to be moved and taken to a different place and time as Chapter 1 explains in its discussion of fiction.

The IB English A Literature Course

IB English A is a course designed to make you appreciate literature all the more. You will read different genres, engage in close-reading activities, discuss the role of context and culture in literary production, appreciate literary conventions and improve your own powers of literary expression as you go along.

The course will hopefully inspire you to keep reading throughout your life, and look at literature in an increasingly critical manner. One of the things you will be doing as you work through it is to develop your understanding of literary criticism.

These are the aims of all Group 1 courses as specified in the IB student guide:

Franz Kafka's prose brought fiction to a new point of literary expression in which, as opposed to the more didactic style of the 19th century, feelings of angst, alienation and anonymity were evoked in the reader.

1. Introduce students to a range of texts from different periods, styles and genres.

2. Develop in students the ability to engage in close, detailed analysis of individual texts and make relevant connections.

3. Develop the students' powers of expression, both in oral and written communication.

4. Encourage students to recognize the importance of the contexts in which texts are written and received.

5. Encourage, through the study of texts, an appreciation of the different perspectives of people from other cultures, and how these perspectives construct meaning.

6. Encourage students to appreciate the formal, stylistic and aesthetic qualities of texts.

7. Promote in students an enjoyment of, and lifelong interest in, language and literature.

IB Learner Profile and links to ToK

The literature course is not only an expression of the human condition, but a chance for you to explore the Learner Profile through it. As you read through works of literature and consider the social, ethical, cultural, artistic and philosophical implications that they have, you are improving your mind, learning about yourself as a reader and widening your awareness of the human condition. The self-aware reader can use literature as much to learn about life as art.

The IB's emphasis on international awareness is something that is brought out strongly in the study of literature, particularly when you approach the topic of works in translation. Indeed, hardly any other form of expression is so powerful as literature, so embodied in a cultural context and at the same time so capable of powerful universality.

Your abilities in critical thinking will be enhanced by studying literature. Remember that accepting critical feedback will make you a better scholar and a better person, and lead to improvements in your intellectual ability. As you read through this book you will see links to Global Perspectives and Theory of Knowledge (ToK). These are there to help you make connections and reflect on interrelationships.

How you will be assessed
Standard Level
Assessment component weighting
External assessment (3 hours) 70 per cent

Paper 1: Guided literary analysis (1 hour 30 minutes)
The paper consists of two passages: one prose and one poetry. Students choose one and write a guided literary analysis in response to two questions.
(20 marks – 20 per cent)

Paper 2: Essay (1 hour 30 minutes)
The paper consists of three questions for each literary genre. In response to one question students write an essay based on at least two works studied in Part 3.
(25 marks – 25 per cent)

Written assignment
Students submit a reflective statement and literary essay on one work studied in Part 1. The reflective statement must be 300–400 words in length. The essay must be 1,200–1,500 words in length.
(25 marks – 25 per cent)

Internal assessment 30 per cent

This component is internally assessed by the teacher and externally moderated by the IB at the end of the course.

Individual oral commentary (10 minutes)
Students present a formal oral commentary and answer subsequent questions on an extract from a work studied in Part 2.
(30 marks – 15 per cent)

Individual oral presentation (10–15 minutes)
The presentation is based on works studied in Part 4. It is internally assessed and externally moderated through the Part 2 internal assessment task.
(30 marks – 15 per cent)

Higher Level

Assessment component weighting
External assessment (4 hours) 70 per cent

Paper 1: Literary Commentary (2 hours)
The paper consists of two passages: one prose and one poetry. Students choose one and write a literary commentary.
(20 marks – 20 per cent)

Paper 2: Essay (2 hours)
The paper consists of three questions for each literary genre. In response to one question students write an essay based on at least two works studied in Part 3.
(25 marks – 25 per cent)

Written assignment
Students submit a reflective statement and literary essay on one work studied in Part 1. The reflective statement must be 300–400 words in length. The essay must be 1,200–1,500 words in length.
(25 marks – 25 per cent)

Internal assessment 30 per cent

This component is internally assessed by the teacher and externally moderated by the IB at the end of the course.

Individual oral commentary and discussion (20 minutes)
Formal oral commentary on poetry studied in Part 2 with subsequent questions (10 minutes), followed by a discussion based on one of the other Part 2 works (10 minutes).
(30 marks – 15 per cent)

Individual oral presentation (10–15 minutes)
The presentation is based on works studied in Part 4. It is internally assessed and externally moderated through the Part 2 internal assessment task.
(30 marks – 15 per cent)

The Extended Essay

If you are considering an extended essay in literature, then you must be ready to do extra reading and follow your passion for literature through to a different level. It is a great opportunity for you to gain some hands-on experience as a young scholar, and a chance for you to learn more about literary expression from a broader perspective. View the Extended Essay and Theory of Knowledge chapters to learn more about this.

Information boxes

Throughout the book, you will see a number of coloured boxes interspersed through each chapter. They may be in the margins or in the main text area. Each of these boxes provides different information and stimulus as follows.

Learning Outcomes

Knowledge and Understanding
- Understand what it means to be an active, close reader
- Consider the importance of a writer's choice of point of view
- Identify the variations of characterization
- Understand the function and importance of plot, setting and time
- Understand theme and structure

Appreciation
- Identify the nuance of a speaker
- Identify and analyze details that create effect
- Appreciate tone such as irony and its relationship to voice
- Determine point of view and effect
- Analyse characterization within the text
- Evaluate stylistic features in fiction

You will find a **Learning Outcomes** box like this at the start of each chapter. They define the learning outcomes for the chapter you are about to read, and they set out what content and aspects of learning are covered in the chapter.

In addition to the ToK chapter, there are **ToK** boxes throughout the book. These boxes are there to stimulate thought and consideration of any ToK issues as they arise and in context. Often they will just contain a question to stimulate your own thoughts and discussion.

The **Interesting Facts** boxes contain interesting information that will add to your wider knowledge, but which does not fit within the main body of the text.

To what extent can we look at works of art as expressions of culture?

Syllogism
A syllogism is a logically constructed argument. For a syllogism to be valid, the conclusion must be drawn from the premise correctly. For example, a valid syllogism would be: 'All men are mortal. Socrates is a man. Therefore Socrates is mortal.' An invalid syllogism would be: 'All men are mortal. Socrates is mortal. Therefore Socrates is a man.' Note that this is wrong because Socrates could be a dog or something else; we have mixed up the category and the rule, unlike in the first example where the correct order has been followed.

The green **Key Facts** boxes contain key facts that are drawn out from the main text and highlighted. This makes them easily identifiable for quick reference. The boxes also enable you to identify the core learning points within a section.

The IB Learner Profile stresses the importance of being a good communicator and someone who can share ideas. The oral presentation can help you develop these qualities.

Examiner's hints provide insight into how to answer a question in order to achieve the highest marks in an examination. They also identify common pitfalls when answering such questions and suggest approaches that examiners like to see.

● **Examiner's hints**
There are only two ways to avoid academic dishonesty:
1. Telling the reader and audience each time you use an idea that is not your own;
2. Using your own ideas.

Examiner's comments boxes provide analysis of sample student essays, helping you to see examples of strong and weak approaches to questions, and where an answer would be situated in the IB markbands. These boxes also give advice on how to pick up additional marks.

Examiner's comments

This answer would probably be situated – roughly – in the 3–4 band of the assessment criteria: 'There is some knowledge and superficial understanding of the content of the work(s) presented.' The description is not very detailed and there is little elaboration on the points made. Furthermore, the response is tentative ('seems to') and does not bring us to any affirmative statements. The understanding is superficial because clearly there is a more subtle and nuanced undertone to the poem than the idea of the end of the world. We need to take it further.

The **Global Perspectives** boxes provide a broader and often international insight into the topic you are studying or the skills you are developing.

GLOBAL PERSPECTIVES

The IB Learner Profile stresses the importance of being a good communicator and someone who can share ideas. The oral presentation can help you develop these qualities.

To access worksheet 1.1 on evaluation of research, please visit www.pearsonbacconline.com and follow the on-screen instructions.

Blue **Online Resources** boxes indicate that online resources are available that relate to this section of the book. These resources might be extension exercises, additional practice questions, interactive material, suggestions for Internal Assessment (IA), Extended Essay (EE) and revision, or other sources of information.

Summary boxes consolidate key passages of information, and bring together ideas covered in the preceding sections. They can act as useful points for revision or clarification.

SUMMARY

Narrative voice cannot be distinguished from narrator. The 'tone of voice' that we associate with any speaker can be used to describe the narrative voice of any fiction text. When we determine voice, we, in a sense, embody the narrator. If that narrator is first person, we have a character, a body, on which to hang that voice. In third person, however, the disembodied voice of the narrator is not without understanding and not without judgement or bias. The only narrative voice that does not judge, that is not embodied, is the objective point of view.

Insights boxes consolidate the material you have studied in the entire chapter. They are handy for reminding yourself of key themes and major points about the study of literature, and to provide guidance on tackling your IB English A course.

INSIGHTS INTO FICTION

So what are the conventions of fiction and what expectations should you have as a reader?

The world of fiction is a world with its own time and place. It has its own weather, its own history and its own moral code. The characters that inhabit these worlds are not to be confused with real people, but they may amuse and frighten or surprise us in much the same way and for many of the same reasons that people do. Fiction writers invite their readers into their worlds and hold them there with stories and characters that engage a reader intellectually and emotionally. When we experience the world of a text, when we engage with it, when we willingly immerse ourselves in that world, we read actively. **It is only through active reading that we can experience a text.**

Introduction to the Conventions chapters

The English A: Literature course will include the study of different types of literature. These types, commonly referred to as 'genres', include drama, fiction, poetry and prose other than fiction (also known as non-fiction). Each of these genres requires different perspectives from you as a reader, and it is important to know what these requirements are so that you can approach your reading with confidence. The key to analysis and interpretation relies on a clear and precise knowledge of each genre's conventions. Conventions, quite simply, are the established 'rules' that writers use. If we read with a sharp understanding of these conventions, then we can know what is expected of us as readers and can judge whether the text before us is representative of a particular genre.

It is critical to understand that each genre has its own particular set of conventions, or expectations. The writers of fiction, for example, use certain strategies to create their narratives. These narrative strategies, or narrative techniques, are particular to the writing of the short story and the novel. As a confident reader, you can approach any work of fiction and come to appreciate that work in terms of its genre. That appreciation comes about through the ability to measure one text in terms of the conventions of that genre. Being aware of these conventions will allow you to respond to the emotional and literary effects of a particular text. It is your awareness of these effects that forms the basis of your analysis and/or interpretation of a work of literature.

The next four chapters will introduce each of the four genres individually and will provide you with knowledge of their conventions. From these chapters, you will learn what each genre expects from you as a reader, what strategies you can expect to encounter as you read, and how these expectations will provide you with a basis for understanding, analyzing, or interpreting a text.

Each Convention chapter includes three sections: Knowledge and Understanding, Appreciation, and Insight:

- In the Knowledge and Understanding section you will learn about the conventions of the genre and the strategies that are available to the writer. These conventions and strategies comprise the expectations that you will have as a reader of the genre.
- In the Appreciation section you will apply those expectations by examining samples from specific textual exercises.
- In the Insight section you will find a series of summary questions that can guide your reading and, subsequently, your analytical approach to the genre.

CONVENTIONS OF FICTION

Learning Outcomes

Knowledge and Understanding
- Understand what it means to be an active, close reader
- Consider the importance of a writer's choice of point of view
- Identify the variations of characterization
- Understand the function and importance of plot, setting and time
- Understand theme and structure

Appreciation
- Identify the nuance of a speaker
- Identify and analyze details that create effect
- Appreciate tone such as irony and its relationship to voice
- Determine point of view and effect
- Analyse characterization within the text
- Evaluate stylistic features in fiction

Knowledge and Understanding

When we read prose fiction, whether a short story or a novel, we most often read alone and in private. The images associated with reading prose – a comfy chair, a quiet space – speak to the nature of the form itself. This genre creates a writer's world bit by bit, over time, through a voice that speaks to the silent reader. The readers' ability to shut out their own world and immerse themselves in the world of prose fiction often determines whether the reading experience is a satisfying one.

The world created within a novel can encompass a range of emotions, from terrifying to amusing, but the satisfying experience of every prose fiction text is built on engaging the reader emotionally, or intellectually, or both. Engaging a reader involves many strategies, and no two novels or short stories are alike in creating the kind of hermetic seal that keeps the reader's external world at bay for those minutes or hours of reading. Short stories are often read in one sitting simply due to their length, but reading novels requires more than one sitting. Novels are picked up and laid aside, sometimes for periods of weeks. Because of variations in the act of reading itself, novelists structure their texts to accommodate this process. Sections, chapters and interstices (white space or gaps on a page) function as natural breaks for the reader, and novelists can use these breaks as part of their narrative strategy.

Short story writers and novel writers share many of the same narrative strategies in creating the worlds of their fiction. Features used by authors of all prose fiction to bring these worlds to life include:

- point of view
- voice
- characterization
- plot
- setting
- theme
- time
- structure

In private moments or shared moments, reading on a park bench or in bed, fiction has the power to transport us into different worlds.

Thinking vs. feeling

When we experience a fiction text, we open ourselves to the effects of the text. Sometimes those effects trigger an emotional response, and other times the effect is intellectual, but a full and satisfying experience incorporates both thinking and feeling. As readers of a genre, we need to be aware of our reactions but also what triggers them. Being conscious of your responses, your reactions, requires close reading of the text. In close reading you focus not only on the literal meaning of the words but also on the subtlety of a writer's style – the use of descriptive language, the pace of sentences, the rhythm of dialogue, all influence a reader's emotional and intellectual responses. Understanding the nuance, or subtlety, of a writer's style will only be possible if you read closely, with an eye to the effect of the writer's choices. The more you practise close reading, the better a close reader you become. The more attuned you become to the strategic choices that writers make, the more you will be able to appreciate each fictional text as a purposeful, unified creation whose effects on readers are specific and intentional.

The Nobel Prize-winning novelist, Toni Morrison, in her essay 'The Reader as Artist' (2006), defines the process of active reading. In this course you are expected to read, as Morrison says, by 'surrender[ing] to the narrator's world while remaining alert inside it.' By remaining 'alert' you can 'dig for the hidden, questioning and relishing the choices the author made.' **Active reading is the guiding principle for the English A: Literature course.**

Far too often, young readers assume that they are reading for the 'story' and nothing more. So, when asked to evaluate the 'story' their response is either 'I liked it' or 'I didn't like it.' Morrison's perspective is that it doesn't matter if you 'like' the text. **What matters is that you can read closely and observe your reactions to the subtleties of the text – you can, in Morrison's words, 'think the text.'**

Aspire to be an active, rather than passive, reader.

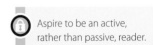

SUMMARY

As a student of literature you bring a willingness to engage with the words on the page. When you open yourself to the writer's language, you allow yourself to imagine the fictional world that the writer has created. Envisioning means just that – you see the characters, hear them speak, and watch their actions. You step into the world of the fiction, yet you are fully conscious of the choices the writer makes. For example, you know that your sympathy or lack thereof is directly influenced by the writer. Your job as an analyst of the fiction, as someone who reads as an artist, is to determine what makes you feel and think as you do about a specific moment within the text.

Considering point of view

Prose fiction writers decide on the manner and method of presenting their text. The primary consideration is just how much information they want to reveal or how much they want to conceal. Point of view is the perspective a writer determines for his reader – something like choosing a camera angle or field of view. The choice is significant.

Imagine the difference in shooting a film from high atop a cliff a mile away from the action, as opposed to shooting the same scene from five metres away. Details in the close-up version would be sharp and clear, but the wider context in which the scene plays out would be unseen. At the same time, the view from the cliff top would offer a perfect view of the panorama but details would be lost. In the same way, a prose fiction writer judiciously selects the angle of vision dependent upon the effects that he or she wants to create for the reader. How close will the writer allow the reader to get to the story? How much will the reader 'know'? How much will the reader have to assume or surmise? Will there be information that the reader will never know? A writer's decision as to the point of view is perhaps the first, and most significant, choice to make.

▶ A chosen angle of vision, just as in point of view, limits what we see as well as what we know. While the close-up angles focus on the gargoyle, only the panoramic angle provides the context, the knowledge that this gargoyle is atop Notre-Dame overlooking Paris.

Types of point of view

- First-person
- Third-person omniscient
- Third-person limited
- Objective

First-person point of view is the internal perspective of one of the characters (either major or minor) in the text, identified through the use of 'I'.

Example: I knew from the moment that I saw her, that my life, as I knew it, would be changed forever.

Third-person omniscient point of view is the perspective of a narrator outside the action of the story, a narrator who knows what the characters think and feel and why they behave as they do. This narrator can potentially tell the reader everything about the characters and the situations of the text, but does not have to.

Example: When they met, they exchanged pleasantries. Susan smiled and grabbed the other's hands, as if she had met an old, dear friend while the other nodded and wrinkled her nose the way she always did when she was nervous. They both knew that their meeting may have been by chance but felt fated nonetheless.

Third-person limited point of view is similar to the perspective of the third-person omniscient narrator, but only with regard to a single character. This narrator can enter the mind and heart of that character and virtually knows everything about him or her, but cannot tell us what other characters are thinking and feeling.

Example: When Susan saw her, there, standing there, looking that beautiful, she knew that she had to say something. Stop, get her attention, say something stupid. Anything. This meeting had to happen sometime and today was destined to be the day. She knew it.

The **objective** point of view is often called 'the fly on the wall' perspective. This narrator observes and describes but does not judge or offer insight into characters or situations within the text.

Example: They stopped suddenly, smiled, and stood aside. One talked. One didn't. The sun was glaring, hot. A hand to the forehead, a smile, gestures offered and denied. They stood together, a part of the crowd.

 Why would a writer choose one point of view over another?

 Is first-person point of view always more engaging than a third-person perspective?

SUMMARY

Point of view is the most significant choice a fiction writer makes because it directly influences how a reader perceives a text. Writers understand that a reader may find particular subject matter alienating, or even disturbing. By choosing to present this material in a first-person point of view, the writer is directly challenging the reader's sensitivity, if not tolerance. Presenting this sensitive material in third-person point of view can allow the reader some distance from which to view it. For example, a violent scene could be described less graphically from the perspective of an omniscient narrator – someone who knows what happened as opposed to the first-hand knowledge of the perpetrator.

Considering voice

Narrative voice is wholly dependent upon the **writer's choice** of narration. The voice can be engaged in the action of the text or detached from it. The tone of the narrator's voice is a critical narrative feature. While a title may grab the attention of a reader, the voice in the opening paragraph can engage the reader so intensely that they don't want to stop reading.

Consider the following example:

> It goes a long way back, some twenty years. All my life I had been looking for something, and everywhere I turned someone tried to tell me what it was. I accepted their answers too, though they were often in contradiction and even self-contradictory. I was naive. I was looking for myself and asking everyone except myself questions which I, and only I, could answer. It took me a long time and much painful boomeranging of my expectations to achieve a realization everyone else appears to have been born with: That I am nobody by myself. But first I had to discover that I am an invisible man!
>
> – From Ralph Ellison, *The Invisible Man* (1952)

In **first-person narration**, like the example above, the voice of the narrator is the voice of the character. While engaging, this voice is subjective, has bias, and is not always believable. Naive narrators are those too young, or too inexperienced, to understand fully the context of events or the motivations of characters. Unreliable narrators, while initially believable, prove to be untrustworthy as the plot progresses.

To identify a naive or unreliable narrator, the reader must be alert to clues that indicate the narrator is unaware of the reality of a situation.

In *Dom Casmurro* by Machado de Assis, the unreliable narrator's rants and ravings throughout the text provide evidence for his unreliability.

> I escaped from the dependent, I escaped from my mother by not going to her room, but I did not escape from myself. I ran to my room, and came in after myself. I talked to myself, I chased after myself, I threw myself on the bed and rolled around with myself, weeping and stifling sobs on the edge of the sheet.
>
> – From Machado de Assis, *Dom Casmurro* (1899)

Third-person narrators, because they have some degree of omniscience, either full or limited omniscience, are often accepted as trustworthy because we believe that they offer honest insights into character, thought and feeling and unbiased assessments of event and situation, when in fact, they may hold biases. The voice of the narrator appears direct and confident – we trust this perspective because the narrator seems familiar with the characters, the setting or the events. It is important, however, to examine the narrator's voice for clues to bias. Information can be revealed sympathetically or disdainfully and the reader's judgement of character and situation is always directed by narrative voice.

As you can see in the following example, the voice of the third-person narrator describes a character in such detail that we accept the description at face value.

> She stood, feet slightly apart, looking directly at him. Not nineteen, but sure of herself. A little paler, a little less healthy than he had first thought. And on closer scrutiny her bright clothes, attractive from a distance, had seen better days.
>
> – From Bao Ninh, *The Sorrow of War* (1991)

In the example below, the narrative voice makes a judgement of the character based on what appears to be close observation over a period of time. This voice is self-assured and is, therefore, believable.

> When he walked, his heels hardly touched the ground and he seemed to walk on springs, as if he was going to pounce on somebody. And he did pounce on people quite

often. He had a slight stammer and whenever he was angry and could not get words out quickly enough, he would use his fists. He had no patience with unsuccessful men. He had had no patience with his father.

– From Chinua Achebe, *Things Fall Apart* (1958)

The voice of an **objective** narrator is often mechanical and disembodied, and lends itself to texts where information is revealed matter-of-factly without opinion or bias. This voice simply reports what it sees.

SUMMARY

Narrative voice cannot be distinguished from narrator. The 'tone of voice' that we associate with any speaker can be used to describe the narrative voice of any fiction text. When we determine voice, we, in a sense, embody the narrator. If that narrator is first person, we have a character, a body, on which to hang that voice. In third person, however, the disembodied voice of the narrator is not without understanding and not without judgement or bias. The only narrative voice that does not judge, that is not embodied, is the objective point of view.

 The choice of point of view is purposeful and strategic. A narrator's distance from the action determines the reader's response to that action.

Appreciation

EXERCISE 1

The following four passages are openings of novels. Examine the speaker of each piece and see how many of the following points you can determine for each. Keep in mind that you will need to read the words carefully, but you may also need to speculate on the information that is presented subtly 'between' the lines. Often, the connotations and images within specific word choice can contribute to the tone.

- Who is the speaker?
- What do you know about the speaker?
- Can you determine what the speaker feels or what the speaker knows?
- Can you determine what situation is the cause of these feelings or this knowledge?
- What do you see when you read this opening? Do you invent details? What are these details?

Passage 1: the opening to *The Old Gringo* by Carlos Fuentes

Now she sits alone and remembers.

She sees, over and over, the specters of Tomas Arroyo and the moon-faced woman and the old gringo cross her window. But they are not ghosts. They have simply mobilized their old pasts, hoping that she would do the same and join them.

But for her it took a long time.

First, she had to stop hating Tomas Arroyo for showing her what she could be and then forbidding her to ever be what she might be. And he knew that she could never be that, and in spite of knowing it, he let her see it.

He always knew that she would return home. But he let her see what would become of her if she remained. She had to purge herself of this hatred. It took her many years to do so. The old gringo was no longer there to help her. Arroyo was not there. Tom Brook. He might have given her a child by that name. She had no right to think this. The moon-faced woman had taken him with her toward their nameless destiny. Tomas Arroyo was over.

So the only moment she had left was when she crossed the border and looked back at the two men, the soldier Inocencio and the boy Pedrito. Behind them, she now thought she saw the dust marshaling itself into some kind of silent chronology that told her to remember; she had come back to her land without memory, and Mexico was no longer available.

Mexico had disappeared forever, but across that bridge, on the other side of the river, a memorious dust insisted on marshaling itself for her, on crossing the frontier and sweeping over the shrub and the wheat fields, the plains and the smoky mountains, the long deep green rivers that the old man had pined for, right up to her walk-up apartment in Washington D.C., on the shores of the Potomac, the Atlantic, the center of the World.

The dust blew and told her that she was alone.

She remembers.

Alone.

Passage 2: the opening to *The Pickup* by Nadine Gordimer

Clustered predators round a kill. It's a small car with a young woman inside it. The battery has failed and taxis, cars, minibuses, vans, motorcycles butt and challenge one another, reproach and curse her, a traffic mob mounting its own confusion. Get going. Stupid bloody woman. Idikazana lomlungu, le! She throws up hands, palms open, in surrender. They continue to jostle and blare their impatience. She gets out of her car and faces them. One of the unemployed black men who beg by waving vehicles into parking bays sidles his way deftly through fenders, signals with his head—Oka-ay, Oka-ay go inside, go!—and mimes control of the steering wheel. Another like him appears, and they push her and her car into a loading bay. The street hustles on. They stand, looking musingly beyond her while she fumbles for her purse, An expert's quick glance at what she has put in his hand assures the street boss that it is more than adequate. She doesn't know how to thank them enough, etc. He hitches his body to get the money stowed in trousers cut to fit somebody else and smiles with his attention on the lookout for the next vehicle seeking a place to park. A woman wearing a towel as a shawl, enthroned on a fruit-box before her stock of hair combs, razor blades, pumice stones, woolen caps and headache powders, yells out to him what must be a teasing remark in a language the young woman doesn't understand.

There. You've seen. I've seen. The gestures. A woman in a traffic jam among those that are everyday in the city, any city. You won't remember it, you won't know who she is.

But I know because from the sight of her I'll find out—as a story—what was going to happen as the consequence of that commonplace embarrassment on the streets; where it was heading for, and what. Her hands thrown up, open.

Passage 3: the opening to *Accident* by Christa Wolf

On a day about which I cannot write in the present tense, the cherry trees will have been in blossom. I will have avoided thinking, 'exploded,' the cherry trees have exploded, although only one year earlier I could not only think but also say it readily, if not entirely with conviction. The green is exploding. Never would such a sentence have been more appropriate in describing the progress of nature than this year, in this spring heat, following the endlessly long winter. I knew nothing yet of the warnings that would circulate much later about eating the fruit, still invisible on the branches of the blossoming trees, on the morning when I was annoyed, as I am every morning, by the bustlings of the neighbor's chickens on our freshly seeded lawn. White leghorns. The only good thing you say about them is that they react to my clapping and hissing with fear, if also confusion. Still, most of them scattered in the direction of the neighboring property. There's a good chance you'll be able to hang on to your eggs now, I thought spitefully, and I intimated to that authority who had begun early on to watch me alertly from a very distant future—a glance, nothing more—that I would not feel bound by anything anymore. Free to do and, above all, not to do as I pleased. That goal in a very distant future toward which all lines had run till now had been blasted away, was smoldering, along with the fissionable material in a nuclear reactor. A rare case . . .

Passage 4: the opening to *Cracking India* by Bapsi Sidhwa

Shall I lament the nightingale, submissively lending my ear?
Am I the rose to suffer its cry in silence year after year?
The fire of verse gives me courage and bids me no more to be faint.
With dust in my mouth, I am abject: to God I make my complaint.
Sometimes You favor our rivals then sometimes with us You are free.
I am sorry to say it so boldly. You are no less fickle than we.
– Muhammad Iqbal: 'Complaint to God'

My world is compressed. Warris Road, lined with rain gutters, lies between Queens Road and Jail Road: both wide, clean, orderly streets at the affluent fringes of Lahore.

Rounding the right-hand corner of Warris Road and continuing on Jail Road is the hushed Salvation Army wall. Set high, at eight-foot intervals, are the wall's dingy eyes. My child's mind is blocked by the gloom emanating from the wire mesh screening the oblong ventilation slits. I feel such sadness for the dumb creatures I imagine lurking behind the wall. I know it is dumb because I have listened to its silence, my ear to the wall.

Jail Road also harbors my energetic Electric-aunt and her adenoidal son . . . large, slow, inexorable. Their house is adjacent to the den of the Salvation Army.

Opposite it, down a bumpy, dusty, earth-packed drive, is the one-and-a-half-room abode of my godmother. With her dwell her docile old husband and her slavesister. This is my haven. My refuge from the perplexing unrealities of my home on Warris Road.

A few furlongs away Jail Road vanishes into the dense bazaars and Mozang Chungi. At the other end a distant canal cuts the road at the periphery of my world.

EXERCISE 2

Each of the following passages, taken from several novels, demonstrates a wide range of points of view and voice. Determine the type of narrative point of view for each passage. Then, determine all that you can about the narrator, including age, gender and tone of voice. Can you sense if the tone of voice of the narrator is sympathetic, detached or indifferent? What specific words or phrases indicate the narrator's attitude towards the subject matter?

What information does the narrator reveal? Is there any evidence that would support the claim that some information is purposely concealed? Identify the specific words and phrases that would support your claims.

1   Her marriage to Leonce Pontellier was purely an accident, in this respect resembling many other marriages which masquerade as the decrees of Fate. It was in the midst of her secret great passion that she met him. He fell in love, as men are in the habit of doing, and pressed his suit with an earnestness and an ardor which left nothing to be desired. He pleased her; his absolute devotion flattered her. She fancied there was a sympathy of thought and taste between them, in which fancy she was mistaken.

   – Kate Chopin, *The Awakening* (1899)

2   Papa was walking toward Jaja. He spoke entirely in Igbo now. I thought he would pull at Jaja's ears, that he would tug and yank at the same pace as he spoke, that he would slap Jaja's face and his palm would make that sound, like a heavy book falling from a library shelf at school. And then he would reach across and slap me on the face with the casualness of reaching for the pepper shaker. But he said, 'I want you to finish that food and go to your rooms and pray for forgiveness,' before turning to go back downstairs. The silence he left was heavy but comfortable, like a well-worn, prickly cardigan on a bitter morning.

   – Chimamanda Adichie, *Purple Hibiscus* (2003)

3   Snowman wakes before dawn. He lies unmoving, listening to the tide coming in, wave after wave sloshing over the various barricades, wish-wash, wish-wash, the rhythm of heartbeat. He would like to believe he is still asleep.

   – Margaret Atwood, *Oryx and Crake* (2003)

4   The people all saw her come because it was sundown. The sun was gone, but he had left his footprints in the sky. It was the time for sitting on porches beside the road. It was the time to hear things and talk. These sitters had been tongueless, earless, eyeless conveniences all day long. Mules and other brutes had occupied their skins. But now, the sun and the bossman were gone, so the skins felt powerful and human. They became lords of sounds and lesser things. They passed notions through their mouths. They sat in judgment.

   – Zora Neale Hurston, *Their Eyes Were Watching God* (1937)

5   All of this happened a long time ago. But not so long ago that everyone who played a part in it is dead. Some can still be met in dark old rooms with nurses in attendance. They look at you and rearrange their thoughts. They say, 'I don't remember.' The occupants of memory have to be protected from strangers. Ask what happened, they say: 'I don't know.' Mention Robert Ross—they look away. 'He's dead,' they tell you. This is not news. 'Tell me about the horses,' you ask. Sometimes, they weep at this. Other times they say: 'that bastard!' Then the nurses nod at you, much to say—you see? It's best to go away and find your information somewhere else. In the end, the only facts you have are public.

     – Timothy Findley, *The Wars* (1977)

6   She had always known the day would come when she would be exposed before the world because of that child of hers. Many a night she had lain awake preparing herself for that day and going over what she would say. In the Kloof over the years everyone, white and Coloured, had had to give way before her tongue; she had made them keep out of Wolwekraal's affairs. The Kloof had got used to the child being with her.

     – Dalene Matthee, *Fiela's Child* (1985)

7   People in delirium rise and sink, rise and sink, in and out of lucidity. The swaying, shuddering, thudding, flinging stops, and the furniture of life falls into place. The vehicle was the fever. Chattering metal and raving dance of loose bolts in the smell of the children's car-sick. She rose from it gradually for longer and longer intervals. At first what fell into place was what had vanished, the past.

     – Nadine Gordimer, *July's People* (1981)

8   Lord Warburton not only spent the night at Gardencourt, but he was persuaded to remain over the second day; and when the second day was ended he determined to postpone his departure till the morrow. During this period he addressed many of his remarks to Isabel, who accepted his evidence of his esteem with a very good grace. She found herself liking him extremely; the first impression he had made on her had weight, but at the end of an evening spent in his society she scarce fell short of seeing him – though quite without lucidity – as a hero of romance.

     – Henry James, *The Portrait of a Lady* (1881)

9   I knew I was not in Saigon. I was not a hospital volunteer. It was not 1968 but 1978. Yet I also knew, as I passed a wall of smoked-glass windows, that I would see the quick movements of green camouflage fatigues, and I knew. I knew the medic insignia on his uniform and I knew, I knew, what I would see next. His face, not the face before the explosion, but the face after, motionless in the liquefied red that poured from a tangle of delicate veins. 'Oh God, oh God, oh my God!' people cried. The doctor, the medic, and the operating-room crew killed in a cramped, battered room reinforced by rows of military-green sandbags. The calm of Saigon had always been unreliable, narcotically unreal. Who could have known before the man was cut up that an unexploded grenade, fired from a launcher—not a dead bullet—had lodged in the hollowness of his stomach?

     – Lan Cao, *Monkey Bridge* (1997)

10   So it was Cash holding to the horse when it come splashing and scrambling up the bank, moaning and groaning like a natural man. When I come to it it was just kicking Cash loose from his holt on the saddle. His face turned up a second when he was sliding back into the water. It was gray, with his eyes closed and a long swipe of mud across his face. Then he let go and turned over in the water. He looked just like a old bundle of clothes kind of washing up and down against the bank. He looked like he was laying there in the water on his face, rocking up and down a little, looking at something on the bottom.

– William Faulkner, *As I Lay Dying* (1930)

EXERCISE 3

Go back to the Considering Point of View section in this chapter (page 4) and, using the ideas about camera angles and narrative perspective, choose the type of camera angle (such as close-up, standard, wide angle or panoramic view) that would work best in filming each of the ten passages above. Be prepared to defend your choices with at least three details from each passage.

Considering characterization

There are two methods of characterization in prose fiction – direct and indirect.

Direct characterization relies on the narrator's descriptions and judgements about a specific character. If a narrator describes a character as tall and thin with a slight limp, we classify that method as direct characterization. If the narrator tells us that a character dislikes small children and avoids them at every opportunity, once again, we have direct characterization. But, if we witness a character struggling up a narrow staircase, or holding his hands over his ears and moving nervously aside when small children run past him screaming with delight, we experience **indirect characterization**. If another character describes a character as 'skinny as a bean pole and not a friend to children,' we classify this observation as indirect characterization as well.

Characters may either be dynamic or static in terms of their presentation within fiction.

Dynamic characters change within the text. Experiences affect these characters and they may act or think differently because of these experiences. The world of the fiction in which these dynamic characters reside, like the world of the reader, challenges pre-established beliefs and provokes reflection, action and reaction. **Static characters**, on the other hand, do not change, although the reader's perception of such a character can change over time. Static characters encounter the opportunity for change through their experiences, but these experiences never provoke change within the character.

Is it possible for a static character to be a protagonist?

A narrator's bias regarding a character must be evaluated in terms of textual evidence to support the truth or falsity of that bias.

EXERCISE 4

In Alice Walker's story, 'Roselily', characterization is masterfully developed via an internal monologue. In this monologue, Walker uses direct and indirect characterization. Through Roselily's thoughts, observations and actions, the reader gains insight not only into her character but her groom's character as well.

As you read this story, make notes about what you come to know about both characters, particularly at each portion of the marriage vow.

For example, in the opening section, the paragraph following 'Dearly Beloved', we learn indirectly that the bride feels like a small girl as she moves with great slow-motion effort across the porch to stand next to the man she is marrying. We also learn, directly, that this man, her groom, does not like the fact that they are marrying on a front porch next to a busy, noisy highway.

'Roselily' by Alice Walker (1973)

Dearly Beloved,

She dreams; dragging herself across the world. A small girl in her mother's white robe and veil, knee raised waist high through a bowl of quicksand soup. The man who stands beside her is against this standing on the front porch of her house, being married to the sound of cars whizzing by on highway 61.

we are gathered here

Like cotton to be weighed. Her fingers at the last minute busily removing dry leaves and twigs. Aware it is a superficial sweep. She knows he blames Mississippi for the respectful way the men turn their heads up in the yard, the women stand waiting and knowledgeable, their children held from mischief by teachings from the wrong God. He glares beyond them to the occupants of the cars, white faces glued to promises beyond a country wedding, noses thrust forward like dogs on a track. For him they usurp the wedding.

in the sight of God

Yes, open house. That is what country black folks like. She dreams she does not already have three children. A squeeze around the flowers in her hands chokes off three and four and five years of breath. Instantly she is ashamed and frightened in her superstition. She looks for the first time at the preacher, forces humility into her eyes, as if she believes he is, in fact, a man of God. She can imagine God, a small black boy, timidly pulling the preacher's coattail.

to join this man and this woman

She thinks of ropes, chains, handcuffs, his religion. His place of worship. Where she will be required to sit apart with covered head. In Chicago, a word she hears when thinking of smoke, from his description of what a cinder was, which they never had in Panther Burn. She sees hovering over the heads of the clean neighbors in her front yard black specks falling, clinging, from the sky. But in Chicago. Respect, a chance to build. Her children at last from underneath the detrimental wheel. A chance to be on top. What a relief, she thinks. What a vision, a view, from up so high.

in holy matrimony.

Her fourth child she gave away to the child's father who had some money. Certainly a good job. Had gone to Harvard. Was a good man but weak because good language meant so much to him he could not live with Roselily. Could not abide TV in the living room, five beds in three rooms, no Bach except from four to six on Sunday afternoons. No chess at all. She does not forget to worry about her son among his father's people. She wonders if the New England climate will agree with him. If he will ever come down to Mississippi, as his father did, to try to right the country's wrongs. She wonders if he will be stronger than his father. His father cried off and on throughout her pregnancy. Went to skin and bones. Suffered nightmares, retching and falling out of bed. Tried to kill himself. Later told his wife he found the right baby through friends. Vouched for, the sterling qualities that would make up his character.

It is not her nature to blame. Still, she is not entirely thankful. She supposes New England, the North, to be quite different from what she knows. It seems right somehow to her that people who move there to live return home completely changed. She thinks of the air, the smoke, the cinders. Imagines cinders big as hailstones; heavy, weighing on the people. Wonders how this pressure finds its way into the veins, roping the springs of laughter.

If there's anybody here that knows a reason why

But of course they know no reason why beyond what they daily have come to know. She thinks of the man who will be her husband, feels shut away from him because of the stiff severity of his plain black suit. His religion. A lifetime of black and white. Of veils. Covered head. It is as if her children are already gone from her. Not dead, but exalted on a pedestal, a stalk that has no roots. She wonders how to make new roots. It is beyond her. She wonders what one does with memories in a brand-new life. This had seemed easy, until she thought of it. 'The reasons why . . . the people who' . . . she thinks, and does not wonder where the thought is from.

these two should not be joined

She thinks of her mother, who is dead. Dead, but still her mother. Joined. This is confusing. Of her father. A gray old man who sold wild mink, rabbit, fox skins to Sears, Roebuck. He stands in the yard, like a man waiting for a train. Her young sisters stand behind her in smooth green dresses, with flowers in their hands and hair. They giggle, she feels, at the absurdity of the wedding. They are ready for something new. She thinks the man beside her should marry one of them. She feels old. Yoked. An arm seems to reach out from behind her and snatch her backward. She thinks of cemeteries and the long sleep of grandparents mingling in the dirt. She believes that she believes in ghosts. In the soil giving back what it takes.

together,

In the city. He sees her in a new way. This she knows, and is grateful. But is it new enough? She cannot always be a bride and virgin, wearing robes and veil. Even now her body itches to be free of satin and voile, organdy and lily of the valley. Memories crash against her. Memories of being bare to the sun. She wonders what it will be like. Not to have to go to a job. Not to work in a sewing plant. Not to worry about learning to sew straight seams in workingmen's overalls, jeans, and dress pants. Her place will be in the home, he has said, repeatedly, promising her rest she had prayed for. But now she wonders. When she is rested, what will she do? They will make babies – she thinks practically about her fine brown body, his strong black one. They will be inevitable. Her hands will be full. Full of what? Babies. She is not comforted.

let him speak

She wishes she had asked him to explain more of what he meant. But she was impatient. Impatient to be done with sewing. With doing everything for three children, alone. Impatient to leave the girls she had known since childhood, their children growing up, their husbands hanging around her, already old, seedy. Nothing about them that she wanted, or needed. The fathers of her children driving by, waving, not waving; reminders of times she would just as soon forget. Impatient to see the South Side, where they would live and build and be respectable and respected and free. Her husband would free her. A romantic hush. Proposal. Promises. A new life! Respectable, reclaimed, renewed. Free! In robe and veil.

or forever hold

She does not even know if she loves him. She loves his sobriety. His refusal to sing just because he knows the tune. She loves his pride. His blackness and his gray car. She loves his understanding of her condition. She thinks she loves the effort he will make to redo her into what he truly wants. His love of her makes her completely conscious of how unloved she was before. This is something; though it makes her unbearably sad. Melancholy. She blinks her eyes. Remembers she is finally being married, like other girls. Like other girls, women? Something strains upward behind her eyes. She thinks of the something as a rat trapped, cornered, scurrying to and fro in her head, peering through the windows of her eyes. She wants to live for once. But doesn't know quite what that means. Wonders if she has ever done it. If she ever will. The preacher is odious to her. She wants to strike him out of the way, out of her light, with the back of her hand. It seems to her he has always been standing in front of her, barring her way.

his peace

The rest she does not hear. She feels a kiss, passionate, rousing, within the general pandemonium. Cars drive up blowing their horns. Firecrackers go off. Dogs come from under the house and begin to yelp and bark. Her husband's hand is like the clasp of an iron gate. People congratulate. Her children press against her. They look with awe and distaste mixed with hope at their new father. He stands curiously apart, in spite of the people crowding about to grasp his free hand. He smiles at them all but his eyes are as if turned inward. He knows they cannot understand that he is not a Christian. He will not explain himself. He feels different, he looks it. The old women thought he was like one of their sons except that he had somehow got away from them. Still a son, not a son. Changed.

She thinks how it will be later in the night in the silvery gray car. How they will spin through the darkness of Mississippi and in the morning be in Chicago, Illinois. She thinks of Lincoln, the president. That is all she knows about the place. She feels ignorant, wrong, backward. She presses her worried fingers into his palm. He is standing in front of her. In the crush of well-wishing people, he does not look back.

 To access worksheet 1.1 on 'Roselily', please visit www. pearsonbacconline.com and follow the on-screen instructions.

Considering plot

If a friend asks you to tell him what a movie was about, you would probably give him a quick summary of the main events of the film. Those main events, linked together through time, create a unified whole – in this example, a film. Aristotle, in his *Poetics*, wrote about plot in this way. He said that plot is the 'imitation of an action' and 'the arrangement of the incidents.' This arrangement would have to be unified: it would have a beginning, middle and an end, and each part could be recognized within a chain of causality better known as cause and effect. Stories have beginnings, and middles, and ends, so is a story the same thing as a plot?

E.M. Forster distinguishes between a story and a plot. He says that a story is 'a narrative of events arranged in their time sequence.' Plot, he continues, 'is also a narrative of events, but the emphasis falls on causality.' He gave this example: 'The king died, and then the queen died,' is a story. 'The king died, and then the queen died of grief,' is a plot. Causality takes precedence over time sequence in plot. Time sequence is still there, but it is secondary to cause and effect.

Novels are developed in such a way that they may have more than one plot. These subplots have a number of functions. They can deepen suspense, serve as ironic contrast to the main plot, or function as a means to develop character. The intricacy of plot within a text is one of the many narrative strategies that fiction writers have at their disposal; they can create simple, unified plot lines, or they can interweave plot and subplot, creating a tangle of action.

Considering setting and time

To render a setting is to create a fictional world that readers can envision. ▶

● **Examiner's hints**
Always pay careful attention to weather references within fiction. These observations can have association to place, time, mood and character development.

Settings, like plots, can be complex or simple. The setting of a novel, for example, can be limited to a single place, or more than one place depending upon the aims of the writer. What is perhaps most important, however, is not the number of settings, but what we might call the 'rendering' of setting within a text. **Setting includes the geographical, historical and social background in which the action takes place.** In some fiction, setting can take on the significance of character or theme. For example, a wall could take on thematic significance if a character witnesses a crime through a crevice in that wall. Every time that character sees that wall, the memory of what he saw or heard is relived; or, perhaps with the passing of time, the wall crumbles like the memory itself.

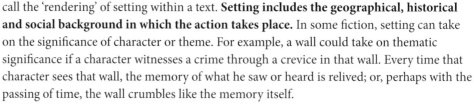

What issues does an unfamiliar setting present to a reader?

Fiction writers create and manipulate setting because it comprises the fictional world in which their characters reside. All action takes place within a setting, but the setting can change with the passage of time.

Time, then, or rather the passing of time within a work of fiction, is relative to other conventions of fiction. What this means is that many aspects of fiction – the characters, the plot, the setting, the revelation of theme, even the structure of a text – relate to the passing of time. Some writers unfold their text as a strict chronology while others break the sequence of time from past to present and to future. One tool writers use to do this is flashback, where the present tense of the action of a text is suspended, to reveal some moment in the past. The significance of such a moment may or may not be apparent when it occurs. As a close reader, your ability to recognize the flashback is key, but even more important is your ability to consider the effect of the flashback. Does that effect inform your understanding of some aspect of the present tense of the text? Is your understanding of a character enhanced through the flashback? Would a series of flashbacks work as a progressive understanding of character in the present tense of the text?

Considering theme

Theme is best understood as a lesson about human nature that emerges from the action and interaction within a text. A work of fiction is not limited by the number of themes that can unfold as you read a text. Essentially there are two types of themes, those that are explicitly stated and those that are subtly implied.

Explicit themes are stated outright by a narrator or a character. In children's literature, explicit themes abound because writers want the message to be absolutely clear, spelled out directly for the child to consider. In more sophisticated reading, the themes are seldom explicit.

Implicit themes are inferred by the reader over time. These messages about human nature are subtle, rather than didactic, and are discovered through examining character action and interaction. At best, the convention of theme emerges as the text unfolds.

The messages, or themes, in children's literature are always clearly stated.

▼

Considering structure

The structure of a novel or short story is a narrative strategy that can greatly affect the reader's understanding of a text. Alice Walker's structuring of 'Roselily' is a case in point; enabling the reader to be inside the mind of the character as her wedding vows are being spoken allows for greater understanding of the character, her situation, her fears and her hopes. Irony is also heightened through the connection of Roselily's thoughts to a particular segment of the vow. The structure of the story creates very specific effects on the reader.

So, if a writer chooses to switch point of view every other chapter, or to use the present time of the novel for the odd-numbered chapters and flashbacks for the even-numbered chapters, they would do so to create very specific effects for the reader. Always consider the structure of a novel – the number of chapters and the use of groupings of chapters within sections of the text may seem arbitrary considerations, but they are not. They are purposeful manipulations of the convention with intended results.

Considering tone

Every work of fiction has an associated tone. Tone is the writer's attitude towards his or her subject matter. It can express the full range of emotions, from passion and anger to boredom and indifference. This attitude is revealed through the action and situation of the text as well as the reactions of characters. A writer's tone, then, is his emotional and intellectual perspective on his characters, the actions they perform and witness, and the situations that prompt reaction. The writer's tone directly affects the reader's perception. Just as tone of voice can soften the effect of a reprimand, the writer's tone can modify or direct a reader's response to a character, action or situation.

EXERCISE 5

Using the ten samples in Exercise 1, assess the tone of each passage. Consider the possibilities of tone as a range of emotion, from detached and objective to reflective, sincere, matter of fact, sympathetic or even ironic.

EXERCISE 6

Read these two short stories, 'The Handsomest Drowned Man in the World', by Gabriel García Márquez and 'A Small, Good Thing', by Raymond Carver, and apply the Insight observations which are listed on pages 37–38. Explore each author's narrative choices, his strategies to engage his readers both emotionally and intellectually. Determine the stylistic features common to each piece and compare the effects created for the reader.

'The Handsomest Drowned Man in the World' by Gabriel García Márquez (1968)

The first children who saw the dark and slinky bulge approaching through the sea let themselves think it was an enemy ship. Then they saw it had no flags or masts and they thought it was a whale. But when it washed up on the beach, they removed the clumps of seaweed, the jellyfish tentacles, and the remains of fish and flotsam, and only then did they see that it was a drowned man.

They had been playing with him all afternoon, burying him in the sand and digging him up again, when someone chanced to see them and spread the alarm in the village. The men who carried him to the nearest house noticed that he weighed more than any dead man they had ever known, almost as much as a horse, and they said to each other that maybe he'd been floating too long and the water had got into his bones. When they laid him on the floor they said he'd been taller than all other men because there was barely enough room for him in the house, but they thought that maybe the ability to keep on growing after death was part of the nature of certain drowned men. He had the smell of the sea about him and only his shape gave one to suppose that it was the corpse of a human being, because the skin was covered with a crust of mud and scales.

They did not even have to clean off his face to know that the dead man was a stranger. The village was made up of only twenty-odd wooden houses that had stone courtyards with no flowers and which were spread about on the end of a desertlike cape. There was so little land that mothers always went about with the fear that the wind would carry off their children and the few dead that the years had caused among them had to be thrown off the cliffs. But the sea was calm and bountiful and all the men fitted into seven boats. So when they found the drowned man they simply had to look at one another to see that they were all there.

That night they did not go out to work at sea. While the men went to find out if anyone was missing in neighboring villages, the women stayed behind to care for the drowned man. They took the mud off with grass swabs, they removed the underwater stones entangled in his hair, and they scraped the crust off with tools used for scaling fish. As they were doing that they noticed that the vegetation on him came from faraway oceans and deep water and that his clothes were in tatters, as if he had sailed through labyrinths of coral. They noticed too that he bore his death with pride, for he did not have the lonely look of other drowned men who came out of the sea or that haggard, needy look of men who drowned in rivers. But only when they finished cleaning him off did they become aware of the kind of man he was and it left them breathless. Not only was he the tallest, strongest, most virile, and best built man they had ever seen, but even though they were looking at him there was no room for him in their imagination.

They could not find a bed in the village large enough to lay him on nor was there a table solid enough to use for his wake. The tallest men's holiday pants would not fit him, nor the fattest ones' Sunday shirts, nor the shoes of the one with the biggest feet. Fascinated by his huge size and his beauty, the women then decided to make him some pants from a large piece of sail and a shirt from some bridal linen so that he could continue through his death with dignity. As they sewed, sitting in a circle and gazing at the corpse between stitches, it seemed to them that the wind had never been so steady nor the sea so restless as on that night and they supposed that the change had something to do with the dead man. They thought that if that magnificent man had lived in the village, his house would have had the widest doors, the highest ceiling, and the strongest floor, his bedstead would have been made from a midship frame held together by iron bolts, and his wife would have been the happiest woman. They thought that he would have had so much authority that he could have drawn fish out of the sea simply by calling their names and that he would have put so much work into his land that springs would have burst forth from among the rocks so that he would have been able to plant flowers on the cliffs. They secretly compared him to their own men, thinking that for all their lives theirs were incapable of doing what he could do in one night, and they ended up dismissing them deep in their hearts as the weakest, meanest and most useless creatures on earth. They were wandering through that maze of fantasy when the oldest woman, who as the oldest had looked upon the drowned man with more compassion than passion, sighed: 'He has the face of someone called Esteban.'

It was true. Most of them had only to take another look at him to see that he could not have any other name. The more stubborn among them, who were the youngest, still lived for a few hours with the illusion that when they put his clothes on and he lay among the flowers in patent leather shoes his name might be Lautaro. But it was a vain illusion. There had not been enough canvas, the poorly cut and worse sewn pants were too tight, and the hidden strength of his heart popped the buttons on his shirt.

After midnight the whistling of the wind died down and the sea fell into its Wednesday drowsiness. The silence put an end to any last doubts: he was Esteban. The women who had dressed him, who had combed his hair, had cut his nails and shaved him were unable to hold back a shudder of pity when they had to resign themselves to his being dragged along the ground. It was then that they understood how unhappy he must have been with that huge body since it bothered him even after death. They could see him in life, condemned to going through doors sideways, cracking his head on crossbeams, remaining on his feet during visits, not knowing what to do with his soft, pink, sea lion hands while the lady of the house looked for her most resistant chair and begged him, frightened to death, sit here, Esteban, please, and he, leaning against the wall, smiling, don't bother, ma'am, I'm fine where I am, his heels raw and his back roasted from having done the same thing so many times whenever he paid a visit, don't bother, ma'am, I'm fine where I am, just to avoid the embarrassment of breaking up the chair, and never knowing perhaps that the ones who said don't go, Esteban, at least wait till the coffee's ready, were the ones who later on would whisper the big boob finally left, how nice, the handsome fool has gone. That was what the women were thinking beside the body a little before dawn.

Later, when they covered his face with a handkerchief so that the light would not bother him, he looked so forever dead, so defenseless, so much like their men that the first furrows of tears opened in their hearts. It was one of the younger ones who began the weeping. The others, coming to, went from sighs to wails, and the more they sobbed the more they felt like weeping, because the drowned man was becoming all the more Esteban for them, and so they wept so much, for he was the most destitute, most peaceful, and most obliging man on earth, poor Esteban. So when the men returned with the news that the drowned man was not from the neighboring villages either, the women felt an opening of jubilation in the midst of their tears. 'Praise the Lord,' they sighed, 'he's ours!' The men thought the fuss was only womanish frivolity. Fatigued because of the difficult night-time inquiries, all they wanted was to get rid of the bother of the newcomer once and for all before the sun grew strong on that arid, windless day. They improvised a litter with the remains of foremasts and gaffs, tying it together with rigging so that it would bear the weight of the body until they reached the cliffs. They wanted to tie the anchor from a cargo ship to him so that he would sink easily into the deepest waves, where fish are blind and divers die of nostalgia, and bad currents would not bring him back to shore, as had happened with other bodies. But the more they hurried, the more the women thought of ways to waste time. They walked about like startled hens, pecking with the sea charms on their breasts, some interfering on one side to put a scapular of the good wind on the drowned man, some on the other side to put a wrist compass on him, and after a great deal of get away from there, woman, stay out of the way, look, you almost made me fall on top of the dead man, the men began to feel mistrust in their livers and started grumbling about why so many main-altar decorations for a stranger, because no matter how many nails and holy-water jars he had on him, the sharks would chew him all the same, but the women kept piling on their junk relics, running back and forth, stumbling, while they released in sighs what they did not in tears, so that the men finally exploded with since when has there ever been such a fuss over a drifting corpse, a drowned nobody, a piece of cold Wednesday meat. One of the women, mortified by so much lack of care, then removed the handkerchief from the dead man's face and the men were left breathless too. He was Esteban. It was not necessary to repeat it for them to recognize him. If they had been told Sir Walter Raleigh, even they might have been impressed with his gringo accent, the macaw on his shoulder, his cannibal-killing blunderbuss, but there could be only one Esteban in the world and there he was, stretched out like a sperm whale, shoeless, wearing the pants of an undersized child, and with those stony nails that had to be cut with a knife.

They only had to take the handkerchief off his face to see that he was ashamed, that it was not his fault that he was so big or so heavy or so handsome, and if he had known that this was going to happen, he would have looked for a more discreet place to drown in, seriously, I even would have tied the anchor off a galleon around my neck and staggered off a cliff like someone who doesn't like things in order not to be upsetting people now with this Wednesday dead body, as you people say, in order not to be bothering anyone with this filthy piece of cold meat that doesn't have anything to do with me. There was so much truth in his manner that even the most mistrustful men, the ones who felt the bitterness of endless nights at sea fearing that their women would tire of dreaming about them and begin to dream of drowned men, even they and others who were harder still shuddered in the marrow of their bones at Esteban's sincerity.

That was how they came to hold the most splendid funeral they could ever conceive of for an abandoned drowned man. Some women who had gone to get flowers in the neighboring villages returned with other women who could not believe what they had been told, and those women went back for more flowers when they saw the dead man, and they brought more and more until there were so many flowers and so many people that it was hard to walk about. At the final moment it pained them to return him to the waters as an orphan and they chose a father and mother from among the best people, and aunts and uncles and cousins, so that through him all the inhabitants of the village became kinsmen.

Some sailors who heard the weeping from a distance went off course and people heard of one who had himself tied to the mainmast, remembering ancient fables about sirens. While they fought for the privilege of carrying him on their shoulders along the steep escarpment by the cliffs, men and women became aware for the first time of the desolation of their streets, the dryness of their courtyards, the narrowness of their dreams as they faced the splendor and beauty of their drowned man. They let him go without an anchor so that he could come back if he wished and whenever he wished, and they all held their breath for the fraction of centuries the body took to fall into the abyss. They did not need to look at one another to realize that they were no longer all present, that they would never be. But they also knew that everything would be different from then on, that their houses would have wider doors, higher ceilings, and stronger floors so that Esteban's memory could go everywhere without bumping into beams and so that no one in the future would dare whisper the big boob finally died, too bad, the handsome fool has finally died, because they were going to paint their house fronts gay colors to make Esteban's memory eternal and they were going to break their backs digging for springs among the stones and planting flowers on the cliffs so that in future years at dawn the passengers on great liners would awaken, suffocated by the smell of gardens on the high seas, and the captain would have to come down from the bridge in his dress uniform, with his astrolabe, his pole star, and his row of war medals and, pointing to the promontory of roses on the horizon, he would say in fourteen languages, look there, where the wind is so peaceful now that it's gone to sleep beneath the beds, over there, where the sun's so bright that the sunflowers don't know which way to turn, yes, over there, that's Esteban's village.

To access worksheet 1.2 on 'The Handsomest Drowned Man in the World', please visit www. pearsonbacconline.com and follow the on-screen instructions.

'A Small, Good Thing' by Raymond Carver (1983)

Saturday afternoon she drove to the bakery in the shopping center. After looking through a loose-leaf binder with photographs of cakes taped onto the pages, she ordered chocolate, the child's favorite. The cake she chose was decorated with a spaceship and launching pad under a sprinkling of white stars, and a planet made of red frosting at the other end. His name, SCOTTY, would be in green letters beneath the planet. The baker, who was an older man with a thick neck, listened without saying anything when she told him the child would be eight years old next Monday. The baker wore a white apron that looked like a smock. Straps cut under his arms, went around in back and then to the front again, where they were secured under his heavy waist. He wiped his hands on his apron as he listened to her. He kept his eyes down on the photographs and let her talk. He let her take her time. He'd just come to work and he'd be there all night, baking, and he was in no real hurry.

She gave the baker her name, Ann Weiss, and her telephone number. The cake would be ready on Monday morning, just out of the oven, in plenty of time for the child's party that afternoon. The baker was not jolly. There were no pleasantries between them, just the minimum exchange of words, the necessary information. He made her feel uncomfortable, and she didn't like that. While he was bent over the counter with the pencil in his hand, she studied his coarse features and wondered if he'd ever done anything else with his life besides be a baker. She was a mother and thirty-three years old, and it seemed to her that everyone, especially someone the baker's age – a man old enough to be her father – must have children who'd gone through this special time of cakes and birthday parties. There must be that between them, she thought. But he was abrupt with her – not rude, just abrupt. She gave up trying to make friends with him. She looked into the back of the bakery and could see a long, heavy wooden table with aluminum pie pans stacked at one end; and beside the table a metal container filled with empty racks. There was an enormous oven. A radio was playing country-western music.

The baker finished printing the information on the special order card and closed up the binder. He looked at her and said, 'Monday morning.' She thanked him and drove home.

On Monday morning, the birthday boy was walking to school with another boy. They were passing a bag of potato chips back and forth and the birthday boy was trying to find out what his friend intended to give him for his birthday that afternoon. Without looking, the birthday boy stepped off the curb at an intersection and was immediately knocked down by a car. He fell on his side with his head in the gutter and his legs out in the road. His eyes were closed, but his legs moved back and forth as if he were trying to climb over something. His friend dropped the potato chips and started to cry. The car had gone a hundred feet or so and stopped in the middle of the road. The man in the driver's seat looked back over his shoulder. He waited until the boy got unsteadily to his feet. The boy wobbled a little. He looked dazed, but okay. The driver put the car into gear and drove away.

The birthday boy didn't cry, but he didn't have anything to say about anything either. He wouldn't answer when his friend asked him what it felt like to be hit by a car. He walked home, and his friend went on to school. But after the birthday boy was inside his house and was telling his mother about it – she sitting beside him on the sofa, holding his hands in her lap, saying, 'Scotty, honey, are you sure you feel all right, baby?' thinking she would call the doctor anyway, he suddenly lay back on the sofa, closed his eyes, and went limp. When she couldn't wake him up, she hurried to the telephone and called her husband at work. Howard told her to remain calm, remain calm, and then he called an ambulance for the child and left for the hospital himself.

Of course, the birthday party was canceled. The child was in the hospital with a mild concussion and suffering from shock. There'd been vomiting, and his lungs had taken in fluid which needed pumping out that afternoon. Now he simply seemed to be in a very deep sleep – but no coma, Dr. Francis had emphasized, no coma, when he saw the alarm in the parents' eyes. At eleven o'clock that night, when the boy seemed to be resting comfortably enough after the many X-rays and the lab work, and it was just a matter of his waking up and coming around, Howard left the hospital. He and Ann had been at the hospital with the child since that afternoon, and he was going home for a short while to bathe and change clothes. 'I'll be back in an hour,' he said. She nodded. 'It's fine,' she said. 'I'll be right here.' He kissed her on the forehead, and they touched hands. She sat in the chair beside the bed and looked at the child. She was waiting for him to wake up and be all right. Then she could begin to relax.

Howard drove home from the hospital. He took the wet, dark streets very fast, then caught himself and slowed down. Until now, his life had gone smoothly and to his satisfaction – college, marriage, another year of college for the advanced degree in business, a junior partnership in an investment firm. Fatherhood. He was happy and, so far, lucky – he knew that. His parents were still living, his brothers and his sister were established, his friends from college had gone out to take their places in the world. So far, he had kept away from any real harm, from those forces he knew existed and that could cripple or bring down a man if the luck went bad, if things suddenly turned. He pulled into the driveway and parked. His left leg began to tremble. He sat in the car for a minute and tried to deal with the present situation in a rational manner. Scotty had been hit by a car and was in the hospital, but he was going to be all right. Howard closed his eyes and ran his hand over his face. He got out of the car and went up to the front door. The dog was barking inside the house. The telephone rang and rang while he unlocked the door and fumbled for the light switch. He shouldn't have left the hospital, he shouldn't have. 'Goddamn it!' he said. He picked up the receiver and said, 'I just walked in the door!'

'There's a cake here that wasn't picked up,' the voice on the other end of the line said.

'What are you saying?' Howard asked.

'A cake,' the voice said. 'A sixteen-dollar cake.'

Howard held the receiver against his ear, trying to understand. 'I don't know anything about a cake,' he said. 'Jesus, what are you talking about?'

'Don't hand me that,' the voice said.

Howard hung up the telephone. He went into the kitchen and poured himself some whiskey. He called the hospital. But the child's condition remained the same; he was still sleeping and nothing had changed there. While water poured into the tub, Howard lathered his face and shaved. He'd just stretched out in the tub and closed his eyes when the telephone rang again. He hauled himself out, grabbed a towel, and hurried through the house, saying, 'Stupid, stupid,' for having left the hospital. But when he picked up the receiver and shouted, 'Hello!' there was no sound at the other end of the line. Then the caller hung up.

He arrived back at the hospital a little after midnight. Ann still sat in the chair beside the bed. She looked up at Howard, and then she looked back at the child. The child's eyes stayed closed, the head was still wrapped in bandages. His breathing was quiet and regular. From an apparatus over the bed hung a bottle of glucose with a tube running from the bottle to the boy's arm.

'How is he?' Howard said. 'What's all this?' waving at the glucose and the tube.

'Dr. Francis's orders,' she said. 'He needs nourishment. He needs to keep up his strength. Why doesn't he wake up, Howard? I don't understand, if he's all right.'

Howard put his hand against the back of her head. He ran his fingers through her hair. 'He's going to be all right. He'll wake up in a little while. Dr. Francis knows what's what.'

After a time, he said, 'Maybe you should go home and get some rest. I'll stay here. Just don't put up with this creep who keeps calling. Hang up right away.'

'Who's calling?' she asked.

'I don't know who, just somebody with nothing better to do than call up people. You go on now.'

She shook her head. 'No,' she said, 'I'm fine.'

'Really,' he said. 'Go home for a while, and then come back and spell me in the morning. It'll be all right. What did Dr. Francis say? He said Scotty's going to be all right. We don't have to worry. He's just sleeping now, that's all.'

A nurse pushed the door open. She nodded at them as she went to the bedside. She took the left arm out from under the covers and put her fingers on the wrist, found the pulse, then consulted her watch. In a little while, she put the arm back under the covers and moved to the foot of the bed, where she wrote something on a clipboard attached to the bed.

'How is he?' Ann said. Howard's hand was a weight on her shoulder. She was aware of the pressure from his fingers.

'He's stable,' the nurse said. Then she said, 'Doctor will be in again shortly. Doctor's back in the hospital. He's making rounds right now.'

'I was saying maybe she'd want to go home and get a little rest,' Howard said. 'After the doctor comes,' he said.

'She could do that,' the nurse said. 'I think you should both feel free to do that, if you wish.' The nurse was a big Scandinavian woman with blond hair. There was the trace of an accent in her speech.

'We'll see what the doctor says,' Ann said. 'I want to talk to the doctor. I don't think he should keep sleeping like this. I don't think that's a good sign.' She brought her hand up to her eyes and let her head come forward a little. Howard's grip tightened on her shoulder, and then his hand moved up to her neck, where his fingers began to knead the muscles there.

'Dr. Francis will be here in a few minutes,' the nurse said. Then she left the room.

Howard gazed at his son for a time, the small chest quietly rising and falling under the covers. For the first time since the terrible minutes after Ann's telephone call to him at his office, he felt a genuine fear starting in his limbs. He began shaking his head. Scotty was fine, but instead of sleeping at home in his own bed, he was in a hospital bed with bandages around his head and a tube in his arm. But this help was what he needed right now.

Dr. Francis came in and shook hands with Howard, though they'd just seen each other a few hours before. Ann got up from the chair. 'Doctor?'

'Ann,' he said and nodded. 'Let's just first see how he's doing,' the doctor said. He moved to the side of the bed and took the boy's pulse. He peeled back one eyelid and then the other. Howard and Ann stood beside the doctor and watched. Then the doctor turned back the covers and listened to the boy's heart and lungs with his stethoscope. He pressed his fingers here and there on the abdomen. When he was finished, he went to the end of the bed and studied the chart. He noted the time, scribbled something on the chart, and then looked at Howard and Ann.

'Doctor, how is he?' Howard said. 'What's the matter with him exactly?'

'Why doesn't he wake up?' Ann said.

The doctor was a handsome, big-shouldered man with a tanned face. He wore a three-piece blue suit, a striped tie, and ivory cuff links. His gray hair was combed along the sides of his head, and he looked as if he had just come from a concert. 'He's all right,' the doctor said. 'Nothing to shout about, he could be better, I think. But he's all right. Still, I wish he'd wake up. He should wake up pretty soon.' The doctor looked at the boy again. 'We'll know some more in a couple of hours, after the results of a few more tests are in. But he's all right, believe me, except for the hairline fracture of the skull. He does have that.'

'Oh, no,' Ann said.

'And a bit of a concussion, as I said before. Of course, you know he's in shock,' the doctor said. 'Sometimes you see this in shock cases. This sleeping.'

'But he's out of any real danger?' Howard said. 'You said before he's not in a coma. You wouldn't call this a coma, then – would you, doctor?' Howard waited. He looked at the doctor.

'No, I don't want to call it a coma,' the doctor said and glanced over at the boy once more. 'He's just in a very deep sleep. It's a restorative measure the body is taking on its own. He's out of any real danger, I'd say that for certain, yes. But we'll know more when he wakes up and the other tests are in,' the doctor said.

'It's a coma,' Ann said. 'Of sorts.'

'It's not a coma yet, not exactly,' the doctor said. 'I wouldn't want to call it coma. Not yet, anyway. He's suffered shock. In shock cases, this kind of reaction is common enough; it's a temporary reaction to bodily trauma. Coma. Well, coma is a deep, prolonged unconsciousness, something that could go on for days, or weeks even. Scotty's not in that area, not as far as we can tell. I'm certain his condition will show improvement by morning. I'm betting that it will. We'll know more when he wakes up, which shouldn't be long now. Of course, you may do as you like, stay here or go home for a time. But by all means feel free to leave the hospital for a while if you want. This is not easy, I know.' The doctor gazed at the boy again, watching him, and then he turned to Ann and said, 'You try not to worry, little mother. Believe me, we're doing all that can be done. It's just a question of a little more time now.' He nodded at her, shook hands with Howard again, and then he left the room.

Ann put her hand over the child's forehead. 'At least he doesn't have a fever,' she said. Then she said, 'My God, he feels so cold, though. Howard? Is he supposed to feel like this? Feel his head.'

Howard touched the child's temples. His own breathing had slowed. 'I think he's supposed to feel this way right now,' he said. 'He's in shock, remember? That's what the doctor said. The doctor was just in here. He would have said something if Scotty wasn't okay.'

Ann stood there a while longer, working her lip with her teeth. Then she moved over to her chair and sat down.

Howard sat in the chair next to her chair. They looked at each other. He wanted to say something else and reassure her, but he was afraid, too. He took her hand and put it in his lap, and this made him feel better, her hand being there. He picked up her hand and squeezed it. Then he just held her hand. They sat like that for a while, watching the boy and not talking. From time to time, he squeezed her hand. Finally, she took her hand away.

'I've been praying,' she said.

He nodded.

She said, 'I almost thought I'd forgotten how, but it came back to me. All I had to do was close my eyes and say, 'Please God, help us – help Scotty,' and then the rest was easy. The words were right there. Maybe if you prayed, too,' she said to him.

'I've already prayed,' he said. 'I prayed this afternoon – yesterday afternoon, I mean – after you called, while I was driving to the hospital. I've been praying,' he said.

'That's good,' she said. For the first time, she felt they were together in it, this trouble. She realized with a start that, until now, it had only been happening to her and to Scotty. She hadn't let Howard into it, though he was there and needed all along. She felt glad to be his wife.

The same nurse came in and took the boy's pulse again and checked the flow from the bottle hanging above the bed.

In an hour, another doctor came in. He said his name was Parsons, from Radiology. He had a bushy moustache. He was wearing loafers, a western shirt, and a pair of jeans.

'We're going to take him downstairs for more pictures,' he told them. 'We need to do some more pictures, and we want to do a scan.'

'What's that?' Ann said. 'A scan?' She stood between this new doctor and the bed. 'I thought you'd already taken all your X-rays.'

'I'm afraid we need some more,' he said. 'Nothing to be alarmed about. We just need some more pictures, and we want to do a brain scan on him.'

'My God,' Ann said.

'It's perfectly normal procedure in cases like this,' this new doctor said. 'We just need to find out for sure why he isn't back awake yet. It's normal medical procedure, and nothing to be alarmed about. We'll be taking him down in a few minutes,' this doctor said.

In a little while, two orderlies came into the room with a gurney. They were black-haired, dark-complexioned men in white uniforms, and they said a few words to each other in a foreign tongue as they unhooked the boy from the tube and moved him from his bed to the gurney. Then they wheeled him from the room. Howard and Ann got on the same elevator. Ann gazed at the child. She closed her eyes as the elevator began its descent. The orderlies stood at either end of the gurney without saying anything, though once one of the men made a comment to the other in their own language, and the other man nodded slowly in response.

Later that morning, just as the sun was beginning to lighten the windows in the waiting room outside the X-ray department, they brought the boy out and moved him back up to his room. Howard and Ann rode up on the elevator with him once more, and once more they took up their places beside the bed.

They waited all day, but still the boy did not wake up. Occasionally, one of them would leave the room to go downstairs to the cafeteria to drink coffee and then, as if suddenly remembering and feeling guilty, get up from the table and hurry back to the room. Dr. Francis came again that afternoon and examined the boy once more and then left after telling them he was coming along and could wake up at any minute now. Nurses, different nurses from the night before, came in from time to time. Then a young woman from the lab knocked and entered the room. She wore white slacks and a white blouse and carried a little tray of things which she put on the stand beside the bed. Without a word to them, she took blood from the boy's arm. Howard closed his eyes as the woman found the right place on the boy's arm and pushed the needle in.

'I don't understand this,' Ann said to the woman.

'Doctor's orders,' the young woman said. 'I do what I'm told. They say draw that one, I draw. What's wrong with him, anyway?' she said. 'He's a sweetie.'

'He was hit by a car,' Howard said. 'A hit-and-run.'

The young woman shook her head and looked again at the boy. Then she took her tray and left the room.

'Why won't he wake up?' Ann said. 'Howard? I want some answers from these people.'

Howard didn't say anything. He sat down again in the chair and crossed one leg over the other. He rubbed his face. He looked at his son and then he settled back in the chair, closed his eyes, and went to sleep.

Ann walked to the window and looked out at the parking lot. It was night, and cars were driving into and out of the parking lot with their lights on. She stood at the window with her hands gripping the sill, and knew in her heart that they were into something now, something hard. She was afraid, and her teeth began to chatter until she tightened her jaws. She saw a big car stop in front of the hospital and someone, a woman in a long coat, get into the car. She wished she were that woman and somebody, anybody, was driving her away from here to somewhere else, a place where she would find Scotty waiting for her when she stepped out of the car, ready to say Mom and let her gather him in her arms.

In a little while, Howard woke up. He looked at the boy again. Then he got up from the chair, stretched, and went over to stand beside her at the window. They both stared out at the parking lot. They didn't say anything. But they seemed to feel each other's insides now, as though the worry had made them transparent in a perfectly natural way.

The door opened and Dr. Francis came in. He was wearing a different suit and tie this time. His gray hair was combed along the sides of his head, and he looked as if he had just shaved. He went straight to the bed and examined the boy. 'He ought to have come around by now. There's just no good reason for this,' he said. 'But I can tell you we're all convinced he's out of any danger. We'll just feel better when he wakes up. There's no reason, absolutely none, why he shouldn't come around. Very soon. Oh, he'll have himself a dilly of a headache when he does, you can count on that. But all of his signs are fine. They're as normal as can be.'

'It is a coma, then?' Ann said.

The doctor rubbed his smooth cheek. 'We'll call it that for the time being, until he wakes up. But you must be worn out. This is hard. I know this is hard. Feel free to go out for a bite,' he said. 'It would do you good. I'll put a nurse in here while you're gone if you'll feel better about going. Go and have yourselves something to eat.'

'I couldn't eat anything,' Ann said.

'Do what you need to do, of course,' the doctor said. 'Anyway, I wanted to tell you that all the signs are good, the tests are negative, nothing showed up at all, and just as soon as he wakes up he'll be over the hill.'

'Thank you, doctor,' Howard said. He shook hands with the doctor again. The doctor patted Howard's shoulder and went out.

'I suppose one of us should go home and check on things,' Howard said. 'Slug needs to be fed, for one thing.'

'Call one of the neighbors,' Ann said. 'Call the Morgans. Anyone will feed a dog if you ask them to.'

'All right,' Howard said. After a while, he said, 'Honey, why don't you do it? Why don't you go home and check on things, and then come back? It'll do you good. I'll be right here with him. Seriously,' he said. 'We need to keep up our strength on this. We'll want to be here for a while even after he wakes up.'

'Why don't *you* go?' she said. 'Feed Slug. Feed yourself.'

'I already went,' he said. 'I was gone for exactly an hour and fifteen minutes. You go home for an hour and freshen up. Then come back.'

She tried to think about it, but she was too tired. She closed her eyes and tried to think about it again. After a time, she said, 'Maybe I *will* go home for a few minutes. Maybe if I'm not just sitting right here watching him every second, he'll wake up and be all right. You know? Maybe he'll wake up if I'm not here. I'll go home and take a bath and put on clean clothes. I'll feed Slug. Then I'll come back.'

'I'll be right here,' he said. 'You go on home, honey. I'll keep an eye on things here.' His eyes were bloodshot and small, as if he'd been drinking for a long time. His clothes were rumpled. His beard had come out again. She touched his face, and then she took her hand back. She understood he wanted to be by himself for a while, not have to talk or share his worry for a time. She picked her purse up from the nightstand, and he helped her into her coat.

'I won't be gone long,' she said.

'Just sit and rest for a little while when you get home,' he said. 'Eat something. Take a bath. After you get out of the bath, just sit for a while and rest. It'll do you a world of good, you'll see. Then come back,' he said. 'Let's try not to worry. You heard what Dr. Francis said.'

She stood in her coat for a minute trying to recall the doctor's exact words, looking for any nuances, any hint of something behind his words other than what he had said. She tried to remember if his expression had changed any when he bent over to examine the child. She remembered the way his features had composed themselves as he rolled back the child's eyelids and then listened to his breathing.

She went to the door, where she turned and looked back. She looked at the child, and then she looked at the father. Howard nodded. She stepped out of the room and pulled the door closed behind her.

She went past the nurses' station and down to the end of the corridor, looking for the elevator. At the end of the corridor, she turned to her right and entered a little waiting room where a Negro family sat in wicker chairs. There was a middle-aged man in a khaki shirt and pants, a baseball cap pushed back on his head. A large woman wearing a housedress and slippers was slumped in one of the chairs. A teenaged girl in jeans, hair done in dozens of little braids, lay stretched out in one of the chairs smoking a cigarette, her legs crossed at the ankles. The family swung their eyes to Ann as she entered the room. The little table was littered with hamburger wrappers and Styrofoam cups.

'Franklin,' the large woman said as she roused herself. 'Is it about Franklin?' Her eyes widened. 'Tell me now, lady,' the woman said. 'Is it about Franklin?' She was trying to rise from her chair, but the man had closed his hand over her arm.

'Here, here,' he said. 'Evelyn.'

'I'm sorry,' Ann said. 'I'm looking for the elevator. My son is in the hospital, and now I can't find the elevator.'

'Elevator is down that way, turn left,' the man said as he aimed a finger.

The girl drew on her cigarette and stared at Ann. Her eyes were narrowed to slits, and her broad lips parted slowly as she let the smoke escape. The Negro woman let her head fall on her shoulder and looked away from Ann, no longer interested.

'My son was hit by a car,' Ann said to the man. She seemed to need to explain herself. 'He has a concussion and a little skull fracture, but he's going to be all right. He's in shock now, but it might be some kind of coma, too. That's what really worries us, the coma part. I'm going out for a little while, but my husband is with him. Maybe he'll wake up while I'm gone.'

'That's too bad,' the man said and shifted in the chair. He shook his head. He looked down at the table, and then he looked back at Ann. She was still standing there. He said, 'Our Franklin, he's on the operating table. Somebody cut him. Tried to kill him. There was a fight where he was at. At this party. They say he was just standing and watching. Not bothering nobody. But that don't mean nothing these days. Now he's on the operating table. We're just hoping and praying, that's all we can do now.' He gazed at her steadily.

Ann looked at the girl again, who was still watching her, and at the older woman, who kept her head down, but whose eyes were now closed. Ann saw the lips moving silently, making words. She had an urge to ask what those words were. She wanted to talk more with these people who were in the same kind of waiting she was in. She was afraid, and they were afraid. They had that in common. She would have liked to have said something else about the accident, told them more about Scotty, that it had happened on the day of his birthday, Monday, and that he was still unconscious. Yet she didn't know how to begin. She stood looking at them without saying anything more.

She went down the corridor the man had indicated and found the elevator. She waited a minute in front of the closed doors, still wondering if she was doing the right thing. Then she put out her finger and touched the button.

She pulled into the driveway and cut the engine. She closed her eyes and leaned her head against the wheel for a minute. She listened to the ticking sounds the engine made as it began to cool. Then she got out of the car. She could hear the dog barking inside the house. She went to the front door, which was unlocked. She went inside and turned on lights and put on a kettle of water for tea. She opened some dog food and fed Slug on the back porch. The dog ate in hungry little smacks. It kept running into the kitchen to see that she was going to stay. As she sat down on the sofa with her tea, the telephone rang.

'Yes!' she said as she answered. 'Hello!'

'Mrs. Weiss,' a man's voice said. It was five o'clock in the morning, and she thought she could hear machinery or equipment of some kind in the background.

'Yes, yes! What is it?' she said. 'This is Mrs. Weiss. This is she. What is it, please?' She listened to whatever it was in the background. 'Is it Scotty, for Christ's sake?'

'Scotty,' the man's voice said. 'It's about Scotty, yes. It has to do with Scotty, that problem. Have you forgotten about Scotty?' the man said. Then he hung up.

She dialed the hospital's number and asked for the third floor. She demanded information about her son from the nurse who answered the telephone. Then she asked to speak to her husband. It was, she said, an emergency.

She waited, turning the telephone cord in her fingers. She closed her eyes and felt sick at her stomach. She would have to make herself eat. Slug came in from the back porch and lay down near her feet. He wagged his tail. She pulled at his ear while he licked her fingers. Howard was on the line.

'Somebody just called here,' she said. She twisted the telephone cord. 'He said it was about Scotty,' she cried.

'Scotty's fine,' Howard told her. 'I mean, he's still sleeping. There's been no change. The nurse has been in twice since you've been gone. A nurse or else a doctor. He's all right.'

'This man called. He said it was about Scotty,' she told him.

'Honey, you rest for a little while, you need the rest. It must be that same caller I had. Just forget it. Come back down here after you've rested. Then we'll have breakfast or something.'

'Breakfast,' she said. 'I don't want any breakfast.'

'You know what I mean,' he said. 'Juice, something. I don't know. I don't know anything, Ann. Jesus, I'm not hungry, either. Ann, it's hard to talk now. I'm standing here at the desk. Dr. Francis is coming again at eight o'clock this morning. He's going to have something to tell us then, something more definite. That's what one of the nurses said. She didn't know any more than that. Ann? Honey, maybe we'll know something more then. At eight o'clock. Come back here before eight. Meanwhile, I'm right here and Scotty's all right. He's still the same,' he added.

'I was drinking a cup of tea,' she said, 'when the telephone rang. They said it was about Scotty. There was a noise in the background. Was there a noise in the background on that call you had, Howard?'

'I don't remember,' he said. 'Maybe the driver of the car, maybe he's a psychopath and found out about Scotty somehow. But I'm here with him. Just rest like you were going to do. Take a bath and come back by seven or so, and we'll talk to the doctor together when he gets here. It's going to be all right, honey. I'm here, and there are doctors and nurses around. They say his condition is stable.'

'I'm scared to death,' she said.

She ran water, undressed, and got into the tub. She washed and dried quickly, not taking the time to wash her hair. She put on clean underwear, wool slacks, and a sweater. She went into the living room, where the dog looked up at her and let its tail thump once against the floor. It was just starting to get light outside when she went out to the car.

She drove into the parking lot of the hospital and found a space close to the front door. She felt she was in some obscure way responsible for what had happened to the child. She let her thoughts move to the Negro family. She remembered the name Franklin and the table that was covered with hamburger papers, and the teenaged girl staring at her as she drew on her cigarette. 'Don't have children,' she told the girl's image as she entered the front door of the hospital. 'For God's sake, don't.'

She took the elevator up to the third floor with two nurses who were just going on duty. It was Wednesday morning, a few minutes before seven. There was a page for a Dr. Madison as the elevator doors slid open on the third floor. She got off behind the nurses, who turned in the other direction and continued the conversation she had interrupted when she'd gotten into the elevator. She walked down the corridor to the little alcove where the Negro family had been waiting. They were gone now, but the chairs were scattered in such a way that it looked as if people had just jumped up from them the minute before. The tabletop was cluttered with the same cups and papers, the ashtray was filled with cigarette butts.

She stopped at the nurses' station. A nurse was standing behind the counter, brushing her hair and yawning.

'There was a Negro boy in surgery last night,' Ann said. 'Franklin was his name. His family was in the waiting room. I'd like to inquire about his condition.'

A nurse who was sitting at a desk behind the counter looked up from a chart in front of her. The telephone buzzed and she picked up the receiver, but she kept her eyes on Ann.

'He passed away,' said the nurse at the counter. The nurse held the hairbrush and kept looking at her. 'Are you a friend of the family or what?'

'I met the family last night,' Ann said. 'My own son is in the hospital. I guess he's in shock. We don't know for sure what's wrong. I just wondered about Franklin, that's all. Thank you.' She moved down the corridor. Elevator doors the same color as the walls slid open and a gaunt, bald man in white pants and white canvas shoes pulled a heavy cart off the elevator. She hadn't noticed these doors last night. The man wheeled the cart out into the corridor and stopped in front of the room nearest the elevator and consulted a clipboard. Then he reached down and slid a tray out of the cart. He rapped lightly on the door and entered the room. She could smell the unpleasant odors of warm food as she passed the cart. She hurried on without looking at any of the nurses and pushed open the door to the child's room.

Howard was standing at the window with his hands behind his back. He turned around as she came in.

'How is he?' she said. She went over to the bed. She dropped her purse on the floor beside the nightstand. It seemed to her she had been gone a long time. She touched the child's face. 'Howard?'

'Dr. Francis was here a little while ago,' Howard said. She looked at him closely and thought his shoulders were bunched a little.

'I thought he wasn't coming until eight o'clock this morning,' she said quickly.

'There was another doctor with him. A neurologist.'

'A neurologist,' she said.

Howard nodded. His shoulders were bunching, she could see that. 'What'd they say, Howard? For Christ's sake, what'd they say? What is it?'

'They said they're going to take him down and run more tests on him, Ann. They think they're going to operate, honey. Honey, they are going to operate. They can't figure out why he won't wake up. It's more than just shock or concussion, they know that much now. It's in his skull, the fracture, it has something, something to do with that, they think. So they're going to operate. I tried to call you, but I guess you'd already left the house.'

'Oh, God,' she said. 'Oh, please, Howard, please,' she said, taking his arms.

'Look!' Howard said. 'Scotty! Look, Ann!' He turned her toward the bed.

The boy had opened his eyes, then closed them. He opened them again now. The eyes stared straight ahead for a minute, then moved slowly in his head until they rested on Howard and Ann, then traveled away again.

'Scotty,' his mother said, moving to the bed.

'Hey, Scott,' his father said. 'Hey, son.'

They leaned over the bed. Howard took the child's hand in his hands and began to pat and squeeze the hand. Ann bent over the boy and kissed his forehead again and again. She put her hands on either side of his face. 'Scotty, honey, it's Mommy and Daddy,' she said. 'Scotty?'

The boy looked at them, but without any sign of recognition. Then his mouth opened, his eyes scrunched closed, and he howled until he had no more air in his lungs. His face seemed to relax and soften then. His lips parted as his last breath was puffed through his throat and exhaled gently through the clenched teeth.

The doctors called it a hidden occlusion and said it was a one-in-a-million circumstance. Maybe if it could have been detected somehow and surgery undertaken immediately, they could have saved him. But more than likely not. In any case, what would they have been looking for? Nothing had shown up in the tests or in the X-rays.

Dr. Francis was shaken. 'I can't tell you how badly I feel. I'm so very sorry, I can't tell you,' he said as he led them into the doctors' lounge. There was a doctor sitting in a chair with his legs hooked over the back of another chair, watching an early-morning TV show. He was wearing a green delivery room outfit, loose green pants and green blouse, and a green cap that covered his hair. He looked at Howard and Ann and then looked at Dr. Francis. He got to his feet and turned off the set and went out of the room. Dr. Francis guided Ann to the sofa, sat down beside her, and began to talk in a low, consoling voice. At one point, he leaned over and embraced her. She could feel his chest rising and falling evenly against her shoulder. She kept her eyes open and let him hold her. Howard went into the bathroom, but he left the door open.

After a violent fit of weeping, he ran water and washed his face. Then he came out and sat down at the little table that held a telephone. He looked at the telephone as though deciding what to do first. He made some calls. After a time, Dr. Francis used the telephone.

'Is there anything else I can do for the moment?' he asked them.

Howard shook his head. Ann stared at Dr. Francis as if unable to comprehend his words.

The doctor walked them to the hospital's front door. People were entering and leaving the hospital. It was eleven o'clock in the morning. Ann was aware of how slowly, almost reluctantly, she moved her feet. It seemed to her that Dr. Francis was making them leave when she felt they should stay, when it would be more the right thing to do to stay. She gazed out into the parking lot and then turned around and looked back at the front of the hospital. She began shaking her head. 'No, no,' she said. 'I can't leave him here, no.' She heard herself say that and thought how unfair it was that the only words that came out were the sort of words used on TV shows where people were stunned by violent or sudden deaths. She wanted her words to be her own. 'No,' she said, and for some reason the memory of the Negro woman's head lolling on the woman's shoulder came to her. 'No,' she said again.

'I'll be talking to you later in the day,' the doctor was saying to Howard. 'There are still some things that have to be done, things that have to be cleared up to our satisfaction. Some things that need explaining.'

'An autopsy,' Howard said.

Dr. Francis nodded.

'I understand,' Howard said. Then he said, 'Oh, Jesus. No, I don't understand, doctor. I can't, I can't. I just can't.'

Dr. Francis put his arm around Howard's shoulders. 'I'm sorry. God, how I'm sorry.' He let go of Howard's shoulders and held out his hand. Howard looked at the hand, and then he took it. Dr. Francis put his arms around Ann once more. He seemed full of some goodness she didn't understand. She let her head rest on his shoulder, but her eyes stayed open. She kept looking at the hospital. As they drove out of the parking lot, she looked back at the hospital.

At home, she sat on the sofa with her hands in her coat pockets. Howard closed the door to the child's room. He got the coffee-maker going and then he found an empty box. He had thought to pick up some of the child's things that were scattered around the living room. But instead he sat down beside her on the sofa, pushed the box to one side, and leaned forward, arms between his knees. He began to weep. She pulled his head over into her lap and patted his shoulder. 'He's gone,' she said. She kept patting his shoulder. Over his sobs, she could hear the coffee-maker hissing in the kitchen. 'There, there,' she said tenderly. 'Howard, he's gone. He's gone and now we'll have to get used to that. To being alone.'

In a little while, Howard got up and began moving aimlessly around the room with the box, not putting anything into it, but collecting some things together on the floor at one end of the sofa. She continued to sit with her hands in her coat pockets. Howard put the box down and brought coffee into the living room.

Later, Ann made calls to relatives. After each call had been placed and the party had answered, Ann would blurt out a few words and cry for a minute. Then she would quietly explain, in a measured voice, what had happened and tell them about arrangements. Howard took the box out to the garage, where he saw the child's bicycle. He dropped the box and sat down on the pavement beside the bicycle. He took hold of the bicycle awkwardly so that it leaned against his chest. He held it, the rubber pedal sticking into his chest. He gave the wheel a turn.

Ann hung up the telephone after talking to her sister. She was looking up another number when the telephone rang. She picked it up on the first ring.

'Hello,' she said, and she heard something in the background, a humming noise. 'Hello!' she said. 'For God's sake,' she said. 'Who is this? What is it you want?'

'Your Scotty, I got him ready for you,' the man's voice said. 'Did you forget him?'

'You evil bastard!' she shouted into the receiver. 'How can you do this, you evil son of a bitch?'

'Scotty,' the man said. 'Have you forgotten about Scotty?' Then the man hung up on her.

Howard heard the shouting and came in to find her with her head on her arms over the table, weeping. He picked up the receiver and listened to the dial tone.

Much later, just before midnight, after they had dealt with many things, the telephone rang again.

'You answer it,' she said. 'Howard, it's him, I know.' They were sitting at the kitchen table with coffee in front of them. Howard had a small glass of whiskey beside his cup. He answered on the third ring.

'Hello,' he said. 'Who is this? Hello! Hello!' The line went dead. 'He hung up,' Howard said. 'Whoever it was.'

'It was him,' she said. 'That bastard. I'd like to kill him,' she said. 'I'd like to shoot him and watch him kick,' she said.

'Ann, my God,' he said.

'Could you hear anything?' she said. 'In the background? A noise, machinery, something humming?'

'Nothing, really. Nothing like that,' he said. 'There wasn't much time. I think there was some radio music. Yes, there was a radio going, that's all I could tell. I don't know what in God's name is going on,' he said.

She shook her head. 'If I could, could get my hands on him.' It came to her then. She knew who it was. Scotty, the cake, the telephone number. She pushed the chair away from the table and got up. 'Drive me down to the shopping center,' she said. 'Howard.'

'What are you saying?'

'The shopping center. I know who it is who's calling. I know who it is. It's the baker, the son-of-a-bitching baker, Howard. I had him bake a cake for Scotty's birthday. That's who's calling. That's who has the number and keeps calling us. To harass us about that cake. The baker, that bastard.'

They drove down to the shopping center. The sky was clear and stars were out. It was cold, and they ran the heater in the car. They parked in front of the bakery. All of the shops and stores were closed, but there were cars at the far end of the lot in front of the movie theater. The bakery windows were dark, but when they looked through the glass they could see a light in the back room and, now and then, a big man in an apron moving in and out of the white, even light. Through the glass, she could see the display cases and some little tables with chairs. She tried the door. She rapped on the glass. But if the baker heard them, he gave no sign. He didn't look in their direction.

They drove around behind the bakery and parked. They got out of the car. There was a lighted window too high up for them to see inside. A sign near the back door said THE PANTRY BAKERY, SPECIAL ORDERS. She could hear faintly a radio playing inside and something creak – an oven door as it was pulled down? She knocked on the door and waited. Then she knocked again, louder. The radio was turned down and there was a scraping sound now, the distinct sound of something, a drawer, being pulled open and then closed.

Someone unlocked the door and opened it. The baker stood in the light and peered out at them. 'I'm closed for business,' he said. 'What do you want at this hour? It's midnight. Are you drunk or something?'

She stepped into the light that fell through the open door. He blinked his heavy eyelids as he recognized her. 'It's you,' he said.

'It's me,' she said. 'Scotty's mother. This is Scotty's father. We'd like to come in.'

The baker said, 'I'm busy now. I have work to do.'

She had stepped inside the doorway anyway. Howard came in behind her. The baker moved back. 'It smells like a bakery in here. Doesn't it smell like a bakery in here, Howard?'

'What do you want?' the baker said. 'Maybe you want your cake? That's it, you decided you want your cake. You ordered a cake, didn't you?'

'You're pretty smart for a baker,' she said. 'Howard, this is the man who's been calling us.' She clenched her fists. She stared at him fiercely. There was a deep burning inside her, an anger that made her feel larger than herself, larger than either of these men.

'Just a minute here,' the baker said. 'You want to pick up your three-day-old cake? That it? I don't want to argue with you, lady. There it sits over there, getting stale. I'll give it to you for half of what I quoted you. No. You want it? You can have it. It's no good to me, no good to anyone now. It cost me time and money to make that cake. If you want it, okay, if you don't, that's okay, too. I have to get back to work.' He looked at them and rolled his tongue behind his teeth.

'More cakes,' she said. She knew she was in control of it, of what was increasing in her. She was calm.

'Lady, I work sixteen hours a day in this place to earn a living,' the baker said. He wiped his hands on his apron. 'I work night and day in here, trying to make ends meet.' A look crossed Ann's face that made the baker move back and say, 'No trouble, now.' He reached to the counter and picked up a rolling pin with his right hand and began to tap it against the palm of his other hand. 'You want the cake or not? I have to get back to work. Bakers work at night,' he said again. His eyes were small, mean-looking, she thought, nearly lost in the bristly flesh around his cheeks. His neck was thick with fat.

'I know bakers work at night,' Ann said. 'They make phone calls at night, too. You bastard,' she said.

The baker continued to tap the rolling pin against his hand. He glanced at Howard. 'Careful, careful,' he said to Howard.

'My son's dead,' she said with a cold, even finality. 'He was hit by a car Monday morning. We've been waiting with him until he died. But, of course, you couldn't be expected to know that, could you? Bakers can't know everything – can they, Mr. Baker? But he's dead. He's dead, you bastard!' Just as suddenly as it had welled in her, the anger dwindled, gave way to something else, a dizzy feeling of nausea. She leaned against the wooden table that was sprinkled with flour, put her hands over her face, and began to cry, her shoulders rocking back and forth. 'It isn't fair,' she said. 'It isn't, isn't fair.'

Howard put his hand at the small of her back and looked at the baker. 'Shame on you,' Howard said to him. 'Shame.'

The baker put the rolling pin back on the counter. He undid his apron and threw it on the counter. He looked at them, and then he shook his head slowly. He pulled a chair out from under the card table that held papers and receipts, an adding machine, and a telephone directory. 'Please sit down,' he said. 'Let me get you a chair,' he said to Howard. 'Sit down now, please.' The baker went into the front of the shop and returned with two little wrought-iron chairs. 'Please sit down, you people.'

Ann wiped her eyes and looked at the baker. 'I wanted to kill you,' she said. 'I wanted you dead.'

The baker had cleared a space for them at the table. He shoved the adding machine to one side, along with the stacks of notepaper and receipts. He pushed the telephone directory onto the floor, where it landed with a thud. Howard and Ann sat down and pulled their chairs up to the table. The baker sat down, too.

'Let me say how sorry I am,' the baker said, putting his elbows on the table. 'God alone knows how sorry. Listen to me. I'm just a baker. I don't claim to be anything else. Maybe once, maybe years ago, I was a different kind of human being. I've forgotten, I don't know for sure. But I'm not any longer, if I ever was. Now I'm just a baker. That don't excuse my doing what I did, I know. But I'm deeply sorry. I'm sorry for your son, and sorry for my part in this,' the baker said. He spread his hands out on the table and turned them over to reveal his palms. 'I don't have any children myself, so I can only imagine what you must be feeling. All I can say to you now is that I'm sorry. Forgive me, if you can,' the baker said. 'I'm not an evil man, I don't think. Not evil, like you said on the phone. You got to understand what it comes down to is I don't know how to act anymore, it would seem. Please,' the man said, 'let me ask you if you can find it in your hearts to forgive me?'

It was warm inside the bakery. Howard stood up from the table and took off his coat. He helped Ann from her coat. The baker looked at them for a minute and then nodded and got up from the table. He went to the oven and turned off some switches. He found cups and poured coffee from an electric coffee-maker. He put a carton of cream on the table, and a bowl of sugar.

'You probably need to eat something,' the baker said. 'I hope you'll eat some of my hot rolls. You have to eat and keep going. Eating is a small, good thing in a time like this,' he said.

He served them warm cinnamon rolls just out of the oven, the icing still runny. He put butter on the table and knives to spread the butter. Then the baker sat down at the table with them. He waited. He waited until they each took a roll from the platter and began to eat. 'It's good to eat something,' he said, watching them. 'There's more. Eat up. Eat all you want. There's all the rolls in the world in here.'

They ate rolls and drank coffee. Ann was suddenly hungry, and the rolls were warm and sweet. She ate three of them, which pleased the baker. Then he began to talk. They listened carefully. Although they were tired and in anguish, they listened to what the baker had to say. They nodded when the baker began to speak of loneliness, and of the sense of doubt and limitation that had come to him in his middle years. He told them what it was like to be childless all these years. To repeat the days with the ovens endlessly full and endlessly empty. The party food, the celebrations he'd worked over. Icing knuckle-deep. The tiny wedding couples stuck into cakes. Hundreds of them, no, thousands by now. Birthdays. Just imagine all those candles burning. He had a necessary trade. He was a baker. He was glad he wasn't a florist. It was better to be feeding people. This was a better smell anytime than flowers.

'Smell this,' the baker said, breaking open a dark loaf. 'It's a heavy bread, but rich.' They smelled it, then he had them taste it. It had the taste of molasses and coarse grains. They listened to him. They ate what they could. They swallowed the dark bread. It was like daylight under the fluorescent trays of light. They talked on into the early morning, the high, pale cast of light in the windows, and they did not think of leaving.

 To access worksheet 1.3 on 'A Small, Good Thing', please visit www.pearsonbacconline.com and follow the on-screen instructions.

INSIGHTS INTO FICTION

So what are the conventions of fiction and what expectations should you have as a reader?

The world of fiction is a world with its own time and place. It has its own weather, its own history and its own moral code. The characters that inhabit these worlds are not to be confused with real people, but they may amuse and frighten or surprise us in much the same way and for many of the same reasons that people do. Fiction writers invite their readers into their worlds and hold them there with stories and characters that engage a reader intellectually and emotionally. When we experience the world of a text, when we engage with it, when we willingly immerse ourselves in that world, we read actively. **It is only through active reading that we can experience a text.**

1   Determining point of view, the perspective through which a story is told, is critical. Once a reader is aware of perspective, he understands the limitations that the point of view may intrinsically provide. A first-person perspective, while immediate and engaging, cannot provide the range of information, and consequently, understanding of a situation and the characters in that situation that an omniscient narration can provide. What is important to realize is that the writer might not want to reveal certain information about a situation or specific understanding about a character. Writers make conscious choices depending upon the way they want the text to be read as well as the way it is understood. Only a naive reader would assume that every writer should tell his or her story in the same way with a straightforward, chronological, omniscient narration.

2   Voice is an essential element of point of view. While point of view is the angle of vision, the perspective from which a story is told – the voice of the narrator – informs that perspective. What this means is that the speaker's tone of voice and attitude directly influence how the reader receives the narration. For example, imagine a sarcastic narrator's account of a serious car accident. Now imagine the same account told by a witness, the mother of the driver. Would the account detailed by a television reporter embrace a substantially different tone? Voice makes a substantive difference in any fiction text.

3 When you examine the structure of a work of fiction, you are actually examining other aspects as well. The structure of the plot relates to the presentation of time within the work as well as the presentation of place. Are events revealed slowly over time? Is the ordering of events chronological? Are chapters within a novel arranged purposefully to accommodate plot? Or, are chapters arranged seemingly at random? In fiction, the text is always purposefully rather than arbitrarily arranged.

4 Consider the writer's development or lack of development of characters. Stereotypical characters, flat as opposed to round characters, stock characters such as evil villains or innocent maidens, are created with specific purposes in mind. Depending on the writer's intention, characters may not engage the reader at all. They may function as representations of character types, or they may function symbolically. Do characters change? Do they differentiate themselves from each other? Are characters vehicles for thematic understanding or social commentary?

5 While it is important to consider the purpose of a fictional text, the themes, messages and lessons about the nature of our world and ourselves are often addressed as simplistic platitudes that have little bearing on the text itself. Assuming that a theme will emerge full blown at the end of a text is absurd. Thematic ideas must always be differentiated from theme. To say that the theme of the story is love is a misstatement. While love, and the ways that we respond to it, may be considered a subject of theme, it is not a theme. A theme is a statement, a complete idea, stated in a complete sentence or several sentences. For example, the theme that love is a gift we give ourselves is a complex statement that requires explanation and elaboration. Themes that are simplistically stated are, more often than not, forced observations that are based on false assumptions about the characters and situations of the fiction.

6 A writer's style is determined by his or her use of language and syntax (sentence structure). Figurative language, language that evokes additional meaning in the mind's eye of the reader (as opposed to the literal, denotative meaning of words), creates imagery, develops symbol and evokes connotation and comparison through the expression of simile, metaphor and personification. Syntactic patterns, the use of complex sentences or even the use of fragments, are also important to note. Is there a prose rhythm created by the pattern of sentences? Does the prose rhythm speed up or slow down as a way to underscore, or emphasize, the fictional situation?

7 Are there any ironies within the fiction? Does the title have a literal as well as a figurative meaning? Is this meaning ironic? Consider the function of irony within the text. Is there situational or verbal irony? Does the irony function to underscore character, theme or both?

2 CONVENTIONS OF DRAMA

Learning Outcomes

Knowledge and Understanding
- Understand drama as performance literature
- Consider the advantages and limitations of staging
- Understand the creation of momentum
- Identify dramatic structure and effect on the audience
- Explore conventions and expectations of drama

Appreciation
- Appreciate drama on both page and stage
- Explore importance of themes, characters and action
- Evaluate the importance of setting and props
- Evaluate the importance of dialogue and sound
- Appreciate and analyze a variety of plays
- Consider the function of stage devices

Knowledge and Understanding

Every play has one common aspect: it is written to be performed. What this means for you as a reader is that you must call upon your imagination to see the characters and to hear the same words, sounds, actions and movements that you would experience as a member of an audience viewing a play.

While drama and prose fiction share the common elements of plot, characters and themes, the ways in which playwrights render these elements are quite distinct. The stage, and the position of the audience in relation to that stage, have limitations which the prose fiction writer does not have. For example, the physical space of the stage restricts the types of action

Theatrical performances are amongst the most immediate forms of literary presentation. The words of a script are meant to be enacted, not simply read from the page.

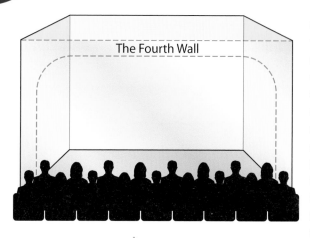

The Fourth Wall

A visual representation of the 'Fourth Wall', the imaginary wall through which the audience witnesses the action of a play.

a playwright can display. While in prose fiction readers can witness descriptions of horses stampeding, elephants parading or characters water-skiing, such action is generally unavailable on stage. Prose fiction writers also have a variety of perspectives or angles of vision to use in their works. The playwright essentially has one point of view, and that is essentially the dramatic perspective of the audience members themselves, sometimes referred to as the 'fourth wall'. If a playwright wants to reveal motivation for an action, and get inside the mind of the character, then that motivation must be revealed directly to the audience. We have to listen and watch the characters to discover their interior thoughts. Dialogue, then, becomes the primary vehicle for the playwright. Character action and interaction, gestures, props, the configuration of the stage itself, lighting and sound – all contribute to the experience of the audience, but words, and how they are spoken by the actors, produce the greatest effects on the audience. Even if you are unable to view a play physically, learning the conventions and expectations of drama will enable you to 'see' the play in your mind's eye as you read it.

Dramatic strategies

A dramatic strategy is one of many tools available to the playwright to create specific effects either on stage or in the reading of a play. These tools are called dramatic conventions.

Bertolt Brecht, the German playwright, was particularly known for the 'alienation effect' in his plays, using techniques to generate distance between the performance and the audience.

Conventions and expectations of drama

Drama as an 'artifice' employs a number of strategies that bring to life the imaginary world of the play. Playwrights might want their audiences to embrace the theatrical world wholly or in part. Realistic drama invites audiences to view the world on stage as a familiar one. The characters, words, actions and stage sets, regardless of culture or time frame, are approachable as opposed to alienating. The character emotions are familiar and so the response of the audience is to some degree sympathetic. The psychological distance between audience and performance is minimized. In these plays, the audience experiences more emotion and participates actively from behind the fourth wall. In these plays, the audience 'suspends disbelief' and accepts that the world on stage before them is realistic and, therefore, can offer them emotional intensity and release.

Other playwrights might want their audiences to be fully aware of the artifice of their presentation, and may consciously work at dissolving the fourth wall so that audiences are reminded throughout the performance that the presentation before them is just that – a presentation that challenges the audience's subjectivity. These types of dramatic experiences keep audiences at a purposeful distance from the emotional impact of the work. A detached, somewhat objective, audience perspective is the goal similar to Bertolt Brecht's 'alienation effect'. The 'alienation effect' seeks to keep audience members well aware that what they are witnessing on stage is purely artificial; in this way, audiences will remain alienated, or emotionally distant, from the world they witness on stage.

The audience's emotional investment in a play can be manipulated by the playwright to great effect. Dramatic irony, for example, when the audience recognizes the truth or falsity of words or actions when characters do not, can heighten the emotional investment of the audience. The tension that such knowledge produces in the audience can drive the play forward as audience members anticipate the eventual revelation of truth.

What are the conventions of drama and what sort of expectations do we bring to plays as audience or readers? For all drama, we have a stage on which actors play out the words and actions of the playwright. Stages come in various shapes and sizes with equally varied configurations of audience seating. The stage is the setting of the play's action, and the

world of character interaction. To stage a play means to bring the play to life. Staging, then, refers to all of the decisions of a play's production, including the positioning of actors, their movements on stage, the construction of the set (including the placement and physical attributes of props), as well as the use of lighting, costume and sound devices.

Your task, as a reader, is to pay attention to every detail of the stage. You must construct the stage in your imagination, noting positions, shapes, colours and sizes of every detail provided in the stage directions. Note where doors and windows are located, because these staging devices differentiate the interior world of the play (on-stage) from its exterior world (off-stage).

Actors assume the roles of characters. Just as in prose fiction, a play can have major and minor characters, foil characters, a protagonist, an antagonist, and, in the case of memory plays, a narrator. You will need to examine characters carefully and pay particular attention to stage directions regarding the way that a character is described initially. Note physical and costume descriptions that appear in the stage directions so that you can imagine a character

Memory plays
Memory plays use a character as a narrator who typically stands off to the side of the stage and provides background exposition, clarification or explanation to the drama unfolding on stage.

A theatre in the round.

Can reading a play provide the same dramatic insight as watching a play?

visually. Also note any stage direction that describes the way a character speaks. Often, the manner in which a line is delivered can be just as important, or more so, than the words themselves. When watching a play, we have the added benefit of the actor's voice, which can suggest subtle meanings beyond the words themselves. When reading, however, voice moderation, accenting and pacing of the playwright's words can only be noted through written stage directions.

Dialogue is a major cause of dramatic momentum, increasing tension between characters or pushing plot development.

Actions on stage, whether overt or subtle, together with the words spoken by characters, serve to advance the plot of the play. Momentum, which drives the play forward, is often associated with increasing tension. As you read, you must be sensitive to those actions or situations that create reaction in one or more characters. These reactions allow you to watch character development unfold before your eyes. By reading closely you can identify what subject matter, action or interaction triggers an explosively tense moment or a moment of absolute silence. Both reactions are important to recognize because in either situation, momentum builds.

Dramatic action can be the fulfilment of rising tension, or can create new tensions in itself.

Silence on stage often prompts complete silence from the audience, as they are waiting for something important to happen or be said.

By creating the forward motion, the momentum, of a play, the playwright allows the audience to invest emotionally in the characters and their situations on stage. Tension, whether overt or subtly presented, extends to the audience. Ideally, the audience embraces the tension, driving forward their engagement with plot. Quite simply, the moment that the audience wants to know what is going to happen next, is the moment that creates momentum.

Dramatic structure

In 1863 German dramatist and novelist Gustav Freytag created his 'Pyramid' to explain the predictable order for the unfolding of a play. The five-part structure was basically as follows:

- Exposition
- Rising action
- Climax/crisis (a turning point)
- Falling action/reversal
- Dénouement

Of course, as drama has developed through the centuries, the structuring of plays has been modified. Rather than beginning with the prescribed exposition or background, many playwrights choose to engage their audience from the outset, seemingly dropping their audiences into the action of the play. This immediate engagement in the middle of action – *in medias res* – is often provocative. Audiences and readers alike have little time to ease into the action of the play. The effects are sometimes startling, or confusing, but the expectation is that spectators are actively engaged from the onset. Passive observation, for these playwrights, is a thing of the past.

The 'well-made play'

One modification of Freytag's traditional five-part structure is the structure 19th-century Norwegian playwright Henrik Ibsen used to great effect – the 'well-made play'. In this format, the plot involves a character withholding a secret. Through a series of events and actions, tension and suspense build steadily to the moment of climax when a secret is revealed and the character's fear of ultimate loss is translated into gain. Death and destruction give way to freedom and understanding – a new life, so to speak, emerges for the character.

A well-made play incorporates many of the following elements:
- A protagonist's secret
- Mistaken identity
- Misplaced documents
- Well-timed entrances and exits
- A battle of wits
- A climactic scene reveals the secret
- Logical dénouement

We will examine these elements later in this chapter in our 'Appreciation' section. In this section, however, you will have the opportunity to apply the concepts of dramatic convention and the subsequent expectations for you as a reader of drama.

A scene from Henrik Ibsen's great play, *A Doll's House*.

Other dramatic classifications

In addition to the realistic play and the well-made play, there are a number of other types of plays that you may study in one or more parts of the programme, including theatre of the absurd, classical or Elizabethan comedy and tragedy (see Chapter 3, Conventions of Poetry), and tragicomedy. Theatre of the Absurd, for example, is a term coined by Martin Esslin and refers to a nonrealistic form of drama. Characters, staging and action all run counter to our expectations of realistic drama. The world of the absurd is peopled with

Here we see Eugène Ionesco, one of the greatest exponents of the Theatre of the Absurd, standing beneath a poster advertising one of his plays.

▼

Patrick Stewart (left) and Sir Ian McKellen perform a scene from Samuel Beckett's *Waiting for Godot*.

confusion, despair, illogicality and incongruity. Action is frequently repetitive or seemingly irrational. Characters are often confused, and metaphysical themes tend to reinforce that the world is incomprehensible. Ionesco's *The Bald Soprano* and Beckett's *Waiting for Godot* are well-known plays of this classification.

SUMMARY

The more realistic the play, the more often the playwright intends to engage the audience emotionally. Less realistic drama, such as absurdist plays, often disregard the emotional sympathies of the audience in favour of their intellectual responses. Do not assume that playwrights always want their audiences to identify with characters and their situations.

Considering theme in drama

Themes in drama, like those in prose fiction, are ideas that express an understanding of some aspect of human nature. Themes express lessons common to the human condition, so the time and place of the play is inconsequential to the lessons about what it means to be human. While thematic ideas can be expressed in single words or short phrases, themes are expressed in sentence form. For example, the word 'fear' is a thematic idea while the statement, 'Anger and rage are often manifestations of fear', would be a statement of theme.

EXERCISE 1

Below are five thematic ideas. Try to describe at least four possible themes for each thematic idea, creating ideas that would translate readily into a theatrical production.

- Jealousy
- Forgiveness
- Love
- Freedom
- Competition

Considering time in drama

How does a playwright account for the passage of time on stage? In some instances, a playwright can use the designation of scenes themselves to indicate that time is passing. Closing the curtain or blacking out the stage between scenes or acts implicitly prompts the audience to assume that there will be changes in either the location of the set or in the time of the next scene. These mechanical devices work in the way that a chapter break works in prose fiction. Audiences anticipate change.

Playwrights can also use props on stage to signify the passage of time. Lighting a lamp, winding a clock, using background lighting or visuals (such as a sunset the audience can view from a window), all are effective means of showing time passing. Characters' words and actions and changes in costume can also signify a time shift. As a reader, you can expect that time will progress within the literal time span of the performance. But time considerations can take on more significance as well. Apart from the passage of time that an audience member observes as it occurs on stage, time can also function in relation to other conventions of drama. For example, the pacing of a scene can influence the momentum of the play itself, as well as how we respond to characters and their interactions. In Ibsen's *A Doll's House*, for example, time functions as an antagonist. Time is Nora's enemy. Ibsen slows specific scenes and quickens the pace of other scenes to enhance the tension that drives the play forward to its resolution.

What constitutes a 'striking theatrical experience'?

When all is said and done, when that curtain comes down, the lights fade, or you turn that last page, what thoughts and feelings do you carry with you? Peter Brook, author and critic of film and theatre, seeks an answer to these questions in his work entitled *The Empty Space*:

> I know of one acid test in the theatre. […] When a performance is over, what remains? Fun can be forgotten, but powerful emotion also disappears and good arguments lose their thread. When emotion and argument are harnessed to a wish from the audience to see more clearly into itself – then something in the mind burns. The event scorches on to the memory of an outline, a taste, a trace, a smell – a picture. It is the play's central image that remains, its silhouette, and if the elements are rightly blended this silhouette will be its meaning, this shape will be the essence of what it has to say. When years later I think of a striking theatrical experience I find a kernel engraved on my memory: two tramps under a tree, an old woman dragging a cart, a sergeant dancing, three people on a sofa in hell – or occasionally a trace deeper than any imagery. I haven't a hope of remembering the meanings precisely, but from the kernel I can reconstruct a set of meanings. Then a purpose will have been served. A few hours could amend my thinking for life. This is almost but not quite impossible to achieve.
> – Peter Brook, *The Empty Space* (1968)

SUMMARY

A striking theatrical experience, as defined by Brook, is often encapsulated into a single moment, a single image onstage, that holds insight into understanding the self.

As you work through the following exercises in drama, consider how your appreciation of the playwright's choices, his dramatic strategies, contribute to your theatrical experience of each text.

Appreciation

A Doll's House by Henrik Ibsen (1879)

Using the following extract from Act 1 of Henrik Ibsen's *A Doll's House*, test your close-reading skills. The prompts that follow the text are designed to guide your approach to this 'well-made play'.

Act 1

[*Scene.– A room furnished comfortably and tastefully, but not extravagantly. At the back, a door to the right leads to the entrance-hall, another to the left leads to Helmer's study. Between the doors stands a piano. In the middle of the left-hand wall is a door, and beyond it a window. Near the window are a round table, arm-chairs and a small sofa. In the right-hand wall, at the farther end, another door; and on the same side, nearer the footlights, a stove, two easy chairs and a rocking-chair; between the stove and the door, a small table. Engravings on the walls; a cabinet with china and other small objects; a small book-case with well-bound books. The floors are carpeted, and a fire burns in the stove.*

It is winter. A bell rings in the hall; shortly afterwards the door is heard to open. Enter Nora, humming a tune and in high spirits. She is in outdoor dress and carries a number of parcels; these she lays on the table to the right. She leaves the outer door open after her, and through it is seen a porter who is carrying a Christmas Tree and a basket, which he gives to the maid who has opened the door.]

NORA:	Hide the Christmas Tree carefully, Helen. Be sure the children do not see it until this evening, when it is dressed. [*To the porter, taking out her purse.*] How much?
PORTER:	Sixpence.
NORA:	There is a shilling. No, keep the change. [*The porter thanks her, and goes out. Nora shuts the door. She is laughing to herself, as she takes off her hat and coat. She takes a packet of macaroons from her pocket and eats one or two; then goes cautiously to her husband's door and listens.*] Yes, he is in. [*Still humming, she goes to the table on the right.*]
HELMER:	[*calls out from his room*]. Is that my little lark twittering out there?
NORA:	[*busy opening some of the parcels*]. Yes, it is!
HELMER:	Is it my little squirrel bustling about?
NORA:	Yes!
HELMER:	When did my squirrel come home?
NORA:	Just now. [*Puts the bag of macaroons into her pocket and wipes her mouth.*] Come in here, Torvald, and see what I have bought.
HELMER:	Don't disturb me. [*A little later, he opens the door and looks into the room, pen in hand.*] Bought, did you say? All these things? Has my little spendthrift been wasting money again?

NORA:	Yes but, Torvald, this year we really can let ourselves go a little. This is the first Christmas that we have not needed to economise.
HELMER:	Still, you know, we can't spend money recklessly.
NORA:	Yes, Torvald, we may be a wee bit more reckless now, mayn't we? Just a tiny wee bit! You are going to have a big salary and earn lots and lots of money.
HELMER:	Yes, after the New Year; but then it will be a whole quarter before the salary is due.
NORA:	Pooh! we can borrow until then.
HELMER:	Nora! [*Goes up to her and takes her playfully by the* ear.] The same little featherhead! Suppose, now, that I borrowed fifty pounds today, and you spent it all in the Christmas week, and then on New Year's Eve a slate fell on my head and killed me, and –
NORA:	[*putting her hands over his mouth*]. Oh! don't say such horrid things.
HELMER:	Still, suppose that happened, – what then?
NORA:	If that were to happen, I don't suppose I should care whether I owed money or not.
HELMER:	Yes, but what about the people who had lent it?
NORA:	They? Who would bother about them? I should not know who they were.
HELMER:	That is like a woman! But seriously, Nora, you know what I think about that. No debt, no borrowing. There can be no freedom or beauty about a home life that depends on borrowing and debt. We two have kept bravely on the straight road so far, and we will go on the same way for the short time longer that there need be any struggle.
NORA:	[*moving towards the stove*]. As you please, Torvald.
HELMER:	[*following her*]. Come, come, my little skylark must not droop her wings. What is this! Is my little squirrel out of temper? [*Taking out his purse.*] Nora, what do you think I have got here?
NORA:	[*turning round quickly*]. Money!
HELMER:	There you are. [*Gives her some money.*] Do you think I don't know what a lot is wanted for housekeeping at Christmas-time?
NORA:	[*counting*]. Ten shillings – a pound – two pounds! Thank you, thank you, Torvald; that will keep me going for a long time.
HELMER:	Indeed it must.
NORA:	Yes, yes, it will. But come here and let me show you what I have bought. And all so cheap! Look, here is a new suit for Ivar, and a sword; and a horse and a trumpet for Bob; and a doll and dolly's bedstead for Emmy, – they are very plain, but anyway she will soon break them in pieces. And here are dress-lengths and handkerchiefs for the maids; old Anne ought really to have something better.
HELMER:	And what is in this parcel?

NORA: [*crying out*]. No, no! you mustn't see that until this evening.

HELMER: Very well. But now tell me, you extravagant little person, what would you like for yourself?

NORA: For myself? Oh, I am sure I don't want anything.

HELMER: Yes, but you must. Tell me something reasonable that you would particularly like to have.

NORA: No, I really can't think of anything – unless, Torvald –

HELMER: Well?

NORA: [*playing with his coat buttons, and without raising her eyes to his*]. If you really want to give me something, you might – you might –

HELMER: Well, out with it!

NORA: [*speaking quickly*]. You might give me money, Torvald. Only just as much as you can afford; and then one of these days I will buy something with it.

HELMER: But, Nora –

NORA: Oh, do! dear Torvald; please, please do! Then I will wrap it up in beautiful gilt paper and hang it on the Christmas Tree. Wouldn't that be fun?

HELMER: What are little people called that are always wasting money?

NORA: Spendthrifts – I know. Let us do as you suggest, Torvald, and then I shall have time to think what I am most in want of. That is a very sensible plan, isn't it?

HELMER: [*smiling*]. Indeed it is – that is to say, if you were really to save out of the money I give you, and then really buy something for yourself. But if you spend it all on the housekeeping and any number of unnecessary things, then I merely have to pay up again.

NORA: Oh but, Torvald –

HELMER: You can't deny it, my dear little Nora. [*Puts his arm round her waist.*] It's a sweet little spendthrift, but she uses up a deal of money. One would hardly believe how expensive such little persons are!

NORA: It's a shame to say that. I do really save all I can.

HELMER: [*laughing*]. That's very true, – all you can. But you can't save anything!

NORA: [*smiling quietly and happily*]. You haven't any idea how many expenses we skylarks and squirrels have, Torvald.

HELMER: You are an odd little soul. Very like your father. You always find some new way of wheedling money out of me, and, as soon as you have got it, it seems to melt in your hands. You never know where it has gone. Still, one must take you as you are. It is in the blood; for indeed it is true that you can inherit these things, Nora.

NORA: Ah, I wish I had inherited many of papa's qualities.

HELMER:	And I would not wish you to be anything but just what you are, my sweet little skylark. But, do you know, it strikes me that you are looking rather – what shall I say – rather uneasy today?
NORA:	Do I?
HELMER:	You do, really. Look straight at me.
NORA:	[*looks at him*]. Well?
HELMER:	[*wagging his finger at her*]. Hasn't Miss Sweet Tooth been breaking rules in town today?
NORA:	No; what makes you think that?
HELMER:	Hasn't she paid a visit to the confectioner's?
NORA:	No, I assure you, Torvald –
HELMER:	Not been nibbling sweets?
NORA:	No, certainly not.
HELMER:	Not even taken a bite at a macaroon or two?
NORA:	No, Torvald, I assure you really –
HELMER:	There, there, of course I was only joking.
NORA:	[*going to the table on the right*]. I should not think of going against your wishes.
HELMER:	No, I am sure of that; besides, you gave me your word – [*Going up to her.*] Keep your little Christmas secrets to yourself, my darling. They will all be revealed tonight when the Christmas Tree is lit, no doubt.

A Doll's House prompts

1 Sketch the stage according to the opening stage directions. Use colour in your drawing. Pay particular attention to the placement of props and doors.

2 Examine character reactions in this extract from Act 1. Often these reactions (either overt or subtle) hint at potential conflicts, issues, secrets and/or mysteries that are later exposed or resolved. This gradual unfolding of mystery is what provides momentum to the play. Note where these reactions occur, and briefly address what seems to lie behind each reaction.

3 Compare and contrast the values/ideals/truths of Nora and Torvald Helmer. Briefly describe what each believes is most important in terms of moral belief. Consider how Nora and Torvald are depicted as 'complementary' to each other in terms of these beliefs. 'Complementary' characters need not be opposites (though they could be); 'complementary' implies connection, balance and working together in some way to make a point that the playwright believes is important.

4 List the props from Act 1. From the extract, choose a prop that you believe has a critical function. Is that function emphatic? Ironic? Satiric? Does Ibsen go so far as to use the prop as a symbol? Explain.

 To access worksheet 2.1 on *A Doll's House* (identifying contextual elements), please visit www. pearsonbacconline.com and follow the on-screen instructions.

EXERCISE 3

'Master Harold' . . . and the Boys by Athol Fugard (1982)

Using the following extract from this one-act play by Athol Fugard, test your close-reading skills. The prompts that follow the text are designed to guide your approach to this realistic drama. The play opens in a restaurant in Port Elizabeth, South Africa, in the year 1950. Willie and Sam work there as waiters and cleaning staff. They are both black men in their early forties. They are joined by Hally, the owner's son, a 17-year-old white boy.

Hally deposits his school case and takes off his raincoat. His clothes are a little neglected and untidy: black blazer with school badge, gray flannel trousers in need of an ironing, khaki shirt and tie, black shoes. Sam has fetched a towel for Hally to dry his hair.

HALLY: God, what a lousy bloody day. It's coming down cats and dogs out there. Bad for business, chaps . . . [*Conspiratorial whisper.*] . . . but it also means we're in for a nice quiet afternoon.

SAM: You can speak loud. Your Mom's not here.

HALLY: Out shopping?

SAM: No, the hospital.

HALLY: But it's Thursday. There's no visiting on Thursday afternoons. Is my Dad okay?

SAM: Sounds like it. In fact, I think he's going home.

HALLY: [*Stopped short by Sam's remark.*] What do you mean?

SAM: The hospital phoned.

HALLY: To say what?

SAM: I don't know. I just heard your Mom talking.

HALLY: So what makes you say he's going home?

SAM: It sounded as if they were telling her to come and fetch him.

Hally thinks about what Sam has said for a few seconds.

HALLY: When did she leave?

SAM: About an hour ago. She said she would phone you. Want to eat?

Hally doesn't respond.

                Hally, want your lunch?

HALLY: I suppose so. [*His mood has changed.*] What's on the menu? . . . as if I don't know.

SAM: Soup, followed by meat pie and gravy.

HALLY: Today's?

SAM: No.

HALLY: And the soup?

SAM: Nourishing pea soup.

HALLY: Just the soup. [*The pile of comic books on the table.*] And these?

SAM: For your Dad. Mr. Kempston brought them.

HALLY: You haven't been reading them, have you?

SAM: Just looking.

HALLY: [*Examining the comics.*] Jungle Jim . . . Batman and Robin . . . Tarzan . . . God, what rubbish! Mental pollution. Take them away.

Sam exits waltzing into the kitchen. Hally turns to Willie.

HALLY: Did you hear my Mom talking on the telephone, Willie?

WILLIE: No, Master Hally. I was at the back.

HALLY: And she didn't say anything to you before she left?

WILLIE: She said I must clean the floors.

HALLY:	I mean about my Dad.
WILLIE:	She didn't say nothing to me about him, Master Hally.
HALLY:	[*With conviction.*] No! It can't be. They said he needed at least another three weeks of treatment. Sam's definitely made a mistake. [*Rummages through his school case, finds a book and settles down at the table to read.*] So, Willie!
WILLIE:	Yes, Master Hally! Schooling okay today?
HALLY:	Yes, okay . . . [*He thinks about it.*] . . . No, not really. *Ag,* what's the difference? I don't care. And Sam says you've got problems.
WILLIE:	Big problems.
HALLY:	Which leg is sore?

Willie groans.

	Both legs.
WILLIE:	There is nothing wrong with my legs. Sam is just making jokes.
HALLY:	So then you *will* be in the competition.
WILLIE:	Only if I can find me a partner.
HALLY:	But what about Hilda?
SAM:	[*Returning with a bowl of soup.*] She's the one who's got trouble with her legs.
HALLY:	What sort of trouble, Willie?
SAM:	From the way he describes it, I think the lady has gone a bit lame.
HALLY:	Good God! Have you taken her to see a doctor?
SAM:	I think a vet would be better.
HALLY:	What do you mean?
SAM:	What do you call it again when a racehorse goes very fast?
HALLY:	Gallop?
SAM:	That's it!
WILLIE:	*Boet* Sam!
HALLY:	'A gallop down the homestretch to the winning post.' But what's that got to do with Hilda?
SAM:	Count Basie always gets there first.

Willie lets fly with his slop rag. It misses Sam and hits Hally.

HALLY:	[*Furious.*] For Christ's sake, Willie! What the hell do you think you're doing?
WILLIE:	Sorry, Master Hally, but it's him . . .
HALLY:	Act your bloody age! [*Hurls the rag back at Willie.*] Cut out the nonsense now and get on with your work. And you too, Sam. Stop fooling around.

Sam moves away.

	No. Hang on. I haven't finished! Tell me exactly what my Mom said.
SAM:	I have. 'When Hally comes, tell him I've gone to the hospital and I'll phone him.'
HALLY:	She didn't say anything about taking my Dad home?

SAM:	No. It's just that when she was talking on the phone . . .
HALLY:	[*Interrupting him.*] No, Sam. They can't be discharging him. She would have said so if they were. In any case, we saw him last night and he wasn't in good shape at all. Staff nurse even said there was talk about taking more X-rays. And now suddenly today he's better? If anything, it sounds more like a bad turn to me . . . which I sincerely hope it isn't. Hang on . . . how long ago did you say she left?
SAM:	Just before two . . . [*His wrist watch.*] . . . hour and a half.
HALLY:	I know how to settle it. [*Behind the counter to the telephone. Talking as he dials.*] Let's give her ten minutes to get to the hospital, ten minutes to load him up, another ten, at the most, to get home and another ten to get him inside. Forty minutes. They should have been home for at least half an hour already. [*Pause – he waits with the receiver to his ear.*] No reply, chaps. And you know why? Because she's at his bedside in hospital helping him pull through a bad turn. You definitely heard wrong.
SAM:	Okay.

As far as Hally is concerned, the matter is settled. He returns to his table, sits down and divides his attention between the book and his soup.

[Hally and Sam discuss Hally's teachers and what he is learning. They debate their 'men of magnitude'.]

HALLY:	Anyway, that's my man of magnitude. Charles Darwin! Who's yours?
SAM:	[*Without hesitation.*] Abraham Lincoln.
HALLY:	I might have guessed as much. Don't get sentimental, Sam. You've never been a slave, you know. And anyway we freed your ancestors here in South Africa long before the Americans. But if you want to thank somebody on their behalf, do it to Mr. William Wilberforce. Come on. Try again. I want a real genius. [*Now enjoying himself, and so is Sam. Hally goes behind the counter and finds himself a chocolate.*]
SAM:	William Shakespeare.
HALLY:	[*No enthusiasm.*] Oh. So you're also one of them, are you? You're basing that opinion on only one play, you know. You've only read my *Julius Caesar* and even I don't understand half of what they're talking about. They should do what they did with the old Bible: bring the language up to date.
SAM:	That's all you've got. It's also the only one *you've* read.
HALLY:	I know. I admit it. That's why I suggest we reserve our judgment until we've checked up on a few others. I've got a feeling, though, that by the end of this year one is going to be enough for me, and I can give you the names of twenty-nine other chaps in the Standard Nine class of the Port Elizabeth Technical College who feel the same. But if you want him, you can have him. My turn now. [*Pacing.*] This is a damn good exercise, you know! It started off looking like a simple question and here it's got us really probing into the intellectual heritage of our civilization.

SAM:	So who is it going to be?
HALLY:	My next man . . . and he gets the title on two scores: social reform and literary genius . . . is Leo Nikolaevich Tolstoy.
SAM:	That Russian.
HALLY:	Correct. Remember the pictue of him I showed you?
SAM:	With the long beard.
HALLY:	[*Trying to look like Tolstoy.*] And those burning, visionary eyes. My God, the face of a social prophet if ever I saw one! And remember my words when I showed it to you? Here's a *man*, Sam!
SAM:	Those were words, Hally.
HALLY:	Not many intellectuals are prepared to shovel manure with the peasants and then go home and write a 'little book' called *War and Peace*. Incidentally, Sam, he was somebody else who, to quote, '. . . did not distinguish himself scholastically.'
SAM:	Meaning?
HALLY:	Meaning he was not good at school.
SAM:	Like you and Winston Churchill.
HALLY:	[*Mirthlessly.*] Ha, ha, ha.
SAM:	[*Simultaneously.*] Ha, ha, ha.
HALLY:	Don't get clever, Sam. That man freed his serfs of his own free will.
SAM:	No argument. He was a somebody, all right. I accept him.
HALLY:	I'm sure Count Tolstoy will be very pleased to hear that. Your turn. Shoot. [*Another chocolate from behind the counter.*] I'm waiting, Sam.
SAM:	I've got him.
HALLY:	Good. Submit your candidate for examination.
SAM:	Jesus.
HALLY:	[*Stopped dead in his tracks.*] Who?
SAM:	Jesus Christ.
HALLY:	Oh, come on, Sam!
SAM:	The Messiah.
HALLY:	*Ja*, but still . . . No Sam. Don't let's get started on religion. We'll just spend the whole afternoon arguing again. Suppose I turn around and say Mohammed?
SAM:	All right.
HALLY:	You can't have them both on the same list!
SAM:	Why not? You like Mohammed, I like Jesus.
HALLY:	I *don't* like Mohammed. I never have. I was merely being hypothetical. As far as I'm concerned, the Koran is as bad as the Bible. No. Religion is out! I'm not going to waste my time again arguing with you about the existence of God. You know perfectly well I'm an atheist . . . and I've got homework to do.
SAM:	Okay, I take him back.
HALLY:	You've got time for one more name.

SAM:	[*After thought.*] I've got one I know we'll agree one. A simple straightforward great Man of Magnitude . . . and no arguments. And *he* really *did* benefit all mankind.
HALLY:	I wonder. After your last contribution I'm beginning to doubt whether anything in the way of an intellectual agreement is possible between the two of us. Who is he?
SAM:	Guess.
HALLY:	Socrates? Alexandre Dumas? Karl Marx? Dostoevsky? Nietzsche?

Sam shakes his head after each name.

	Give me a clue.
SAM:	The letter P is important . . .
HALLY:	Plato!
SAM:	. . . and his name begins with an F.
HALLY:	I've got it. Freud and Psychology.
SAM:	No. I didn't understand him.
HALLY:	That makes two of us.
SAM:	Think of mouldy apricot jam.
HALLY:	[*After a delighted laugh.*] Penicillin and Sir Alexander Fleming! And the title of the book: *The Microbe Hunters*. [*Delighted.*] Splendid, Sam! Splendid. For once we are in total agreement. The major breakthrough in medical science in the Twentieth Century. If it wasn't for him, we might have lost the Second World War. It's deeply gratifying, Sam, to know that I haven't been wasting my time in talking to you. [*Strutting around proudly*.] Tolstoy may have educated his peasants, but I've educated you.
SAM:	Standard Four to Standard Nine.
HALLY:	Have we been at it as long as that?

[Hally, Sam and Willie talk about when they first met seven years ago. Hally would tell Sam about what he had learnt and they would play games together, which Willie would always lose unless they let him win. Hally recounts his favourite memory, which was when Sam built him a kite that he loved to see fly.]

The telephone rings. Sam answers it.

SAM:	St. George's Park Tea Roon . . . Hello, Madam . . . Yes, Madam, he's here . . . Hally, it's your mother.
HALLY:	Where is she phoning from?
SAM:	Sounds like the hospital. It's a public telephone.
HALLY:	[*Relieved.*] You see! I told you. [*The telephone.*] Hello, Mom . . . Yes . . . Yes no fine. Everything's under control here. How's things with poor old Dad? . . . Has he had a bad turn? . . . What? . . . Oh, God! . . . Yes, Sam told me, but I was sure he'd made a mistake. But what's all this about, Mom? He didn't look at all good last night. How can he get better so quickly? . . . Then very obviously you must say no. Be firm with him. You're the boss. . . . You know what it's going to be like if he comes home. . . . Well, then, don't blame me when I fail my exams at

the end of the year. . . . Yes! How am I expected to be fresh for school when I spend half the night massaging his gammy leg? . . . So am I! . . . So tell him a white lie. Say Dr. Colley wants more X-rays of his stump. Or bribe him. We'll sneak in double tots of brandy in future. . . . What? . . . Order him to get back into bed at once! If he's going to behave like a child, treat him like one. . . . All right, Mom! I was just trying to . . . I'm sorry. . . . I said I'm sorry. . . . Quick, give me your number. I'll phone you back. [*He hangs up and waits a few seconds.*] Here we go again! [*He dials.*] I'm sorry, Mom. . . . Okay . . . But now listen to me carefully. All it needs is for you to put your foot down. Don't take no for an answer. . . . Did you hear me? And whatever you do, don't discuss it with him. . . . Because I'm frightened you'll give in to him. . . . Yes, Sam gave me lunch. . . . I ate all of it! . . . No, Mom not a soul. It's still raining here. . . . Right, I'll tell them. I'll just do some homework and then lock up. . . . But remember now, Mom. Don't listen to anything he says. And phone me back and let me know what happens. . . . Okay. Bye, Mom. [*He hangs up. The men are staring at him.*] My Mom says that when you're finished with the floors you must do the windows. [*Pause.*] Don't misunderstand me, chaps. All I want is for him to get better. And if he was, I'd be the first person to say: 'Bring him home.' But he's not, and we can't give him the medical care and attention he needs at home. That's what hospitals are there for. [*Brusquely.*] So don't just stand there! Get on with it!

Sam clears Hally's table.

You heard right. My Dad wants to go home.

'Master Harold' . . . and the Boys prompts

1   Construct Hally's 'emotional map' from these selected portions of the play. An emotional map records the progression of a character's emotions from his emotional status when he first enters the play to his final emotional condition. You should indicate in chart form: (1) initial state of mind; (2) events or words that change the character's state of mind; and (3) the character's resulting emotional state.

2   Choose a moment in the selected section when Willie's character functions as a foil either to Sam or Hally, or both. What does Willie's character allow us to understand more fully about the character he is foiling?

3   Speculate on the effect of the 'man of magnitude' discussion. What subtleties of characterization emerge for Sam and Hally? What does their discussion indicate about their ability to communicate openly? Does a theme emerge about the nature of communication?

4   Identify two examples of verbal (surprising, incongruous statements), dramatic (the audience has knowledge that the characters on stage do not have) or situational (those situations that are surprising, shocking, or incongruous) irony. What effects do these ironies produce in terms of characterization directly or indirectly?

 To access worksheet 2.2 on *'Master Harold' . . . and the Boys* (constructing a metaphorical character map), please visit www.pearsonbacconline.com and follow the on-screen instructions.

EXERCISE 4

The Visit by Friedrich Dürrenmatt (1956)

Using this extract from the first act of Friedrich Dürrenmatt's play, test your close reading skills. The prompts that follow the reading are designed to guide your approach to this tragicomedy.

Act 1 opens at the train station in Guellen in Germany, where a group of people await the arrival of the multi-millionairess, Claire Zachanassian. Claire was born in Guellen and the townspeople are hoping that she will give some money to improve the town, and Ill, an old friend and lover of Claire, is there to ask for her help. They reminisce about their past relationship and how good it was. The mayor addresses the town in a welcome ceremony for Claire.

MAYOR: My dear lady, fellow citizens. Forty-five years have flowed by since you left our little town, our town founded by Crown Prince Hasso the Noble, our town so pleasantly nestling between Konrad's Village Wood and Pückenried Valley. Forty-five years, more than four decades, it's a long time. Many things have happened since then, many bitter things. It has gone sadly with the world, sadly with us. And yet we have never, my dear lady – our Claire (*applause*) – never forgotten you. Neither you, nor your family. Your mother, that magnificent and robustly healthy woman (*Ill whispers something to him*) tragically and prematurely torn from our midst by tuberculosis, and your father, that popular figure, who built the building by the station which experts and laymen still visit so often (*Ill whispers something to him*) – still admire so much, they both live on in our thoughts, for they were of our best, our worthiest. And you too, my dear lady: who, as you gambolled through our streets – our streets, alas, so sadly decrepit nowadays – you a curly-headed, blonde (*Ill whispers something to him*) – redheaded madcap, who did not know you? Even then, everyone could sense the magic in your personality, foresee your approaching rise to humanity's dizzy heights. (*Takes out his notebook.*) You were never forgotten. Literally never. Even now, the staff at school hold up your achievements as an example to others, and in nature studies – the most essential ones – they were astonishing, a revelation of your sympathy for every living creature, indeed of all things in need of protection. And even then, people far and wide were moved to wonder at your love of justice, at your sense of generosity. (*Huge applause.*) For did not our Claire obtain food for an old widow, buying potatoes with that pocket-money so hardly earned from neighbours, and thereby save the old lady from dying of hunger, to mention but one of her deeds of charity. (*Huge applause.*) My dear lady, my dear Guelleners, that happy temperament has now developed from those tender seeds to an impressive flowering, and our redheaded madcap has become a lady whose generosity stirs the world: we need only to think of her social work, of her maternity homes and her soup kitchens, of her art foundations and her children's nurseries, and now, therefore, I ask you to give three cheers for the prodigal returned: Hip, Hip, Hip, Hurrah! (*Applause.*)

(*Claire Zachanassian gets to her feet.*)

CLAIRE ZACHANASSIAN: Mister Mayor, Guelleners. I am moved by your unselfish joy at my visit. As a matter of fact I was somewhat different from the child I seemed to be in the mayor's speech. When I went to school, I was thrashed. And I stole potatoes for Widow Boll, aided by Ill; not to save the old bawd from dying of hunger, but just for once to sleep with Ill in a more comfortable bed than Konrad's Village Wood or Petersens' Barn. None the less, as my contribution to this joy of yours, I want to tell you that I'm ready to give Guellen one million.

Five hundred thousand for the town and five hundred thousand to be shared among each family.

(*Deathly silence.*)

MAYOR: (*stammers*). One million.

(*Everyone still dumbstruck.*)

CLAIRE ZACHANASSIAN: On one condition.

(*Everyone bursts into indescribable jubilation, dancing round, standing on chairs, Gymnast performing acrobatics, etc. Ill pounds his chest enthusiastically.*)

ILL: There's Clara for you! What a jewel! She takes your breath away! Just like her, O my little sorceress!

(*Kisses her.*)

MAYOR: Madam: you said, on one condition. May I ask, on what condition?

CLAIRE ZACHANASSIAN: I'll tell you on what condition. I'm giving you a million, and I'm buying myself justice.

(*Deathly silence.*)

MAYOR: My dear lady, what do you mean by that?

CLAIRE ZACHANASSIAN: What I said.

MAYOR: Justice can't be bought.

CLAIRE ZACHANASSIAN: Everything can be bought.

MAYOR: I still don't understand.

CLAIRE ZACHANASSIAN: Boby. Step forward.

(*Butler steps forward, from right to centre, between the three tables. Takes off his dark glasses.*)

BUTLER: I don't know if any of you here still recognise me.

SCHOOLMASTER: Chief Justice Courtly.

BUTLER: Chief Justice Courtly. Forty-five years ago, I was Lord Chief Justice in Guellen. I was later called to the Kaffigen Court of Appeal until, twenty-five years ago it is now, Madame Zachanassian offered me the post of Butler in her service. A somewhat unusual career, indeed, I grant you, for an academic man, however, the salary involved was really quite fantastic . . .

CLAIRE ZACHANASSIAN: Get to the point, Boby.

BUTLER: As you may have gathered, Madame Claire Zachanassian is offering you the sum of one million pounds, in return for which she insists that justice be done. In other words, Madame Zachanassian will give you all a million if you right the wrong she was done in Guellen. Mr Ill, if you please.

(*Ill stands. He is pale, startled, wondering.*)

ILL: What do you want of me?

BUTLER: Step forward, Mr Ill.

ILL: Sure.

(*Steps forward, to front of table, right. Laughs uneasily. Shrugs.*)

BUTLER: The year was nineteen ten. I was Lord Chief Justice in Guellen. I had a paternity claim to arbitrate. Claire Zachanassian, at the time Claire Wascher, claimed that you, Mr Ill, were her child's father.

(*Ill keeps quiet.*)

At that time, Mr Ill, you denied paternity. You called two witnesses.

ILL: Oh, it's an old story. I was young, thoughtless.

CLAIRE ZACHANASSIAN: Toby and Roby, bring in Koby and Loby.

(*The two gum-chewing giants lead a pair of blind eunuchs on to centre of stage, blind pair gaily holding hands.*)

BLIND PAIR: We're on the spot, we're on the spot!

BUTLER: Do you recognise these two, Mr Ill?

(*Ill keeps quiet.*)

BLIND PAIR: We're Koby and Loby, we're Koby and Loby.

ILL: I don't know them.

BLIND PAIR: We've changed a lot, we've changed a lot!

BUTLER: Say your names.

FIRST BLIND MAN:
Jacob Chicken, Jacob Chicken.

SECOND BLIND MAN: Louis Perch, Louis Perch.

BUTLER: Now, Mr Ill.

ILL: I know nothing about them.

BUTLER: Jacob Chicken and Louis Perch, do you know Mr Ill?

BLIND PAIR: We're blind, we're blind.

BUTLER: Do you know him by his voice?

BLIND PAIR: By his voice, by his voice.

BUTLER: In nineteen ten, I was Judge and you the witnesses. Louis Perch and Jacob Chicken, what did you swear on oath to the court of Guellen?

BLIND PAIR: We'd slept with Clara, we'd slept with Clara.

BUTLER: You swore it on oath, before me. Before the court. Before God. Was it the truth?

BLIND PAIR: We swore a false oath, we swore a false oath.

BUTLER: Why, Jacob Chicken and Louis Perch?

BLIND PAIR: Ill bribed us, Ill bribed us.

BUTLER: With what did he bribe you?

BLIND PAIR: With a pint of brandy, with a pint of brandy.

CLAIRE ZACHANASSIAN: And now tell them what I did with you, Koby and Loby.

BUTLER: Tell them.

BLIND PAIR: The lady tracked us down, the lady tracked us down.

BUTLER: Correct. Claire Zachanassian tracked you down. To the ends of the earth. Jacob Chicken had emigrated to Canada and Louis Perch to Australia. But she tracked you down. And then what did she do with you?

BLIND PAIR: She gave us to Toby and Roby, she gave us to Toby and Roby.

BUTLER: And what did Toby and Roby do with you?

BLIND PAIR: Castrated and blinded us, castrated and blinded us.

BUTLER: And there you have the full story. One Judge, one accused, two false witnesses: a miscarriage of justice in the year nineteen ten. Isn't that so, plaintiff?

CLAIRE ZACHANASSIAN: (*Stands.*) That is so.

ILL: (*Stamping on floor.*) It's over and done with, dead and buried! It's an old, crazy story.

BUTLER: What happened to the child, plaintiff?

CLAIRE ZACHANASSIAN: (*Gently.*) It lived one year.

BUTLER: What happened to you?

CLAIRE ZACHANASSIAN: I became a prostitute.

BUTLER: What made you one?

CLAIRE ZACHANASSIAN: The judgment of that court made me one.

MRS ILL: Freddy!

ILL: My little sorceress! You can't ask that! It was long ago. Life went on.

CLAIRE ZACHANASSIAN: Life went on, and I've forgotten nothing, Ill. Neither Konrad's Village Wood, nor Petersens' Barn; neither Widow Boll's bedroom, nor your treachery. And now we're old, the pair of us. You decrepit, and me cut to bits by the surgeon's knives. And now I want accounts between us settled. You chose your life, but you forced me into mine. A moment ago you wanted time turned back, in that wood so full of the past, where we spent our young years. Well I'm turning it back now, and I want justice. Justice for a million.

BUTLER: And now you desire justice, Claire Zachanassian?

CLAIRE ZACHANASSIAN: I can afford it. A million for Guellen if someone kills Alfred Ill.

(*Deathly silence. Mrs Ill rushes to Ill, flings her arms round him.*)

(*Mayor stands, pale, dignified.*)

MAYOR: Madame Zachanassian: you forget, this is Europe. You forget, we are not savages. In the name of all citizens of Guellen, I reject your offer; and I reject it in the name of humanity. We would rather have poverty than blood on our hands.

(*Huge applause.*)

CLAIRE ZACHANASSIAN: I'll wait.

To access worksheet 2.3 on *The Visit* (identifying contextual elements), please visit www. pearsonbacconline.com and follow the on-screen instructions.

The Visit prompts

1   Define tragicomedy. To what degree does this extract from the first act of the play demonstrate the characteristics of tragicomedy? Use two or three specific references to the text to support your argument.

2   Sound and silence are both used to powerful dramatic effect in this play. Identify a particular sound effect and trace its progressive effect on the audience/reader. Consider how silence functions in this extract from Act 1. Identify a specific instance and discuss the function of silence within dialogue. Does silence 'speak'? If so, what is its message?

3   Discuss the function of the physical stage/set as a means of establishing an actor's physical space. What do we learn and/or experience emotionally and intellectually as we witness the visual spectacle that Dürrenmatt creates in this extract?

4   The theme of morality is presented in Act 1 of *The Visit*, when Claire Zachanassian demands that 'justice' be carried out for the wrong done to her by Ill, which caused her to lose the man she loved and become a prostitute. Justice, for her, means Ill's death. Which character do you think is morally right, and why?

INSIGHTS INTO DRAMA

So what are the conventions of drama and what expectations should you have as you read a play? All plays possess three elements: actors who perform dramatic action; a stage on which the performance takes place; and the words of the playwright. Beyond these basic elements, playwrights can include many more theatrical strategies to create their dramatic vision, and to provide their audience with a full and satisfactory understanding of that vision.

The list below explores the dramatic strategies that playwrights can use. Understanding these strategies and recognizing them as you read will enable you to evaluate their varying functions and the effects they produce within the play. Whether you are writing about plays or speaking about them in your course of study, the principle common to analysis is **close reading** – observing the stylistic strategies of the writer and determining their effects.

1   In stage directions, playwrights can establish full or partial descriptions of characters, and state the way that actors should deliver specific lines. In addition, descriptions of costumes, facial expressions and gestures enable a reader to have a clearer visual picture of the characters on stage. As a reader, you will have to imagine the tone of voice of a character with the help of specific stage directions.

2   While playwrights make use of monologues, soliloquies and asides, the primary vehicle of expression on stage is dialogue. Pay attention to those moments when one character dominates the stage. Is that domination a result of the frequency of his or her speech or something else? Does the use of questioning have a significant function? Does the use of questioning establish tension? Is there a power struggle between two or more characters?

3   Dramatic action includes physical movement of the characters, such as when and where they enter or exit a scene. Pay attention to characters that are referred to even though they are off-stage. Sound effects can accompany these off-stage scenes and the audience will be particularly curious about what they hear but cannot see, or what they see but cannot hear.

4   Themes can emerge directly or indirectly. Characters can serve as the mouthpiece of the playwright. Without biographical insights, however, denoting a character as a mouthpiece is purely speculative. Remember, too, that themes develop and build as the play unfolds.

5   Irony, particularly dramatic irony, has a powerful function in drama. As a reader you must also be sensitive to those characters that use sarcasm or speak in asides.

6   Stage props can have symbolic value. While some symbols are traditional – darkness as a symbol of hopelessness, a cross as a symbol of Christianity, water as a symbol of rebirth, light as a symbol of insight or understanding – other symbols are particular to a text. Symbolic value is only established by the frequency and significance of use within the dramatic action of the play.

7   The events of the play and the ordering of those events determine the plot. Be aware that subplots often function in comparison or contrast to the main plot for purposes of character or thematic development.

8   The design of the stage set and the use of lighting and sound effects are all functional elements of the drama. Changes to the set in scene changes, the use of lighting or sound effects (including music), must be noted. The decision of the playwright to include these elements at a particular moment in the dramatic action is important. What effects are produced in the audience? How do these effects impact on meaning or understanding?

CONVENTIONS OF POETRY

3

Learning Outcomes

Knowledge and Understanding

- Understand what makes poetry, poetry
- Explore the conventions of poetry in relation to context
- Understand the variations of poetic form
- Understand the differences in types of poetry
- Differentiate between speaker and persona
- Explore the use of sound and figurative language

Appreciation

- Identify types of poems
- Evaluate situation and speaker/persona
- Identify the function of irony
- Evaluate the structural framework and metrical patterns of poems
- Identify the effects of sound and figurative language
- Apply the guidelines for reading poetry

Knowledge and Understanding

In Chapter 1, we noted that different genres of literature contain varying expectations of their readers. While you might snuggle down in your favourite comfy chair to read a novel, a short story could be read on a park bench or a commuter train. And even though plays are written as performance literature, few of us have the opportunity to witness plays as audience members, and so we read them either silently or aloud, trying our best to imagine all of the sights and sounds that take place on the world of the playwright's stage.

Poetry, like fiction and drama genres, has its own particular set of conventions that set it apart. Your ability to recognize these conventions in any given poem is important, but you should not equate recognition with analysis. While you need to be able to observe a poet's use of specific conventions within a poem, analysis requires that you draw inferences about the effects that these conventions, also called features, techniques or strategies, create. Through close reading, your observations will lead you to understand about the function and consequent effect of the poet's choices.

Since poetry is written to be read aloud, sound is neither secondary nor incidental to meaning. Every poem has a sound all its own – think of it as a kind of auditory

Poetry readings provide an immediate encounter with the rhythm, rhyme and metre of a poem. Here 'beat' poet and social activist Jack Hirschman performs a reading of one of his own works.

The sound of a poem, when read aloud, establishes an 'auditory fingerprint' unique to that particular poem.

> *When we met first and loved, I did not build*
> *Upon the event with marble. Could it mean*
> *To last, a love set pendulous between*
> *Sorrow and sorrow? Nay, I rather thrilled,*
> *Distrusting every light that seemed to gild*
> *The onward path, and feared to overlean*
> *A finger even. And, though I have grown serene*
> *And strong since then, I think that God has willed*
> *A still renewable fear . . .*

A song book literally puts music to poetry, but poems have a musicality of their own even without instruments accompanying them.

'fingerprint'. Pauses, rhythms and rhymes all contribute to the sounds that words make when you read a poem aloud.

Apart from sound, however, what makes poetry, poetry? This question may sound ridiculous, but as modern poetry has evolved, many readers assume that poetry has to look and sound a certain way to be called poetry. These readers believe that poetry as a genre consists of a rigid, unchangeable form. They assume that a poem must rhyme, and that the lines of poetry are arranged in fixed, regimented stanzas, much like lyrics in a song book.

Certainly the history of poetry, like that of any other genre of literature, reveals vast changes between the early forms and the modern forms. The appearance of poetry on the page, its physical arrangement, coupled with variations in rhyme and metre, leave no question that poetry has evolved.

EXERCISE 1

1 Examine the form, or shape, of each of the following poems. What do you **see** that is different in the visual form of each?

2 Now, read them aloud. What do you **hear** that makes one poem different from another?

'London' by William Blake (1794)

> I wander through each chartered street,
> Near where the chartered Thames does flow,
> And mark in every face I meet
> Marks of weakness, marks of woe.
>
> In every cry of every Man,   5
> In every Infant's cry of fear,
> In every voice, in every ban,
> The mind-forged manacles I hear.

How the Chimney-sweeper's cry
Every black'ning Church appalls;   10
And the hapless Soldier's sigh
Runs in blood down Palace walls.

But most through midnight streets I hear
How the youthful Harlot's curse
Blasts the new-born Infant's tear,   15
And blights with plagues the Marriage hearse.

'We Wear the Mask' by Paul Laurence Dunbar (1896)

We wear the mask that grins and lies,
It hides our cheeks and shades our eyes, –
This debt we pay to human guile;
With torn and bleeding hearts we smile,
And mouth with myriad subtleties.   5

Why should the world be over-wise,
In counting all our tears and sighs?
Nay, let them only see us, while
    We wear the mask.

We smile, but, O great Christ, our cries   10
To thee from tortured souls arise.
We sing, but oh the clay is vile
Beneath our feet, and long the mile;
But let the world dream otherwise,
    We wear the mask!   15

'Planetarium' by Adrienne Rich (1968)

(Thinking of Caroline Herschel, 1750–1848, astronomer, sister of William; and others)

A woman in the shape of a monster
a monster in the shape of a woman
the skies are full of them

a woman   'in the snow
among the Clocks and instruments   5
or measuring the ground with poles'

in her 98 years to discover
8 comets

she whom the moon ruled
like us   10
levitating into the night sky
riding the polished lenses

Galaxies of women, there
doing penance for impetuousness
ribs chilled   15
in those spaces   of the mind

An eye,
　　'virile, precise and absolutely certain'
　　from the mad webs of Uranisborg
　　　　　　encountering the NOVA　　　　　　20

every impulse of light exploding
from the core
as life flies out of us

　　Tycho whispering at last
　　'Let me not seem to have lived in vain'　　25

What we see, we see
and seeing is changing

the light that shrivels a mountain
and leaves a man alive

Heartbeat of the pulsar　　　　　　　　30
heart sweating through my body

The radio impulse
pouring in from Taurus

　　I am bombarded yet　　I stand

I have been standing all my life in the　　35
direct path of a battery of signals
the most accurately transmitted most
untranslatable language in the universe
I am a galactic cloud so deep　　so invo-
luted that a light wave could take 15　　　40
years to travel through me　　And has
taken　　I am an instrument in the shape
of a woman trying to translate pulsations
into images　　for the relief of the body
and the reconstruction of the mind.　　　45

QUESTION

In examining each of these three poems, written over a period of nearly 200 years, visual form and sound are widely divergent. What accounts for the differences in these poems? And is there anything that we can say is a common feature of poetry?

Donald Hall (writer of 15 poetry books, Poet Laureate of his home state, New Hampshire in 1984–89, and US Poet Laureate in 2006) in his essay 'Poetry: The Unsayable Said', tries to define poetry in terms of the poets who 'publish in their work the unsayable said.' Hall makes several statements in his essay which will help you in your study of poetry:

> *We must never assume that the poem, appearing simple, hides an intellectual statement that only professors are equipped to explicate.*

Anyone, not just professional academics, can read a poem and extract meaning and emotion from it. The effect may not be exactly the same for everyone, but poems are often ambiguous. Debating the meaning and outcome of poems and defending your opinion can develop your interpretative and analytical skills.

We come to poetry for the pleasure of its body and for the accuracy and confirmation of its feeling. [...]

Mostly we read poetry for the love of it [...] In the act of reading, we exercise or practice emotion [...] as if poems were academies of feelings, as if in reading poems we practiced emotions and understandings of emotion.

Hall believes that while 'most poems end by saying something', there is much more to poetry than the words themselves – there is the 'unsayable', which makes the reader feel emotion and pleasure when he or she studies the poem. The order and meaning of the words, and the way the poem sounds as it trips off the tongue, are all part of the experience. When reading a poem, therefore, consider what the poet might have been feeling, or what he/she might want you to feel.

Poetry is not talk [...] poetry is talk altered into art, speech slowed down and attended to, words arranged for the reader who contracts to read them for their whole heft of association and noise.

If we try reading poetry with our eyes, as we learn to read newspapers, we miss its bodiliness as well as the history bodied into its words. Reading with care, so that a wholeness of language engages a wholeness of reading body and mind, we absorb poetry not with our eyes only nor with our ears at a reading: We read with our mouths that chew on vowel and consonant; we read with our limbed muscles that enact the dance of the poem's rhythm; we read alert to the history and context of words.

The way a poem is written, the way it appears on the page, the way it sounds when it is read, word order, poetic devices and structure, can all heighten the reader's appreciation of a poem. Remember that each word, punctuation mark, rhyme, sound, etc. was chosen for a reason, and consider what that reason might be. Also reflect on the context of the poem and what you know about the poet (e.g., the time or place in which the poem was written).

The secret room is something to acknowledge, accept, and honour in a silence of assent; the secret room is where the unsayable gathers, and it is poetry's uniqueness.

The 'secret room' in Donald Hall's essay houses the 'unsayable', and is the reason that we take from some poems more than just the words and their meaning. Poetry gives us more than many other types of writing because it aims to activate all our senses, so that we remember it with our minds and bodies.

When we wish to embody in language a complex of feelings or sensations or ideas, we fall into inarticulateness; attempting to speak, in the heat of love or argument, we say nothing or we say what we do not intend.

You might feel conflicting emotions sometimes and be unable to express them; poetry can be a way of getting past this obstacle, and reading poems can be a way of identifying with how the speaker or the persona (see the definitions on pages 67–68) may be feeling. Think about some thematic ideas present in the poems you have read: love, hate, jealousy, death, etc. are all feelings we have encountered or are likely to encounter in our own lives. Consider whether you think that poetry expresses these themes better than other types of writing.

The poet Marianne Moore also tries to define what poetry is in the form of a poem. Are her ideas about poetry similar in any way to Donald Hall's opinions?

'POETRY' BY MARIANNE MOORE (1924)

I, too, dislike it: there are things that are important beyond all this fiddle.
  Reading it, however, with a perfect contempt for it, one discovers in
  it after all, a place for the genuine.
    Hands that can grasp, eyes
      that can dilate, hair that can rise   5
        if it must, these things are important not because a

high-sounding interpretation can be put upon them but because they are
  useful. When they become so derivative as to become unintelligible,
  the same thing may be said for all of us, that we
    do not admire what   10
    we cannot understand: the bat
      holding on upside down or in quest of something to

eat, elephants pushing, a wild horse taking a roll, a tireless wolf under
  a tree, the immovable critic twitching his skin like a horse that feels a flea, the baseball fan, the statistician –   15
    nor is it valid
      to discriminate against 'business documents and

school-books'; all these phenomena are important. One must make a distinction
  however: when dragged into prominence by half poets, the result is not poetry,
  nor till the poets among us can be   20
    'literalists of
      the imagination' – above
        insolence and triviality and can present

for inspection, 'imaginary gardens with real toads in them,' shall we have
  it. In the meantime, if you demand on the one hand,   25
  the raw material of poetry in
    all its rawness and
    that which is on the other hand
      genuine, you are interested in poetry.

QUESTION

What does Moore mean when she references 'imaginary gardens with real toads in them'?

Regardless of how you may define it, poetry, just like fiction and drama, has a particular set of strategies, or conventions, which poets use to create meaning from experience. And while Hall references the uniqueness of poetry as 'unsayable', Moore recognizes a kind of 'genuine rawness'.

What makes poetry, then? For one thing, poems are shorter than other genres of the literary imagination. And, the language of poetry is much more concentrated than the language of prose fiction, prose non-fiction or drama. In poetry, experience is distilled into fewer words, and so those words must have more impact, more dimension, more potency.

Remember these points as you approach any poem for the first time:

- The subject matter of poetry is no different than any other genre of literature. If a human being can have an experience, that experience can serve as the subject of a poem.

- Experiences translate into feelings. Some poets explore or confront feelings, rationalize feelings or intellectualize feelings, but poetry is the vehicle for conveying emotion, either directly or indirectly.
- In order to experience a poem you must be willing to experience the form. Read the poem aloud, if possible, several times. Read strictly according to the syntax (sentence structure). Let the punctuation of the poem determine your pauses and stops. The end of a line does not automatically signal a full stop unless there is a period; a slight pause is indicated otherwise.
- If you don't know the meaning of a word, stop and look it up. Every word in a poem has been carefully chosen for a reason, so you need to understand them all.
- Think about the speaker of the poem and also about the situation that the speaker is referring to. What do you know about each?
- Think about the title and determine if it refers to the situation or the speaker either directly or indirectly.

Considering types of poetry: lyric, narrative and dramatic

Lyric poems were originally composed to be sung or chanted. Today, lyric poems are the largest group and include highly personal, subjective and melodic reflections about ideas, abstractions, people or places. Odes and elegies are considered specific types of lyric poem. An elegy is written on the occasion of someone's death, and an ode is typically a longer lyric that uses elevated language to describe a serious, often abstract, subject.

Narrative poems tell stories, and so, like fiction, contain plot, setting, characters and point of view. The longest of these narrative poems are called epics. Shorter, highly rhythmic narratives called ballads often have repeated lines, like a refrain in song.

Dramatic poems have an invented speaker, or persona, who speaks in a dramatic monologue as a soliloquy or in a scene from a play.

Considering structure and language
A word about translation

Poems in translation will require you to understand that the artistry of the translator governs the choices he or she makes in translating specific words. A translator's understanding of the original language with its nuances and meanings allows for a faithful rendering of a poem. Subtleties, including the original poet's use of specific conventions and their effects, are not ignored by the translator. The translated poem, however, is not regarded as identical to the original. The fluid nature of language, as well as the translator's intentions, create something new. The translator's artistry stands on its own merit.

Speaker and persona

Speaker and persona – what's the difference? The difference relies upon the use of pronouns in a given poem. If a first-person 'I' voice is used, we can assume that either the poet is speaking directly to us, as he or she would in a diary entry, or that the speaker is a character the poet has created with a singular personality and perspective.

It is problematic and even dangerous to assume that the 'I' voice of the poem is the poet. Such an assumption would mean that the poet is confessing his or her feelings, admitting actions or proclaiming an understanding in a completely self-conscious manner. To assume that the persona, the 'I' voice, is the poet, is the same as assuming that any first-person narrator is, in fact, the writer speaking directly to the reader. Only extensive biographical information could confirm that the 'I' voice is that of the poet speaking directly about his or her own experience. It is always best to assume that the persona is a voice created by the poet, to render the experience of the poem in a personal, immediate and engaged manner.

Sometimes, the voice of the poem is termed 'speaker', despite the pronouns used in the poem. A voice that references 'he', 'she', 'it' or 'they' is called a speaker. This speaker functions in a similar way to a third-person narrator in prose fiction. This voice is less personal, less intimate and less immediate than the voice of the persona.

To access worksheet 3.1 on speaker or persona, please visit www. pearsonbacconline.com and follow the on-screen instructions.

Time and place

Determining the speaker or persona of a poem is only part of your assessment. Where the speaker is located, when he or she is speaking, if anyone else is present, and why they are even speaking – all are significant questions that you will need to answer. Some poems require you to have knowledge of an actual time, place or historical event. Often, a direct allusion to a literary or historical figure carries with it an equally specific emotional meaning.

EXERCISE 2

Read the following poem by Eavan Boland and answer the questions that follow.

'Patchwork' by Eavan Boland (1990)

I have been thinking at random
on the universe
or rather, how nothing in the universe
is random—

(there's nothing like presumption late at night.)   5

My sumptuous
trash bag of colors—
Laura Ashley cottons—
waits to be cut
and stitched and patched   10

but there's a mechanical feel
about the handle
of my secondhand sewing machine,
with its flowers
and Singer painted orange on it.   15
And its iron wheel.

My back is to the dark.
Somewhere out there
are stars and bits of stars
and little bits of bits.   20
And swiftness and brightness and drift.

But is it craft or art?

I will be here
till midnight,
cross-legged in the dining-room,   25
logging triangles and diamonds,
cutting and aligning,
finding greens in pinks
and burgundies in whites
until I finish it.   30

There's no reason in it.

Only when it's laid
right across the floor,
sphere on square
and seam on seam,   35
in a good light—
a night-sky spread—
will it start to hit me.

These are not bits.
They are pieces.   40

And the pieces fit.

	QUESTIONS
1	What do you know about this speaker or persona?
2	How does time function in this poem?
3	What effect does the structure produce?
4	What is the tone of this poem?
5	How does punctuation function in this poem?

Diction

Flowery, ornate language has often been associated with poetry, but as a student of poetry you will see that not all poems are written in elevated language. Many poems are expressed with simple, straightforward, even colloquial language. In older poems, you will often encounter archaic terms or phrasings that are unfamiliar. A dictionary is a necessity when you read poetry.

Another consideration of diction in poetry is the way in which poets use the connotation of a word. Connotations – implied meanings – are loaded with emotion. Poets use these emotional connotations to add impact and create intensity for the speaker or for the situation the speaker addresses.

Syntax

No matter how a poem may look on the page, as a reader you must read the poem with full awareness of its syntax. Poets often vary word order to change rhyme schemes or rhythm patterns, such as introducing metrical variations. The order of the words within sentences affects not only how the words sound, but also how they suggest meaning. This order can

Diction refers to the specific vocabulary used by a writer or speaker to express his or her point of view.

Syntax refers to the way that words and phrases are arranged to form phrases, clauses and sentences.

therefore alter our understanding of a poem. Inversion – reversing accepted syntactic patterns such as subject, verb and object – creates emphasis, or stress, on a particular word.

Briefly consider the first four poems in this chapter as examples of variations in syntax. 'London' has a regular and consistent syntactic pattern; each stanza, with four lines, contains a single sentence that works to enhance rhythm and rhyme. In 'We Wear the Mask', the syntax is a bit more varied. While the initial stanza is comprised of one sentence, the second and third stanzas have two sentences each – the variation of line lengths within the stanzas produce an interesting effect when compared to 'London'. While Dunbar's poem has a clear rhyme pattern, the effect of the unrhymed final line in the second and third stanzas emphasizes the unpredictable, stressing the unseen masks worn by African Americans as they struggled against the racist 'Jim Crow' laws of the late 19th century.

Adrienne Rich's 'Planetarium' is composed of only one sentence, though many sentences are implied through capitalization and spacing. Moore's 'Poetry' offers even more variation of syntax. Some sentences stop at the end of lines and others seem to run on for many lines. Moore's use of enjambment (run on, no end stop lines) between stanzas signals to the reader that enjambed stanzas must be regarded as a single unit of meaning, and consequently, a single unit of understanding.

To access worksheet 3.2 on examining syntax in 'Patchwork', please visit www.pearsonbacconline.com and follow the on-screen instructions.

Figurative language – metaphor, simile, personification

Figures of speech attempt to define something in terms of comparison to something else which is more familiar. Metaphor, simile and personification are all useful to poets who are trying to convey meaning and emotion to their readers. In **similes**, the comparison is stated using the words 'like' or 'as'. **Metaphors** make the same comparison but without the comparative words. To say that 'his fist is a hammer' (metaphor) or 'his fist was like a hammer' (simile) convey the same meaning. This meaning is produced through the comparison of two essentially unlike things expressed directly in metaphor and indirectly through simile. In personification, an abstraction is defined with human qualities. To say that 'love sat patiently by the door, waiting' works through a comparison of the animate and inanimate. Such a comparison creates a picture in the mind, but it also functions by forming meaning. Abstract concepts are made concrete through such comparisons.

Figurative language helps the reader create a picture within the mind's eye, and while that picture, or image, is most often visual, it can also be auditory or tactile. Figurative language becomes a way for us to imagine more clearly, more precisely. By using figurative language, poets enable their readers to access their senses more fully.

Sound – onomatopoeia, assonance, consonance, alliteration

As we noted at the beginning of this chapter, poems are meant to be read aloud, because the sound of the words on the page is central to the poem's meaning. Sound devices, then, are significant and you must train your ear to 'hear' them.

Onomatopoeia is a wonderful device in which the word sounds like what it describes – 'splat', 'bubble', 'gurgle' and 'murmur' are all onomatopoeic words.

Assonance is the repetition of vowel sounds within a line or series of lines in a poem. Assonance creates a rhythmic effect, as when E.E. Cummings writes 'on a pr**ou**d r**ou**nd cl**ou**d in wh**i**te h**i**gh n**i**ght'.

Consonance is the repetition of a consonant sound within a line of poetry, as can be seen in these lines from the Emily Dickinson poem ''Twas later when the summer went …':

> 'T was sooner when the cricket went
> Than when the winter came,
> Yet that pathetic pendulum
> Keeps esoteric time.

Alliteration in a line of poetry involves the repetition of the beginning consonant sound in a series of two or more words, such as in this line from a Robert Frost poem, 'Acquainted with the Night': 'I have stood still and stopped the sound of feet' – note the repetition of the 's' sound.

Assonance, consonance and alliteration are significant because the manipulation of sound creates an effect on the reading experience – words can be stressed and rhythms can be either intensified or broken.

EXERCISE 3

Read the following poem by Gerard Manley Hopkins and answer the questions that follow.

'God's Grandeur' by Gerard Manley Hopkins (1877)

> The world is charged with the grandeur of God.
>   It will flame out, like shining from shook foil;
>   It gathers to a greatness, like the ooze of oil
> Crushed. Why do men then now not reck his rod?
> Generations have trod, have trod, have trod;   5
>   And all is seared with trade; bleared, smeared with toil;
>   And wears man's smudge and shares man's smell: the soil
> Is bare now, nor can foot feel, being shod.
>
> And for all this, nature is never spent;
>   There lives the dearest freshness deep down things;   10
> And though the last lights off the black West went
>   Oh, morning, at the brown brink eastward, springs—
> Because the Holy Ghost over the bent
>   World broods with warm breast and with ah! bright wings.

QUESTIONS

1 How many different types of poetic conventions can you spot in this poem? What effects do they have on tone?

2 What is the effect of the assonance in line 6, and how does it underscore what is being described?

3 What is the message of this poem and how do specific images and sounds contribute to this message?

> **ⓘ Symbol – traditional and poetic**
> Flags, logos, even religious images like a cross, are regarded as traditional symbols because they represent something beyond themselves. In poetry, objects, actions and events can be given symbolic significance. The meaning of these symbols is controlled by the context of their use in the poem, and not necessarily by any widely accepted secondary meaning.

Structure – narrative, discursive, descriptive, reflective/meditative

The organizational frameworks for poems are determined by the poet's message, and his or her intention. Some organizational principle will guide the presentation of ideas. For example, stories are told within a chronological framework, regardless of their genre. So, if a poet's intention is narrative, some kind of chronology will form the 'spine' of the body of this poem.

This type of chronology is not typical of poems that are reflective in nature. When we think about any subject, when we reflect on a specific incident or even an abstraction, our minds often move randomly, switching from one sensory impression to another seemingly without reason. Thus, reflective poems are typically more randomly structured than those that seek to narrate a story.

If the poet's message is to create a clear and accurate portrayal, we say that the poem has a descriptive framework or structure. Such descriptive structures will rely on vivid, often visual detail to sketch the poem's subject into the mind of the reader.

Likewise, in the presentation of argument, what is known as the discursive framework, the poet needs to be convincing. Often poets will choose to dramatize an event that will argue a point more subtly. A vivid, detailed account of a scene can then become the structural framework of their argument.

Rhyme scheme

A rhyme scheme is the pattern of rhyme established by a poem, based on the sound at the end of each line. Looking across history, there are dozens of different formulaic rhyme schemes in use, strictly laid down by the conventions of the type of poem. Alternatively, some poems will avoid a regular rhyme scheme altogether.

Rhyme schemes are commonly mapped out using a system of letters, each letter denoting a different rhyme sound. For example, here is John Donne's 'Death be not Proud', with the rhyme scheme mapped out:

Death be not proud, though some have called thee	a
Mighty and dreadfull, for, thou art not soe,	b
For, those, whom thou think'st, thou dost overthrow,	b
Die not, poore death, nor yet canst thou kill mee.	a
From rest and sleepe, which but thy pictures bee,	a
Much pleasure, then from thee, much more must flow,	b
And soonest our best men with thee doe goe,	b
Rest of their bones, and soules deliverie.	a
Thou art slave to Fate, Chance, kings, and desperate men,	c
And dost with poyson, warre, and sicknesse dwell,	d
And poppie, or charmes can make us sleepe as well,	d
And better then thy stroake; why swell'st thou then?	c
One short sleepe past, wee wake eternally,	e
And death shall be no more; death, thou shalt die.	f

Remember, it is not enough in poetic analysis just to describe the rhyme scheme; you must also say what effect the rhyme scheme has, and how it contributes to meaning. Does the rhyme accent certain lines, and hence emphasize certain meanings? Does it produce a peaceful or a dissonant effect? Reading the poem aloud will help you to sense the poetic effect more clearly.

Metre

Poets use sound to create meaning and to elicit emotion in the reader. One way that poets create meaning is through the purposeful, patterned arrangement of stressed and unstressed syllables in words. A stressed syllable has more emphasis, more sound, than an unstressed syllable, so if words are arranged in a set pattern of stressed and unstressed syllables, a rhythm is created. Scansion is the process of scanning a line of poetry to determine this pattern of rhythm. By measuring the basic unit of a line, called a foot, we can describe the pattern. A foot consists of one stressed and one or two unstressed syllables, and they fall into the following categories:

- The **iamb** is an unstressed syllable followed by a stressed syllable: e.g. 'enough'
- The **trochee** is a stressed syllable followed by an unstressed syllable: e.g. 'dearly'
- The **anapaest** (also spelt anapest) is composed of two unstressed syllables followed by a stressed syllable: e.g. 'understand'
- The **dactyl** is a stressed syllable followed by two unstressed syllables: e.g. 'desperate'
- And, a **spondee** is formed by two stressed syllables: e.g. 'help me'

A line is measured by the number of feet it contains:

- Monometer – one foot
- Dimeter – two feet
- Trimeter – three feet
- Tetrameter – four feet
- Pentameter – five feet
- Hexameter – six feet
- Heptameter – seven feet
- Octameter – eight feet

The most common metre in English poetry is based on iambic feet. Shakespeare's blank verse is essentially unrhymed iambic pentameter. End-stopped lines, run-on lines and enjambed lines all affect the rhythm of the poem.

As with rhyme, you should think about how the metre contributes to the overall tone and meaning of a poem. Does it make, for example, the poem rushed and breathless, or slow and steady, and how do these effects shape or emphasize the content of the poem?

Stanza forms – terza rima, villanelle, sonnet, free verse, concrete poems

As with rhyme schemes and metre, poetry has throughout its history also adopted several formulaic stanza forms. Part of the poet's skill has been to demonstrate his own flair and originality, but within the confines of a particular pattern of stanzas. The following are the most common of the stanza forms.

Terza rima consists of a series of three-line stanzas (tercets) with the rhyme scheme aba, bcb, cdc, ded, and so on. At the end of the poem, an extra line is often added to complete the structure: yzy z.

A **villanelle** is a poem of 19 lines, written in iambic pentameter. The poem is composed of five triplets (three lines) and a quatrain (four lines). Line 1 is repeated as lines 6, 12 and 18. Line 3 is repeated as lines 9, 15, and 19. The entire poem moves on only two rhymes: aba aba aba aba aba abaa.

There are many variations of **sonnet**, including the English or Shakespearean sonnet and the Italian, or Petrarchan, sonnet. Both are 14 lines in length, but the difference is in structure. In the first, the sonnet divides into three units of four lines each (three quatrains) followed by a final two-line unit (rhyming couplet). In the second, the fundamental break is between the first eight lines (an octave) and the last six (a sestet). The rhyme scheme in the Shakespearean sonnet is typically abab, cdcd, efef, gg, while the Petrarchan is typically abbaabba cdecde. Traditional sonnets are written in iambic pentameter. A sonnet is a perfect form for arguing a point that is brought to conclusion at the end.

EXERCISE 4

Below is Shakespeare's Sonnet 130. Read it through and define what you think is the core message. Then explain how poetic devices, metre and rhyme contribute to expressing that message. Are the three stanzas of four lines, followed by a rhyming couplet as the last stanza, a good way of presenting an argument?

My mistress' eyes are nothing like the sun;
Coral is far more red than her lips' red;
If snow be white, why then her breasts are dun;
If hairs be wires, black wires grow on her head.

I have seen roses damask'd, red and white,   5
But no such roses see I in her cheeks;
And in some perfumes is there more delight
Than in the breath that from my mistress reeks.

I love to hear her speak, yet well I know
That music hath a far more pleasing sound;   10
I grant I never saw a goddess go;
My mistress, when she walks, treads on the ground:

And yet, by heaven, I think my love as rare
As any she belied with false compare.

– William Shakespeare, Sonnet 130 (1609)

Poems written in **free verse** avoid regular metre and consequently have no obviously perceivable rhythm. These poems often have highly irregular line lengths, but may also use repetition of words or phrases.

Concrete poems often draw their meaning less from the words used in the poem and more from the physical arrangement or shape on the page. These shapes are visually recognizable.

Appreciation

When you read poetry, you are using your imagination, your senses, your intelligence and your emotions. Reading poetry requires you to hear the sound of it, even if you cannot read the poem aloud. It also requires you to pay attention to every detail, from line length, to punctuation, to lack of punctuation, to capitalization, to rhyming words, to words that look like they should rhyme but don't – everything. Every word, every line, every space is purposeful. Nothing in a poem is arbitrary.

And so, to be alert, to be prepared to observe the poem, you need to read slowly and purposefully. For all of the poems that follow in this section, you will be asked to focus on a few details. Because interpretation is based on analysis, and analysis is based on keen observation or description, close reading in poetry requires that you are able to observe the poet's strategies. Some of these strategies, like subject matter, are obvious. Other strategies are less so. The subtlety of a shift in verb tense, for instance, may not be apparent on a first reading. The use of enjambment, or the placement of a caesura, can be equally significant because in all instances, these subtle details create effects that translate into meaning, into understanding and into feeling.

Understanding the type of poem may provide you with some quick insight as to the type of subject matter and tone. For example, a lyric, which by definition will have rhythm, will often be reflective, and will offer a highly emotional insight into an individual, an experience, or an event.

Caesura

A caesura is defined as a stop in a line of poetry, often but not always indicated by punctuation such as full stops and semi-colons, or by a natural break in breathing. An example would be this line from Alexander Pope: 'To err is human; to forgive, divine'.

As you work through these poems, focus on your own emotional or intellectual reactions. You might find that by reading carefully and patiently, you discover that access point where the poem 'opens' for you, where you find the 'secret room' of the 'unsayable', or where you find the pleasure in reading poetry.

Guidelines for reading poetry

The following list provides a kind of road map for reading poetry. You can use these guidelines to approach any poem as the first step in analysis:

1. Read the poem, preferably aloud, several times.
2. Pay attention to the title. Has your understanding of the title changed as a result of reading the poem?
3. Do you perceive a speaker or a persona? What do you know about him or her? Is gender important? Does the speaker have personality or does he or she seem detached or disembodied? Do you respond personally to this voice? Does it engage you emotionally? Intellectually? Does the speaker address someone else in the poem? Can you determine their relationship to each other?
4. What is the situation in the poem? Does it take place at a specific time or place? Is location important?
5. How is imagery used in regard to defining both the situation and the speaker? What images strike you as particularly effective in terms of creating tone/attitude? Which of your senses are evoked through imagery – visual, auditory, tactile, olfactory, gustatory, kinaesthetic, organic?
6. What tones are created? A few to consider include: reflective, nostalgic, playful, ironic, sad, bitter, humorous, sincere, objective, formal, informal, solemn, satiric or serious.
7. What is the central purpose? To describe, to persuade, to tell a story, to reveal a moment in time, to reflect, to philosophize? Something else?
8. Does the poet draw your attention to a specific word, either through placement, repetition, allusion or connotation? Do some words take on metaphorical or symbolic meaning?
9. What sound devices are used in the poem? Consider: onomatopoeia, alliteration, assonance, consonance and rhyme. Is there a regular or irregular rhythm? If the rhythm is established through a metrical pattern, identify any breaks and/or shifts in that metrical pattern.
10. How does the shape of the poem, its structure and its architecture, work to underscore meaning? What effect does enjambment or punctuation produce? Does the physical structure of the poem reveal meaning?

EXERCISE 5

For all the following poems, answer these questions or perform these tasks , in addition to the individual questions after each poem.

1 Identify the type of poem (lyric, narrative or dramatic).

2 Identify the speaker or persona.

3 In which of the poems is knowledge of a particular time or place essential for understanding the poem?

4 Which of the poems use irony to great effect?

5 Identify which poems use sound devices. What effects are created?

6 Which poems use metaphor, simile and personification? How does the comparison aid in understanding? What image is created in the mind's eye?

7 Determine the structural framework.

8 Answer the questions that follow each of these poems.

9 Go back to the first three poems in this chapter, and, using the guidelines for reading poetry, evaluate each of them.

'Blood' by Naomi Shihab Nye (1986)

'A true Arab knows how to catch a fly in his hands,'
 my father would say. And he'd prove it,
cupping the buzzer instantly
while the host with the swatter stared.

In the spring our palms peeled like snakes.   5
True Arabs believed watermelon could heal fifty ways.
I changed these to fit the occasion.

Years before, a girl knocked,
wanted to see the Arab.
I said we didn't have one.   10
After that, my father told me who he was,
'Shihab' – 'shooting star' –
a good name, borrowed from the sky.
Once I said, 'When we die, we give it back?'
He said that's what a true Arab would say.   15

Today the headlines clot in my blood.
A little Palestinian dangles a toy truck on the front page.
Homeless fig, this tragedy with a terrible root
is too big for us. What flag can we wave?
I wave the flag of stone and seed,   20
table mat stitched in blue.

I call my father, we talk around the news.
It is too much for him,
neither of his two languages can reach it.
I drive into the country to find sheep, cows,   25
to plead with the air;
Who calls anyone *civilized*?
Where can the crying heart graze?
What does a true Arab do now?

QUESTIONS

1 What do you know about the speaker/persona?

2 What is the speaker/persona's attitude?

3 Examine the use of punctuation in this poem. What effects are produced?

4 What is the situation in this poem?

'My Son, My Executioner' by Donald Hall (1955)

My son, my executioner,
    I take you in my arms,
Quiet and small and just astir,
    And whom my body warms.

Sweet death, small son, our instrument   5
    Of immortality,
Your cries and hungers document
    Our bodily decay.

We twenty-five and twenty-two,
    Who seemed to live forever,   10
Observe enduring life in you
    And start to die together.

QUESTIONS

1 What 'unsayable' is said in this poem?

2 What is the tone of this poem?

3 Comment on the paradoxical nature of the title.

4 Examine the regular metre and rhyme scheme of this poem. What is it and why is it used?

'The Writer' by Richard Wilbur (1976)

In her room at the prow of the house
Where light breaks, and the windows are tossed with linden,
My daughter is writing a story.

I pause in the stairwell, hearing
From her shut door a commotion of typewriter-keys   5
Like a chain hauled over a gunwale.

Young as she is, the stuff
Of her life is a great cargo, and some of it heavy:
I wish her lucky passage.

But now it is she who pauses,   10
As if to reject my thought and its easy figure.
A stillness greatens, in which

The whole house seems to be thinking,
And then she is at it again with a bunched clamor
Of strokes, and again is silent.   15

I remember the dazed starling
Which was trapped in that very room, two years ago;
How we stole in, lifted a sash

And retreated, not to affright it;
And how for a helpless hour, through the crack of the door,   20
We watched the sleek, wild, dark

And iridescent creature
Batter against the brilliance, drop like a glove
To the hard floor, or the desk-top.

And wait then, humped and bloody,   25
For the wits to try it again; and how our spirits
Rose when, suddenly sure,

It lifted off from a chair-back,
Beating a smooth course for the right window
And clearing the sill of the world.   30

It is always a matter, my darling,
Of life or death, as I had forgotten. I wish
What I wished you before, but harder.

QUESTIONS

1   What do you know about this speaker/persona?
2   Does the tone shift in this poem?
3   How does imagery contribute to tone?
4   Describe the effect of punctuation in this poem.

'Digging' by Seamus Heaney (1980)

Between my finger and my thumb
The squat pen rests; snug as a gun.

Under my window, a clean rasping sound
When the spade sinks into gravelly ground:
My father, digging. I look down   5

Till his straining rump among the flowerbeds
Bends low, comes up twenty years away
Stooping in rhythm through potato drills
Where he was digging.

The coarse boot nestled on the lug, the shaft   10
Against the inside knee was levered firmly.
He rooted out tall tops, buried the bright edge deep
To scatter new potatoes that we picked
Loving their cool hardness in our hands.

By God, the old man could handle a spade.   15
Just like his old man.

My grandfather cut more turf in a day
Than any other man on Toner's bog.
Once I carried him milk in a bottle
Corked sloppily with paper. He straightened up   20
To drink it, then fell to right away

Nicking and slicing neatly, heaving sods
Over his shoulder, going down and down
For the good turf. Digging.

The cold smell of potato mould, the squelch and slap   25
Of soggy peat, the curt cuts of an edge
Through living roots awaken in my head.
But I've no spade to follow men like them.

Between my finger and my thumb
The squat pen rests.   30
I'll dig with it.

QUESTIONS

1 Explain how the title could function metaphorically.

2 What is the tone of this poem?

3 What do you know about the speaker/persona?

'Cinderella' by Anne Sexton (1970)

You always read about it:
the plumber with twelve children
who wins the Irish Sweepstakes.
From toilets to riches.
That story.   5

Or the nursemaid,
some luscious sweet from Denmark
who captures the oldest son's heart.
From diapers to Dior.
That story.   10

Or a milkman who serves the wealthy,
eggs, cream, butter, yogurt, milk,
the white truck like an ambulance
who goes into real estate
and makes a pile.   15
From homogenized to martinis at lunch.

Or the charwoman
who is on the bus when it cracks up
and collects enough from the insurance.
From mops to Bonwit Teller.   20
That story.

Once
the wife of a rich man was on her deathbed
and she said to her daughter Cinderella:
Be devout. Be good. Then I will smile   25
down from heaven in the seam of a cloud.

The man took another wife who had
two daughters, pretty enough
but with hearts like blackjacks.
Cinderella was their maid. 30

She slept on the sooty hearth each night
and walked around looking like Al Jolson.
Her father brought presents home from town,
jewels and gowns for the other women
but the twig of a tree for Cinderella. 35
She planted that twig on her mother's grave
and it grew to a tree where a white dove sat.
Whenever she wished for anything the dove
would drop it like an egg upon the ground.
The bird is important, my dears, so heed him. 40

Next came the ball, as you all know.
It was a marriage market.
The prince was looking for a wife.
All but Cinderella were preparing
and gussying up for the event. 45
Cinderella begged to go too.
Her stepmother threw a dish of lentils
into the cinders and said: Pick them
up in an hour and you shall go.
The white dove brought all his friends; 50
all the warm wings of the fatherland came,
and picked up the lentils in a jiffy.
No, Cinderella, said the stepmother,
you have no clothes and cannot dance.
That's the way with stepmothers. 55

Cinderella went to the tree at the grave
and cried forth like a gospel singer:
Mama! Mama! My turtledove,
send me to the prince's ball!
The bird dropped down a golden dress 60
and delicate little slippers.
Rather a large package for a simple bird.
So she went. Which is no surprise.
Her stepmother and sisters didn't
recognize her without her cinder face 65
and the prince took her hand on the spot
and danced with no other the whole day.

As nightfall came she thought she'd better
get home. The prince walked her home
and she disappeared into the pigeon house 70
and although the prince took an axe and broke
it open she was gone. Back to her cinders.
These events repeated themselves for three days.
However on the third day the prince
covered the palace steps with cobbler's wax 75
And Cinderella's gold shoe stuck upon it.

Now he would find whom the shoe fit
and find his strange dancing girl for keeps.
He went to their house and the two sisters
were delighted because they had lovely feet.   80
The eldest went into a room to try the slipper on
but her big toe got in the way so she simply
sliced it off and put on the slipper.
The prince rode away with her until the white dove
told him to look at the blood pouring forth.   85
That is the way with amputations.
They don't just heal up like a wish.
The other sister cut off her heel
but the blood told as blood will.
The prince was getting tired.   90
He began to feel like a shoe salesman.
But he gave it one last try.
This time Cinderella fit into the shoe
like a love letter into its envelope.

At the wedding ceremony   95
the two sisters came to curry favor
and the white dove pecked their eyes out.
Two hollow spots were left
like soup spoons.

Cinderella and the prince   100
lived, they say, happily ever after,
like two dolls in a museum case
never bothered by diapers or dust,
never arguing over the timing of an egg,
never telling the same story twice,   105
never getting a middle-aged spread,
their darling smiles pasted on for eternity
Regular Bobbsey Twins.
That story.

QUESTIONS

1   What is the tone of this poem?
2   What do you know about the speaker?
3   Examine the use of irony in this poem.
4   How does repetition function in this poem?

Extended metaphor

Sometimes poets use the technique of 'extended metaphor', when a metaphor is developed through the whole poem. Consider the effect of the extended metaphor in 'My Papa's Waltz'.

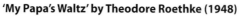

'My Papa's Waltz' by Theodore Roethke (1948)

The whiskey on his breath
Could make a small boy dizzy;
But I hung on like death:
Such waltzing was not easy.

We romped until the pans   5
Slid from the kitchen shelf;
My mother's countenance
Could not unfrown itself.

The hand that held my wrist
Was battered on one knuckle;   10
At every step you missed
My right ear scraped a buckle.

You beat time on my head
With a palm caked hard by dirt,
Then waltzed me off to bed   15
Still clinging to your shirt.

QUESTIONS

1   What do you know about the speaker of this poem?
2   What is the situation?
3   What is the speaker's attitude towards this situation?
4   How does rhyme function in this poem?

'Buffalo Bill's' by E. E. Cummings (1923)

Buffalo Bill's
defunct
        who used to
        ride a watersmooth-silver
                                  stallion   5
and break onetwothreefourfive pigeonsjustlikethat
                                          Jesus
he was a handsome man
                      and what i want to know is
how do you like your blueeyed boy   10
Mister Death

QUESTIONS

1   What do you know about the speaker of this poem?
2   What effect does the absence of punctuation have?
3   Describe how rhythm is created in this poem.

'How Everything Happens' by May Swenson (1967)

(Based on a Study of the Wave)

                                        happen.
                                    to
                                up
                            stacking
                        is   5
                    something
When nothing is happening

When it happens
            something
                    pulls   10
                    back
                        not
                        to
                            happen.

When   has happened.   15
        pulling back   stacking up
                happens

        has happened   stacks up.
When it   something   nothing
                    pulls back while   20

Then nothing is happening.

                            happens.
                        and
                    forward
                    pushes   25
            up
        stacks
    something
Then

'In the Rear-View Mirror' by Robert Shaw (1999)

Thinking about them as you saw them last,
you see them standing there behind your back,
leaning out into the road to wave goodbye,
lingering even as growing speed and distance
diminish them until they neatly fit   5
head to foot in the mirror-strip you glance at.
Tiny in your lengthening wake, still waving,
they could be nameless people on a postcard,
too far away for you to make out faces.
Then, at the first turn, they're lost completely,   10
places taken by someone's windbreak pines,
a split-rail fence, and then, as the wheel straightens,
nothing but empty road. Ahead of you
are towns where you will never know a soul,
exits following exits you will pass   15
and never take, amassing a stiff toll
finally to make good on. Fortunately
you carry along with you that higher-powered
reflective instrument that you can use
no matter how far down the road you've gone   20
to bring them back in view as large as life,
putting yourself in the picture, too, which makes
thinking about them as you saw them lasting.

QUESTIONS

1   How is the title used as a metaphor?
2   What do you know about this speaker?
3   Does the shape of the poem underscore its meaning?
4   Examine the two caesuras in this poem. How does their use create emphasis?

'A Lesson for this Sunday' by Derek Walcott (1962)

The growing idleness of summer grass
With its frail kites of furious butterflies
Requests the lemonade of simple praise
In scansion gentler than my hammock's swings
And rituals no more upsetting than a   5
Black maid shaking linen as she sings
The plain notes of some Protestant hosanna –
Since I lie idling from the thought in things –

Or so they should, until I hear the cries
Of two small children hunting yellow wings,   10
Who break my Sabbath with the thought of sin.

Brother and sister, with a common pin,
Frowning like serious lepidopterists.
The little surgeon pierces the thin eyes.
Crouched on plump haunches, as a mantis prays   15
She shrieks to eviscerate its abdomen.
The lesson is the same. The maid removes
Both prodigies from their interest in science.
The girl, in lemon frock, begins to scream
As the maimed, teetering thing attempts its flight.   20
She is herself a thing of summery light,
Frail as a flower in this blue August air,
Not marked for some late grief that cannot speak.

The mind swings inward on itself in fear
Swayed towards nausea from each normal sign.   25
Heredity of cruelty everywhere,
And everywhere the frocks of summer torn,
The long look back to see where choice is born,
As summer grass sways to the scythe's design.

QUESTIONS

1   What do you know about the speaker?

2   What is the situation?

3   Can you paraphrase this poem completely? If not, which lines defy paraphrase?

4   Examine the use of stanza. What is the progression in terms of subject matter and tone?

5   How do specific images work in this poem to intensify meaning?

'Water' by Robert Lowell (1976)
It was a Maine lobster town –
each morning boatloads of hands
pushed off for granite
quarries on the islands,

and left dozens of bleak   5
white frame houses stuck
like oyster shells
on a hill of rock,

and below us, the sea lapped
the raw little match-stick   10
mazes of a weir,
where the fish for bait were trapped.

Remember? We sat on a slab of rock.
From this distance in time,
it seems the color   15
of iris, rotting and turning purpler,

but it was only
the usual gray rock
turning the usual green
when drenched by the sea.   20

The sea drenched the rock
at our feet all day,
and kept tearing away
flake after flake.

One night you dreamed   25
you were a mermaid clinging to a wharf-pile,
and trying to pull
off the barnacles with your hands.

We wished our two souls
might return like gulls   30
to the rock. In the end,
the water was too cold for us.

To access worksheet 3.3 on additional questions on poetry, please visit www.pearsonbacconline.com and follow the on-screen instructions.

QUESTIONS

1 What do you know about the speaker?

2 What do you know about the situation?

3 How does imagery create tone?

4 What is the type and purpose of this poem?

INSIGHTS INTO POETRY

Remember that poetry in its essence is pleasurable. Saying words, shaping them in your mouth, engages us on a very primal level. Consider the pleasure that children have in listening to the sounds of words. Rhymes amuse us as children listening to a story, and continue to do so as we learn to read the words and make the sounds ourselves. Sound, then, lies at the heart of this genre.

Other helpful insights as you explore this genre include:

- Initially, you need to determine all that you can about the speaker/persona and their tone of voice.

- Consider that the tone of that voice reflects the speaker's attitude towards the situation of the poem.

- Don't be afraid to look up a word you don't know or investigate a reference or allusion to a person, place or event in history or myth. You must feel confident that you know what all the words mean, at least denotatively.

- Much in the same way, do not be afraid to experience the situation the poet presents or the emotions that accompany it. Just as in other genres, be open to possibility, give yourself permission to think and to feel.

Because of the many dimensions of the language of poetry and the vast number of poetic strategies/conventions that a poet has to use, accept that reading and re-reading a poem many times has value. As you observe which strategies or conventions a poet uses, you can apply those observations to understand how the interaction of form and subject matter creates specific effects. To understand these effects and their functions within the poem is to produce analysis.

4 CONVENTIONS OF PROSE OTHER THAN FICTION

Learning Outcomes

Knowledge and Understanding

- Understand the main differences between 'prose other than fiction' (i.e. non-fiction), and fiction
- Consider the importance of audience and context
- Understand the principal features of persuasive techniques including rhetoric
- Consider the importance of register
- Explore the main conventions and types of non-fiction texts

Appreciation

- Discuss the relationship between form and content when looking at non-fiction
- Discuss the different ways that authors of non-fiction get their points across
- Appreciate the way that sample non-fiction texts have been constructed
- Analyse key features that are typical of the non-fiction genre
- Identify the effects of these features on the reader
- Consider past examination questions on the genre

Knowledge and Understanding

Prose other than fiction is prose (i.e. continuous text, not poetry) that is factual, more commonly known as 'non-fiction'. In other words, non-fiction will be texts such as:

- Essays
- Letters
- Memoirs
- Diaries
- Philosophical texts: treatises, maxims, aphorisms
- Manifestos
- Chronicles
- Annals
- Speeches
- Autobiographies
- Biographies

In fact, we could argue that just about any piece of writing that is not a poem, dramatic work or a piece of fictional story-telling is classified as non-fiction. Signs, instructions, pamphlets, job descriptions, textbooks, advertising billboards, manuals, documentaries, reports, newspapers, journal and magazine articles, are all examples.

As opposed to short stories and novels, which create imagined worlds, non-fiction presents ideas that are facts or believed to be facts. Non-fiction is writing about the real world, not the make-believe one.

The recognizable techniques of a genre, as we have seen, are called 'literary conventions'. For non-fiction, these conventions are:

- Audience and context
- Persuasive techniques
- Register

These three conventions are important because they differentiate non-fiction from fiction quite clearly. Let's look at them one by one.

Audience and context

Non-fiction is one of the broadest genres, incorporating everything from essays to signs, manifestos to newspapers.

Audience is important to consider because unlike fiction, where in the majority of cases the reader is not known, most pieces of non-fiction have an intended reader or viewer in mind. This type of writing is crafted with the objective to attract and draw in a specific reader or audience in some way.

The following key features of a non-fiction work will tell you much about its intended audience:

- The date of publication or delivery
  Knowing when a speech was made or when a letter was published can give you important contextual background information, including historical events taking place at the time and who exactly was being addressed.
- The type of register used (see pages 90–91 on register)
  If the register is highly formal it tells you that the author is addressing educated, high-status people in some official or formal capacity (politicians, members of a senate, congress or parliament, academics, members of a board and so on). Formal register will be used on solemn occasions too. Highly informal register might suggest that the target audience is young, lower-class and less decorous. Informal register tends to be used at events such as mass gatherings.
- The tone
  Tone tells you something about the design the author has to convince the audience: sarcasm will be used to discredit and ridicule something, accusation to indict and prosecute, inflammatory speech to stir up strong emotions.

Note that non-fiction doesn't have to be remote from the conventions of fiction. Non-fiction can include literary features found in fiction, such as dramatic visual imagery and a narrative structure. Some pieces of non-fiction, however, use the second-person narrative ('you'). This is a fairly rare narrative device in fiction, but one that can draw in the reader quite effectively in letter writing or advertising.

Audience is an important element to consider when looking at speeches, for speeches are made in a specific context with a live audience in mind. Churchill's war speeches, such as 'We shall fight them on the beaches' or 'Blood, sweat and tears', cannot be separated from the context of Britain being at war with Germany, and the audience's emotions needing to be roused for them to fight and make sacrifices. Similarly, Martin Luther King Jr's famous speech 'I Have a Dream' had a particular audience in mind, and was delivered at the time of the Civil Rights Movement during the 1960s, when themes of social justice and racial equality moved listeners to action. We will come back to speeches later.

The intended audience often determines the tone, register and narrative structure of a piece of non-fiction. Understanding the intended audience can help you analyze the choices the author makes.

Persuasive techniques

Another important convention of non-fiction is how the author tries to persuade or manipulate the audience. In fiction, the literary conventions are concerned largely with characterization, plot and narrative. In non-fiction, however, since the author has a particular audience in mind from the start, he or she can use a number of techniques to convince the reader.

One persuasive device is known as rhetoric. Throughout Greek, Roman and medieval times, rhetoric was one of the most important subjects taught to young people, and great figures from the ancient world, such as the Greek statesman Pericles and the Roman orator Cicero, were famous for their rhetoric (for more about rhetoric see pages 93–94).

The Greek philosopher Aristotle divided persuasion into three categories: the use of logically constructed argument (logos), the use of emotional argument (pathos) and standpoints that are ethically or morally credible (ethos).

Logos is typical of essays, articles and reports. It comes from the ancient Greek meaning 'word' and/or 'speech'. When an author uses logically constructed arguments to make a point, then we can speak of logos. For example, an argument in favour of economic measures such as lower taxes or increased inflation will most likely make use of logic. When you talk about 'reason' in Theory of Knowledge, you will see how logical constructs such as syllogisms, and inductive and deductive reasoning, can be used to make a point in language. Logos is more prominent in non-fiction than fiction itself because we are dealing with facts and real-life situations, so the nature of persuasion tends to be fairly logical (like a lawyer arguing in a court case) rather than lyrical or imaginary.

Cicero was famous for his speeches in favour of the Roman Republic.

The Greek philosopher Aristotle was renowned for his persuasive use of logic, emotion and ethical argument.

Syllogism
A syllogism is a logically constructed argument. For a syllogism to be valid, the conclusion must be drawn from the premise correctly. For example, a valid syllogism would be: 'All men are mortal. Socrates is a man. Therefore Socrates is mortal.' An invalid syllogism would be: 'All men are mortal. Socrates is mortal. Therefore Socrates is a man.' Note that this is wrong because Socrates could be a dog or something else; we have mixed up the category and the rule, unlike in the first example where the correct order has been followed.

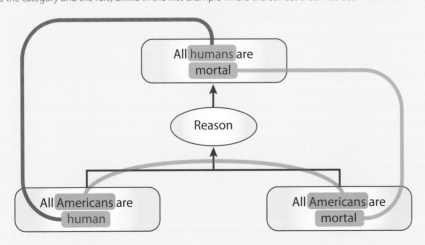

Think how inductive and deductive reasoning can be used to persuade a reader or audience. Can you think of any important recent political examples where reason has been used to persuade a large body of people?

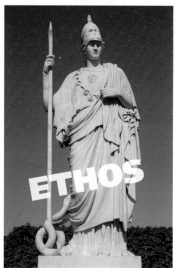

Pathos is a method of persuading the reader by appealing to the emotions. It comes from the ancient Greek for 'suffering' or 'experience'. Pathos goes beyond non-fiction into drama, poetry and fiction, since any type of art will always evoke the emotions. Pathos will affect the language used by the author; features such as strong imagery, hyperbole (exaggeration), an emotionally arousing tone and powerful symbolism are common features of the use of pathos. Speeches, for example, often have to generate big emotions in a crowd and will often make use of pathos. One of the things to consider when looking at pathos is how the author allows the reader or audience to sympathize and empathize with the case or plea in question.

Ethos is the ancient Greek for 'character'. It is basically the technique of establishing credibility as a speaker or writer by making ethically sound statements. When we speak of the ethos of a school, for instance, we mean the values that it stands for. Unlike fiction, where ideas and artistic sentiment take precedence, in non-fiction ethos means the ethical standpoint taken by the speaker. Depending on the argument, both speeches and essays tend to use various degrees of ethos to establish credibility and make points.

SUMMARY

Whether looking at a piece of non-fiction as part of an oral commentary or in an essay, it is important to consider the way that the author uses emotion, reason and ethical argument to convince the reader/audience. At least one of these will always be used.

Register

Register is the style of language that is used in certain social contexts. The way we speak varies according to the setting, and knowing which register to use under specific circumstances is an important skill for any student of literature. Consider the way you talk with your friends as opposed to the way you speak when doing a formal presentation in class. In each case you are using a different register.

The choice of register is an essential factor to consider when looking at non-fiction, as it tells us something about the intended audience and the manner in which the speaker wishes to make points and to whom. As such, a speech made to a gathering of politicians will contain a very different register to one made to a gathering of manual labourers; similarly, the register used in addressing fans of pop music would be different to that used with university professors.

There are six basic different types of register:

Archaic – when the language is old-fashioned and from an earlier period to the one in which it is being used.

Technical – when the language used is specific to a type of technology or discipline.

Formal – when the language is 'smart' and appropriate for formal occasions, such as meetings with figures of authority.

Informal – when the language is casual, without special attention paid to the type of idiom or vocabulary used, although it is still mainstream and reasonably polite.

Colloquial – when the language used is characterized by the words and structures of everyday speech (in other words, the type of language that you would use in the corridor when speaking to a friend, but not when addressing a teacher or writing an essay).

Slang – when terms are faddish and popular amongst a specific social group, but not necessarily understandable to others outside that group.

To make it clearer, here is an example of how a single term can be expressed through these five different types of register:

Archaic: The man is filled with love unto himself.

Technical: The subject is narcissistic.

Formal: That gentleman is self-centred.

Informal: The chap's full of himself.

Colloquial: The guy's a navel-gazer.

Slang: The dude is totally into himself.

Key elements of non-fiction
Three elements to consider with prose non-fiction: audience, persuasive techniques and register.

SUMMARY

Register is a key feature of prose other than fiction: it tells you about the audience being addressed and the type of affiliations and support groups the author is attempting to attract. With the advent of electronic communication, such as blogs, wikis and texting, a highly informal register is used on an increasingly wide scale.

What does register tell you about language and power? The French philosopher Michel Foucault (1926–84) argued that language is mostly used to exert power, especially in historical writing. Think about how the writing of the history of your country could be considered an act of power.

Literary features of repetition

Many speeches use figures of repetition to create rhetorical effect. Here are some common ones:

Anadiplosis: repetition of a word at the end of one clause and the beginning of the following clause.

> Example: 'We stand here before you today. Today when the tide is turning. Turning it is and turn it will.'

Epizeuxis: incremental repetition.

> Example: '... never, never, never, never give up.' (Winston Churchill)

Anaphora: repetition of a word or phrase at the beginning of different clauses.

> Example: 'We are a people in a quandary about the present. We are a people in search of our future. We are a people in search of a national community.' (Barbara Jordan)

Different types of non-fiction
Essays

The essay form was invented by Michel de Montaigne when he published 107 pieces of writing under that name in 1580. The word itself is derived from the French meaning 'try' or 'attempt'.

An essay is a logically constructed piece of writing that usually makes an argument for or against something. Essays follow various conventions when it comes to the way that they are constructed, but will tend to start with an introduction that posits a basic argument, followed by the main body that gives examples and elaboration of that argument, finishing with a synthetic conclusion (summing up the main body). This much said, the form of the essay can be modified greatly, and it is a flexible and adaptable form. Essays can be in the first or the third person. The most common type of essay will be a few hundred lines long, but in some cases entire books are called essays, such as John Locke's *An Essay on Human Understanding*.

The history of the essay has witnessed continental European writers using it for political, polemic and moral argument. Some of the philosophers who have used the essay form to these ends include Montesquieu, Virginia Woolf, Jean-Paul Sartre, Albert Camus, Bertrand Russell, Susan Sontag, Arundhati Roy and André Malraux. The following opening paragraphs are from an essay by the famous French existentialist philosopher Albert Camus:

FROM ALBERT CAMUS, 'THE MYTH OF SISYPHUS' (1942)

The gods had condemned Sisyphus to ceaselessly rolling a rock to the top of a mountain, whence the stone would fall back of its own weight. They had thought with some reason that there is no more dreadful punishment than futile and hopeless labor.

If one believes Homer, Sisyphus was the wisest and most prudent of mortals. According to another tradition, however, he was disposed to practice the profession of highwayman. I see no contradiction in this. Opinions differ as to the reasons why he became the futile laborer of the underworld. To begin with, he is accused of a certain levity in regard to the gods. He stole their secrets. Egina, the daughter of Esopus, was carried off by Jupiter. The father was shocked by that disappearance and complained to Sisyphus. He, who knew of the abduction, offered to tell about it on condition that Esopus would give water to the citadel of Corinth. To the celestial thunderbolts he preferred the benediction of water. He was punished for this in the underworld. Homer tells us also that Sisyphus had put Death in chains. Pluto could not endure the sight of his deserted, silent empire. He dispatched the god of war, who liberated Death from the hands of her conqueror.

It is said that Sisyphus, being near to death, rashly wanted to test his wife's love. He ordered her to cast his unburied body into the middle of the public square. Sisyphus woke up in the underworld. And there, annoyed by an obedience so contrary to human love, he obtained from Pluto permission to return to earth in order to chastise his wife. But when he had seen again the face of this world, enjoyed water and sun, warm stones and the sea, he no longer wanted to go back to the infernal darkness. Recalls, signs of anger, warnings were of no avail. Many years more he lived facing the curve of the gulf, the sparkling sea, and the smiles of earth. A decree of the gods was necessary. Mercury came and seized the impudent man by the collar and, snatching him from his joys, led him forcibly back to the underworld, where his rock was ready for him.

You have already grasped that Sisyphus is the absurd hero. He is, as much through his passions as through his torture. His scorn of the gods, his hatred of death, and his passion for life won him that unspeakable penalty in which the whole being is exerted toward accomplishing nothing. This is the price that must be paid for the passions of this earth. Nothing is told us about Sisyphus in the underworld. Myths are made for the imagination to breathe life into them. As for this myth, one sees merely the whole effort of a body straining to raise the huge stone, to roll it, and push it up a slope a hundred times over; one sees the face screwed up, the cheek tight against the stone, the shoulder bracing the clay-covered mass, the foot wedging it, the fresh start with arms outstretched, the wholly human security of two earth-clotted hands. At the very end of his long effort measured by skyless space and time without depth, the purpose is achieved. Then Sisyphus watches the stone rush down in a few moments toward that lower world whence he will have to push it up again toward the summit. He goes back down to the plain.

It is during that return, that pause, that Sisyphus interests me. A face that toils so close to stones is already stone itself! I see that man going back down with a heavy yet measured step toward the torment of which he will never know the end. That hour like a breathing-space which returns as surely as his suffering, that is the hour of consciousness. At each of those moments when he leaves the heights and gradually sinks toward the lairs of the gods, he is superior to his fate. He is stronger than his rock.

QUESTION

Try to sum up the central idea of this passage in a sentence. What philosophical point is the author making?

SUMMARY

The key features of an essay to think about are that it tends to proceed by logical argument, it is used to put forward philosophical, political or social positions, and it is usually written with a clear introduction and conclusion. Look again at the extract from 'The Myth of Sisyphus'. We could say that Camus' elaborate description of Sisyphus' fate illustrates how a person who strives for life against powerful forces can achieve a heroic stoicism.

Speeches

Speeches are spoken pieces of rhetoric used to raise awareness, rally people around a cause or inspire. The speech differs from numerous other types of non-fiction in that it is intended for an audience to hear rather than read.

The art of making speeches, and using language for public verbal persuasion, was known traditionally as 'rhetoric', and was one of the most important aspects of an education in the ancient world. From the days of Cicero in ancient Rome right up until the 19th century, rhetoric was taught to young people, and was divided into the following processes:

- Invention (finding a topic to speak about)
- Arrangement (organizing the speech)
- Style (choosing the register of the speech)
- Memory (techniques on how to remember the speech)
- Delivery (actually making the speech, projecting the voice and body accordingly)

Some of the famous speech-makers of the past include Cicero, Winston Churchill and Adolf Hitler. Politicians are not the only ones to make speeches, though, and there are a host of examples of powerful speeches made by human rights activists such as Emmeline Pankhurst and Martin Luther King Jr, and feminists such as Helen Keller:

Orwell's essays
George Orwell wrote a series of essays early in the 20th century, and they are good examples of the form, using a combination of ethos, pathos and logos to construct argumentative pieces on colonialism. Some of the most poignant examples of Orwell's essays are 'A Hanging' (1931) in which he gives a chilling description of the ruthlessness of British colonial rule, 'Shooting an Elephant' (1936), a graphic description of how Orwell kills an elephant, spurred on by a mob, and 'Politics and the English Language' (1946), an analytical piece on how language and power are intertwined.

George Orwell

Emmeline Pankhurst (1858–1928) was a brilliant orator and leader of the Suffragettes movement – an organization that rallied for women to have the right to vote in Britain. She was a radical militant and is widely considered as one of the most significant feminists of all time. Her most famous speech is 'Freedom or Death' (1913) – see pages 110–11.

FROM HELEN KELLER, 'STRIKE AGAINST WAR' (1916)

We are not free unless the men who frame and execute the laws represent the interests of the lives of the people and no other interest. The ballot does not make a free man out of a wage slave. There has never existed a truly free and democratic nation in the world. From time immemorial men have followed with blind loyalty the strong men who had the power of money and of armies. Even while battlefields were piled high with their own dead they have tilled the lands of the rulers and have been robbed of the fruits of their labor. They have built palaces and pyramids, temples and cathedrals that held no real shrine of liberty.

QUESTION

As you can deduce from reading this extract, Helen Keller was a militant feminist who spoke at a time when women had few rights. She was deaf and blind, but these physical constraints did not stop her from speaking passionately about freedom and rights. How would you describe the tone and symbolism she uses to get her points across in this short extract?

SUMMARY

Speeches tend to use a variety of devices to persuade and control their audience. These devices include rhetorical questions (questions that are posed without actually expecting an answer, but are there to provoke), figures of repetition (such as anaphora) and variations in register suited to the audience in question and, in general, the first-person narrative structure. One of the key points to keep in mind when analyzing a speech is how the author attempts to convince the audience.

It was in 1964 at the Rivonia Trial that Nelson Mandela made his famous 'I am Prepared to Die' speech before being sentenced to prison where he spent 27 years, making the world turn apartheid-based South Africa against its laws of racial discrimination.

It was directly as a consequence of Nikita Khrushchev's so-called 'Secret Speech' made in 1956 that Joseph Stalin's crimes against humanity were recognized more openly and the Soviet system became less repressive.

GLOBAL PERSPECTIVES

Speeches have been made throughout history in different parts of the world to change political structures, raise awareness about social plights, and promote human rights. Great speeches have changed the shape of history across frontiers.

Letters

Letters are the most personally directed examples of non-fiction, in that they have a very clearly intended reader and are often written for one specific person. Sometimes the form is used for public statements, however. The Romans divided letters into two categories: private letters (*personalis*) and business letters or letters of affairs (*negotialis*). We can add to these a third category, which would be the open letter, written to the public at large. 'Letters' are sometimes used to describe ancient historical accounts, as we see in the observations of Seneca the Younger, Pliny the Younger and Pliny the Elder.

Letters have been used by historians to find out more about the lives of famous people. The letters of Van Gogh, Mozart, Keats and Flaubert, to mention but a few, have allowed theories about their lifestyles to flourish.

Letters employ the first-person narrative. The essential elements to grasp when thinking of letters (or the 'epistolary form') is that they can have an extremely loose structure, because they are not following structural conventions in the way that speeches or essays do. Letters make use of context without necessarily feeling the need to explain things in great detail to the uninformed reader, as they are written in the expectation that the events discussed will be known to the reader. Hence, the tone of letters tends to be very personal. A famous example of an intimate and highly autobiographical letter is 'De Profundis' (1905) by Oscar Wilde to his lover, Lord Alfred Douglas. Here is an example of its personal style:

FROM OSCAR WILDE, 'DE PROFUNDIS' (1905)

A week later, I am transferred here. Three more months go over and my mother dies. No one knew how deeply I loved and honoured her. Her death was terrible to me; but I, once a lord of language, have no words in which to express my anguish and my shame. She and my father had bequeathed me a name they had made noble and honoured, not merely in literature, art, archaeology, and science, but in the public history of my own country, in its evolution as a nation. I had disgraced that name eternally. I had made it a low by-word among low people. I had dragged it through the very mire. I had given it to brutes that they might make it brutal, and to fools that they might turn it into a synonym for folly.

Wilde's letter is full of strong emotional language ('anguish', 'shame', 'brutal'), making it poignant to the reader. Hard-hitting judgemental phrases such as 'dragged it through the very mire' and 'make it brutal', when referring to his name, make the letter stand out as an example of guilt-ridden confession.

When authors use the epistolary form to make a more public announcement, as was the case with Martin Luther King in his 'Letter from a Birmingham Jail' (see page 101) the form is used to communicate ideas through a personal, intimate style even if the reader is not known to the author.

Epistolary novel
Writing novels (fiction rather than non-fiction) in the form of letters became popular in the 18th century. Examples of the 'epistolary novel' are *Pamela* (1740) and *Clarissa* (1748) by Samuel Richardson and *Les Liaisons Dangereuses* (1782) by Choderlos de Laclos. Be sure not to confuse real letters with fictional letters.

Diaries

Diaries are personal records that can vary in the type of information given, but tend to log that information on a daily or other periodic basis. They range from intimate journals to more historical or anecdotal accounts of a time and place. Samuel Pepys (1633–1703) is famous for his lively and vivid account of London during famous historical events such as the Great Plague (1665) and Great Fire (1666). These are recounted in his Diary:

Samuel Pepys

Anne Frank

SEPTEMBER 2, 1666

So down [I went], with my heart full of trouble, to the Lieutenant of the Tower, who tells me that it began this morning in the King's baker's house in Pudding Lane, and that it hath burned St. Magnus's Church and most part of Fish Street already. So I rode down to the waterside, ... and there saw a lamentable fire... Everybody endeavouring to remove their goods, and flinging into the river or bringing them into lighters that lay off; poor people staying in their houses as long as till the very fire touched them, and then running into boats, or clambering from one pair of stairs by the waterside to another. And among other things, the poor pigeons, I perceive, were loth to leave their houses, but hovered about the windows and balconies, till they some of them burned their wings and fell down.

– Diary of Samuel Pepys (1666)

Other examples of anecdotal diaries or journals include those of Charles Greville and Thomas Creevey. *The Diary of Anne Frank* is another example of diary writing that deals with important historical events, in this case descriptions of life under the Nazi occupation in Holland, but it could be classed more in the 'intimate' category, as it deals with personal emotions and observations. Similar intimate diaries include those by the Russian author Leo Tolstoy and the French novelist André Gide. Journals are essentially the same as diaries, the main difference being that they are not usually as emotionally revealing.

SUMMARY

Diaries tend to be informal in register, as they are intended as logs of information without a specific reader in mind. In this way they are rather different to most other types of non-fiction. Modern types of diary, however, include tweets and blogs – these contrast with the classic diary in that they are written with an intended, albeit unspecified, audience in mind.

Biographies

A biography is an account of someone's life by someone else. The famous poet John Dryden defined biographies as 'the history of particular men's lives'. Biographies have become very popular in recent times and have explored increasingly personal themes and details. They tend to be fairly neutral in tone, with an emphasis on events and factual information. Biographies are some of history's most ancient writings, since one way of mapping important historical events was through the lives of famous people. Old Testament stories and ancient epics from Greece, Scandinavia and Mesopotamia, for example, were partly composed from the stories of real people's lives. One of the earliest examples of such a work comes from the ancient Greek writer Xenophon, who wrote about the life of Socrates in his *Memorabilia*, as did Plato in different writings.

The life of Socrates (below) comes to us through the writings of Xenophon and Plato.

Some biographies are not flattering to the subject. This extract concerning Florence Nightingale from Lytton Strachey's 1918 book *Eminent Victorians* is a case in point:

Everyone knows the popular conception of Florence Nightingale. The saintly, self-sacrificing woman, the delicate maiden of high degree who threw aside the pleasures of a life of ease to succour the afflicted, the Lady with the Lamp, gliding through the horrors of the hospital at Scutari, and consecrating with the radiance of her goodness the dying soldier's couch – the vision is familiar to all. But the truth was different. The Miss Nightingale of fact was not as facile fancy painted her.

Autobiographies

The famous literary wit Dr Johnson is believed to have said that no man is better qualified to write his life than himself (although we could doubt this quite seriously). Autobiographies are accounts of a life written by that person. For this reason they are always in the first person, unless we are dealing with fictional autobiographies that explore different narrative structures, such as J.M. Coetzee using the third person to speak about himself in the fictional autobiographies *Boyhood* and *Youth*.

The first famous autobiography was the *Confessions* by the 4th-century philosopher St Augustine. In it he discussed deep and intimate questions of guilt, and this perspective laid the foundations for the confessional mode of many subsequent autobiographies. Other great autobiographies include *Childhood* by Maxim Gorky (1913), *Seven Pillars of Wisdom* by T.E. Lawrence (1926), *Long Walk to Freedom* by Nelson Mandela (1994) and *An Angel at My Table* by Janet Frame (1984).

An autobiographical work can contain just a portion of a person's life. For example, *If This is a Man* (1979) by Primo Levi is an autobiographical description of the author's experience in a concentration camp. Here is how it opens, *in medias res* (meaning 'in the middle of things'):

> I was captured by the fascist militia on 13 December 1943. I was twenty-four, with little wisdom, no experience and a decided tendency – encouraged by the life of segregation forced on me for the previous four years by the racial laws – to live in an unrealistic world of my own, a world inhabited by civilized Cartesian phantoms, by sincere male and bloodless female friendships.
>
> – Primo Levi, *If This is a Man* (1979)

 Do you think that autobiographies are reliable sources of information? Which pressures shape the way people write about others or themselves?

Levi does not begin his account at the beginning of his life, but instead plunges the reader straight into wartime Italy in 1943, and his incarceration by the 'fascist militia'. This opening carries with it great power, and an immediate shock to the reader.

Historical accounts

We have already seen how diaries and journals, but also biographies and autobiographies, deal with historical information, but historical accounts are amongst the greatest works of non-fiction. Famous historians include Herodotus (*The Histories*), Thucydides (*The Peloponnesian Wars*), Livy (*History of Rome*), Suetonius (*The Twelve Caesars*) and Edward Gibbon (*The Decline and Fall of the Roman Empire*). What they have in common is the pursuit of truthful analysis based on factual observation and record. Here are some other forms that are specifically dedicated to recording history:

Annals

Annals are historical accounts that should be, technically speaking, yearly records of events, but the term can be used for the official reports of an organization or society. The most noted examples of annals are those of the Roman writer Tacitus, who was famous for his caustic and forthright statements, written between AD 14 and 15:

> When after the destruction of Brutus and Cassius there was no longer any army of the Commonwealth, when Pompeius was crushed in Sicily, and when, with Lepidus pushed aside and Antonius slain, even the Julian faction had only Caesar left to lead it, then, dropping the title of triumvir, and giving out that he was a Consul, and was satisfied with a tribune's authority for the protection of the people, Augustus won

> over the soldiers with gifts, the populace with cheap corn, and all men with the sweets of repose, and so grew greater by degrees, while he concentrated in himself the functions of the Senate, the magistrates, and the laws. (Book 1)
>
> – Tacitus, *Annals* (AD 14–15)

Tacitus is describing the transition from the end of the Roman Republic through the breaking down of Julius Caesar's grip on power to the reign of the first Roman Emperor, Augustus. Note how he sums up economic and social factors with economy and great synthesis.

Chronicles

Chronicles are linear (chronological) records of events. They should be contemporaneous with the events recorded (in other words, chronicles are written at the time of the events rather than after). Whereas the forms of historical writing mentioned above need not follow any strict chronology, but can make substantial jumps in time and jumble events for effect, the chronicle tends to follow the unfolding of real events in the style of reportage. Famous examples include the numerous chronicles written by William of Malmesbury in the Middle Ages and those of Raphael Holinshed whose *Chronicles* (1577) inspired Shakespeare.

Here is an excerpt from William of Malmesbury's account of the battle of Lincoln in 1142:

> The time of decision came on the very day of the Purification of the most blessed Mary [2 Feb. 1141], beside the river that flowed between the two armies, named Trent, which was then so much swollen by a heavy fall of rain as well as water from its source that there was no possibility of fording it. Only then did the earl disclose his intention to his son-in-law, who had met him with a strong body of troops, and the rest of his followers, adding that he had long since made up his mind that nothing should ever compel him to retreat; he would die or be captured if he did not win the victory. All filled him with good hope, and so – wonderful to hear – he resolved to risk a battle at once, and swam across the racing current of the river mentioned above with all his men. So eager was the earl to make an end of the troubles, that he would sooner face the final danger than have the kingdom's misfortune prolonged. For the king on his side had broken off the siege and offered battle with spirit, accompanied by very many earls and an active body of knights. The royalists first attempted that prelude to the fight which is called jousting, for in this they were accomplished. But when they saw that the 'earlists', if the expression may be allowed, were fighting not with lances at a distance but with swords at close quarters and, charging with their banners in the van, were breaking through the king's line, then all the earls to a man sought safety in flight.

SUMMARY

The different types of historical text mentioned above all express information in different ways, but they have a few points in common that you should think about: the information tends to be factual and without any great affectation or stylistic extravagance – the aim is to describe events clearly. (There are exceptions – see Edward Gibbon and Simon Schama for examples of historical writing that is quite florid.)

Philosophical texts

Philosophical texts can be considered non-fiction and will usually use the form of the essay. However, there are other types of prose that philosophers often use. They are:

- Treatises
- Maxims
- Aphorisms

Treatises

The treatise is a fairly formal work that goes about discussing or investigating a subject and its principles in a systematic way. Some of the famous examples include Aristotle's *Poetics* (4th century BC), where he examines literary tragedy in detail; Francis Bacon's *Novum Organum* (1620), an explication of his scientific method; and David Hume's famous *Treatise of Human Nature* (1740). Aristotle's study of comedy has not survived, but his study of tragedy is still a reference for students of drama:

> Poetry in general seems to have sprung from two causes, each of them lying deep in our nature. First, the instinct of imitation is implanted in man from childhood, one difference between him and other animals being that he is the most imitative of living creatures, and through imitation learns his earliest lessons; and no less universal is the pleasure felt in things imitated. We have evidence of this in the facts of experience. Objects which in themselves we view with pain, we delight to contemplate when reproduced with minute fidelity: such as the forms of the most ignoble animals and of dead bodies. The cause of this again is, that to learn gives the liveliest pleasure, not only to philosophers but to men in general; whose capacity, however, of learning is more limited. Thus the reason why men enjoy seeing a likeness is, that in contemplating it they find themselves learning or inferring, and saying perhaps, 'Ah, that is he.' For if you happen not to have seen the original, the pleasure will be due not to the imitation as such, but to the execution, the coloring, or some such other cause.
>
> – Aristotle, *Poetics*, Book II

Maxims

Maxims are philosophical propositions that are extremely short and to-the-point, stating something fundamental about human nature. Maxims do not usually run for more than a sentence or two and many are anonymous. The most famous writer of maxims was the French philosopher La Rochefoucauld, whose *Maximes* (1665) are still studied by many students of literature today. Examples are:

- 'Old people are fond of giving good advice: it consoles them for no longer being able to set a bad example.' – La Rochefoucauld
- 'It is better to light a candle than to curse the darkness.' – Eleanor Roosevelt
- 'Genius is one percent inspiration and ninety-nine percent perspiration.' – Thomas Edison

Aphorisms

The aphorism is like the maxim in that it is succinct and discusses philosophical themes, but whereas the maxim tends to focus on the human condition and therefore leans towards moral truths, the aphorism outlines any truth, be it human or not. Furthermore, the aphorism is often more poetic, whereas the maxim is frequently ironic and critical. Here are some examples of aphorisms:

'For everything you have missed, you have gained something else; and for everything you gain, you lose something else.' – Ralph Waldo Emerson

'Paradox though it may seem, it is none the less true that life imitates art far more than art imitates life.' – Oscar Wilde

SUMMARY

Philosophical texts can take a variety of different forms, but the common thread they share is an expressive form that deals with abstractions, concepts and ideas. Philosophical texts usually use ethos and logos more than pathos.

Emerging technologies

The internet has introduced a number of non-fiction text types into the world. They include e-mails, discussion forums, e-mail chats, blogs, wikis, tweets and RSS feeds. The general pattern that we can see in the use of language on these electronic platforms is a tendency for informal register, contractions, acronyms and shorter sentence structure. Just think of the e-mails you write, the blog postings you read off the web and the way that language tends to be truncated in this type of usage.

New communications technology are changing the way we look at language itself.

Does fiction or non-fiction portray a stronger idea of truth?

Academic monograph

One type of very common non-fiction text is the academic monograph (such as this book). Textbooks, journals and reviews tend to be written in a formal, clear language that might be specific to a particular discipline (for example, a science journal will contain language specific to the sciences, and the discipline within the sciences). Academic publications will usually focus on research using evidence-based, expository argument, whereas textbooks are made up of exercises and passages designed to clarify concepts.

Appreciation

To access worksheet 4.1 and view responses to the questions in Exercise 1, please visit www. pearsonbacconline.com and follow the on-screen instructions.

EXERCISE 1

The following extracts from different non-fiction texts are intended for different audiences. Each one makes use of persuasive techniques in different ways and each employs a certain type of register. Read and compare the short extracts and answer the questions that follow.

---

1   From Martin Luther King, 'Letter from a Birmingham Jail' (1963)

My Dear Fellow Clergymen:

While confined here in the Birmingham city jail, I came across your recent statement calling my present activities 'unwise and untimely.' Seldom do I pause to answer criticism of my work and ideas. If I sought to answer all the criticisms that cross my desk, my secretaries would have little time for anything other than such correspondence in the course of the day, and I would have no time for constructive work. But since I feel that you are men of genuine good will and that your criticisms are sincerely set forth, I want to try to answer your statement in what I hope will be patient and reasonable terms.

2   From George Orwell, 'Shooting an Elephant' (1936)

When I pulled the trigger I did not hear the bang or feel the kick – one never does when a shot goes home – but I heard the devilish roar of glee that went up from the crowd. In that instant, in too short a time, one would have thought, even for the bullet to get there, a mysterious, terrible change had come over the elephant. He neither stirred nor fell, but every line of his body had altered. He looked suddenly stricken, shrunken, immensely old, as though the frightful impact of the bullet had paralysed him without knocking him down. At last, after what seemed a long time – it might have been five seconds, I dare say – he sagged flabbily to his knees. His mouth slobbered. An enormous senility seemed to have settled upon him. One could have imagined him thousands of years old. I fired again into the same spot. At the second shot he did not collapse but climbed with desperate slowness to his feet and stood weakly upright, with legs sagging and head drooping. I fired a third time. That was the shot that did for him. You could see the agony of it jolt his whole body and knock the last remnant of strength from his legs. But in falling he seemed for a moment to rise, for as his hind legs collapsed beneath him he seemed to tower upward like a huge rock toppling, his trunk reaching skyward like a tree. He trumpeted, for the first and only time. And then down he came, his belly towards me, with a crash that seemed to shake the ground even where I lay.

3   From Jonathan Swift, 'A Modest Proposal' (1729)

It is a melancholy object to those who walk through this great town or travel in the country, when they see the streets, the roads, and cabin doors, crowded with beggars of the female sex, followed by three, four, or six children, all in rags and importuning every passenger for an alms. These mothers, instead of being able to work for their honest livelihood, are forced to employ all their time in strolling to beg sustenance for their helpless infants: who as they grow up either turn thieves for want of work, or leave their dear native country to fight for the Pretender in Spain, or sell themselves to the Barbadoes.

4   From Michel de Montaigne, 'Of Cannibals' (1562)

They have I know not what kind of priests and prophets, who very rarely present themselves to the people, having their abode in the mountains. At their arrival, there is a great feast, and solemn assembly of many villages: each house, as I have described, makes a village, and they are about a French league distant from one another. This prophet declaims to them in public, exhorting them to virtue and their duty: but all their ethics are comprised in these two articles, resolution in war, and affection to their wives. He also prophesies to them events to come, and the issues they are to expect from their enterprises, and prompts them to or diverts them from war: but let him look to't; for if he fail in his divination, and anything happen otherwise than he has foretold, he is cut into a thousand pieces, if he be caught, and condemned for a false prophet: for that reason, if any of them has been mistaken, he is no more heard of.

Divination is a gift of God, and therefore to abuse it, ought to be a punishable imposture. Among the Scythians, where their diviners failed in the promised effect, they were laid, bound hand and foot, upon carts loaded with furze and bavins, and drawn by oxen, on which they were burned to death. Such as only meddle with things subject to the conduct of human capacity, are excusable in doing the best they can: but those other fellows that come to delude us with assurances of an extraordinary faculty, beyond our understanding, ought they not to be punished, when they do not make good the effect of their promise, and for the temerity of their imposture?

● **Examiner's hints**
It is important to go beyond identifying literary features to analyzing them, saying what effect they have on the reader and the meaning of the text.

QUESTIONS

1   What sort of intended audience do you think each author had in mind, and what makes you think this?

2   Identify some of the persuasive techniques (logos, pathos or ethos) that each extract uses to engage the reader. Give examples.

3   Describe the register of each extract, with examples.

4   How would you summarize the main messages the authors are trying to get across in each text?

To access worksheet 4.2 and view responses to the questions in Exercise 2, please visit www. pearsonbacconline.com and follow the on-screen instructions.

EXERCISE 2

The following is a famous essay by Arthur Miller on Tragedy. Read it and answer the questions that follow.

From Arthur Miller, 'Tragedy and the Common Man' (1949)

In this age few tragedies are written. It has often been held that the lack is due to a paucity of heroes among us, or else that modern man has had the blood drawn out of his organs of belief by the skepticism of science, and the heroic attack on life cannot feed on an attitude of reserve and circumspection. For one reason or another, we are often held to be below tragedy – or tragedy above us. The inevitable conclusion is, of course, that the tragic mode is archaic, fit only for the very highly placed, the kings or the kingly, and where this admission is not made in so many words it is most often implied.

I believe that the common man is as apt a subject for tragedy in its highest sense as kings were. On the face of it this ought to be obvious in the light of modern psychiatry, which bases its analysis upon classific formulations, such as the Oedipus and Orestes complexes, for instance, which were enacted by royal beings, but which apply to everyone in similar emotional situations.

More simply, when the question of tragedy in art is not at issue, we never hesitate to attribute to the well-placed and the exalted the very same mental processes as the lowly. And finally, if the exaltation of tragic action were truly a property of the highbred character alone, it is inconceivable that the mass of mankind should cherish tragedy above all other forms, let alone be capable of understanding it.

As a general rule, to which there may be exceptions unknown to me, I think the tragic feeling is evoked in us when we are in the presence of a character who is ready to lay down his life, if need be, to secure one thing – his sense of personal dignity. From Orestes to Hamlet, Medea to Macbeth, the underlying struggle is that of the individual attempting to gain his 'rightful' position in his society.

Sometimes he is one who has been displaced from it, sometimes one who seeks to attain it for the first time, but the fateful wound from which the inevitable events spiral is the wound of indignity, and its dominant force is indignation. Tragedy, then, is the consequence of a man's total compulsion to evaluate himself justly.

In the sense of having been initiated by the hero himself, the tale always reveals what has been called his 'tragic flaw,' a failing that is not peculiar to grand or elevated characters. Nor is it necessarily a weakness. The flaw, or crack in the character, is really nothing – and need be nothing – but his inherent unwillingness to remain passive in the face of what he conceives to be a challenge to his dignity, his image of his rightful status. Only the passive, only those who accept their lot without active retaliation, are 'flawless'. Most of us are in that category.

But there are among us today, as there always have been, those who act against the scheme of things that degrades them, and in the process of action, everything we have accepted out of fear or insensitivity or ignorance is shaken before us and examined, and from this total onslaught by an individual against the seemingly stable cosmos surrounding us – from this total examination of the 'unchangeable' environment – comes the terror and the fear that is classically associated with tragedy.

More important, from this total questioning of what has been previously unquestioned, we learn. And such a process is not beyond the common man. In revolutions around the world, these past thirty years, he has demonstrated again and again this inner dynamic of all tragedy.

Insistence upon the rank of the tragic hero, or the so-called nobility of his character, is really but a clinging to the outward forms of tragedy. If rank or nobility of character was indispensable, then it would follow that the problems of those with rank were the particular problems of tragedy. But surely the right of one monarch to capture the domain from another no longer raises our passions, nor are our concepts of justice what they were to the mind of an Elizabethan king.

The quality in such plays that does shake us, however, derives from the underlying fear of being displaced, the disaster inherent in being torn away from our chosen image of what and who we are in this world. Among us today this fear is as strong, and perhaps stronger, than it ever was. In fact, it is the common man who knows this fear best.

Now, if it is true that tragedy is the consequence of a man's total compulsion to evaluate himself justly, his destruction in the attempt posits a wrong or an evil in his environment. And this is precisely the morality of tragedy and its lesson. The discovery of the moral law, which is what the enlightenment of tragedy consists of, is not the discovery of some abstract or metaphysical quantity.

The tragic right is a condition of life, a condition in which the human personality is able to flower and realize itself. The wrong is the condition which suppresses man, perverts the flowing out of his love and creative instinct. Tragedy enlightens – and it must, in that it points the heroic finger at the enemy of man's freedom. The thrust for freedom is the quality in tragedy which exalts. The revolutionary questioning of the stable environment is what terrifies. In no way is the common man debarred from such thoughts or such actions.

Seen in this light, our lack of tragedy may be partially accounted for by the turn which modern literature has taken toward the purely psychiatric view of life, or the purely sociological. If all our miseries, our indignities, are born and bred within our minds, then all action, let alone the heroic action, is obviously impossible.

And if society alone is responsible for the cramping of our lives, then the protagonist must needs be so pure and faultless as to force us to deny his validity as a character. From neither of these views can tragedy derive, simply because neither represents a balanced concept of life. Above all else, tragedy requires the finest appreciation by the writer of cause and effect.

No tragedy can therefore come about when its author fears to question absolutely everything, when he regards any institution, habit, or custom as being either everlasting, immutable, or inevitable. In the tragic view the need of man to wholly realize himself is the only fixed star, and whatever it is that hedges his nature and lowers it is ripe for attack and examination. Which is not to say that tragedy must preach revolution.

The Greeks could probe the very heavenly origin of their ways and return to confirm the rightness of laws. And Job could face God in anger, demanding his right, and end in submission. But for a moment everything is in suspension, nothing is accepted, and in 'this stretching and tearing apart of the cosmos, in the very action of so doing, the character gains "size,"' the tragic stature which is spuriously attached to the royal or the highborn in our minds. The commonest of men may take on that stature to the extent of his willingness to throw all he has into the contest, the battle to secure his rightful place in his world.

There is a misconception of tragedy with which I have been struck in review after review, and in many conversations with writers and readers alike. It is the idea that tragedy is of necessity allied to pessimism. Even the dictionary says nothing more about the word than that it means a story with a sad or unhappy ending. This impression is so firmly fixed that I almost hesitate to claim that in truth tragedy implies more optimism in its author than does comedy, and that its final result ought to be the reinforcement of the onlooker's brightest opinion of the human animal.

For, if it is true to say that in essence the tragic hero is intent upon claiming his whole due as a personality, and if this struggle must be total and without reservation, then it automatically demonstrates the indestructible will of man to achieve his humanity.

The possibility of victory must be there in tragedy. Where pathos rules, where pathos is finally derived, a character has fought a battle he could not possibly have won. The pathetic is achieved when the protagonist is, by virtue of his witlessness, his insensitivity, or the very air he gives off, incapable of grappling with a much superior force.

Pathos truly is the mode for the pessimist. But tragedy requires a nicer balance between what is possible and what is impossible. And it is curious, although edifying, that the plays we revere, century after century, are the tragedies. In them, and in them alone, lies the belief – optimistic, if you will – in the perfectibility of man.

It is time, I think, that we who are without kings took up this bright thread of our history and followed it to the only place it can possibly lead in our time – the heart and spirit of the average man.

QUESTIONS

1 How does Miller draw the reader into his argument? What are the elements of pathos, logos and ethos at work?

2 Can you summarize Miller's argument in a short sentence?

3 How would you describe the register in this essay? What is the relationship between the register and the message?

● **Examiner's hints**
To show knowledge and understanding of a text, you should be able to sum up its main message clearly.

GLOBAL PERSPECTIVES

Arthur Miller, best known as a playwright, argues across ethnicities, culture and gender to give a truly universal message about the fallen hero in this essay, even if the references are primarily Greek and English.

EXERCISE 3

Compare and contrast the two extracts from famous speeches below. Look specifically at how the authors use imagery to create effect, and comment on the emotional impact these speeches have on the reader.

To access worksheet 4.3 – an example of how you might go about this exercise – please visit www.pearsonbacconline.com and follow the on-screen instructions.

1 **From Martin Luther King, 'I have a Dream' (1963)**

Five score years ago, a great American, in whose symbolic shadow we stand, signed the Emancipation Proclamation. This momentous decree came as a great beacon light of hope to millions of Negro slaves who had been seared in the flames of withering injustice. It came as a joyous daybreak to end the long night of captivity.

But one hundred years later, we must face the tragic fact that the Negro is still not free. One hundred years later, the life of the Negro is still sadly crippled by the manacles of segregation and the chains of discrimination. One hundred years later, the Negro lives on a lonely island of poverty in the midst of a vast ocean of material prosperity. One hundred years later, the Negro is still languishing in the corners of American society and finds himself an exile in his own land. So we have come here today to dramatize an appalling condition.

In a sense we have come to our nation's capital to cash a check. When the architects of our republic wrote the magnificent words of the Constitution and the declaration of Independence, they were signing a promissory note to which every American was to fall heir. This note was a promise that all men would be guaranteed the inalienable rights of life, liberty, and the pursuit of happiness.

It is obvious today that America has defaulted on this promissory note insofar as her citizens of color are concerned. Instead of honoring this sacred obligation, America has given the Negro people a bad check which has come back marked 'insufficient funds.' But we refuse to believe that the bank of justice is bankrupt. We refuse to believe that there are insufficient funds in the great vaults of opportunity of this nation. So we have come to cash this check – a check that will give us upon demand the riches of freedom and the security of justice. We have also come to this hallowed spot to remind America of the fierce urgency of now. This is no time to engage in the luxury of cooling off or to take the tranquilizing drug of gradualism. Now is the time to rise from the dark and desolate valley of segregation to the sunlit path of racial justice. Now is the time to open the doors of opportunity to all of God's children. Now is the time to lift our nation from the quicksands of racial injustice to the solid rock of brotherhood.

2   From Winston Churchill, 'We will Fight them on the Beaches' (1940)

We have found it necessary to take measures of increasing stringency, not only against enemy aliens and suspicious characters of other nationalities, but also against British subjects who may become a danger or a nuisance should the war be transported to the United Kingdom. I know there are a great many people affected by the orders which we have made who are the passionate enemies of Nazi Germany. I am very sorry for them, but we cannot, at the present time and under the present stress, draw all the distinctions which we should like to do. If parachute landings were attempted and fierce fighting attendant upon them followed, these unfortunate people would be far better out of the way, for their own sakes as well as for ours. There is, however, another class, for which I feel not the slightest sympathy. Parliament has given us the powers to put down Fifth Column activities with a strong hand, and we shall use those powers subject to the supervision and correction of the House, without the slightest hesitation until we are satisfied, and more than satisfied, that this malignancy in our midst has been effectively stamped out.

Turning once again, and this time more generally, to the question of invasion, I would observe that there has never been a period in all these long centuries of which we boast when an absolute guarantee against invasion, still less against serious raids, could have been given to our people. In the days of Napoleon the same wind which would have carried his transports across the Channel might have driven away the blockading fleet. There was always the chance, and it is that chance which has excited and befooled the imaginations of many Continental tyrants. Many are the tales that are told. We are assured that novel methods will be adopted, and when we see the originality of malice, the ingenuity of aggression, which our enemy displays, we may certainly prepare ourselves for every kind of novel stratagem and every kind of brutal and treacherous manoeuvre. I think that no idea is so outlandish that it should not be considered and viewed with a searching, but at the same time, I hope, with a steady eye. We must never forget the solid assurances of sea power and those which belong to air power if it can be locally exercised.

I have, myself, full confidence that if all do their duty, if nothing is neglected, and if the best arrangements are made, as they are being made, we shall prove ourselves once again able to defend our Island home, to ride out the storm of war, and to outlive the menace of tyranny, if necessary for years, if necessary alone. At any rate, that is what we are going to try to do. That is the resolve of His Majesty's Government – every man of them. That is the will of Parliament and the nation. The British Empire and the French Republic, linked together in their cause and in their need, will defend to the death their native soil, aiding each other like good comrades to the utmost of their strength. Even though large tracts of Europe and many old and famous States have fallen or may fall into the grip of the Gestapo and all the odious apparatus of Nazi rule, we shall not flag or fail. We shall go on to the end, we shall fight in France, we shall fight on the seas and oceans, we shall fight with growing confidence and growing strength in the air, we shall defend our Island, whatever the cost may be, we shall fight on the beaches, we shall fight on the landing grounds, we shall fight in the fields and in the streets, we shall fight in the hills; we shall never surrender, and even if, which I do not for a moment believe, this Island or a large part of it were subjugated and starving, then our Empire beyond the seas, armed and guarded by the British Fleet, would carry on the struggle, until, in God's good time, the New World, with all its power and might, steps forth to the rescue and the liberation of the old.

Taking it to another dimension

In order to stretch your imagination into non-verbal signs and to get a feeling for the atmosphere created in each of the speeches, draw a symbol that expresses the feelings in each of these extracts. Look at them and give each one a name. This exercise can help you get away from a straightforward explication into an analysis. By converting the texts into symbols you are thinking in terms of connotation rather than denotation. It can also help you sum up the essence or main points of the texts.

EXERCISE 4

From Barack Obama's inaugural address (2009)

In what ways is writing a speech like writing a play?

Homes have been lost, jobs shed, businesses shuttered. Our health care is too costly, our schools fail too many, and each day brings further evidence that the ways we use energy strengthen our adversaries and threaten our planet.

These are the indicators of crisis, subject to data and statistics. Less measurable, but no less profound, is a sapping of confidence across our land; a nagging fear that America's decline is inevitable, that the next generation must lower its sights.

Today I say to you that the challenges we face are real, they are serious and they are many. They will not be met easily or in a short span of time. But know this America: They will be met. On this day, we gather because we have chosen hope over fear, unity of purpose over conflict and discord.

On this day, we come to proclaim an end to the petty grievances and false promises, the recriminations and worn-out dogmas that for far too long have strangled our politics.

We remain a young nation, but in the words of Scripture, the time has come to set aside childish things. The time has come to reaffirm our enduring spirit; to choose our better history; to carry forward that precious gift, that noble idea, passed on from generation to generation: the God-given promise that all are equal, all are free, and all deserve a chance to pursue their full measure of happiness.

In reaffirming the greatness of our nation, we understand that greatness is never a given. It must be earned. Our journey has never been one of shortcuts or settling for less.

It has not been the path for the faint-hearted, for those who prefer leisure over work, or seek only the pleasures of riches and fame.

Rather, it has been the risk-takers, the doers, the makers of things – some celebrated, but more often men and women obscure in their labor – who have carried us up the long, rugged path towards prosperity and freedom.

For us, they packed up their few worldly possessions and traveled across oceans in search of a new life. For us, they toiled in sweatshops and settled the West, endured the lash of the whip and plowed the hard earth.

For us, they fought and died in places Concord and Gettysburg; Normandy and Khe Sanh.

Time and again these men and women struggled and sacrificed and worked till their hands were raw so that we might live a better life. They saw America as bigger than the sum of our individual ambitions; greater than all the differences of birth or wealth or faction.

This is the journey we continue today. We remain the most prosperous, powerful nation on Earth. Our workers are no less productive than when this crisis began. Our minds are no less inventive, our goods and services no less needed than they were last week or last month or last year. Our capacity remains undiminished. But our time of standing pat, of protecting narrow interests and putting off unpleasant decisions – that time has surely passed.

QUESTIONS

1 Looking at the extract from Barack Obama's inaugural address above, think about the sentence structure. How does Obama convey logos, pathos and ethos through the way that he constructs his phrases?

2 In this speech, can you see any of these figures of repetition mentioned on page 91? What is the effect of their being employed?

EXERCISE 5

To access worksheet 4.4 and view responses to the questions in Exercise 5, please visit www. pearsonbacconline.com and follow the on-screen instructions.

Both Betty Friedan (1921–2006) and Emmeline Pankhurst (1858–1928) reflected upon women's place in society. In the extracts below, they did this through different forms and through different techniques. Read the two texts and answer the questions that follow.

1 From Betty Friedan, *The Feminine Mystique* (1963)

The problem lay buried, unspoken, for many years in the minds of American women. It was a strange stirring, a sense of dissatisfaction, a yearning that women suffered in the middle of the twentieth century in the United States. Each suburban wife struggled with it alone. As she made the beds, shopped for groceries, matched slipcover material, ate peanut butter sandwiches with her children, chauffeured Cub Scouts and Brownies, lay beside her husband at night – she was afraid to ask even of herself the silent question – 'Is this all?'

For over fifteen years there was no word of this yearning in the millions of words written about women, for women, in all the columns, books and articles by experts telling women their role was to seek fulfillment as wives and mothers. Over and over women heard in voices of tradition and of Freudian sophistication that they could desire no greater destiny than to glory in their own femininity. Experts told them how to catch a man and keep him, how to breastfeed children and handle their toilet training, how to cope with sibling rivalry and adolescent rebellion; how to buy a dishwasher, bake bread, cook gourmet snails, and build a swimming pool with their own hands; how to dress, look, and act more feminine and make marriage more exciting; how to keep their husbands from dying young and their sons from growing into delinquents. They were taught to pity the neurotic, unfeminine, unhappy women who wanted to be poets or physicists or presidents. They learned that truly feminine women do not want careers, higher education, political rights – the independence and the opportunities that the old-fashioned feminists fought for. Some women, in their forties and fifties, still remembered painfully giving up those dreams, but most of the younger women no longer even thought about them. A thousand expert voices applauded their femininity, their adjustment, their new maturity. All they had to do was devote their lives from earliest girlhood to finding a husband and bearing children.

By the end of the nineteen-fifties, the average marriage age of women in America dropped to 20, and was still dropping, into the teens. Fourteen million girls were engaged by 17. The proportion of women attending college in comparison with men dropped from 47 per cent in 1920 to 35 per cent in 1958. A century earlier, women had fought for higher education; now girls went to college to get a husband. By the mid-fifties, 60 per cent dropped out of college to marry, or because they were afraid too much education would be a marriage bar. Colleges built dormitories for 'married students,' but the students were almost always the husbands. A new degree was instituted for the wives – 'Ph.T.' (Putting Husband Through).

Then American girls began getting married in high school. And the women's magazines, deploring the unhappy statistics about these young marriages, urged that courses on marriage, and marriage counselors, be installed in the high schools. Girls started going steady at twelve and thirteen, in junior high. Manufacturers put out brassieres with false bosoms of foam rubber for little girls of ten. And an advertisement for a child's dress, sizes 3–6x, in the *New York Times* in the fall of 1960, said: 'She Too Can Join the Man-Trap Set.'

By the end of the fifties, the United States birthrate was overtaking India's. The birth-control movement, renamed Planned Parenthood, was asked to find a method whereby women who had been advised that a third or fourth baby would be born dead or defective might have it anyhow. Statisticians were especially astounded at the fantastic increase in the number of babies among college women. Where once they had two children, now they had four, five, six. Women who had once wanted careers were now making careers out of having babies. So rejoiced *Life* magazine in a 1956 paean to the movement of American women back to the home.

. . .

For over fifteen years, the words written for women, and the words women used when they talked to each other, while their husbands sat on the other side of the room and talked shop or politics or septic tanks, were about problems with their children, or how to keep their husbands happy, or improve their children's school, or cook chicken or make slipcovers. Nobody argued whether women were inferior or superior to men; they were simply different. Words like 'emancipation' and 'career' sounded strange and embarrassing; no one had used them for years. When a Frenchwoman named Simone de Beauvoir wrote a book called *The Second Sex*, an American critic commented that she obviously 'didn't know what life was all about,' and besides, she was talking about French women. The 'woman problem' in America no longer existed.

If a woman had a problem in the 1950s and 1960s, she knew that something must be wrong with her marriage, or with herself. Other women were satisfied with their lives, she thought. What kind of a woman was she if she did not feel this mysterious fulfillment waxing the kitchen floor? She was so ashamed to admit her dissatisfaction that she never knew how many other women shared it. If she tried to tell her husband, he didn't understand what she was talking about. She did not really understand it herself.

The suburban housewife – she was the dream image of the young American women and the envy, it was said, of women all over the world. The American housewife – freed by science and labor-saving appliances from the drudgery, the dangers of childbirth and the illnesses of her grandmother. She was healthy, beautiful, educated, concerned only about her husband, her children, her home. She had found true feminine fulfillment. As a housewife and mother, she was respected as a full and equal partner to man in his world. She was free to choose automobiles, clothes, appliances, supermarkets; she had everything that women ever dreamed of.

2 From Emmeline Pankhurst, 'Freedom or Death' (1913)

I do not come here as an advocate, because whatever position the suffrage movement may occupy in the United States of America, in England it has passed beyond the realm of advocacy and it has entered into the sphere of practical politics. It has become the subject of revolution and civil war, and so tonight I am not here to advocate woman suffrage. American suffragists can do that very well for themselves.

I am here as a soldier who has temporarily left the field of battle in order to explain – it seems strange it should have to be explained – what civil war is like when civil war is waged by women. I am not only here as a soldier temporarily absent from the field at battle; I am here – and that, I think, is the strangest part of my coming – I am here as a person who, according to the law courts of my country, it has been decided, is of no value to the community at all; and I am adjudged because of my life to be a dangerous person, under sentence of penal servitude in a convict prison.

It is not at all difficult if revolutionaries come to you from Russia, if they come to you from China, or from any other part of the world, if they are men. But since I am a woman it is necessary to explain why women have adopted revolutionary methods in order to win the rights of citizenship. We women, in trying to make our case clear, always have to make as part of our argument, and urge upon men in our audience the fact – a very simple fact – that women are human beings.

Suppose the men of Hartford had a grievance, and they laid that grievance before their legislature, and the legislature obstinately refused to listen to them, or to remove their grievance, what would be the proper and the constitutional and the practical way of getting their grievance removed? Well, it is perfectly obvious at the next general election the men of Hartford would turn out that legislature and elect a new one.

But let the men of Hartford imagine that they were not in the position of being voters at all, that they were governed without their consent being obtained, that the legislature turned an absolutely deaf ear to their demands, what would the men of Hartford do then? They couldn't vote the legislature out. They would have to choose; they would have to make a choice of two evils: they would either have to submit indefinitely to an unjust state of affairs, or they would have to rise up and adopt some of the antiquated means by which men in the past got their grievances remedied.

Your forefathers decided that they must have representation for taxation, many, many years ago. When they felt they couldn't wait any longer, when they laid all the arguments before an obstinate British government that they could think of, and when their arguments were absolutely disregarded, when every other means had failed, they began by the tea party at Boston, and they went on until they had won the independence of the United States of America.

It is about eight years since the word militant was first used to describe what we were doing. It was not militant at all, except that it provoked militancy on the part of those who were opposed to it. When women asked questions in political meetings and failed to get answers, they were not doing anything militant. In Great Britain it is a custom, a time-honoured one, to ask questions of candidates for parliament and ask questions of members of the government. No man was ever put out of a public meeting for asking a question. The first people who were put out of a political meeting for asking questions, were women; they were brutally ill-used; they found themselves in jail before 24 hours had expired.

We were called militant, and we were quite willing to accept the name. We were determined to press this question of the enfranchisement of women to the point where we were no longer to be ignored by the politicians.

You have two babies very hungry and wanting to be fed. One baby is a patient baby, and waits indefinitely until its mother is ready to feed it. The other baby is an impatient baby and cries lustily, screams and kicks and makes everybody unpleasant until it is fed. Well, we know perfectly well which baby is attended to first. That is the whole history of politics. You have to make more noise than anybody else, you have to make yourself more obtrusive than anybody else, you have to fill all the papers more than anybody else, in fact you have to be there all the time and see that they do not snow you under.

QUESTIONS

1 Compare Friedan's and Pankhurst's use of imagery, saying how it gives a different slant to each text and the way the message is transferred to the reader or audience.

2 The first text is an extract from a book, the second from a speech. How does contrast in format affect the use of narrative structure?

3 Consider how both texts use pathos, logos and ethos, comparing and contrasting them for each of these.

PRACTICE QUESTIONS

Consider the following questions, extracted from IB Higher Level exams on prose other than fiction and apply them to the non-fiction texts that you are studying:

'Our true natures are revealed by the ways in which we face adversity.' Consider in at least two works you have studied how far writers have used adversity to point to certain features of the topics or the voices in their works. (Nov 2009)

In prose other than the novel and short story, content is more important than style. To what extent does this statement apply to at least two of the works you have studied? (May 2009 TZ1)

Discuss the treatment of poverty in at least two of the works in your study. (May 2009 TZ1)

Prose works (other than novels and short stories) often deal with transitions in the lives of the writers or other characters. Discuss the role of such transitions and the ways in which they are presented in at least two of the works you have studied. (May 2009 TZ2)

Writers may choose a formal or informal style of writing to express their ideas. Characterize the style selected by at least two of the writers you have studied, and discuss how that choice affects the work as a whole. (May 2009 TZ2)

Situations involving dilemmas or difficult choices are often the subject of prose other than fiction. What role have these kinds of situations played in at least two works you have studied, and how have they contributed to the meaning of those works? (Nov 2008)

'If a work has no clear structure, a reader is more often bewildered than enlightened.' How far do at least two works in your study lead you to agree or disagree with this statement? (Nov 2008)

A writer usually attempts to create a bond of trust between writer and reader. How and to what extent have at least two writers you have studied been able to elicit your trust? (May 2008 TZ1)

What are the questions that underlie at least two of the works that you have read and how have the authors sought to answer those questions? (May 2008 TZ1)

'Daily life is the stuff of which high sanctity can be made.' Discuss how far and in what ways at least two of the prose works you have studied have treated daily life in such a way as to raise it above the 'everyday'. (May 2008 TZ2)

Prose other than the novel or short story often expresses strong political and/or ethical views. To what extent is this true of at least two of the works you have studied, and in what ways and to what extent have the writers made such views convincing? (May 2008 TZ2)

In many forms of prose other than fiction, writers discuss things at both a literal level and also at a 'deeper' or sub-textual level in order to convey their views or stances on certain issues they hold dear. Using at least two works you have studied, discuss the writer's handling of these two levels of discourse. (Nov 2007)

'Ordinary life is commonplace whereas life in literature bristles with energy.' Explore this view in at least two works you have studied, showing to what extent the writers have invested the works with an energy that makes the material 'bristle'. (Nov 2007)

With reference to two or three works you have studied, discuss techniques authors have used to persuade readers to sympathize with their ideas. (May 2007)

INSIGHTS INTO NON-FICTION

Summing up what we have covered in this chapter, there are a number of points to keep in mind. The essential point to retain is that non-fiction is unique in that it is often (although not always) written with a specific audience or reader in mind. Persuasion is also a common imperative behind non-fiction. Unlike fiction, which can be purely expressive, non-fiction is very frequently there to argue a point and/or sensitize the reader or audience to a particular situation.

There are a plethora of different types of non-fiction: it is an extremely diverse genre, with many interesting forms. For a work to be considered literature, on the other hand, it must contain artistic merit and this is what distinguishes literary non-fiction from instructions, signs, pamphlets and pieces of text that have no real stylistic quality.

Here are some points to consider and retain when exploring this genre and its conventions:

- Non-fiction is essentially characterized by three fundamental elements: its intended audience, its register and its use of persuasive techniques.

- One of the most prominent persuasive techniques is called 'rhetoric'. Aristotle outlined three strands of rhetoric: pathos, logos and ethos. Remember that rhetoric is not confined to non-fiction alone even if it is most frequently found in speeches.

- Register tells you something about the intended audience and the kind of rapport that the speaker or author wishes to establish with his or her audience. The six types of register are archaic, technical, formal, informal, colloquial and slang.

- Essays are traditionally used for philosophic discourse and authors tend to use the form to posit logically constructed arguments.

- Letters convey a sense of the intimate and the highly personal, even if they are 'open letters' for the public.

- Remember that speeches are intended to be heard and not read, so when we analyze a speech we are looking at a transcription of something that should be appreciated live. Remembering that speeches should be heard more than read can help you appreciate the quality of the conventions of speech writing, such as rhetorical figures and figures of repetition.

- Autobiographies and biographies evoke key ethical and psychological questions of truth, confession, authenticity and purpose, and these broader philosophical ideas should not be lost when reading such texts.

COMMENTARY

5

Learning Outcomes

Knowledge and Understanding

- Understand the role of commentary in assessment
- Discuss the differences between commentary and guided literary analysis
- Examine the structure and components of commentary
- Explore colour-marking as a strategy for commentary preparation
- Approach commentaries on Shakespearean drama

Appreciation

- Evaluate examples of commentary
- Utilize colour-marking in commentary preparation
- Practise writing commentaries in relation to the assessment criteria
- Evaluate examples of guided literary analysis
- Review the specifics of the commentary and the guided literary analysis

Knowledge and Understanding

The English A: Literature course guide talks of the artistry of literature, and the student's appreciation of that artistry, through the close study of individual texts and passages. This appreciation includes the ability to analyze language, structure, technique and style, and to evaluate their effects on the reader. At the higher level, students are expected to show a deeper understanding of content and a writer's techniques, including the formal, stylistic and aesthetic features of texts. Commentary is the primary tool for demonstrating such understanding.

In terms of your formal IB assessments, the commentary, whether spoken or written, is central to your success in this course.

In Part 2 of the programme (Detailed Study), at both SL and HL, you will be required to deliver a ten-minute oral commentary. At SL, the commentary is based on an extract from one of the works studied in Part 2; at HL, the commentary is based on a single poem studied in Part 2, followed by a discussion on one of the other two works studied.

In Part 4 (Options) assessment, the Individual Oral Presentation (IOP), at both SL and HL, you could opt to present an oral commentary from a passage in a work that you studied in Part 4. For exam Paper 1, at SL, you must be prepared to write a **guided literary analysis** on an unseen prose extract or poem. The analysis must demonstrate a sustained and convincing interpretation of the text. It has to show an appreciation of the ways in which the writer has used language, structure, technique and style to shape meaning.

At HL, students are required to write a **literary commentary** on an unseen poem or prose passage for Paper 1. A literary commentary refers to a **close reading** of a passage or poem that is **presented in the form of an essay**. In these essays, you will explore a text's content, style, structure, theme and language. The assessment of commentary is based on your showing an understanding and an interpretation of the passage, and supporting your interpretation through detailed references to the text. You must also analyze and explain how the passage achieves its effects on the reader.

SUMMARY

SL students write a guided literary analysis for Paper 1, while HL students write a literary commentary for Paper 1. The purpose of both exercises is to demonstrate close-reading skills as a vehicle for understanding a literary text.

What is a guided literary analysis?

As with the commentary, exam Paper 1 contains two unseen passages and students write a guided literary analysis on one of these passages. One passage will be poetry, and the other will be prose – a novel, short story, essay, biography, or journalistic piece of writing. **Two guiding questions are provided – one focused on understanding and interpretation, the other on style.** Students are required to respond to **both** questions, but not necessarily in sequence. You could respond with two separate answers, or you could write a single answer that includes a response to both questions. You can decide how to structure your response most effectively.

The essential difference between a literary commentary and a guided literary analysis is one of organization and development of ideas, as opposed to the nature of the analysis. In both tasks, students are asked to demonstrate an understanding of the thought and feeling within the passage, as well as show an appreciation for the ways in which a writer shapes his or her meaning through specific **choices of language, structure, technique and style.** A commentary, however, involves developing an argument based on a well-supported interpretation of a piece of literature, while the SL guided literary analysis is just that, an analysis, not an argument. The ideas in the guided literary analysis are presented coherently, and the two guiding questions help students to do this. In the commentary, the introduction and conclusion set the framework of the argument. In the guided literary analysis, SL students are not required to present their own perspectives on the prose passage or poem.

What is a commentary?

According to the Language A guide, there are many ways to approach and to structure a literary commentary, but a 'good commentary explains, rather than merely summarizing content or listing effects.' Commentaries should be 'continuous and developed.' This continuous development means that the commentary, like any essay, requires a reasoned, purposeful structure as opposed to a more random organization.

Commentary, as a form of response, accounts for at least 40 per cent of the HL assessment in the English A: Literature course. Consequently, learning how to write and to deliver a spoken commentary is critical.

The commentary is actually a specific type of essay. In the commentary, the focus is on the writer and the choices he or she has made stylistically within a prose passage or a poem to create an intended effect. Your job in commentary is to 'comment' as to how, i.e. in what ways, the writer has contributed to meaning through specific stylistic choices. For example, the poet's use of punctuation, or the prose fiction writer's use of dialogue may serve to produce effects that underscore meaning.

You might like to believe that there is a pre-set format for commentary, a kind of pattern or formulaic approach that works like a template, but this is not the case.

Every passage or poem has its own 'architecture', its own shape, and within this shape or form is an **internal** as well as **external** structure (see below for an explanation). In the simplest terms, each extract for commentary has a beginning, middle and an end. Your task is to determine how the extract is 'built', how it is put together both in terms of content/subject matter and literary conventions and then to determine how those conventions are manipulated by the writer to create an intended effect on the reader.

The purposeful stylistic choices of writers and their manipulation of the conventions of the genre are not isolated from meaning. As a close reader, you will observe the relationship of form to meaning and appreciate how the writer has made specific choices to create specific effects. This essay focused on close reading is called a commentary.

Later, in this chapter, you will learn about several strategies for examining the relationship between style and meaning. Before we approach these strategies, however, it is important for you to know and understand several key terms.

What is the architecture/structure/form of an extract?

Extracts of prose, including drama and poetry, have an architecture, a shape or a form that is observable to the eye. This **external structure** could include the number of stanzas or sentences in a poem, or the number of paragraphs in a prose passage. Analyzing punctuation, too, is important in terms of close reading. By assessing the presence or absence of full stops, question marks, quotation marks and dashes, just to name a few, we can discover individual words or phrases that the poet seeks to draw our attention to simply by their placement in a sentence.

Punctuation also controls rhythm and pace. Commas, ellipses, the absence of a full stop at the end of a stanza – all create rhythm, and control not only the sound of the poem but the form (shape/architecture) of the poem as well. For example, when a poet uses enjambment, he or she is forcing the reader to acknowledge that the stanzas, even though there may be space between them, are not to be read separately but as a continuation of each other. You might then comment on why you think the poet has done this, and the emotional effects of the form.

In addition to the external, visible, structure of a passage or poem, there is also what might be called an **internal structure**, the meaning and suggestions conveyed in the words themselves. Within this concept of an internal structure is the development of subject matter/content and the shift in tone that may (or may not) accompany this progression.

In the Appreciation section of this chapter, several poems and prose extracts are used to illustrate pre-writing activities that will help you achieve the close reading required for good commentary, including determining external and internal structures.

How to write a commentary

It is always a good idea to read a poem or prose passage several times. If you are working with a text in a classroom setting, as opposed to a test situation, use a dictionary if you are not familiar with specific terms. Know what all the words mean – literally.

Once you understand all terms, can you paraphrase the passage or poem? (Put the passage or poem into your own words.) Be sure to note those particular phrases or lines that are difficult to paraphrase. The lines that prove resistant to paraphrase are often those that are essential to meaning. The ambiguity of their expression, the fact that they refuse to allow straightforward or simplistic summarizing, are indications that the 'heart' of the poem, what you may offer as an interpretation of the poet's message, may lie within them. Now can you venture an observation about the meaning of the poem? Does the title itself provide any clue?

If you are familiar with colour-marking, now is the time to use that process to help you read closely, and identify image patterns, motives, unusual or interesting word choices and sound devices such as rhyme, rhythm and alliteration.

If you are not familiar with the colour-marking process, a brief description follows:

Colour-marking prose and poetry – a way into commentary

Before looking at the specifics of the colour-marking process, first we must define our terms:

- **Image**: a word (or more than one word) appealing to at least one of our senses, and thereby generating a response in the reader. Of our five senses (visual, auditory, olfactory, tactile and gustatory), the visual is generally the strongest.
- **Image patterns**: the repetition of these images, not necessarily in uninterrupted succession.
- **Motif**: a repeated pattern of any type within a text. Note that an image pattern is a motif, but a motif is not always an image pattern. An image pattern is a repeated reference to a particular sense, and, since a motif is a repeated pattern, we can say that an image pattern is a motif.

  We cannot, however, say that the reverse is true. Any repeated pattern, say a repetition of references to time, is indeed a motif. But although we have senses of sight, sound, smell, etc., we do not have a sense called 'time'. Our understanding of time is, however, perceived through many of our senses – the ticking of a clock or the rising of the sun. (Note also that motif is defined variously in reference sources.) When the term is used in this course, use the above definition.

Now, we'll look through a literary microscope at a passage to understand the writer's techniques, whether they be narrative (as in prose fiction), poetic or dramatic. The process below applies to all genres, poetry and prose.

Mark with different colours each type of image/image pattern/motif noted in the given passage. If the text is an extract from a larger work that you have studied, think about the context surrounding the extract, and how that helps you clarify its meaning.

Based on your colour-marking, ask these questions:
- Is one colour predominant? Why?
- Is there some logical progression of imagery/motif, from one type to another? Is the progression illogical? Why?

- How do the imagery/motifs reinforce and/or illustrate the content of the passage? If you prefer, what is the relationship of the scene to the imagery/motifs used to describe it? Imagery reinforces content by giving it emphasis, by making it fresh through an unusual or creative use of imagery, and/or by adding irony (imagery appears to contradict the content or describe it in terms of its opposite qualities).
- Is a specific tone or mood created by the marked material?

Based on your answers to these questions and any others you think appropriate, code each colour-marked poem with inferences you draw about the use of that image/image pattern/motif.

Consider the following poem by Sylvia Plath.

'Two Sisters of Persephone' (1956)

Two girls there are: within the house
One sits; the other, without.
Daylong a duet of shade and light
Plays between these.

In her dark wainscoted room   5
The first works problems on
A mathematical machine.
Dry ticks mark time

As she calculates each sum.
At this barren enterprise   10
Rat-shrewd go her squint eyes,
Root-pale her meager frame.

Bronzed as earth, the second lies,
Hearing ticks blown gold
Like pollen on bright air. Lulled   15
Near a bed of poppies,

She sees how their red silk flare
Of petaled blood
Burns open to sun's blade.
On that green altar   20

Freely become sun's bride, the latter
Grows quick with seed.
Grass-couched in her labor's pride,
She bears a king. Turned bitter

And sallow as any lemon,   25
The other, wry virgin to the last,
Goes graveward with flesh laid waste,
Worm-husbanded, yet no woman.

Now examine the same poem colour-marked, below. You will see that the colour-marking process provides a 'way in' to the poem, a way to observe details that could be significant in your commentary or guided literary analysis. Remember, however, that every observation may not contribute to your analysis, but in terms of close reading it is important to exhaust the passage of all the strategies that the poet used. In addition to the colour-marking, the passage also includes key notes about important stylistic and thematic points.

Colour-marked text

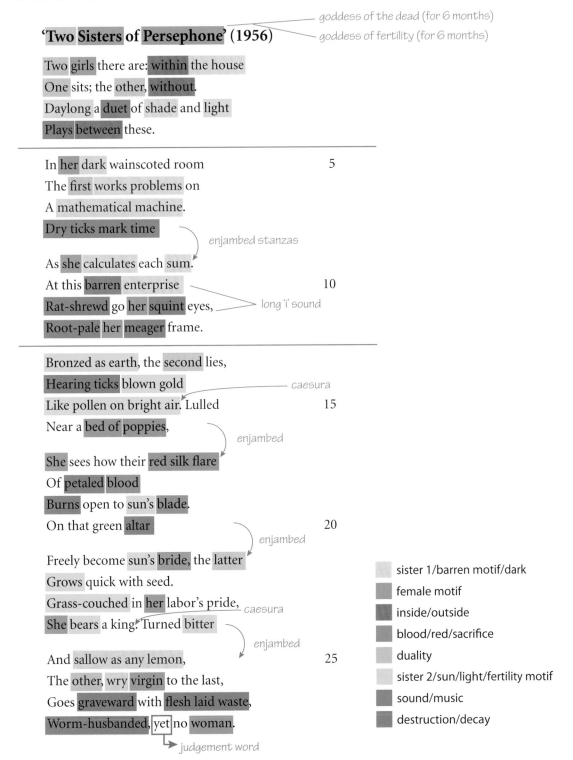

goddess of the dead (for 6 months)
goddess of fertility (for 6 months)

'Two Sisters of Persephone' (1956)

Two girls there are: within the house
One sits; the other, without.
Daylong a duet of shade and light
Plays between these.

In her dark wainscoted room   5
The first works problems on
A mathematical machine.
Dry ticks mark time

enjambed stanzas

As she calculates each sum.
At this barren enterprise   10
Rat-shrewd go her squint eyes,

long 'i' sound

Root-pale her meager frame.

Bronzed as earth, the second lies,
Hearing ticks blown gold

caesura

Like pollen on bright air. Lulled   15
Near a bed of poppies,

enjambed

She sees how their red silk flare
Of petaled blood
Burns open to sun's blade.
On that green altar   20

enjambed

Freely become sun's bride, the latter
Grows quick with seed.
Grass-couched in her labor's pride,

caesura

She bears a king. Turned bitter

enjambed

And sallow as any lemon,   25
The other, wry virgin to the last,
Goes graveward with flesh laid waste,
Worm-husbanded, yet no woman.

judgement word

sister 1/barren motif/dark
female motif
inside/outside
blood/red/sacrifice
duality
sister 2/sun/light/fertility motif
sound/music
destruction/decay

Perhaps one of the most helpful aspects of the colour-marking analytical strategy is that it helps to provide a structure for the commentary.

Once the architecture/shape of the passage is determined, that shape can establish a pattern for discussion. If you pay attention, the shape of the poem can form your response to it – your commentary. For example, in Plath's poem, an examination of the external structure reveals that the poem's shape is arranged in four parts.

- The first part is composed of the opening four-lined, end-stopped stanza.
- The second part is composed of enjambed stanzas two and three.
- The third part is composed of enjambed stanzas four, five, six, and seven.
- Where, then, is the fourth part?

The fourth part comes in the last line of stanza six. Only after examining the internal structure and noting the key caesura (see Chapter 3, page 74) in line 24, is the student aware of Plath's critical positioning of the line, 'Turned bitter . . .'. The position of this phrase after the caesura, signals to the reader that the line is significant in terms of the meaning of the poem.

The other caesura, located on line 15 is equally significant. The position of the word 'Lulled' stresses the fact that the 'second' sister, while seemingly fully conscious of herself, and therefore her decisions, actually may not be fully self-aware. The reference to 'bed of poppies' in line 16, provides further evidence for this claim.

What about the title? Does it offer insight to the poem's meaning? Aside from providing an explanation for the seasons, the myth of Persephone also connects to Hades, the god of the Underworld; Demeter, Persephone's mother; the sun god Apollo; and the thematic ideas of trickery, choice, obligation and fertility. These allusions surface to some degree within the context of the poem, so, yes, the title does offer insight into the meaning and content of the poem.

What about the internal structure of this poem? What observations can we make about the movement/shift/progression of subject matter and the associated shifts in tone?

Initially, we see that the four-part structure that we identified earlier is consistent with the subject matter of the two distinct 'sisters' referenced in the poem. In part one, the opening stanza, both sisters are introduced with imagery that will accompany them throughout the poem. One sister is associated with images of light, the other with darkness. Yet in addition to the duality of the seemingly opposing 'sisters' is the idea of connection between the sisters established with the musical imagery of 'duet' and 'plays'.

In the second section, stanzas two and three, sister number one is presented. Images of the working mind, the calculating and mathematical ('works problems on/A mathematical machine') characterize her. She works in darkness, at a 'barren enterprise'. Her physical body is diminished, shrunken, 'pale', a 'meager frame'. The single auditory image in this section, 'Dry ticks mark time' leads the enjambed line, connecting the physical work and work space to the physical body of the sister. The 'rat-shrewd' eyes show complete and utter devotion to her mental tasks, even at the body's 'root-pale' cost.

In the lengthy third section of the poem the focus shifts from sister one to sister two. In this section, the imagery is lush and fertile, but not without threat. References to 'altar', 'sun's blade', 'petaled blood' and 'burns open' are richly contrasted to the dry barrenness of sister one in the opening section. The contrast in fertility is underscored through the physical 'work' of sister two as compared to the intellectual problem-solving or 'creation' of sister one. The 'labor' of the second sister is in her giving birth to a 'king', the seed of the sun. In the abundant images of the natural world, she hears 'ticks blown gold/ Like pollen on bright air'. The time is right; she is programmed for fertility, and so, 'Lulled/ Near a bed of poppies', she sacrifices herself. The implication we can read through the imagery here is that she did not choose sacrifice so much as acquiesce to it.

One sister works; the other creates. But are their efforts mutually exclusive? Consider the opening stanza's reference to the 'duet of shade and light [that] plays between these'. What are the different connotations of these words?

Plath's careful placement of 'Turned bitter' at the end of the sixth stanza provides an interesting link in terms of meaning, through the connection provided by enjambment. Consider the final stanza as a kind of assertion, a declaration of the effects of choices made. Does the caesura on line 24 provide a clue as to the speaker's judgement of the 'two sisters of Persephone'?

Is either sister unscathed? Persephone has no sister in the myth, so who are these sisters? Are they representative of two paths for women? Two paths for Plath herself? While biography may shed some light on the situations in Plath's life that might be 'confessed' in the poem, the poem can and does stand alone, without the necessity of biographical input.

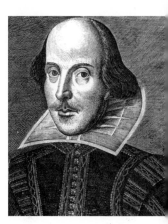

To access worksheet 5.1 on dualities within poems, please visit www.pearsonbacconline.com and follow the on-screen instructions.

How to approach analyses of Shakespeare passages

In terms of analysis, Shakespearean extracts, other than soliloquies, offer an interesting challenge. While soliloquies read essentially as poems, other extracts from these plays include dramatic as well as poetic strategies. Analysis of an extract from a Shakespearean play requires close attention, not only to the language and poetry of Shakespeare, but to the acting strategies that dramatize those words – an actor's movement, a prop, a costume, a gesture, a tone of voice cannot be ignored. Consequently, the analysis has to be sensitive to both the poetic and dramatic features employed by the playwright.

The list below, while not exhaustive, may provide you with some close reading points to explore when you attempt to write or speak a commentary on a Shakespearean extract.

Shakespeare analysis

- **Know context**: Be able to 'frame' the passage specifically by act and scene.
- **Know content**: What is the passage about? What is happening? What do we learn?
- **Know significance**: Why is the passage significant? What do we learn about the character(s) and their interaction? What do we learn about human nature? How is this message, lesson or understanding delivered?

Tie understanding of the passage to dramatic AND poetic features; each has distinctive effects.

Dramatic features	Poetic features
Dramatic/situational/verbal irony	Metre/rhythm
Physical movement	Poetry/prose
Sound	Tone
Lighting	Metaphor/simile
Costume	Imagery/motives
Location	Duality
Aside	Juxtaposition
Soliloquy	Paradox/oxymoron
Props	Sound devices: alliteration, consonance, assonance, onomatopoeia, rhyme

Now, take a look at a passage for commentary from Shakespeare's *The Tempest*.

Prospero's speech, Act 5, Scene 1

You elves of hills, brooks, standing lakes, and groves,

And you that on the sands with printless foot

Do chase the ebbing Neptune, and do fly him

When he comes back; you demi-puppets that

By moonshine do the green sour ringlets make,   5

Whereof the ewe not bites; and you whose pastime

Is to make midnight mushrumps, that rejoice

To hear the solemn curfew; by whose aid,

Weak masters though you be, I have bedimmed

The noontide sun, called forth the mutinous winds,   10

And 'twixt the green sea and the azured vault

Set roaring war, to the dread rattling thunder

Have I given fire, and rifted Jove's stout oak

With his own bolt; the strong-based promontory

Have I made shake, and by the spurs plucked up   15

The pine and cedar; graves at my command

Have waked their sleepers, oped, and let 'em forth

By my so potent art. But this rough magic

I here abjure and when I have required

Some heavenly music, which even now I do,   20

To work mine end upon their sense that

This airy charm is for, I'll break my staff,

Bury it certain fathoms in the earth,

And deeper than did ever plummet sound

I'll drown my book.   25

A dramatic artistic impression of a scene from Shakespeare's *The Tempest*.

Here is an example of the same passage, but with colour-marking. Study it carefully, then look at the sample student essays below:

Prospero's speech, Act 5, Scene 1

You elves of hills, brooks, standing lakes, and groves,

And you that on the sands with printless foot

Do chase the ebbing Neptune, and do fly him

When he comes back; you demi-puppets that

By moonshine do the green sour ringlets make,   5

Whereof the ewe not bites; and you whose pastime

Is to make midnight mushrumps, that rejoice

euphony (harmony)

To hear the solemn curfew; by whose aid,

Weak masters though you be, I have bedimmed

The noontide sun, called forth the mutinous winds,   10

And 'twixt the green sea and the azured vault

Set roaring war, to the dread rattling thunder

Have I given fire, and rifted Jove's stout oak

With his own bolt; the strong-based promontory

Have I made shake, and by the spurs plucked up   15

The pine and cedar; graves at my command

Have waked their sleepers, oped, and let 'em forth

By my so potent art. But this rough magic

cacophony (holds on to power)

I here abjure and when I have required

Some heavenly music, which even now I do,   20

To work mine end upon their sense that

This airy charm is for, I'll break my staff,

euphony (relinquishes power)

Bury it certain fathoms in the earth,

And deeper than did ever plummet sound

I'll drown my book.   25

- nature
- sound imagery
- art/magic
- day/night
- master/servant
- strength/potency

To access worksheet 5.2 on sound and metre, please visit www.pearsonbacconline.com and follow the on-screen instructions.

EXERCISE 1

Evaluate each of the following sample student commentaries. Consider the overall effectiveness of the student's understanding of the passage:

- Does the student seem to understand the thoughts and feelings expressed in the passage (in a literal sense)?
- Does the student offer an interpretation of the passage and support that interpretation with references to the passage?
- Does the analysis show an awareness of and an appreciation for the writer's poetic strategies?
- Are the ideas developed systematically and expressed in clear, concise, accurate sentences?

Rank three samples according to the quality of the commentary, from the most satisfactory to the least. Be prepared to provide specific details to support your assessments and discuss your findings, relating them to the assessment criteria.

Sample student commentary 1

Prospero makes this speech when he decides to stop using his art. It is a very important speech because his magic is so powerful and it has driven most of the major events in the play. In this passage Shakespeare is very conscious of sound and rhythm which he uses to show the power that Prospero possesses along with other imagery.

The passage is divided into two sentences, in which Prospero discusses very different things. The first sentence, that makes up most of the passage, describes the wonders on the island and the effect that Prospero can have on them. Shakespeare uses a lot of visual imagery in describing the 'green sea' and the 'azured vault' and alliteration in 'midnight mushrumps' to emphasize every part of Prospero's world. He also uses the motifs of gods and power to underscore how mighty he truly is. Prospero mentions Neptune, who controls the sea, and Jove, who rules his kingdom with his 'own bolt'.

Both of these all-powerful beings share many things with Prospero who can 'set roaring war' with 'mutinous winds' as well as control everyone else on the island. Shakespeare also uses sound and rhythm to highlight the strength of Prospero's magic. The use of words like 'roaring' and 'rattling' emphasize the loud and destructive nature of the 'rough magic'. The extra syllables in lines 3 and 13 also emphasize the the words 'fly' and 'Jove's stout oak.' This emphasis again links Prospero to a god.

The second sentence in the passage represents a shift in tone. Prospero decides to change his ways. While the tone of the first section seems proud, the tone at the end is different. Here it seems that Prospero is more humble and regrets what he has done. The change occurs in line 18 where there is a caesura. Shakespeare puts the period in the middle of the line to stress how important this change is. There must be a pause between the phrases 'potent art' and 'rough magic' to show the contrast between them. If the line simply stops at the end of the line, it does not feel quite as significant.

Another difference that occurs after Prospero swears to give up magic comes with cacophony and euphony. When Prospero describes the land at the beginning of his speech, there are phrases like 'spurs plucked up' which do not sound pleasing and emphasize how harsh the magic can be. After the caesura, the sounds of the words are almost entirely euphonic. The use of words like 'airy charm' and the ease with which they flow together create a more peaceful image. Additionally, Shakespeare breaks the iambic pentameter once more in line 20. This time the extra syllables emphasize the words 'I do' which indicate that Prospero is still a powerful man, but is perhaps now more willing to use his abilities in better ways.

Sample student commentary 2

Shakespeare, over the course of this speech by Prospero, uses almost every poetic device possible to convey the meaning in his words. Through his use of devices to alter the pace, he manipulates the tone of Prospero's speech. Throughout the first and last sections of the speech, in which he describes the feats of the 'weak masters' (line 9) and how he will forsake magic, lines often break from iambic pentameter. In the first section, on lines 3 and 6, the added syllable disrupts the poetic pace, a stark contrast to the airy images provided. Also lines 1 and 7 invert accented and unaccented syllables, furthering the disruption with jarring sounds. The breaks in iambic pentameter diminish the poetry and, by their extent, also diminish the mysticism of Prospero's words; he seems less sincere. In the third section, when he talks about forsaking magic, the lines become irregular, implying Prospero's potential discomfort, or perhaps, even, his surprise at the thought of living without magic. The concept is unfamiliar and, therefore, the poetry's irregularity underscores this point.

Sound also plays an extremely important role in conveying the changing tone of the passage, from controlling to repentant. The motif of control dominates the first 16 lines of the passage, as Prospero uses his 'potent art' (18) to 'bedim' (9) the sun, '[call] forth' (10) the winds and to 'rift' (13) Jove's oak. Sound reinforces the motif by using euphony to diminish the spirits' powers and using cacophony to enhance Prospero's might. Plosives abound when Prospero speaks of his own magic. The 'dread rattling thunder' (12) is not only a stark image, but the sound is harsh as well. Shakespeare reinforces Prospero's control in this way. Phonetic intensives, too, support Prospero's power. The 'roaring war' (12) and 'strong-based promontory' (14) feature a long 'o' sound, a frightening, dire sound. These sound devices firmly establish the tone of the first part of the poem, but around line 18, everything changes. Prospero, at this point, condemns his 'rough magic', (18) a cacophonous phrase in itself, which helps to solidify his change of mind. Now the description of his powers diminishes to 'an airy charm' (22). Also, the cacophony of 'break my staff' (line 22) draws even more attention to the finality of his decision. A new found resolve occurs with the shift on line 18.

Sample student commentary 3

Shakespeare's four-hour masterpiece, The Tempest, draws to a close. Prospero finally has all of his enemies writhing with torture and prepares to bring them all together to culminate his revenge when his servant, the spirit Ariel, reminds him of the simplicity of compassion and the nobility of forgiveness. Suddenly, Prospero experiences a complete paradigm shift, and the revenge which once seemed so sweet now appears bitter. Prospero realizes the difficulty, and therefore the nobility, of forgiveness and gathers his enemies into a magic circle to break his charms and heal them of their suffering. In this passage, Prospero calls on all of his powers one last time, finally for the purpose of doing good instead of harm, before he gives up magic forever. Shakespeare employs sound devices to emphasize how distasteful magic has become to Prospero, how beautiful his newfound freedom will be, and how powerful Prospero's magic was. The use of sound underscores Prospero's personal transformation.

Shakespeare uses alliteration, assonance, and consonance, to create cacophony and euphony to underscore meaning. In line 1, the repetition of the 'l' sound creates euphony, which suggests that the elves are innocent. As the passage continues, Shakespeare reminds readers and audiences alike that Prospero's dark arts are far from innocent. In lines 12 and 13, Shakespeare uses alliteration and consonance of the 't', 'v', 'z', and 'r' sounds to create cacophony. The 't' strikes the tongue and ear while the 'v' and 'z' unpleasantly buzz, and the 'r' sound suggests a terrible rending. All of this consonance and cacophony underscore the powerful image Shakespeare creates in these lines with visual and auditory imagery, commanding words, and repeated, unpleasant ideas. In the middle of a 'rattling' (12) and 'roaring' (12) storm, Prospero 'rift[s]' (13) the god 'Jove's' (13) own 'oak' (13) with 'his own bolt' (14). Prospero's allusion to the lightning god suggests that, at the height of his power, Prospero was more powerful even than the gods themselves. The cacophony in these two lines reminds the reader that Prospero usually employs his arts for destructive purposes.

Shakespeare also deviates in metre during this passage. One place where Prospero's words aren't in pentameter, line 18, particularly emphasizes his change in viewpoint. The extra unstressed syllable draws the eye to the end of the line, where Prospero declares his magic 'rough' (18). At the same time, this extra unstressed syllable also changes the way that line hits the ear. The words 'potent art' (18) with their strong consonance and their stressed syllables hit the ear more strongly than the words 'rough magic' (18). When this phenomenon is considered in combination with the caesura in the middle of the line, this line embodies the entire meaning of the passage. The strong beginning emphasizes the importance Prospero used to place on magic, while the unstressed end parallels Prospero's promise to give up magic. The caesura in the middle of the line represents Prospero's turning point; it stands between the two conflicting descriptions of magic, 'potent' (18) and 'rough' (18), between the two ways Prospero views magic, and between the two contrasting ways with which the sound of the line hits the ear.

Two lines later, Shakespeare places euphony created by 'm' and 'n' alliteration to underscore that Prospero's choice is the 'right' choice. And finally, Shakespeare ends with a final sound, the phonetically intensive 'plummet' (24) whose low vowel suggests plunging. He suggests that Prospero's magic, like his plays, will become obsolete as it falls into oblivion.

Examiner's comments

In attempting to rank these commentaries, pay careful attention to the Literary Commentary assessment criteria at the end of this chapter. Even if you are not familiar with Shakespeare's *The Tempest*, you can determine the degree to which each sample does each of the following:

Descriptor A: Understanding and interpretation
Does each commentary reveal understanding of the content of the passage?

Does each also offer an interpretation, stated either as an assertion or claim that is then supported with evidence from the passage?

Descriptor B: Appreciation of the writer's choices
Does each commentary identify the writer's specific stylistic choices of language, structure, techniques and style; and does the commentary go on to show how those specific choices shape meaning through the effects they produce?

Descriptor C: Organization and development
Does each commentary show a clear organization?

Are ideas developed in a coherent and logical manner?

Descriptor D: Language
Does each commentary use appropriate language which is clear, accurate, and varied?

Does each commentary use grammar, vocabulary, and sentence structure effectively?

Appreciation

In this section you will find samples of commentaries and guided literary analysis, plus additional examples of the colour-marking strategy. Examine the colour-marking provided prior to reading, and then assess the student sample. Use the HL, Paper 1 assessment criteria located at the end of this chapter for the sample commentaries, and the SL, Paper 1 assessment criteria for the guided literary analysis sample.

'Child and Insect' by Robert Druce (1980)

He cannot hold his hand huge enough.
How can he cage the sudden clockwork fizz
he has snatched from the grassblades ?
He races back, how quick he is,
look! to his mother   5
through the shrieking meadow.
But kneeling at her side
finds only a silence in his fearful clutch.
Revealed, the grasshopper
lies broken on his palm.   10

          It is
nothing now: its dead struts snapped
even the brittle lidless eyes
crushed into the tangle.
          Sunlight   15
and the landscape flood away
in tears.
For horror he dare not
look at what is cradled in his fingers
and will not be comforted.   20
          O,
will not.

Yet quick and now
as if by magic the undead insect
with a flick re-   25
assemble itself
          throbs
and is latched to a leaf a yard away.
And once again incredibly it skirls unspoilt
its chirruping music.   30
He weeps, sick with relief and rage.
'There now, my love. It wasn't hurt at all.'
His mother laughs and puts an arm
around him.
          Tearfully   35

he shakes her off.
He will not rejoice (in time he may
but that is not yet certain) after
such betrayal of his grief.
                He must not   40
have tears torn from him
by petty trickery.
Before his mother's eyes he would not care
to do it (and perhaps not ever)
but gladly in this instant he   45
could snatch the creature up and
shatter it
for leaving him so naked.

Colour-marked text

'Child and Insect' by Robert Druce (1980)

He cannot hold his hand huge enough.
How can he cage the [sudden clockwork fizz]
he has snatched from the grassblades ?
He races back, how quick he is,
look! to his mother   5
through the (shrieking meadow.)
But kneeling at her side
finds only [a silence] in his fearful clutch.
Revealed, the grasshopper
lies broken on his palm.   10

              *It is
nothing now: [its dead struts snapped]
even [the brittle lidless eyes
crushed] into the tangle.
           * Sunlight   15
and the landscape flood away
in tears.
For horror he dare not
look at what is cradled in his fingers
and will not be comforted.   20
           *O,
will not.

Legend:
- body parts motif
- kinaesthetic imagery/motion image pattern
- visual/auditory imagery
- anger motif
- grief motif
- vulnerability
- time progression/cause and effect
- [ ] metaphor
- ( ) personification

*note the word/line placement/ erratic extensions

Yet quick and now
as if by magic the undead insect
with a flick re-   25
assembles itself
                    *   throbs
and is latched to a leaf a yard away.
And once again incredibly it skirls unspoilt
its chirruping music.   30
He weeps, sick with relief and rage.
'There now, my love. It wasn't hurt at all.'
His mother laughs and puts an arm
around him.
                    * Tearfully   35

he shakes her off.
He will not rejoice (in time he may
but that is not yet certain) after
such betrayal of his grief.
                    * He must not   40
have (tears torn) from him
by petty trickery.
Before his mother's eyes he would not care
to do it (and perhaps not ever)
but gladly in this instant he   45
could snatch the creature up and
shatter it
for leaving him so naked.

Sample student commentary 1

The poem 'Child and Insect' by Robert Druce documents a short interaction between
a child and the grasshopper he catches. The poem, which conveys the emotions of the
child, uses this microcosm of a relationship to make much bolder statements about
humankind's reactions to death as a perceived betrayal.

The title of the poem provides the first indication it is much more than a quaint story.
The two major figures in the poem are referred to only as 'child' (with no articles or
qualifiers) and 'insect' (similarly without any superfluous information). Throughout the
poem, the speaker never indentifies the name of the boy or his mother. The characters,
then, seem representative, perhaps even universal.

From here Druce begins to expand on the themes of the poem. He uses several poetic
techniques to accomplish this. The first and predominant technique is the duality of
sound and silence and death and rejuvenation. The 'sudden clockwork fizz' (2) is the
first mention of the grasshopper. This phrase is remarkably auditory and conjures
a lively, loud insect. A few lines later, 'silence' (8) suddenly prevails, coupled with the
discovery of the 'broken' (10) grasshopper. The child must confront death. His initial
excitement gives way to a 'flood' (16) of tears. The return of the sound, however, does

not reestablish happiness. Even when the grasshopper 're-assembles itself' (lines 25–26) and its song once again 'skirls unspoilt' (29), the child is furious because he mourned its death, and, in doing so, made himself vulnerable.

Only after the child expresses his indignation and rage, do we understand the greater relationship of grief and betrayal. Because the child does 'not rejoice' (37) in the grasshopper's return to life, it seems that to 'shatter it' (47) would provide him with the satisfaction of revenge. By tricking him, by tricking the child's emotions, the grasshopper has betrayed him. Vulnerable to pain, to grief, the child blames himself for the death only to feel foolish when the grasshopper 'as if by magic [is] undead' (24). Childish pride gives way to violence.

In the final three stanzas, two phrases stand in sharp counterpoint to the child's rage. The interjected phrases on lines 37, 38, and 44 come directly from the speaker. While the child cradles his pride, the speaker allows the possibility of humility. Though the child's fate is 'not yet certain' (38), the speaker hopes for a reversal from this violent manifestation of loss. His visceral reaction horrifies, but 'in time' (37) he may be able to express loss without rage.

Sample student commentary 2

The poem 'Child and Insect' by Robert Druce is packed full of emotion and detail. The reader is thrust into the world of the poet's imagination through Druce's attention to detail. It is impossible not to sympathize with the youth in the poem, because his emotions beat strongly though this literary work.

Druce uses sensory imagery to entice the reader with a detailed, familiar world. On earth, there are no doubt fields of grass, children, and grasshoppers, however, the poet attributes a certain emotional aspect to each description in the poem. There are fields, but how often is one described as a 'shrieking meadow' (6). A reader may never have experienced a 'fearful clutch' (8), but surely knows exactly what one would feel like.

The poet uses the adjective 'naked' to describe how the 'petty trickery' (42) of the insect left the young boy feeling. Druce's word here is intended to strike the reader to the bone. The word is the final word of the poem, so the lonely emotion that it carries permeates the reader even longer, because they have no other emotions to read to take this word's place. Most people can relate to this child, and that is likely why the reader feels so connected. The boy tried to show his love for the insect, yet the bug deceived him. He dropped his emotional walls in front of his mother to weep for his 'friend', and it turns out that the insect was just toying with his feelings. Even though the grasshopper cannot have enough cognitive ability to actually trick the boy, the poet still manages to convince the reader to back up the child in his lust for revenge in lines 43 to 45.

The title of the poem 'Child and Insect' may at first appear to have no deeper meaning than being a simple description of the two characters who cause conflict in the poem; the child fears that he has killed the insect; the insect tricks the child. The idea that Robert Druce, the poet who wrote this tantalizing poem full of detail, emotion, and deep meaning, would give his poem such a bland title seems ridiculous. Upon further inspection, it can be deduced that the title can be interpreted as a reminder to the reader that the boy is only a child, and grasshopper is only an insect. As a child, understanding emotions as well as life and death is a struggle. In some cases it can never fully be understood. The fact that the child is so upset over the death of an insect reflects this struggle, and the title itself helps the reader reflect on the simplicity of the situation.

The child that is so vital to the poem is a representation of the fickleness found in many children. The excitement he feels when he has the 'clockwork fizz' (2) grasped in his hand shifts to pure horror when he believes that he has taken the life of the grasshopper.

Druce builds up excitement leading up to the realization that the insect may be dead by using short, energetic words in the lines before. As the insect pulls itself together and comes back to life, the words once again are presented in a fashion that flows quickly. The child becomes full of 'relief and rage' (31) while describing how he would take revenge on his back-stabbing friend, and the poet conveys this by directly stating it in the text. Finally, when Druce writes that the child is left 'naked' (48), it is conveyed that the boy has been stripped of all of his emotions due to how frantically his feelings shifted in just the short period of the poem.

Sample student guided literary analysis

Question (a): Discuss the appropriateness of the title.

Question (b): Comment on the poet's use of sensory imagery.

The poem 'Child and Insect' by Robert Druce is loaded with emotion. The reader is thrust into the world of the poet's imagination through attention to detail. It is impossible not to sympathize with the young boy in the poem because his emotions are direct and evocative. The title sets in motion the confrontation that we know must come to pass. Druce seems to believe that any child and any insect will do. They are in opposition from the very start – almost to suggest that the scene and the emotions that unfold are perfectly natural. The child will possess the insect and will have power over it. The child's rage, in part, seems to come from the fact that he thinks that he has accidentally killed it. The insect wasn't supposed to die. And, when he sees the insect 'undead' and it 'reassembles itself' in front of him, he feels tricked, betrayed by his own belief, his own visual evidence that the insect was dead.

The title really doesn't indicate any of the emotional impact that is to come in the poem. It is matter of fact, simple, a naming only. What shocks the reader in this poem is that the mother and her child, like the child and his insect, do not understand the violence that betrayal triggers. As the mother pulls her child close and laughs a knowing, somewhat sympathetic little laugh, the child's rage builds. His true thoughts are hidden. His tears are not what they seem.

Druce uses sensory imagery to entice the reader with a detailed, familiar world. The world of the poem, like our own, is filled with fields of grass, young children, and grasshoppers. The poet, however, attributes a certain emotional aspect to each description in the poem. The fields are 'shrieking' (16). This shrieking mirrors the wild joy that the boy feels when he captures the insect – perhaps for the first time in his life.

It is the 'petty trickery' (4) of the insect that leaves the boy 'naked' (48). The final word of the poem strikes the reader to the bone. The unprotected vulnerability of the child's nakedness leaves the reader feeling sympathetic. The boy tries to show his joyful love of the insect, yet it deceives him. He drops his emotional walls in front of his mother, weeping openly, 'sick with relief and rage' (31). The reference to relief is straightforward enough. The child in some sense is relieved that the insect is not dead. The child did not accidentally kill the insect by grasping it too tightly in his small fist. The insect did not die as the child ran shrieking to show his mother what he had captured. The reference to rage, however, is where the poem's meaning takes a turn. This is not simply a poem about gaining experience or losing innocence. The poem seems to consider the possibility that this child, this young boy, has the potential for violence, for destruction, for murder, within him. Ironically, it is his pride that triggers these emotions—emotions far older than the child, emotions programmed from our

● **Examiner's hints**

If necessary, use the examiner's comments on page 126 to aid your evaluation of these two commentaries. Also be sure to examine the colour-marking carefully and try to assess which of the two commentaries used it more effectively.

ancient desires, our ancient drives. Druce seems to be saying that the impulse for violence lies dormant within us all, and, even more ironically, loss, coupled with pride, triggers the impulse.

Examiner's comments

This sample of a guided literary analysis demonstrates a keen understanding of both the content and the feeling expressed in the poem. The essay's attempts to show an appreciation of the writer's stylistic choices, and how those choices 'shape' meaning, however, are not adequate. The second guiding question is neither fully addressed nor developed. In balance, the language is clear and effective, and the ideas are well organized and coherent.

'Night Crossing' by Sylvia Kantaris (1989)

I caught the boat just once
by some strange mismanagement
and stood as it slid out of harbor
silently, unpiloted.
There were no people waving on the shore.   5
And up and down from end to end
the passengers sat stiff in rows.
None of them had any kind of luggage
or newspapers. They stared at air.
I could have gone on easily with them   10
but for the drumming in my smuggled suitcase.
Someone tugged the long communication cord.
I still don't know whose noisy heart
reminded me to stop the boat
and moonstep across the strip of marshland   15
just in time to catch the last train
back here from the border,
or whether there is any point
in sailing out in order to come back
on tracks that disappear under   20
a smooth, unwinding sheet of blank water.

Colour-marked text

'Night Crossing' by Sylvia Kantaris (1989)

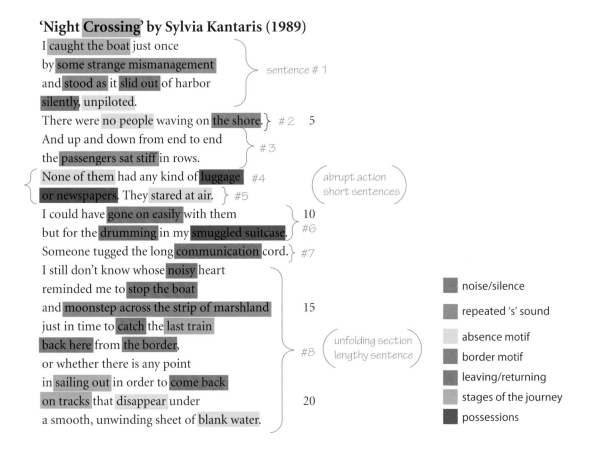

I caught the boat just once
by some strange mismanagement
and stood as it slid out of harbor
silently, unpiloted.
                                 sentence # 1

There were no people waving on the shore. *# 2* 5
And up and down from end to end
the passengers sat stiff in rows. *# 3*
None of them had any kind of luggage *#4*   *abrupt action*
or newspapers. They stared at air. *# 5*   *short sentences*
I could have gone on easily with them 10
but for the drumming in my smuggled suitcase. *#6*
Someone tugged the long communication cord. *#7*
I still don't know whose noisy heart
reminded me to stop the boat
and moonstep across the strip of marshland 15
just in time to catch the last train
back here from the border,   *unfolding section*
or whether there is any point *#8* *lengthy sentence*
in sailing out in order to come back
on tracks that disappear under 20
a smooth, unwinding sheet of blank water.

Legend:
- noise/silence
- repeated 's' sound
- absence motif
- border motif
- leaving/returning
- stages of the journey
- possessions

EXERCISE 3

Sample student (HL) commentary

While the poet, Sylvia Kantaris, deals with a very traditional poetic theme, the journey, she chooses to relay the details of an unsuccessful attempt rather than a successful one. The poem focuses on an 'unpiloted' (4) boat filled with 'stiff' (7) and unfettered passengers. These two images bring to light the primary motif of absence. The passengers on the boat, due to their lack of 'luggage or newspapers' (8–9) appear without distinct identities. Just as the boat has no pilot, they, too, left their possessions, and seemingly, their memories and their pasts behind. They appear to sail without purpose, without intention. This image heavily contrasts with the persona. She, unlike the other passengers, brings a 'smuggled suitcase' (11) which ultimately forces her to leave the boat. The suitcase stands, in a metaphorical sense, for her ties to her home and her past. The suitcase gives her an identity and gives her the strength to return to it.

The 'smuggled suitcase' (11) also plays a key role in the dichotomy between silence and sound which permeates the poem. The boat travels 'silently' (4) over 'blank water' (21). The passengers seem to '[stare] at air' (9) and make no noise or movements. The oppressive silence of the initial lines of the poem works to emphasize the sudden 'drumming' (11) in the persona's suitcase. This sound breaks the silence as well as the persona's resolve to continue on. The unknown 'noisy heart' (14), perhaps the call of friends and family, separates her from the other passengers both physically and emotionally.

Since the poem revolves around the concept of leaving and returning, the different types of transport in the poem are important in shaping the poet's message. The boat, which represents leaving, possesses an ethereal quality as the '[silent], unpiloted' (4) mode of transport. 'The last train' (16) which represents returning, is a much more substantial presence as it travels over land quickly and loudly. The boat's 'tracks that disappear' (20) also contrast those of a train, which root firmly and permanently in the ground. The boat, therefore, becomes a vehicle for those who wish to forget. The persona ends up on the train returning from 'the border' (17) because she chooses to remain connected to the past that her suitcase represents. In making this choice, the persona is choosing life. The interplay between the two vehicles, the two choices, life and death, allows the reader to understand the decision she makes – the decision to remain 'here' (17) with life and the living.

Examiner's comments

While a somewhat short HL response, the student demonstrates excellent understanding of the subtleties of this poem and articulates ideas effectively and clearly. The student's interpretation is well supported with details from the text, and he/she indicates a keen understanding of the poet's choices and their effects. The organization is well structured and coherent, but additional development could elevate this commentary to the highest level.

Sample student (SL) guided literary analysis 1

Question (a): What do you find unusual about the boat and its passengers?

Question (b): What effects arise from the poet's use of imagery?

What is so unusual about the boat and its passengers is its seeming lack of existence. The boat is unpiloted and slides out of harbour in silence. The shore from which this boat departs is abandoned. The passengers are unmoving, caught 'stiff in rows' (7) as they stare into the air.

The speaker describes the departure with an ominous tone. The passengers seem to understand where they are going and why. They accept their destination, but the speaker does not. The boat is fearsome; the passengers anonymous. The boat seems to serve a single purpose – to take the passengers away and not bring them back. But to where? Why won't they return? Why do they have no luggage, no possessions, with them? The speaker does not say because she doesn't seem to have the answers to these questions. In fact, she seems to have appeared on this boat quite by accident, by 'some strange mismanagement' (2). The speaker only remarks on the epiphany that prevents her from joining the other passengers on a voyage into seeming oblivion.

It is only the 'drumming' (11) of her heart that prompts her to flee the boat, the passengers, the destination.

The poet's use of imagery further amplifies the foreboding nature of the poem. The speaker is alone as she observes the boat and those present on it. The people on board do not acknowledge one another. There are no tearful goodbyes, no shouts of promises of reunions. Especially significant is the imagery in the final line of the poem. Here a train track disappears under a 'smooth, unwinding sheet' (21) of water. The water is imagined as still in the night, black ice. There is no fog, no waves that beat against the boat. There is only the boat taking its passengers to the great beyond, like the dead who quietly accept their fate on the river Styx. The speaker, however, 'just in time' (16) catches the train back, refusing to join the others on this 'night crossing'.

Sample student (SL) guided literary analysis 2

At first glance, this poem seems to be a description of a strange boat ride that the speaker starts to take, but on second thoughts, decides not to, opting instead to return by train. The poem, however, is an extended metaphor. The speaker is describing her experience when she almost crossed into the afterlife. Because this idea is a complex one, Kantaris uses the metaphor in this poem to describe an abstract, mysterious experience in concrete, detailed terms. In addition, she uses highly visual language to insure that her reader imagines the journey as a real trip. By using metaphor and visual and auditory imagery, Kantaris describes the journey to the afterlife.

The extended metaphor may not be obvious on a first reading, but there are a number of clues that lead to that conclusion. The first is the title, 'Night Crossing'. For the speaker, this 'crossing' was undertaken 'by some strange mismanagement' (2) meaning that the speaker was not meant to be on the boat; some mistake was made; she was not 'ready'. Another clue is that the speaker gets off the boat before it crosses the 'border' (17). Her death would be premature in some sense, so she must go back to the living. The border represents the point of no return, after which the boat's passengers have passed into the afterlife.

When the speaker disembarks and 'moonsteps across the strip of marshland' (15), she turns away from death and back to life. She is neither dead nor fully alive; perhaps she is in a comatose state. Both visual and auditory imagery reinforce this idea. The title itself connotes silent darkness. The passengers sit 'stiff in rows' (7) and do not speak or move. Immediately, the speaker is in contrast to the others on the boat. The speaker is neither stationary nor stiff, silent nor without luggage. The others seem dreamlike; the boat is silent; the setting is mysterious. The night is silent except for the drumming in the speaker's 'smuggled suitcase' (11). This drumming noise could be a metaphor of the speaker's heart which is still beating, now loud enough to rouse the speaker to get off this boat from which there is no return.

Examiner's comments

While both guided analyses respond to each of the guiding questions, which do you believe achieves the higher level of understanding? Does one sample show a stronger understanding of the effects of specific stylistic choices by the poet? Is the level of language similar or different? Are the ideas in one essay better organized or more coherent?

'The Sleeping Zemis' by Lorna Goodison (HL Paper 1, 1998)

He kept the zemis under his bed for years
after the day he came upon them in a cave
which resembled the head of a great stone god
the zemis placed like weights at the tip of its tongue.

Arawaks* had hidden them there when they fled,   5
or maybe the stone god's head was really a temple.
Now under his bed slept three zemis,
wrought from enduring wood of ebony.

The first was a man god who stood erect, his arms
folded below his belly. The second was a bird god   10
in flight. The third was fashioned in the form
of a spade, in the handle a face was carved.

A planting of the crops zemi,
a god for the blessing of corn,
for the digging of the sweet cassava†   15
which requires good science

to render the white root safe food.
And over the fields the john crows wheel
and the women wait for the fishermen
to return from sea in boats hollowed from trees.   20

Under his bed the zemis slept.
Where were they when Columbus
and his men, goldfever and quicksilver
on the brain, came visiting destruction?

Man god we gave them meat, fish and cassava.   25
Silent deity we mended their sails, their leaking
ships, their endless needs we filled even with
our own lives, our own deaths.

Bird god, we flew to the hills,
their tin bells tolling the deaths   30
of our children, their mirrors
foreshadowing annihilation to follow.

Spade god we perished.
Our spirits wander wild and restless.
There was no one left to dig our graves,   35
no guides to point us the way to Coyaba.

He turned them over to the keepers of history,
they housed them in glass-sided caves.
Then he went home to sleep without the gods
who had slumbered under his bed for years.   40

*Arawaks: an Indian people formerly occupying most of the Greater Antilles
†cassava: a starchy root vegetable of the tropics

Colour-marked text

'The Sleeping Zemis' by Lorna Goodison (HL Paper 1, 1998)

He kept the zemis under his bed for years
after the day he came upon them in a cave
which resembled the head of a great stone god
the zemis placed like weights at the tip of its tongue.

⎱ 1st section

Arawaks* had hidden them there when they fled,   5
or maybe the stone god's head was really a temple.
Now under his bed slept three zemis,
wrought from enduring wood of ebony.

The first was a man god who stood erect, his arms
folded below his belly. The second was a bird god   10
in flight. The third was fashioned in the form
of a spade, in the handle a face was carved.

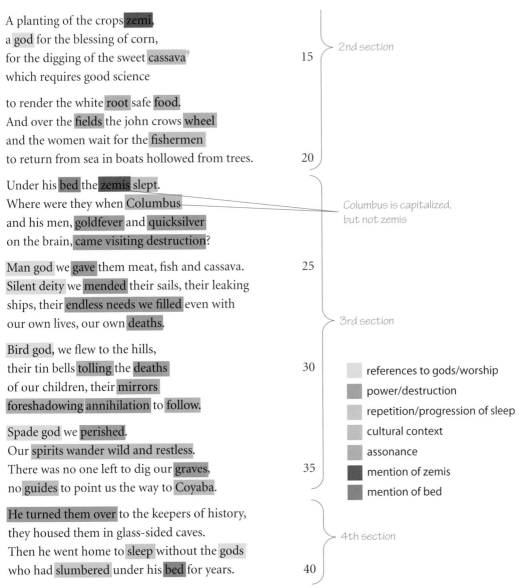

A planting of the crops zemi,
a god for the blessing of corn,
for the digging of the sweet cassava†
which requires good science

to render the white root safe food.
And over the fields the john crows wheel
and the women wait for the fishermen
to return from sea in boats hollowed from trees.

Under his bed the zemis slept.
Where were they when Columbus
and his men, goldfever and quicksilver
on the brain, came visiting destruction?

Man god we gave them meat, fish and cassava.
Silent deity we mended their sails, their leaking
ships, their endless needs we filled even with
our own lives, our own deaths.

Bird god, we flew to the hills,
their tin bells tolling the deaths
of our children, their mirrors
foreshadowing annihilation to follow.

Spade god we perished.
Our spirits wander wild and restless.
There was no one left to dig our graves,
no guides to point us the way to Coyaba.

He turned them over to the keepers of history,
they housed them in glass-sided caves.
Then he went home to sleep without the gods
who had slumbered under his bed for years.

15

20

Columbus is capitalized, but not zemis

2nd section

25

3rd section

30

references to gods/worship
power/destruction
repetition/progression of sleep
cultural context
assonance
mention of zemis
mention of bed

35

4th section

40

*Arawaks: an Indian people formerly occupying most of the Greater Antilles
†cassava: a starchy root vegetable of the tropics

EXERCISE 4

Sample student commentary

Lorna Goodison includes this poem in her collection Archipelago: New Caribbean Writing as a reflection on the fate of one (and by extension, all) tribe who met their downfall with the arrival of Columbus. The zemis are the gods of the Arawaks, rediscovered by a modern man. This modern perspective allows the poet to consider the role and power of the zemis, 'where were they' (22) when they were needed most? The speaker ultimately provides a stark realization of the power of gods compared to the power of 'Columbus/ and his men' (lines 22–23).

The poem appears to have four major sections: the first two stanzas, the next three, the next four, and the final stanza. Stanza 3 establishes the progression of the poem by using caesura to the three major 'god' figures. The division of the stanzas reflects the tone and subject matter shifts. The speaker first describes another man's discovery, the 'He' of line 1, of the zemis and then paints a scene from their history.

With the third section, however, the tone shifts from remembering to lamenting, and by the last stanza, the tone is resigned. The shift in tone begins to occur with the arrival of Columbus when the focus shifts to the 'destruction' (24), 'deaths' (28) and 'annihilation' (32) that his arrival causes. And when the man who discovered them '[turns the zemis] over' (37) at the end of the poem, his gesture acknowledges his belief in their futile, empty power.

This gesture of returning home 'without the gods' (39) establishes the theme of the poem: men control fate more than the gods do. Aside from the progression of tone, the poet uses several techniques to drive her point home. First is the repetition throughout the poem of the zemis who 'under his bed . . . slept' (7) for several years. The picture of a sleeping zemi, so prominent it appears in the title, implies a sort of negligence or inattention. In the sixth through ninth stanzas, too, the impersonal speaker contrasts the sleeping zemi with the flurry of action and desperation following Columbus' arrival. They '[mend]', (26) 'fly', (29) and '[perish]' (33) all under the aegis of the 'man god', (25) 'bird god', (29) and 'spade god' (33) who do nothing to help. The tone shift instigated by the question on line 24 signals a change in the speaker. Until this point, the speaker seems objective and impersonal, but after line 24, the speaker speaks from a collective perspective. This new persona internalizes the struggle to explain why the zemis sleep through the crisis. The fact that the gods do not aid the Arawaks repeatedly suggests either their complacency or their impotence.

Unlike the zemis, Columbus and his men have power and impose a quick, destructive change in the lives of the Arawaks. The dichotomy between the organic nature of the zemis and the brutal nature of the explorers serves to futher establish a hierarchy. The zemis are made of 'wood of ebony' (8) stowed in a 'stone god' (3) cave. On the other hand, the speaker associates the men with 'goldfever and quicksilver' (23); they drive off the natives with 'tin bells' (30). The dominance of metal over wood and stone appears throughout history in matters of war, and so it appears here too. The zemis control 'the blessing of corn', (13) but the explorers override them with the power of destruction.

The resignation of the persona appears as early as line 27 with the paradoxical statement 'endless needs we filled' (27), which places the persona in a position of servitude that seems inescapable. The last stanza is extremely important as not only does the man give up the gods, he gives them to 'the keepers of history' (37). He plainly admits the defeat of his spirituality in light of his consideration of all that's passed. And he also gives the gods to men to '[house]' (38) as they please. Men, both those who release and receive, can manipulate and dismiss gods as they wish.

An important caveat, though, is that man's domination is bittersweet. It leads to the oppression witnessed in the previous stanzas and a man who sleeps alone, far from the nostalgic vision of the second section where 'women wait' (19) on the banks for men and their men and the memory of 'sweet cassava' (15). The gentle, peaceful tone created in stanzas four and five though enjambment and run-on lines linking random memories together, is long forgotten by the end of the poem. Because the man loses hope in his gods, a reasonable reaction, he also loses the connection to that part of history, his history, the history of man. They are all one and the same according to Goodison.

Examiner's comments

This commentary is truly exceptional in that it reveals a superb degree of understanding, as well as extensive examination of and appreciation for the writer's stylistic choices. The organization of the response is fluid and the development is thorough. Both of these features, as well as a masterful use of language and syntax, contribute to this evocative and persuasive response.

Using the instructions for colour-marking provided earlier in the chapter, and the models provided, prepare the following two prose passages and the poem for commentary. Remember to exhaust any and all narrative or poetic strategies, colour-mark thoroughly (if you are using a school textbook, check with your teacher first how he or she wants to approach this – don't start marking your book until you have done so), identify external as well as internal structures, progressions of subject matter/content focus and shifts in tones, if applicable.

Once you have prepared adequately, go ahead and write a practice commentary on each.

Prose passage extracted from Toni Morrison's *Beloved* (1987)

'Your love is too thick,' he said, thinking, That bitch is looking at me; she is right over my head looking down through the floor at me.

'Too thick?' she said, thinking of the Clearing where Baby Suggs' commands knocked the pods off horse chestnuts. 'Love is or it ain't. Thin love ain't love at all.'

'Yeah. It didn't work, did it? Did it work?' he asked.

'It worked,' she said.

'How? Your boys gone you don't know where. One girl dead, the other won't leave the yard. How did it work?'

'They ain't at Sweet Home. Schoolteacher ain't got em.'

'Maybe there's worse.'

'It ain't my job to know what's worse. It's my job to know what is and to keep them away from what I know is terrible. I did that.'

'What you did was wrong, Sethe.'

'I should have gone on back there? Taken my babies back there?'

'There could have been a way. Some other way.'

'What way?'

'You got two feet, Sethe, not four,' he said, and right then a forest sprang up between them; trackless and quiet.

Later he would wonder what made him say it. The calves of his youth? or the conviction that he was being observed through the ceiling? How fast he had moved from his shame to hers. From his cold-house secret straight to her too-thick love.

Meanwhile the forest was locking the distance between them, giving it shape and heft.

He did not put his hat on right away. First he fingered it, deciding how his going would be, how to make it an exit not an escape. And it was very important not to leave without looking. He stood up, turned and looked up the white stairs. She was there all right. Standing straight as a line with her back to him. He didn't rush to the door. He moved slowly and when he got there he opened it before asking Sethe to put supper aside for him because he might be a little late getting back. Only then did he put on his hat.

To access worksheet 5.3 on prose devices, please visit www.pearsonbacconline.com and follow the on-screen instructions.

Sweet, she thought. He must think I can't bear to hear him say it. That after all I have told him and after telling me how many feet I have, 'goodbye' would break me to pieces. Ain't that sweet.

'So long,' she murmured from the far side of the trees.

HL paper 1, 1996 exam, from Peter Carey's *Oscar and Lucinda* (1988)

Oscar hurried after the black, umbrella-humped figure. He waved back. And he made such a comic figure, his hat pushed back on his head, as he leaped across a puddle, waved an umbrella, jumped to avoid some oxen droppings, that the men all laughed, but not maliciously. They walked back to their barrel smiling and shaking their heads. Their new master was an odd bird, but not a knave.

Oscar felt he had opened a door into her life. He would like to sit somewhere, a place with marble tables. If it had been London they would go to the Café Lux in Regent Street. A glass of port wine for the lady. Or merely China tea, and then they could talk about this glass business of hers.

It had never occurred to him that a process of manufacture could be beautiful. Had you, an hour before, asked him to tell you what he would call beautiful he would have drawn on the natural world, and named the species along the lanes of Devon,[1] or brought up for you, plunging his hands into the rock pools of memory, the anemone his father had drawn and named, these fine soulless creatures which had, just the same, been made by God. He would have shown you the Stratton's harvest stooks[2] (and forgotten they had scratched his arms and made them itch all night) or the rolling, dangerous sea seen through a familiar window with a two-foot-thick sill. He would never have led you into a building with a rusting, corrugated roof, or taken you between lanes made from bottle crates, or littered with glittering shards. In these places you expected foulness, stink, refuse, and not, certainly not, wonder.

But it was wonder that he had found, and he had felt it in his water, before he saw anything to wonder at, that this dry, swept place—he knew this the minute he was inside the door—contained something exceptional.

They led him to a glory-hole,[3] had him look in, into the protean world where you could not distinguish between the white of pure heat, the white of the crucible, and the white of the molten glass which they named 'metal'. When Arthur had said, 'metal', Oscar had understood 'tin' or 'silver' or 'gold'. And when the gatherer drew out the substance it could have been all these things. The red-hot orb at the end of the long rod which he watched, passing from man to man, from glory-hole to glory-hole, acquiring more metal, being blown a little, swung, handed on, until it came to that largest, most slovenly of all of them. And then he who dubbed himself (privately, whispered it in Oscar's ear) to be none other than the famous knight Sir Piss-and-Wind, took the long road and was, at once, drum major, bagpipe master, trumpeter, transmuter, as he transformed the metal into a tankard. He sat himself at last on his wooden throne and rolled the long rod back and forth across its arms whilst he smoothed a base with wet pear wood which hissed and steamed in clouds around his tea-and-ale-stained whiskers. He took a snake of red elastic glass from the third gatherer and, lifting it high—where it looked as angry as a snake in an eagle's claws—made it, with a flourish, into a question mark, and thence, a handle. It was all so fine, so precise, and it was a wonder that this miracle was wrought by a whiskered Falstaff with a fat belly and grubby singlet showing through the layers of wet, sour hessian.

'I am a human bellows, sir,' Arthur claimed, waving his hand for someone to come and take his creation from him. 'That is what I have made of myself.'

But it was not this that thrilled Oscar about glass, that a man had made his body to comply with the needs of manufacturing, but that a man so obviously gross and imperfect could produce something so fine.

Glass. Blinding white. Glowing red. Elastic. Protean. Liquid. Vessel for light.

[1]Devon: a rural county in south-west England
[2]stooks: bundles of straw
[3]glory-hole: an opening in the wall of a blast-furnace

'Penelope' by Carol Ann Duffy (1999)

At first, I looked along the road
hoping to see him saunter home
among the olive trees,
a whistle for the dog
who mourned him with his warm head on my knees.
Six months of this
and then I noticed that whole days had passed
without my noticing.
I sorted cloth and scissors, needle, thread,

thinking to amuse myself,
but found a lifetime's industry instead.
I sewed a girl
under a single star—cross-stitch, silver silk
running after childhood's bouncing ball.
I chose between three greens for the grass;
a smoky pink, a shadowy grey
to show a snapdragon gargling a bee.
I threaded walnut brown for a tree,

my thimble like an acorn
pushing up through umber soil.
Beneath the shade
I wrapped a maiden in a deep embrace
with heroism's boy
and lost myself completely
in a wild embroidery of love, lust, loss, lessons learnt;
then watched him sail away
into the loose gold stitching of the sun.

And when the others came to take his place,
disturb my peace,
I played for time.
I wore a widow's face, kept my head down,
did my work by day, at night unpicked it.
I knew which hour of the dark the moon
would start to fray,
I stitched it.

Grey threads and brown
pursued my needle's leaping fish
to form a river that would never reach the sea.
I tricked it. I was picking out
the smile of a woman at the centre
of this world, self-contained, absorbed, content,
most certainly not waiting,
when I heard a far-too-late familiar tread outside the door.
I licked my scarlet thread
and aimed it surely at the middle of the needle's eye once more.

Assessment criteria

Paper 1: Literary commentary

There are four assessment criteria at HL.

Criterion A	Understanding and interpretation	5 marks
Criterion B	Appreciation of the writer's choices	5 marks
Criterion C	Organization and development	5 marks
Criterion D	Language	5 marks
	Total	20 marks

Criterion A: Understanding and interpretation

How well does the student's interpretation reveal understanding of the thought and feeling of the passage?

How well are ideas supported by references to the passage?

Marks	Level descriptor
0	The work does not reach a standard described by the descriptors below.
1	There is basic understanding of the passage but virtually no attempt at interpretation and few references to the passage.
2	There is some understanding of the passage, with a superficial attempt at interpretation and some appropriate references to the passage.
3	There is adequate understanding of the passage, demonstrated by an interpretation that is supported by appropriate references to the passage.
4	There is very good understanding of the passage, demonstrated by sustained interpretation supported by well-chosen references to the passage.
5	There is excellent understanding of the passage, demonstrated by persuasive interpretation supported by effective references to the passage.

Criterion B: Appreciation of the writer's choices

To what extent does the analysis show appreciation of how the writer's choices of language, structure, technique and style shape meaning?

Marks	Level descriptor
0	The work does not reach a standard described by the descriptors below.
1	There are few references to, and no analysis or appreciation of, the ways in which language, structure, technique and style shape meaning.
2	There is some mention, but little analysis or appreciation, of the ways in which language, structure, technique and style shape meaning.
3	There is adequate analysis and appreciation of the ways in which language, structure, technique and style shape meaning.
4	There is very good analysis and appreciation of the ways in which language, structure, technique and style shape meaning.
5	There is excellent analysis and appreciation of the ways in which language, structure, technique and style shape meaning.

Criterion C: Organization and development

How well organized, coherent and developed is the presentation of ideas?

Marks	Level descriptor
0	The work does not reach a standard described by the descriptors below.
1	Ideas have little organization; there may be a superficial structure, but coherence and development are lacking.
2	Ideas have some organization, with a recognizable structure; coherence and development are often lacking.
3	Ideas are adequately organized, with a suitable structure; some attention is paid to coherence and development.
4	Ideas are effectively organized, with very good structure, coherence and development.
5	Ideas are persuasively organized, with excellent structure, coherence and development.

Criterion D: Language

How clear, varied and accurate is the language?

How appropriate is the choice of register, style and terminology? ('Register' refers, in this context, to the student's use of elements such as vocabulary, tone, sentence structure and terminology appropriate to the commentary.)

Marks	Level descriptor
0	The work does not reach a standard described by the descriptors below.
1	Language is rarely clear and appropriate; there are many errors in grammar, vocabulary and sentence construction, and little sense of register and style.
2	Language is sometimes clear and carefully chosen; grammar, vocabulary and sentence construction are fairly accurate, although errors and inconsistencies are apparent; the register and style are to some extent appropriate to the commentary.
3	Language is clear and carefully chosen, with an adequate degree of accuracy in grammar, vocabulary and sentence construction despite some lapses; register and style are mostly appropriate to the commentary.
4	Language is clear and carefully chosen, with a good degree of accuracy in grammar, vocabulary and sentence construction; register and style are consistently appropriate to the commentary.
5	Language is very clear, effective, carefully chosen and precise, with a high degree of accuracy in grammar, vocabulary and sentence construction; register and style are effective and appropriate to the commentary.

Paper 1: Guided literary analysis

There are four assessment criteria at SL.

Criterion A	Understanding and interpretation	5 marks
Criterion B	Appreciation of the writer's choices	5 marks
Criterion C	Organization	5 marks
Criterion D	Language	5 marks
	Total	20 marks

Criterion A: Understanding and interpretation

How well does the student's interpretation reveal understanding of the thought and feeling of the passage?

How well are ideas supported by references to the passage?

Marks	Level descriptor
0	The work does not reach a standard described by the descriptors below.
1	There is very basic understanding of the passage, with mainly irrelevant and/or insignificant interpretation.
2	There is some understanding of the passage but little attempt at interpretation, with few references to the passage.
3	There is adequate understanding of the passage, demonstrated by an interpretation that is mostly supported by references to the passage.
4	There is good understanding of the passage, demonstrated by convincing interpretation that is fully supported by references to the passage.
5	There is very good understanding of the passage, demonstrated by sustained and convincing interpretation that is supported by well-chosen references to the passage.

Criterion B: Appreciation of the writer's choices

To what extent does the analysis show appreciation of how the writer's choices of language, structure, technique and style shape meaning?

Marks	Level descriptor
0	The work does not reach a standard described by the descriptors below.
1	There is virtually no reference to the ways in which language, structure, technique and style shape meaning.
2	There is some reference to, but no analysis of, the ways in which language, structure, technique and style shape meaning.
3	There is adequate reference to, and some analysis and appreciation of, the ways in which language, structure, technique and style shape meaning.
4	There is good analysis and appreciation of the ways in which language, structure, technique and style shape meaning.
5	There is very good analysis and appreciation of the ways in which language, structure, technique and style shape meaning.

Criterion C: Organization

How well organized and coherent is the presentation of ideas?

Marks	Level descriptor
0	The work does not reach a standard described by the descriptors below.
1	Ideas have little organization and virtually no coherence.
2	Ideas have some organization, but coherence is often lacking.
3	Ideas are adequately organized, with some coherence.
4	Ideas are well organized and coherent.
5	Ideas are effectively organized, with very good coherence.

Criterion D: Language

How clear, varied and accurate is the language?

How appropriate is the choice of register, style and terminology?('Register' refers, in this context, to the student's use of elements such as vocabulary, tone, sentence structure and terminology appropriate to the task.)

Marks	Level descriptor
0	The work does not reach a standard described by the descriptors below.
1	Language is rarely clear and appropriate; there are many errors in grammar, vocabulary and sentence construction, and little sense of register and style.
2	Language is sometimes clear and carefully chosen; grammar, vocabulary and sentence construction are fairly accurate, although errors and inconsistencies are apparent; the register and style are to some extent appropriate to the task.
3	Language is clear and carefully chosen, with an adequate degree of accuracy in grammar, vocabulary and sentence construction despite some lapses; register and style are mostly appropriate to the task.
4	Language is clear and carefully chosen, with a good degree of accuracy in grammar, vocabulary and sentence construction; register and style are consistently appropriate to the task.
5	Language is very clear, effective, carefully chosen and precise, with a high degree of accuracy in grammar, vocabulary and sentence construction; register and style are effective and appropriate to the task.

INSIGHTS INTO COMMENTARY

Remember that commentary is a type of essay, and it requires organization and continuity. The type of organization, however, depends on the passage or poem itself. Each extract for commentary has its own meaning and that meaning is created by the writer through a series of strategic choices. These choices vary, depending upon the intentions of the writer and the effects he or she seeks to produce.

Your job in producing a commentary is to understand the connection between the form and the content in any given passage. To articulate that connection requires careful, detailed examination of both the language of the extract or poem and the stylistic features, the conventions, used by the writer. You are examining the artistry of the passage, so your focus is on the writer's technique. The writer's name should appear frequently in your commentary because your focus is on the choices that he or she made in constructing the poem or prose passage.

Using literary terms in your analysis of this artistry is fine as long as you use them accurately, but it is not necessary. What is necessary is that you see and identify the device and its effects. Simply identifying the device is not enough. You must appreciate what the use of a device produces within the passage or poem – its effect.

Your aim is to be convincing, and your tone should be confident but not arrogant. If you encounter ambiguity in the passage, don't ignore it. Simply reference the ambiguity and offer a possible reading, or understanding. In this way, the examiner will know that you read carefully, even if your understanding is incomplete.

Clearly, you want to demonstrate that you understand the passage literally (see Criterion A), but you also need to demonstrate that you can go beyond the literal, surface meaning and offer an interpretation. This interpretation must be grounded in the language of the passage or poem itself. Always avoid speculation beyond the words on the page!

Support for your interpretation, then, requires that you cite from the passage or poem. These references may take the form of direct citations of specific words or phrases, or you may cite indirectly through summary statements. Either is acceptable, but you must convince through textual evidence.

INSIGHTS INTO THE GUIDED LITERARY ANALYSIS

The guided literary analysis is also an essay, in which you respond to the two questions posed on a particular poem or prose extract. The title of the assignment is helpful in understanding the nature of the task. First of all, the response is 'guided' in the sense that the SL candidate has two questions that they must answer with regard to the chosen passage. These two questions guide the analysis, giving it focus and direction. The task is literary, the focus is on the poem or passage along with an analysis of the ways that meaning is created by the writer. The difference between commentary and guided literary analysis is minimal – both require the student to read closely, attuned to the writer's manipulation of language, structure, literary techniques and style.

6 COMPARATIVE ESSAY

Knowledge and Understanding

In terms of the assessment in the English A: Literature course, the comparative essay is second only to the commentary in terms of importance. Exam Paper 2, which assesses the texts studied in Part 3 of the programme, Literary Genres, requires students to compare the similarities and differences between the chosen works of a particular genre. Ideally, the works selected for Part 3 will demonstrate the wide variation of literary conventions within the genre. Paper 2 will allow students to show an understanding of the variety of ways that writers can deliver content within the conventions of the selected genre. Students must select **one question out of three** and must use **at least two** of the texts studied in Part 3 (three works at SL; four works at HL) in their essay response.

At both SL and HL, students are assessed on the basis of these questions:

- How much knowledge and understanding have they shown on the Part 3 works studied in relation to the question answered?
- How well has the student understood the specific demands of the question?
- To what extent has the student responded to these demands?
- How well have the works been compared and contrasted in relation to the demands of the question?
- To what extent does the student identify and appreciate the use of literary conventions in relation to the question and works used?
- How well organized, coherent and developed is the presentation of ideas?
- How clear, varied and accurate is the language?
- How appropriate is the choice of register, style and terminology? (Register refers, in this context, to the student's use of elements such as vocabulary, tone, sentence structure and terminology appropriate to the task.)

Understanding the process of comparison/contrast

The process of determining similarity and difference is central to our understanding of the world. We are constantly bombarded with bits of information, and yet somehow we manage to make sense of this information. Often, we are able to understand what something is, or what something means, by connecting its relationship to something that we already know or understand. Instead of describing every detail of the new bit of information, we shortcut the process by comparison. We place a bit of information side by side with other data and draw conclusions about what we see as essentially similar or markedly different. By evaluating in this way, we understand more quickly and more completely.

In evaluating literature, we often use the process of comparison/contrast to aid in our understanding of a text, and evaluate how representative it is of a particular genre. While every novel, for example, works within a set of narrative conventions (also known as narrative strategies or narrative techniques), fiction writers use these conventions in various ways to create specific effects within their texts. The writer's choice of one type of point of view over another can have a critical effect within a prose fiction text. That effect, that choice, can control how much information is revealed, or concealed, in a given text.

Literary analysis often involves training your eye to spot similarity and difference within a particular genre.

SUMMARY

The eye will naturally respond to distinctions – either in shape, size, mass, colour or functionality. Consequently, the 'reader's eye' can observe distinctions within genre conventions – when something stands out, consider why it has been used.

The comparative process and exam Paper 2

Exam Paper 2 requires students to compare and contrast at least two of the Part 3 works studied in regard to one of three genre-specific questions. The question will limit the scope of comparison so that the time allotted is appropriate to the task – two hours at HL and one hour and 30 minutes at SL.

After reading each question carefully, choose the question that appeals to you in some way. This appeal could be based on the focus of the question, or it could be based on the analytical appeal of specific texts that you have studied. Sometimes one question may not seem as straightforward as another, or it may intrigue you by its degree of ambiguity.

Whatever the reason, successful analytical writing can and should challenge you to move beyond your comfort zone and 'grapple with' or explore less-familiar ideas if you feel confident in doing so. In this way, you can avoid responding to a question with a familiar or pre-determined response. Part of the expectation for this task is that students offer a 'personal response', which means that you approach the question with fresh insights based on your knowledge and understanding of the texts. Choosing a question that interests or engages you on more than one level is always a wise option.

Steps to writing a comparison/contrast essay

The question you select determines the focus and, therefore, the intention or objective of your essay. Examine the two drama questions below:

a 'In dramatic construction there must be variation of pace and rhythm, monotony of any kind being certain to induce boredom.'

Comparing **at least two** plays you have studied in the light of this statement, show how variations of pace and rhythm have been used to attract or heighten the interest of the audience.

b To what extent can the plays you have studied be seen to have, directly or indirectly, a social or political purpose? Refer to **two** or **three** plays, exploring how they achieve their purposes.

For a successful comparison/contrast essay, a common ground for comparison must exist. It makes little sense to compare completely dissimilar things because the essay would simply describe the obvious, and there is little value in such an approach.

So the first thing to do is to find the common ground of the comparison – significant ideas or strategies that two texts share. Comparing one writer's view of love to another writer's ideas about conformity can yield little. But, closer examination of the two texts may reveal less obvious similarities about the treatment of women or the effects of lighting.

In question (a), for example, the focus of the comparison/contrast, its common ground, is the pacing or rhythm of the plays and how the playwrights have used pace to engage the audience, maintain their interest and even heighten their interest at various points. In the second example, the shared focus of the comparative essay is how playwrights, either directly or indirectly, convey a social or political agenda.

In both questions, the common ground is clear, but the specifics of similarity and difference determine the overall effectiveness of the essay. Once you have established a basis of comparison, you will examine the two texts carefully, taking notes and deciding what to say. The next decision you will need to make is to determine how to structure or organize your material.

Describing similarity or difference

Keep in mind that even in seemingly dissimilar works, a workable basis for comparison/contrast can be found. Perhaps two poems approach the same topic, or two plays use the same three-act form, or two protagonists develop a similar attitude towards a specific subject. By using close-reading skills, you can make observations that show subtle similarities. Drawing inferences from these observations and identifying common ground produce engaging and thoughtful comparative analysis.

● **Examiner's hints**

SL and HL students share identical exam Paper 2 questions; they each choose a question from the same three choices. Different evaluative descriptors (see end of chapter) address differences in response expectations for SL and HL.

To access worksheet 6.1 on finding common ground in drama, please visit www.pearsonbacconline. com and follow the on-screen instructions.

It is also true that obviously similar topics, forms or attitudes expressed within two texts of the same genre can yield interesting and engaging comparisons/contrasts. Rather than simply expound upon the obvious similarity, focus instead on the less obvious, the subtle differences that emerge on closer observation.

Evaluating similarity or difference

To access worksheet 6.2 on observing similarity and difference in all genres, please visit www. pearsonbacconline.com and follow the on-screen instructions.

The questions posed in Paper 2 sometimes ask you to evaluate the superiority of one text over another. For example, a question can ask which fiction text uses point of view more effectively than another, or which text is superior to another in relation to the theme or topic in the question.

These types of questions ask you to establish a hierarchy in which you order or rank the texts. Anytime that you are asked to determine which aspect of one text is more effective than the same aspect in another text, you are making a judgement. A judgement based on your observations of two or more texts establishes a hierarchy. It is important to support your judgement with appropriate textual evidence.

● **Examiner's hints**
The most successful exam Paper 2 response measures an aspect of one text against another, rather than simply describing the aspect in each text.

Make sure you are fully aware of the implications of the question that sets up your comparative essay. **Describing** similarity or difference and **evaluating** similarity or difference are not the same exercise.

The following summary point can direct you through the process of comparison/contrast, and the creation of an evaluative thesis.

First, we define our terms:

To **compare**: to show/describe/demonstrate how something is **similar**.

To **contrast**: to show/describe/demonstrate how something **differs** from something else.

An **evaluative thesis**: your opinion, your claim, your thesis; this statement forms the basis of your argument regarding similarity and difference in two texts. An evaluative thesis always takes a stand – it argues a position about the works rather than describing the similar or differing aspect of two texts.

Then:
1. Carefully examine all texts under consideration. Are they more similar than different? Or more different than similar? Decide. Then formulate a general conclusion of *either* similarity *or* difference. This generalization may, perhaps, state the obvious, the self-evident. For example, two drama texts might use a single setting for the staging of their plays.
2. From that generalization, explore the subtle similarities or differences that emerge. If your generalization observes similarity, then focus on the subtle differences; if the generalization observes difference, then focus on the subtle similarities.
   For example: Even though two plays might use a single setting, in one text that setting takes on more dramatic significance as the props are revealed to hold more meaning as the play progresses, while in the other play, the props remain static. This difference underscores the relationship of characters to props and the subtle use of props to heighten or diminish tension in character interaction. Also consider the importance the playwright has placed on context.

   Your exploration here *must* lead you *beyond* the obvious, because a discussion of self-evident conclusions is both pointless and boring. The idea is to illuminate areas formerly dark ... to enlighten. Brainstorm and be creative in your approach to the texts. Then formulate conclusions about the subtle similarities or differences.

3. Now, you begin to structure your thoughts:

   a Your introductory paragraph includes the generalization of *either* similarity *or* difference, with appropriate supporting examples from each text. In longer essays that have no time restraints, these examples could be numerous, perhaps extending to a fully developed body paragraph with textual citations. In timed writings, such as Paper 2, confine these examples to the introductory paragraph.

   b After these supporting details from the texts come the conclusions about subtle similarities or differences that emerge from the generalization. These subtleties comprise your thesis; therefore, they must be arguable, they must take a stand. To say simply that 'differences exist' is descriptive, not arguable. To construct an arguable thesis, you must characterize those similarities or differences in some fashion that engenders literary disagreement. Your essay becomes, with your arguable thesis, *either* comparison *or* contrast but *not both*.

   c Each of your body paragraphs cites carefully selected details from *each* text to support each subtle similarity or difference noted in your thesis. Remember: it takes more than a single textual reference to support an argument. Even two points of support could be dismissed as coincidental. Three or more references from the text would indicate that your claim is valid and supportable.

   d Each body paragraph's topic sentence is an arguable assertion, a conclusion you can draw from the subtle similarities or differences in the texts. This style of comparative essay, in which texts are discussed together in the same paragraph is called a 'point-by-point' analysis. It has several advantages over the 'subject-by-subject' approach where one text is treated separately from the other. This second type of structure produces two mini-essays on the texts, compartmentalizing rather than synthesizing the texts.

   e The concluding paragraph is a fresh, insightful, appropriate finish to an enlightening essay. Avoid mechanical restatements; they weaken impact and bore your reader. You might consider the main effect produced on the reader or the audience (in drama texts). Remember, this effect could be intellectual, emotional or both. Does the point of comparison render a powerful effect on the reader/audience? What emotion or idea remains when the text is closed?

   f Finally, check to see that your introductory paragraph – the generalization of similarity or difference – and the statements of subtle differences (or similarities) are all arguable conclusions that are assertions rather than plot statements.

SUMMARY

Your thesis is ARGUABLE. It is not a plot statement (a true statement that cannot be argued), a self-evident conclusion, a description, or an assertion that cannot be argued with textual evidence.

Imagine a question as a form of suitcase, which when opened reveals numerous other questions and issues that have to be addressed.

▼

Appreciation

In this section of the chapter you will have the opportunity to examine sample questions from exam Paper 2 and read several sample student responses that demonstrate effective comparative analyses. This section will also discuss how to 'unpack' the question, that is, determine what the question is asking you to describe and/ or evaluate in your comparative essay. Only by systematically approaching the question can you be assured that you have not overlooked an element of this comparative task.

'Unpacking' the Paper 2 essay question

The most important thing to remember about the Paper 2 comparative essay is that the question will almost certainly ask you to focus on the conventions of the genre that you studied in Part 3 of the course. The conventions, which are reviewed extensively in the first four chapters, are used by writers to produce specific effects. Your job is to understand the question and the expectations that it places upon you as you compare and contrast two or three of the representative texts of the genre that you studied in Part 3.

Typically questions can be set in two forms. The first is a quotation that makes a generalization about the genre, idea, concept or theme, asserted in such a way as to draw a reaction. Below are several examples of such questions taken from past exams:

Prose: The Novel and the Short Story: 'A novel's setting, its home ground, very often plays a more active part in the plot than is first apparent.' How far does this remark apply to three (3) of the works you have studied?

Poetry: 'Poetry, like music, is to be heard.' Consider the ways in which at least two poets you have studied use the sound of their words to affect our response to their ideas.

Drama: 'As the action of the play unfolds, dramatic tension is often produced by the contrast of concealment and revelation.' Compare at least two of the plays which you have studied in light of this statement.

Prose other than the Novel and Short Story: 'A well-written piece of prose should be unified.' Say how far you agree that a single unified impression is important to two or three works you have studied.

The second type of question set does not include a quotation. These questions may or may not ask you to evaluate the success of the strategy in two or three of the texts that you have read. Consider these examples:

Prose: The Novel and Short Story: Symbols and/or motifs are an essential element of many novels and short stories. How have either or both of these devices been used and, in your opinion, how successfully, in two or three of the works you have studied?

Drama: Some dramatists make more significant use of physical elements such as stage scenery than do others. Discuss the extent of the use of such features and their impact on meaning in two or three plays you have studied.

Poetry: How does the poet exploit language and imagery to develop meaning? Comment in detail upon two or three poems by differing poets.

Prose other than the Novel and Short Story: Explore the ways in which two or three prose works, other than the novel or short story, you have studied have used characters to enhance your enjoyment of the works.

EXERCISE 1

Using your texts, plan your response for each of the appropriate genre questions above. Consider this a practice exercise for Paper 2.

- When you examine the language of the question, do you see more than one question being asked of you? Are these questions stated directly or implied?
- Do you understand all of the words in the question? Look them up if you do not.
- When you list your texts, do two texts stand out in your mind as particularly suited to comparison?
- Can you establish a foundation for comparison? Can you generalize either subtle similarities or differences depending on this foundation?

- Map out the specific details from each text that will support your evaluative comparison.
- Outline the structure of your essay, determining which format (point-by-point or subject-by-subject) will lend itself to your argument.
- Write a full comparative response within the prescribed exam time limit if possible.

Sample student responses (comparative essays)

Each of the following samples are preparation essays for Paper 2, which accounts for the number of texts used in the comparison/contrast essays as well as the nature of the questions themselves. Examine each essay and evaluate its merit using the descriptors that follow.

Sample 1

Question: Compare/contrast how each of the writers uses the relationship of major to minor characters to specific effects and/or function within their work.

Minor characters play a major role in these texts. From the well-depicted character like Comrade Pillai to the shadowy image of Kafka's boarders, minor characters carry a great deal of literary weight. The writers utilize minor characters as foils to enhance certain attributes of major characters in their works. Betrayals of major characters by minor characters also function as points of tension and contribute to literary themes about betrayal within the works. Foils, important characters that contrast aspects of major characters, occur frequently in these works. In *The God of Small Things*, Comrade Pillai acts as a foil to Chako. These 'comic book adversaries' (Roy 266) compare and contrast in peculiar ways. Comrade Pillai's house is the 'Ayemenem office' (Roy 15) of the Communist Party, and he is the Marxist leader of Ayemenem. Chako is the boss of a factory, yet a 'self-proclaimed Marxist' (Roy 62) who encourages the unionization of his workers. Both men are well-educated, and ultimately come to blows in the scandal over Velutha. The similarity of the two men highlights the dogmatic nature of their Marxist rhetoric, and the idea that politics supersedes (for better or worse) the needs of individuals. The betrayal of Velutha in the name of the 'organization's interest' (Roy 271) further cements the impersonal nature of politics in Kerala.

The Metamorphosis and *The Awakening* both feature less predominant foils. The three boarders directly parallel Gregor in the way they 'examine' (Kafka 44) their food prior to eating, and compare in their pretentions to the manager in part 1. The row they cause over Gregor actively prompts Grete's declaration of Gregor as a 'monster', (Kafka 44) the final betrayal of his human dignity. Similarly, in *The Awakening*, Alcee Arobin functions as a foil to Leonce Pontellier, as a source of his betrayal. Alcee is a young, flirtatious man, who writes letters to women that 'should never have been written' (Chopin 27) and propositions Edna throughout her time in New Orleans. Alcee loves horse racing, a pastime Leonce is apt to 'discourage' (Chopin 94). The 'flaming torch' (Chopin 112) Arobin kindles within Edna only highlights the impotence of Leonce in her life, especially when she feels 'neither shame nor remorse' (Chopin 113) over the betrayal. Arobin enables the portrayal of Leonce Pontellier as a failed husband, both in will and passion.

Minor characters foil the protagonists by actively participating in the betrayals that manifest the primary conflict of each novel. Their roles create irony and increase tension as the texts unfold.

Sample 2

Question: Compare/contrast physical, emotional or spiritual borderlines in three of the works you have studied in Part 3. To what extent do borderlines underscore communal values in each work? Must borderlines be crossed? Is the crossing more or less significant than the journey to the borderline?

In Arundhati Roy's *The God of Small Things*, Jean Rhys' *Wide Sargasso Sea*, and Kate Chopin's *The Awakening*, the characters must cross borderlines. Each novel contains both literal and metaphorical borderlines that the characters must cross physically, spiritually, or psychologically in order to achieve their goals and dreams. In all three novels, the borderlines underscore the values of the society in which the characters function. In *The God of Small Things and The Awakening*, the borderlines underscore the values of two very different communities. Although the journey to the borderline is important in each of these novels, in *Wide Sargasso Sea* and *The Awakening* this journey is more important than the actual crossing, while in *The God of Small Things*, the crossing of the borderlines themselves is the action that facilitates the conflict of the novel.

The borderlines in each of these novels underscore the values of the society in which the characters function. In *The Awakening*, the physical borderline of the sea and the metaphorical borderline of Edna Pontellier's independence both emphasize the communal constraint that women cannot live independent and happy lives without feeling indebted to their husbands and children. Edna cannot swim, so the sea is a borderline which she cannot cross at first. She still feels its allure. 'The voice of the sea [is] seductive' and 'whispering' (Chopin 57) like the voices of the forbidden lovers that Edna entertains. On the night of the dinner party, Edna and the other guests go to the beach, where she feels overtaken by the sudden urge to 'swim far out', and to go where 'no woman' has ever swum (Chopin 73).

Chopin uses diction purposefully as she phrases the sentence with 'woman' instead of 'man' or 'person' to emphasize to readers that Edna wants to be free of the constraints of being a woman and to outdo all other women to prove her worth. Edna has consciously chosen to stand apart. Initially, Edna feels tied to her husband, but she crosses the borderline from dependence to independence on the night when she refuses to come in from the hammock.

Her husband is angry, emphasizing the societal expectation that a woman listen to her husband and obey his wishes. Edna refuses to obey Leonce, and instead chooses to stay in the hammock rather than accompanying her husband to bed. Leonce 'can't permit' her to 'stay out there', but she replies that she 'mean[s] to stay' and tells him to 'go to bed' without her (Chopin 78).

In *Wide Sargasso Sea*, the borderlines between Granbois and England ironically underscore the values of each society. Rochester feels uncomfortable in Granbois. He feels threatened surrounded by so much wide, untamed nature. He says that everything is 'too much' (Rhys 64) and that the native people speak a 'horrible' (Rhys 85) language. His disgust shortly turns to fear and eventually he returns to England, with Antoinette, who he has now renamed Bertha. In England, Bertha is imprisoned within 'thick walls' with only a single window.

Without access to the world beyond her tower prison, her madness increases. The borderline in Rhys' novel is the psychological bond of physical space. Comfort and peace are clearly marked behind geographic and cultural lines. In *The God of Small Things*, the caste system itself creates a borderline between Ammu and Velutha. Because Velutha is a Paravan and Ammu is a divorced woman, the 'Love Laws' (Roy 33) dictate that these two characters can never love each other. Traditional orthodoxy overrules the love that these two share. Velutha's nightly crossing of the Meenschal River, a physical borderline, to meet Ammu and cross the borderline of love, further emphasize the relative 'smallness' of love. When these two characters cross these borderlines, they cross into the potential of death and destruction.

In each of these novels, the borderlines must be crossed. Edna must 'swim far out' (Chopin 73) into the sea to achieve independence. After that moment, Edna begins to realize that she can rely on herself rather than Leonce. The borderlines of the sea and

Edna's independence lose their distinction as the novel progresses. Edna's stepping into the sea and learning to swim far out, signify her willingness to succumb to the 'intoxication' and 'newly conquered power' (Chopin 74). Likewise, when Velutha and Ammu challenge the Love Laws and step across the caste borderline, they dared to love each other, dared to share the "small things" in those moments of tenderness on the verandah of the History House. The psychological and geographical borderlines in *Wide Sargasso Sea* are crossed as well, and for each character the crossing intensifies the isolation they feel.

In *Wide Sargasso Sea* and *The Awakening*, the journey to the borderlines is more important than the crossing, while in *The God of Small Things*, the crossing itself is most important. The consequences, as we see in Estha and Rahel, are irreversible and will affect generations.

Sample 3

Question: In what way(s) does the setting of a work (its geographic, cultural, and historical landscape) function in two of the works you have read? Consider functions of landscape in relation to character, plot, and/or thematic development.

In both Jean Rhys's *Wide Sargasso Sea* and Arundhati Roy's *The God of Small Things*, the setting is a crucial part of the work's development. In *The God of Small Things*, the setting is primarily the beginning of the summer in Ayemenem. In *Wide Sargasso Sea*, the setting goes from the Caribbean shortly after the abolition of slavery briefly to Victorian England for the conclusion. In both novels, the settings contribute to the building of tension and progression of plot while also serving to facilitate the social commentary.

In *Wide Sargasso Sea*, the key setting Rhys uses is the Caribbean. Antoinette spends various parts of her childhood in different parts of the islands and after marriage lives in Granbois with her husband (implied to be Rochester of Bronte's *Jane Eyre*). This setting is crucial to the building of tension in both the novel and the marriage; as Rochester is thrust into this brave new world of the Caribbean he suffers from sensory overload and the 'alien, disturbing' (Rhys 87) feel of everything he is encountering. Rochester has spent his whole life in England and is now surprised to find that 'everything is too much' (Rhys 70) in this new setting. This swollen feeling contributes to the sense that tension is building and that everything is ready to burst.

Similarly, Arundhati Roy uses a setting of heightened tension from the first page of *The God of Small Things*. She immediately informs the reader that 'Ayemenem is a hot, brooding' (Roy 3) place and that the city is 'suffused with sloth' (Roy 3). This location adds to the slow and tense atmosphere from the very beginning of the work. Roy depicts Ayemenem in this way to foreshadow the conflict and The Terror that lies in the later parts of the book.

Roy further uses Ayemenem in the development of The Terror in that the social setting is absolutely critical to the plot progression. The caste system and the 'laws that lay down who should be loved' (Roy 33) is what forces Vellya Paapen's 'story of [Ammu and Velutha] standing together in the moonlight' (Roy 242) that causes Mammachi's fury and forces the climax of the novel. The fragmentation of society in this novel creates the conflict between society and the relationship Ammu and Velutha form. Society deems their love 'unthinkable' (Roy 242) and condemns both of them to shattered lives as a result. In using this setting, Roy creates an absolutely ominous air as she gradually foreshadows and then reveals that Ammu and Velutha have defied centuries of tradition.

Rhys too uses the setting to foreshadow and advance the plot in *Wide Sargasso Sea*. Unlike Roy's work, where the conflict rises from the desires of some of the main characters clashing with those of society as a whole, *Wide Sargasso Sea* contains a single character in a setting where he is a stranger, and as a result lashing out against not only the setting but also the characters native to it. Rochester 'hated the place' (Rhys 172) of Granbois, and this seems somewhat to bring about his disdain for Antoinette. This is crucial as the conflict between Rochester and Antoinette is the crux of the plot of the book. Rochester, from the beginning, appears to be overly suspicious of the island and its inhabitants, and as a result feels as if 'he[d] expected' (Rhys 99) Antoinette to be afflicted with madness. Rochester is continuously condescending to the natives of Granbois, and as a result Antoinette as well.

This condescending attitude that Rochester possesses towards the people of the Caribbean is a key part of Rhys's social commentary. Rhys attempts to criticize the patronizing nature of the colonial attitude that many British took to the people of the islands. Rochester condescendingly tells Antoinette that because he '[thinks] of [her] as Bertha' (Rhys 135) he is going to call her that, despite her protests, as though he is her master and has the power to give her whatever slave name he so desires. For Rhy's purposes of condemning prejudiced attitudes towards those in the West Indies, the setting is absolutely essential.

The setting is of similar relevance in *The God of Small Things*. Roy uses Ayemenem to criticize globalization, of which she is an ardent opponent. Roy portrays American culture as an evil polluting the culture of India, and uses the setting to symbolize this. The river water is 'thick and toxic' (Roy 119) because of the Western hotel exploiting the town for tourist purposes, and now 'the smell of shit' (Roy 119) fills the surrounding area from the river. Roy uses this degradation and powerful descriptive imagery to characterize Ayemenem as a dirty place, one that the corrupt Western culture has sullied. This is a recurring theme throughout the book, and one that simply would not be possible without setting.

Both authors use their settings and their developments to parallel the ongoing developments in their novels' plots. The settings build tension and are also crucial to the progression of the plots of the novels. The authors rely heavily on their settings not only in the execution of their stories, but also in the creation of social commentaries. The two settings, May in Ayemenem and the Islands of the Caribbean in the 19th century, are iconic and essential parts of *The God of Small Things* and *Wide Sargasso Sea*, and have central functions in both books.

Examiner's comments

When you are examining each of the samples, be sure to use the appropriate HL or SL descriptors at the end of this chapter. Also, consider the following as you attempt to establish the merit of each sample comparative essay.

In evaluating Criterion A: Knowledge and understanding, ask yourself if this student appears to know detailed information about the text.

For Criterion B: Response to the question, it is important to determine if the student answered the question fully and if the works were compared and contrasted.

For Criterion C: Appreciation of the literary conventions of the genre, be sure to examine if the student referred to literary conventions within the texts and if these conventions, in relation to the question, demonstrate a clear understanding of the effects produced.

For Criterion D: Organization and development, examine the organization of the essay. Are the ideas coherent and well developed?

For Criterion E: Language, focus on the clarity of expression as well as the appropriateness of register and style.

Paper 2: Essay assessment criteria, SL

There are five assessment criteria at SL.

Criterion A	Knowledge and understanding	5 marks
Criterion B	Response to the question	5 marks
Criterion C	Appreciation of the literary conventions of the genre	5 marks
Criterion D	Organization and development	5 marks
Criterion E	Language	5 marks
	Total	25 marks

Criterion A: Knowledge and understanding

How much knowledge and understanding has the student shown of the Part 3 works studied in relation to the question answered?

Marks	Level descriptor
0	The work does not reach a standard described by the descriptors below.
1	There is little knowledge and no understanding of the Part 3 works in relation to the question answered.
2	There is some knowledge but little understanding of the Part 3 works in relation to the question answered.
3	There is adequate knowledge and some understanding of the Part 3 works in relation to the question answered.
4	There is good knowledge and understanding of the Part 3 works in relation to the question answered.
5	There is very good knowledge and understanding of the Part 3 works in relation to the question answered.

Criterion B: Response to the question

How well has the student understood the specific demands of the question?

To what extent has the student responded to these demands?

How well have the works been compared and contrasted in relation to the demands of the question?

Marks	Level descriptor
0	The work does not reach a standard described by the descriptors below.
1	The student shows virtually no awareness of the main implications of the question, and ideas are mostly irrelevant or insignificant. There is no meaningful comparison of the works used in relation to the question.
2	The student shows limited awareness of the main implications of the question, and ideas are sometimes irrelevant or insignificant. There is little meaningful comparison of the works used in relation to the question.

3	The student responds to most of the main implications of the question, with relevant ideas. A comparison is made of the works used in relation to the question, but it may be superficial.
4	The student responds to the main implications of the question, with consistently relevant ideas. An appropriate comparison is made of the works used in relation to the question.
5	The student responds to the main implications and some subtleties of the question, with relevant and carefully explored ideas. An effective comparison is made of the works used in relation to the question.

Criterion C: Appreciation of the literary conventions of the genre

To what extent does the student identify and appreciate the use of literary conventions in relation to the question and the works used?

Marks	Level descriptor
0	The work does not reach a standard described by the descriptors below.
1	Virtually no literary conventions are identified, and there is no development relevant to the question and/or the works used.
2	Examples of literary conventions are sometimes correctly identified, but there is little development relevant to the question and the works used.
3	Examples of literary conventions are mostly correctly identified, and there is some development relevant to the question and the works used.
4	Examples of literary conventions are clearly identified and effectively developed, with relevance to the question and the works used.
5	Examples of literary conventions are clearly identified and effectively developed, with clear relevance to the question and the works used.

Criterion D: Organization and development

How well organized, coherent and developed is the presentation of ideas?

Marks	Level descriptor
0	The work does not reach a standard described by the descriptors below.
1	Ideas have virtually no organization or structure, and coherence and/or development are lacking.
2	Ideas have some organization and structure, but there is very little coherence and/or development.
3	Ideas are adequately organized, with a suitable structure and some attention paid to coherence and development.
4	Ideas are well organized, with a good structure, coherence and development.
5	Ideas are effectively organized, with a very good structure, coherence and development.

Criterion E: Language

How clear, varied and accurate is the language?

How appropriate is the choice of register, style and terminology? ('Register' refers, in this context, to the student's use of elements such as vocabulary, tone, sentence structure and terminology appropriate to the task.)

Marks	Level descriptor
0	The work does not reach a standard described by the descriptors below.
1	Language is rarely clear and appropriate; there are many errors in grammar, vocabulary and sentence construction, and little sense of register and style.

2	Language is sometimes clear and carefully chosen; grammar, vocabulary and sentence construction are fairly accurate, although errors and inconsistencies are apparent; the register and style are to some extent appropriate to the task.
3	Language is clear and carefully chosen, with an adequate degree of accuracy in grammar, vocabulary and sentence construction despite some lapses; register and style are mostly appropriate to the task.
4	Language is clear and carefully chosen, with a good degree of accuracy in grammar, vocabulary and sentence construction; register and style are consistently appropriate to the task.
5	Language is very clear, effective, carefully chosen and precise, with a high degree of accuracy in grammar, vocabulary and sentence construction; register and style are effective and appropriate to the task.

Paper 2: Essay assessment criteria, HL

There are five assessment criteria at HL.

Criterion A	Knowledge and understanding	5 marks
Criterion B	Response to the question	5 marks
Criterion C	Appreciation of the literary conventions of the genre	5 marks
Criterion D	Organization and development	5 marks
Criterion E	Language	5 marks
	Total	25 marks

Criterion A: Knowledge and understanding

How much knowledge and understanding has the student shown of the Part 3 works studied in relation to the question answered?

Marks	Level descriptor
0	The work does not reach a standard described by the descriptors below.
1	There is some knowledge but virtually no understanding of the Part 3 works in relation to the question answered.
2	There is mostly adequate knowledge and some superficial understanding of the Part 3 works in relation to the question answered.
3	There is adequate knowledge and understanding of the Part 3 works in relation to the question answered.
4	There is good knowledge and understanding of the Part 3 works in relation to the question answered.
5	There is perceptive knowledge and understanding of the Part 3 works in relation to the question answered.

Criterion B: Response to the question

How well has the student understood the specific demands of the question?

To what extent has the student responded to these demands?

How well have the works been compared and contrasted in relation to the demands of the question?

Marks	Level descriptor
0	The work does not reach a standard described by the descriptors below.
1	The student shows little awareness of the main implications of the question, and ideas are mainly irrelevant and/or insignificant. There is little meaningful comparison of the works used in relation to the question.

2	The student responds to some of the main implications of the question with some relevant ideas. There is a superficial attempt to compare the works used in relation to the question.
3	The student responds to most of the main implications of the question with consistently relevant ideas. There is adequate comparison of the works used in relation to the question.
4	The student responds to the main implications and some subtleties of the question, with relevant and carefully explored ideas. The comparison makes some evaluation of the works used in relation to the question.
5	The student responds to all the implications, as well as the subtleties of the question, with convincing and thoughtful ideas. The comparison includes an effective evaluation of the works in relation to the question.

Criterion C: Appreciation of the literary conventions of the genre

To what extent does the student identify and appreciate the use of literary conventions in relation to the question and the works used?

Marks	Level descriptor
0	The work does not reach a standard described by the descriptors below.
1	Some literary conventions are identified but there is limited development relevant to the question and/or the works used.
2	Examples of literary conventions are sometimes correctly identified and developed, with some relevance to the question and the works used.
3	Examples of literary conventions are satisfactorily identified and developed, with relevance to the question and the works used.
4	Examples of literary conventions are clearly identified and effectively developed, with relevance to the question and the works used.
5	Examples of literary conventions are perceptively identified and persuasively developed, with clear relevance to the question and the works used.

Criterion D: Organization and development

How well organized, coherent and developed is the presentation of ideas?

Marks	Level descriptor
0	The work does not reach a standard described by the descriptors below.
1	Ideas have little organization; there may be a superficial structure, but coherence and/or development are lacking.
2	Ideas have some organization, with a recognizable structure, but coherence and development are often lacking.
3	Ideas are adequately organized, with a suitable structure and attention paid to coherence and development.
4	Ideas are effectively organized, with a very good structure, coherence and development.
5	Ideas are persuasively organized, with excellent structure, coherence and development.

Criterion E: Language

How clear, varied and accurate is the language?

How appropriate is the choice of register, style and terminology? ('Register' refers, in this context, to the student's use of elements such as vocabulary, tone, sentence structure and terminology appropriate to the task.)

Marks	Level descriptor
0	The work does not reach a standard described by the descriptors below.
1	Language is rarely clear and appropriate; there are many errors in grammar, vocabulary and sentence construction, and little sense of register and style.
2	Language is sometimes clear and carefully chosen; grammar, vocabulary and sentence construction are fairly accurate, although errors and inconsistencies are apparent; the register and style are to some extent appropriate to the task.
3	Language is clear and carefully chosen, with an adequate degree of accuracy in grammar, vocabulary and sentence construction despite some lapses; register and style are mostly appropriate to the task.
4	Language is clear and carefully chosen, with a good degree of accuracy in grammar, vocabulary and sentence construction; register and style are consistently appropriate to the task.
5	Language is very clear, effective, carefully chosen and precise, with a high degree of accuracy in grammar, vocabulary and sentence construction; register and style are effective and appropriate to the task.

INSIGHTS INTO THE COMPARATIVE ESSAY

The comparative essay is specifically intended as a vehicle to demonstrate your ability to synthesize your knowledge of texts. Rather than viewing the Part 3 genre texts as somehow compartmentalized, as individual works studied under a generic heading as 'apples and oranges', this assessment requires you to measure one text against another. In doing so, you demonstrate how much you know about the genre and its conventions as well as how much you understand about the texts themselves.

One important consideration that goes without saying is that the experience of reading the text is an individual experience. Do your best to be aware of your process, noting what controls your intellectual and emotional responses to the text. When, for example, do you anticipate a crisis on stage? Or, what image appears again and again within a poet's work only to be used with highly different connotations? What makes you want to laugh out loud in one prose text, or prompts you to rage in a matter of pages in another? Being aware of yourself, of your own reactions is essential to the task of comparison/contrast.

Rather than a dry exercise in 'apples and oranges', think of the comparative process as one that truly demonstrates your awareness of what makes one text both predictable and idiosyncratic, displaying characteristic trademarks of the genre and yet being original within that genre.

Think, too, of the genre as an evolving, living form. Some of the changes within the genre can be traced to changes over time. In the novel, for example, the nature of the self-conscious narrator has changed substantially over the years. When Charlotte Brontë's Jane Eyre said 'Dear Reader, I married him' (*Jane Eyre*), she spoke to the reader with the confidence of an old friend. The guarded, and somewhat defensive revelations of Nick Carraway about what 'did in' Jay Gatsby 'in the end', are tinged with the self-conscious fears about 20th-century America. The genre conventions, while predictable in some sense, are wholly unpredictable because of the nature of the artist who must challenge and embrace the genre to make it their own.

THE INDIVIDUAL ORAL PRESENTATION

Learning Outcomes

Knowledge and Understanding
- Understand the purpose of the oral presentation
- Examine the learning outcomes of this part of the course
- Familiarize yourself with the assessment criteria of the oral presentation
- Explore ways of achieving high scores on this component of the literature course

Appreciation
- Consider the different types of presentation
- Consider how to establish the topic of your presentation
- Explore strategies to express yourself effectively and engage your audience
- Examine effective ways of planning and structuring your presentation
- Appreciate new textualities in relation to the oral presentation

Knowledge and Understanding
The Individual Oral Presentation

Welcome to one of the most inspirational, fun and innovative parts of the course. Here you will be able to express your creativity in all sorts of dynamic ways. Furthermore, you will develop fundamental skills that go well beyond the classroom, teaching you how to present material effectively to a large audience, an essential skill in the workplace.

In a nutshell, the oral presentation is something that you do either by yourself or in a group. You can spend as much time as you want preparing for it. You might be given time in class, but the chances are that most of the preparation will take place in your own time. The oral presentation can be based on one or more of the three texts that you are studying for Part 4 of the English A course. You will be expected to speak for 10–15 minutes. If you are working in a group, then each individual should speak for this long.

When you study the three works in Part 4 of your course, there are a few things you should keep in the back of your mind:

The Learning Outcomes – What you are expected to demonstrate once you have finished studying the three works. We will go through these in more detail in this chapter.

The Assessment – The oral presentation will be worth 15 per cent of your final IB English score, and so it is important to do a good job on it. You need to study the assessment criteria, and in this chapter we will go through each of them in detail, giving examples of how you can achieve marks in the top of each level descriptor.

The Type of Presentation – This involves having some idea of the exciting creative opportunities you have for the oral presentation. We will look at this aspect in the 'Appreciation' section of the chapter.

Good Delivery – This aspect of the oral presentation is also dealt with in the 'Appreciation' section of the chapter.

A band descriptor is what examiners look at when deciding where to place your mark for a particular criterion.

● **Examiner's hints**
Remember that you need to do a presentation in many other subjects or courses in the diploma programme. The Theory of Knowledge presentation is an important part of your course; the Group 4 presentation needs to be done in science and you will no doubt perform a number of presentations in other subjects, such as languages and humanities. It is also easy to validate this skill in terms of further education and the workplace.

The aim of this chapter is to give you a detailed insight into how to go about the oral presentation on Part 4 of your course, but also for you to see that it is a generally important part of your learning.

The Part 4 presentation is an opportunity for you to grow as a presenter, a skill that you will keep for life.

The learning outcomes for the presentation

Let's think why being able to do a good presentation is an important skill. The art of presenting to a group of people comes back to the principles of rhetoric, which we discussed in Chapter 4. Knowing how to convince a group of people can be very important. University applications and job interviews, for instance, might involve an interview with a single person or a panel of people, in which you have to convince others of your merit in a short space of time.

In specific types of work, presentation skills become the bread and butter of professional life, so nurturing those skills early on is worthwhile. Reflect on the importance of being able to structure a presentation effectively and persuade an audience in the following professions:

- Law
- Politics
- Academia
- Teaching
- Salesmanship
- Management

Being confident about yourself in front of a group of people is essential in a number of artistic areas such as:

- Acting (theatre or film)
- Musical performance
- Recital

Hopefully you are convinced that the oral presentation is much more than simply scoring marks for the diploma programme – it is helping you prepare for life.

Let's look at the learning outcomes of this part of the course. In the subject guide it is stipulated that students should:

- Acquire knowledge and understanding of the works studied
- Present an individual, independent response to works studied
- Acquire powers of expression through oral presentation
- Learn how to interest and hold the attention of an audience

Acquire knowledge and understanding of the works studied

Linguistic determinism, put forward by thinkers such as Ludwig Wittgenstein, is the theory that it is impossible to think without language. This would mean that it is impossible to think about a work of literature without some form of linguistic presentation, either oral or written. Do you agree?

One of the things that the oral presentation will be testing you on is how well you know the work or works you are discussing. Being able to articulate yourself is an important measure of your understanding of the subject matter. In many ways here is the key test of a person's understanding of anything: how well and clearly they can speak about it. This means that you will need to plan your presentation carefully and make sure that you have understood the works and can elaborate on their main ideas confidently and convincingly. In the oral presentation you can spend time being creative, looking for patterns and interesting points on structure, and you can use a number of exciting and original analogies to represent abstract and conceptual approaches to the text.

Present an individual, independent response to works studied

● **Examiner's hints**

There are only two ways to avoid academic dishonesty:

1. Telling the reader and audience each time you use an idea that is not your own;
2. Using your own ideas.

Remember that the teacher is looking for a personal response to the work, and this is where creativity is important. It is pointless copying someone else's theory, since all you will be doing then is repeating something and not showing a dynamic, interesting response as a sensitive reader. Furthermore, using someone else's analysis (for example going onto the internet and simply regurgitating ready-made notes or copying a critic's ideas from a book) can cause you to run into problems of academic honesty.

If you are referring to someone else's ideas, you will have to reference their work clearly, this way making it clear that the response is not your own. Make sure that if you do use others' (referenced) work, you apply it as a springboard to present your own viewpoints, rather simply offering it as a substitute for original thinking.

Make no mistake, you are allowed to reference other people's ideas, and in the Extended Essay you are expected to do this, especially in a literature Extended Essay where you need to show that you are a budding young scholar capable of developing your own understanding of an area by researching existing theories.

For the oral presentation, however, it is not necessary to look for established critical theories, as these will make the task more complicated and could get in the way of what you are trying to do, which is give personal response. The key words to remember in this learning objective are **individual** and **independent**, priorities that will be pushed through the teaching of these texts.

Acquire powers of expression through oral presentation

The oral presentation will help develop your powers of expression. Being able to express yourself well will give you an advantage in roles that go far beyond the list of professions given above – it is a skill that is used daily. Effective communication is crucial to how you develop as a person in society. Look at the presentation as an opportunity to test your verbal powers in a formal setting. To express yourself clearly and powerfully you need to make sure that you structure your work carefully so that the audience is 'on board' at all times.

A separate section of this chapter in the 'Appreciation' section has been dedicated to looking at the different ways that you can go about the oral presentation, with tips on how to deliver one effectively.

Learn how to interest and hold the attention of an audience

This is where the oral presentation can be a lot of fun. Getting your audience hooked on what you have to say and leading them through your ideas is a gratifying, exciting experience. If you take the time to make your presentation original and sparkly, exhilarating and stimulating, it will remain as one of the strongest points of your English course.

Too many speakers go down the beaten track of PowerPoint, or reading from a script, standing in front of a group of people and talking to them in a rather dull manner. Here is your chance to take it to another level and do something that is so original and creative that it remains imprinted in the minds of your audience for a long time.

Is meaning constructed by words alone? What is the role of emotion in creating meaning?

Stimulating different emotions of your audience is a good way of convincing them of your argument and keeping them enthralled by what you have to say.

SUMMARY

The learning outcomes of the oral presentation are there to help you develop into an excellent presenter who will be able to hold the attention of those you are speaking to in the appropriate manner. Acquiring this skill can take you far.

This is what the subject guide says about the oral presentation:

FOCUS OF THE INDIVIDUAL ORAL PRESENTATION

The focus of each oral presentation will depend on the nature and scope of the topic chosen. Whatever the topic and type of presentation chosen, students will be expected to show:

- knowledge and understanding of the works
- thorough appreciation of the aspect discussed
- good use of strategies to engage an audience
- delivery of the presentation in a manner that is appropriate to the task

So all in all there is a fair amount of flexibility in the process and you are given substantial autonomy in coming up with your plan. Make sure that you talk to your teacher about what it is that you plan to do, so that there are no nasty surprises!

● **Examiner's hints**
Whether it is demanded by the teacher or not, make sure that you consult him or her on your oral presentation decisions before you get too involved with the planning, to make sure that you are on the right track.

Assessment

The assessment of the oral presentation will be done according to the published assessment criteria from the guide. This means that you have the opportunity to study how you will be evaluated before you even start planning, to ensure that when you start you know what you need to do to achieve high marks in the different criteria.

The presentation is marked out of 30. The three criteria are weighted equally, so you need to strike a balance between each of them when delivering. The assessment criteria for the oral presentation are different from those used in the Individual Oral Commentary, even though the marks for both are added and moderated together.

Criterion A: Knowledge and understanding of the work(s)

How much knowledge and understanding does the student show of the work(s) used in the presentation?

Marks	Level descriptor
0	The work does not reach a standard described by the descriptors below.
1–2	There is little knowledge or understanding of the content of the work(s) presented.
3–4	There is some knowledge and superficial understanding of the content of the work(s) presented.
5–6	There is adequate knowledge and understanding of the content and some of the implications of the work(s) presented.
7–8	There is very good knowledge and understanding of the content and most of the implications of the work(s) presented.
9–10	There is excellent knowledge and understanding of the content and the implications of the work(s) presented.

Criterion A is worth 10 points. In order to reach for the highest marks you need to show outstanding knowledge and understanding not only of the content (the book, books or collection of poems/short stories/texts), but also the implications of the work studied. This means that beyond factual knowledge and the ability to sum up the plot and characterization, you must demonstrate that you can see what the author/s is/are implying through the choices made.

Furthermore, you will need to consider the aspect that you will discuss, in other words the focus that you will bring to the work. You will have to show that you have understood this focus thoroughly and have mastered it conceptually.

● **Examiner's hints**
Whenever you consider doing a presentation on a work of literature, make 100 per cent sure that you have understood it yourself before you launch into the activity.

To access worksheet 7.0 – an example of how you could go about Exercise 1 – please visit www.pearsonbacconline.com and follow the on-screen instructions.

EXERCISE 1

As a short practice exercise for the kind of work you need to do to get good marks for this criterion, look at the poem below and answer the following questions:

William Butler Yeats, 'The Second Coming' (1919)

> Turning and turning in the widening gyre
> The falcon cannot hear the falconer;
> Things fall apart; the centre cannot hold;
> Mere anarchy is loosed upon the world,
> The blood-dimmed tide is loosed, and everywhere   5

The ceremony of innocence is drowned;
The best lack all conviction, while the worst
Are full of passionate intensity.

Surely some revelation is at hand;
Surely the Second Coming is at hand.   10
The Second Coming! Hardly are those words out
When a vast image out of Spiritus Mundi
Troubles my sight: a waste of desert sand;
A shape with lion body and the head of a man,
A gaze blank and pitiless as the sun,   15
Is moving its slow thighs, while all about it
Wind shadows of the indignant desert birds.

The darkness drops again but now I know
That twenty centuries of stony sleep
Were vexed to nightmare by a rocking cradle,   20
And what rough beast, its hour come round at last,
Slouches towards Bethlehem to be born?

QUESTIONS

1   Sum up the overall meaning of this poem in a few sentences to show that you have understood its central themes.

2   Define those lines that need to be explained in detail to show that you have really come to grips with the poem.

3   What would you say are the implications of the poem? What is Yeats suggesting about the human condition through this poem?

Student answer 1

The Second Coming is a description of an apocalyptic scene where religious and mythological images of animals are used to suggest that we are approaching the end of the world. The poet is saying that the second coming of Christ is at hand but seems to be implying in the last stanza that the world is to be awakened from some sort of sleep.

Examiner's comments

This answer would probably be situated – roughly – in the 3–4 band of the assessment criteria: 'There is some knowledge and superficial understanding of the content of the work(s) presented.' The description is not very detailed and there is little elaboration on the points made. Furthermore, the response is tentative ('seems to') and does not bring us to any affirmative statements. The understanding is superficial because clearly there is a more subtle and nuanced undertone to the poem than the idea of the end of the world. The student needs to take it further.

Student answer 2

The Second Coming was written directly after the First World War and can be read as a spiritual, symbolic expression of angst at the future of mankind after this terrible event in world history. This overshadows much of the imagery, tone and symbolism of the poem. Yeats plays with two Christian symbols (Bethlehem – the birthplace of Christ and the very reference to the Second Coming from the book of the Apocalypse where it is stated that Jesus will return to earth at the end of the world). However, he implies that the Antichrist will precede that second coming with the disturbing image of a slouching 'rough beast'. The references to anarchy and the idea of the widening gyre have specific resonance in Yeats' world, as they relate to his ideas about history being like a vortex, or gyre, and the anarchical sentiment that prevailed in many European countries including Ireland leading up to the First World War. The image of the falcon no longer hearing the falconer indicates a lack of unity and cogency in society. This is echoed in the lines 'the centre cannot hold' and the image of the sphinx-like chimera that lives out its duality in a disharmonious grotesqueness. With references to blood and drowning on the one hand and the desert and a pitiless sun on the other, Yeats creates a tone of solemn anguish and distress. Overall the poem, using the first person narrative to mirror the apocalyptic scene in a highly dramatic scene of personal crisis, is a statement about humanity losing its direction utterly and veering towards destruction.

● **Examiner's hints**

This example is quite academic and gives you an idea of the level of analysis that you might wish to consider. It would need to be presented in a lively, creative manner in the oral presentation.

Examiner's comments

Here is a paragraph that would reach in the top mark for Criterion A: 9–10 'There is excellent knowledge and understanding of the content and the implications of the work(s) presented.' The description is thorough and affirmative and shows clear knowledge and understanding of the poem. We learn about various nuances in the poem and the speaker is willing to go into some detail to explain the overall significance of it.

SUMMARY

Criterion A requires you to show that you have mastered two things: knowledge and understanding of the text or texts on which you are presenting. To show knowledge you need to be able to go into considerable detail about the structure, language and meaning of the text, and for understanding you must show that you have considered the implications, subtleties and nuances of the meaning. Criterion A requires thorough substantiation and illustration.

Criterion B: Presentation

How much attention has been given to making the delivery effective and appropriate to the presentation?

To what extent are strategies used to interest the audience (for example, audibility, eye contact, gesture, effective use of supporting material)?

Marks	Level descriptor
0	The work does not reach a standard described by the descriptors below.
1–2	Delivery of the presentation is seldom appropriate, with little attempt to interest the audience.
3–4	Delivery of the presentation is sometimes appropriate, with some attempt to interest the audience.
5–6	Delivery of the presentation is appropriate, with a clear intention to interest the audience.
7–8	Delivery of the presentation is effective, with suitable strategies used to interest the audience.
9–10	Delivery of the presentation is highly effective, with purposeful strategies used to interest the audience.

Criterion B is also worth 10 points. In other words it is equally weighted with Criterion A. What you are being assessed on here is your ability to present material in a coherent, cogent, articulate manner. Because this is an oral exercise, there is an added need for liveliness and audience response that must be taken into account. As you can see from looking at the assessment criteria, the marks are given for more than appropriate structure, but also 'strategies' that interest the viewers.

Structure

For a presentation to be effective, it must have a discernible structure, even if it is a creative piece of work. Remember that you are trying to get a point across and you should not become so caught up in the nuts and bolts of the presentation that you lose sight of this goal.

A useful exercise is visualizing where you want to take the presentation. Think of the text(s) you are studying in Part 4, on which you are going to do your presentation. Narrow your ideas down to the theme or the character that you will be talking about. Now close your eyes and ask yourself: what exactly do you want to get across, what is your argument? You should be able to come up with a sentence or two that sums up the core principle of your presentation. For example: 'The work is a play by Shakespeare; the character is the protagonist; what I want to show my audience is that the character is in love with himself.'

The point or points that you are trying to get across will be your argument, and this argument will drive the main body of your presentation. You will come back to your argument frequently as the presentation unfolds, to give your presentation a clear message for the audience.

Linking devices

Between each new point you make in the presentation, you should use a structural linking device, so that there is some natural flow and continuity to your piece. Your presentation should look for a continuation of the same idea or effect from one point to the next or, if not, a clear contrast.

Good linking devices to start off each point:

Continuity
- 'Continuing with the theme of . . . , the use of metaphors in the extract/poem creates a similar effect.'
- 'Not only is the theme of death highlighted by the use of punctuation, but also through the use of objectification.'
- 'Similar to the effect created by the tone, a grotesque effect is created by the use of imagery.'

Contrast
- 'While the use of symbolism contributes to the overall theme of love, the use of syntax points in a quite different direction.'
- 'Conversely, the use of similes creates a quite different effect on the reader.'
- 'If the tone of the poem suggests that ambition is a fundamentally negative human attribute, the atmosphere connotes far more positive ideas of success, drive and will-power.'

Start planning your presentation by working out the 'destination' where you want to take your audience and planning the steps back to the beginning. This way you can ensure that your presentation develops purposefully.

Think of the linking devices that you can employ during your individual oral presentation; like the objects shown here, you are looking for balance, interlocking patterns, and a central structure from which your points are developed.

Strategies

You need to think about the strategies listed in the assessment criteria (audibility, eye contact, gesture, effective use of supporting material) and how you will integrate these into your presentation to make it successful. The following list of tips and ideas might be of use:

Audibility

- Find the person farthest away from you in the room and pretend that you are speaking to him or her. That way you can be sure that everyone in the room can hear you.
- Speak slowly. Most people speak too quickly in public and do not realize it. You would do well to speak in a deliberate, steady manner with short pauses between full stops.
- Make sure that you lift your head up and face your audience when you speak, so that you are not speaking to the floor or into your chest.

Eye contact and gesture

- Try to make eye contact with the whole class, including the teacher, at some point in your presentation. It makes you more credible and dramatic.
- Avoid reading an entire text from a piece of paper or index cards. You should have rehearsed your spoken parts enough to direct most of it at the audience.
- Body language is important, as through it you communicate with your audience subliminally. Without realizing it, you are saying quite a lot with your hand gestures and postures, so that aspect is worth thinking about.
- Avoid pointing at people – it is aggressive and rude.
- Do not stand with your hands limp on either side of you, as it makes you appear passive.
- Use your hands creatively to suggest patterns, processes and ideas.
- Try to move around the room a little and not stand in one place for the entire length of the presentation. Of course, you should not overdo movement, as this could have an irritating and distracting effect.

Effective use of supporting material

- Try to find more creative ways of presenting your work than through PowerPoint. If you are using PowerPoint, the slides should feature mostly diagrams and images (not text) to stimulate further ideas and associations in your audience.

- If you are considering using audiovisual material, then be sure to keep it short and relevant. Before the presentation, practise using the technology – you do not want to waste time by sorting out problems during the presentation itself.
- Consider using artwork, posters, diagrams and charts if you feel that these can advance your presentation well. Make sure that if you are using visual material, it clarifies a point or makes visible a process that would be cumbersome to put in words.

Think of your presentation as a ladder: your aim is to take the audience to the top of it step by step.

EXERCISE 2

Act out!

With a friend or friends, act out what your think a poor presentation would look like. This should reinforce what you must do to make your presentation successful. Make a note of your strengths so that you utilise them effectively when giving your oral presentation.

GLOBAL PERSPECTIVES

Some types of body language are culturally insensitive. Avoid those that might offend your listeners – for example, beckoning with a forefinger, pointing, showing the palm of an open hand, using the thumbs-up sign or indicating a circle with your thumb touching your index finger.

SUMMARY

Criterion B is looking at two essential aspects of your presentation: the structure and the strategies you use to enhance your work. Strategies refers to the way you communicate with your audience in terms of voice projection, body language, eye contact and the use of extra materials. There is more on this at the end of the 'Appreciation' section of this chapter.

Criterion C: Language

How clear and appropriate is the language?

How well is the register and style suited to the choice of presentation? ('Register' refers, in this context, to the student's use of elements such as vocabulary, tone, sentence structure and terminology appropriate to the presentation.)

Marks	Level descriptor
0	The work does not reach a standard described by the descriptors below.
1–2	The language is rarely appropriate, with a very limited attempt to suit register and style to the choice of presentation.
3–4	The language is sometimes appropriate, with some attempt to suit register and style to the choice of presentation.
5–6	The language is mostly clear and appropriate, with some attention paid to register and style that is suited to the choice of presentation.
7–8	The language is clear and appropriate, with register and style consistently suited to the choice of presentation.
9–10	The language is very clear and entirely appropriate, with register and style consistently effective and suited to the choice of presentation.

In this assessment criterion, weighted equally with the previous two we looked at, your powers of expression will be assessed according to their clarity, appropriateness, register and style.

The oral presentation is a formal task for which you have had time to prepare, so you are expected to speak well. You should command a technical, formal style of language that nonetheless allows you to get your points across powerfully and simply.

To access worksheet 7.1 – a response to and analysis of Exercise 3 – please visit www. pearsonbacconline.com and follow the on-screen instructions.

EXERCISE 3

Language appropriate to the presentation

Place the following words on the spectrum ranging from appropriate to inappropriate:

Appropriate --- Inappropriate

- Lousy
- Excellent
- Tempestuous
- Grotesque
- Transformative
- Brilliant
- Transcendent

Some words should never feature in an oral presentation at this level, as they are too informal and have no technical resonance. Anything that resembles slang, colloquial language or informal register should be avoided. Here is a list of some of those words that students commonly use, and that you should avoid:

- Horrible
- Scary
- Crazy
- Mad
- Guy
- People
- Thing
- Stuff
- Nice
- Super
- Great
- Amazing
- A lot
- Loads of

Can you think of more?

Verbal ticks such as 'kind of' and 'like' can get in the way of formal expression and should be eradicated from your speech when you are presenting formally. Similarly, too many 'ums' can be distracting. We are not robots, though, and teachers understand this, so do not panic too much if you hear yourself slipping into verbal ticks, but remember that they are something to be avoided.

We looked at different types of register in Chapter 4. Consider the table below – it shows some examples of informal (inappropriate) register and formal (appropriate) register for a presentation:

● **Examiner's hints**
The literary essay and commentary tend to be composed in the simple present tense. The same goes for the oral presentation. Speak about characters as if they were living people to make your appreciation more mature and immediate.

INFORMAL INAPPROPRIATE REGISTER	FORMAL APPROPRIATE REGISTER
The main character is angry most of the time. He hates women and beats up his wife. I really don't like him.	The main character exudes a violent tension throughout the majority of the novel. His misogynistic tendencies lead him to brutalize his wife, and hence the reader is distanced from him.
The scene is totally out there with all sorts of stuff going on in the background. It's kind of freaky and the people described are all scary.	The author creates a surrealistic atmosphere intensified by a flurry of seemingly chaotic instances that serve as backdrop. The effect created is somewhat sinister and the inhabitants of this strange setting are for the most part disturbing.
The story goes round in circles; the last chapter is like the next but with some different details each time.	The plot is constructed cyclically with each chapter interlocking with the next by covering the same material but with a slightly different angle in each instance.

SUMMARY

Style (use of language) can be broken down into lexis, register, grammatical construction and spelling. You need to remain formal, technical and literary to reach into the higher marks on this criterion. Avoid verbal ticks and colloquialisms.

> **Lexis**
> 'Lexis' is a technical term for vocabulary. When we say 'lexical field' we are referring to the vocabulary used by an author in a given text.

Appreciation
Types of presentation

Now that we have looked at the learning outcomes of the oral presentation, and the way that it is assessed, let's turn to the type of presentation you might want to consider.

Start with the main objective of your presentation: what is it you want to achieve? Once you have a clear idea of this goal, the style of presentation that you choose will make more sense to you. For instance, imagine you want to go into depth discussing a character. In this case you might choose role play to dramatize certain aspects of the character's personality. A 'Socratic dialogue' or 'Socratic method' (where a question-and-answer structure is used to elaborate on a topic) might lend itself well to handling an ethical dilemma of conflict in the texts, and would effectively engage your audience.

EXERCISE 4

Considering different types of presentation

Below are some examples of presentation type given in the English A subject guide, with some suggestions for their use. Think about each of them in turn, asking how they would suit the objectives of the presentation you might be considering and how you could apply them imaginatively.

A critique of the student's own writing that has been produced in the style of one of the literary genres studied

For this presentation type, you could take what you have learned about a specific genre and reproduce it through a piece of creative writing. You could write a poem, scene from a play, fictional piece or non-fiction text (an essay or speech, for example). Once you have composed your creative piece, you could use it in the presentation to exercise your analytical skills by interpreting the creative work, explaining the use of literary features, the effects created and connotations evoked. Your presentation would be a critical examination of your own work!

Example: Imagine you have studied the sonnets of William Shakespeare. You would write your own sonnet using Shakespeare's style, structure and imagery. After reading the poem to the class and letting your peers view the poem, you would analyze the poem's literary features, themes and general message, in the same way you would in a Paper 1 answer. Questions and answers at the end of the presentation would allow you to elaborate on the exercise and why you chose certain approaches, how they echo Shakespeare's style and so on.

An explanation of a particular aspect of an author's work

Here you would focus on a specific aspect of a writer's work and examine it in great detail, showing in-depth understanding and appreciation. This type of presentation would give you an opportunity to investigate your subject in a cohesive and specific manner. 'Particular aspect' could mean literary features, plot and/or style, or something thematic. It may be that you wish to look at the way your author or authors use imagery, tone, symbolism, characterization, metaphor, mood, time or plot. Alternatively, you could tackle something broader and more philosophical, such as the way that he or she treats themes such as death, love, youth, jealousy, hatred, ambition, nostalgia, the past, appearance versus reality, and so on.

Example: Imagine that you have studied a novel and noticed that the author has a predilection for the colour yellow. You have charted the way that the colour is used and what it seems to represent. After taking note of all of the instances where the colour is mentioned and analyzing how and why it is used, you could present on the symbolism of the colour yellow in the work.

The examination of a particular interpretation of a work

● **Examiner's hint**
Remember that personal response and personal engagement are crucial in determining a good English oral presentation. If you start to look at existing schools of literary criticism, make sure that you do not merely duplicate those ideas. You will have to integrate the main ideas and then use them in your own original way during the presentation.

The extent to which you have studied existing interpretations of works depends on the way that your course is being taught. If you find you are fascinated by an established critical approach, and you want to take it further, then ask for advice about different schools of literary criticism. By placing different interpretative grids on a work you will yield varying and distinctive interpretations. You might want to consider Marxist, feminist and/or postcolonial interpretations. Once you have looked through some of these schools you could choose to elaborate on one of them, making the presentation personal and lively.

Literary criticism
A school of literary criticism is an established way of approaching literature. For example, a 'Marxist school' will emphasize socio-economics and the means of production (who has financial control) in a text, while a 'feminist school' will look at gender and the treatment of women (for example, a feminist reading of Shakespeare's *Hamlet* will focus, critically, on the way that Gertrude and Ophelia are viewed from a chauvinistic male perspective). The 'postcolonial school' looks at power relations within the context of colonialism, discussing alternative power sites of discourse and meaning (for example, Caliban in *The Tempest* or the character of Othello will be viewed as outsiders in a politically repressive structure).

Example: The table below gives you a quick idea of how Albert Camus' *The Outsider* could be viewed through different reading grids:

MARXIST	FEMINIST	POSTCOLONIAL
Meursault represents the subaltern. He is not in control of the mode of production (he needs to ask permission from his boss to miss work) and belongs to a disempowered proletarian class, seconded by other proletarians like Raymond and Salamano. His trial is a display of the power of religion and economics over the individual: he is fettered by the discourse and cannot emancipate himself from it through any other way than death.	Meursault is a male chauvinist who has little regard for his mother or girlfriend, Marie. He objectifies Marie and has total disregard for her views. Furthermore, Camus presents women in an almost consistently negative light, ranging from the 'little woman' in Céleste's café to the noseless Arab nurse in the morgue. Women do not have a real voice in *The Outsider* and their sole spokesperson, Marie, is superficial and something of a cliché of the light-headed girl.	Camus treats the 'Other' (the Arab) with fear and distrust. As is the case in Joseph Conrad's *Heart of Darkness*, natives are given no voice whatsoever in *The Outsider* and the killing of the Arab on the beach by Meursault is a subconscious act anchoring his colonialist views forcibly and aggressively. The fact that the Arab's death is by-passed during the trial shows how deeply ingrained this colonialist mindset is: the Arab is expendable and of secondary importance.

The interpretation of a work of art can easily be taken for granted, but with careful reflection you will realize that interpretation often comes from a certain established set of beliefs and discourses.

The setting of a particular writer's work against another body of material, for example, details on social background or political views

Here is a chance for you to expand your knowledge and understanding of a text by setting it in the context of its historical or social background. This approach can help the reader appreciate the subtleties of the work in greater detail. There are a number of ways of going about this. Here are some ideas:

OBJECTIVE	STRATEGY
Explore a theme in a work set against a contemporaneous political movement (revolution, protest, wave of reform, etc.).	Make a poster summing up the main points for consideration in the political movement. Present on the theme in the work studied with this poster in mind, making references to it and drawing parallels when and where appropriate.
Appreciate a passage from a work with reference to the specific socio-economic climate of the time (for example, a passage from Steinbeck's novel *The Grapes of Wrath* in relation to the Great Depression).	Role Play: pretend that you are someone suffering through the Great Depression. Read the passage and comment on it with facts and figures pertaining to the Great Depression that you have extracted from a properly referenced source.
Look at a character in a play in terms of the social hierarchy of the time (for instance, the role of Tiresias the blind prophet in Sophocles' Oedipus the King and Antigone).	Map out a pyramid representing the social hierarchy at the time. This can be a visual support (electronic slide, poster, sketch, model) or, if there are many of you in the group, a specifically organized spatial arrangement (students standing in the order of the character's importance, forming a triangle and so on). The visual aid or configuration of speakers would be referenced with sources and would be used to support points in the presentation itself.
A deeper understanding of the cultural setting when presenting on a particular theme within a work.	A short oral summary of an anthropological or historical study. Distribute the summary to the audience for further cross-referencing during a formal oral presentation.
Insights into a philosophical debate at the time the work was written, and how this debate relates to the topic on which you are presenting.	Class debate: divide the group into two sides of the debate (for instance, pro- and anti-abolitionists), and get them to cross-examine you on your presentation once you have finished, each side posing questions from their respective perspectives.

GLOBAL PERSPECTIVES

Presenting on a work can become a rich, far-reaching experience if you decide to examine your theme within a social, political, historical or cultural setting.

A commentary on the use of a particular image, idea or symbol in one text or in a writer's work

Here you would use your close-reading skills, developed in Paper 1 and Part 2, to look at a passage in great detail, elaborating on the chosen image, idea or symbol so as to make interesting connections and creative associations.

Example: You could chart the development of a symbol through the work (an object, action, colour, animal or natural element) to show how it develops and gives depth to the text. You might consider a motif and present on its overall significance.

To remind yourself about the key skills involved in close reading, look at Chapter 5 again and reflect on how you could use this skill in an oral presentation.

A performance or a pastiche of a poem being studied – this activity should be followed by some explanation and discussion of what the student attempted to do

The idea with this exercise is to transpose the meaning of the poem into a performance. Remember that you will not be assessed on your acting style but on the validity and creativity of your ideas and what your pastiche is saying about the text:

Pastiche
An artistic work in a style that imitates that of another work, artist or period.

To access worksheet 7.2 – an example of how you could go about Exercise 5 – please visit www.pearsonbacconline.com and follow the on-screen instructions.

EXERCISE 5

Stretching into non-verbal signs

Look at the following poem, read through it a few times and reflect on the kind of performance or pastiche you would give to bring across the feelings, connotations and ideas it evokes. Try to go beyond merely acting out the action. Convert it into a physical symbol that expresses its main meaning in different ways; for example, you could dance the poem or use body movements to express the way the energy of the poem grows and changes. Once you have finished the performance, you will need to explain it through a short but purposeful rationale, so that the audience can appreciate its point.

Samuel Taylor Coleridge, 'Kubla Khan or, a Vision in a Dream: A Fragment' (1816)

In Xanadu did Kubla Khan
  A stately pleasure-dome decree:
Where Alph, the sacred river, ran
Through caverns measureless to man
  Down to a sunless sea.   5
So twice five miles of fertile ground
With walls and towers were girdled round:
And there were gardens bright with sinuous rills,
Where blossomed many an incense-bearing tree;
And here were forests ancient as the hills,   10
Enfolding sunny spots of greenery.

But oh! that deep romantic chasm which slanted
Down the green hill athwart a cedarn cover!
A savage place! as holy and enchanted
As e'er beneath a waning moon was haunted   15
By woman wailing for her demon-lover!
And from this chasm, with ceaseless turmoil seething,

As if this earth in fast thick pants were breathing,
A mighty fountain momently was forced:
Amid whose swift half-intermitted burst   20
Huge fragments vaulted like rebounding hail,
Or chaffy grain beneath the thresher's flail:
And 'mid these dancing rocks at once and ever
It flung up momently the sacred river.
Five miles meandering with a mazy motion   25
Through wood and dale the sacred river ran,
Then reached the caverns measureless to man,
And sank in tumult to a lifeless ocean:
And 'mid this tumult Kubla heard from far
Ancestral voices prophesying war!   30

    The shadow of the dome of pleasure
    Floated midway on the waves;
    Where was heard the mingled measure
    From the fountain and the caves.
It was a miracle of rare device,   35
A sunny pleasure-dome with caves of ice!

    A damsel with a dulcimer
    In a vision once I saw:
    It was an Abyssinian maid,
    And on her dulcimer she played,   40
    Singing of Mount Abora.
    Could I revive within me
    Her symphony and song,
    To such a deep delight 'twould win me,
That with music loud and long,   45
I would build that dome in air,
That sunny dome! those caves of ice!
And all who heard should see them there,
And all should cry, Beware! Beware!
His flashing eyes, his floating hair!   50
Weave a circle round him thrice,
And close your eyes with holy dread,
For he on honey-dew hath fed,
And drunk the milk of Paradise.

A comparison of two passages, two characters or two works

The key word here is 'comparison'. Make sure that you have thought through how you will compare and contrast the characters or passages so that what you have to say is balanced, incisive and relevant. If you are comparing two main characters, protagonists, antagonists or minor characters, make sure that there are solid points of comparison before you launch into your preparation and that you will not find yourself trying to compare apples with pears!

Characters
In the chapter on fiction, we looked at major and minor characters in direct and indirect ways. Another dimension of character to consider is the idea of the protagonist (the character who drives the plot forward) and the antagonist (the character who gets in the way of the protagonist and tries to foul his or her plans). Take note that the protagonist is not necessarily the 'goody' and the antagonist is not necessarily the 'baddy'.

Example: The main character of one of Shakespeare's plays (*Othello* or *Macbeth* for instance) could hardly be compared to a minor character in a novel who only appears for a few pages – this would create an unhelpful asymmetry.

Likewise, if you are going to compare and contrast two passages, make sure that they are of equal or near-equal significance or structure. For example, you might want to compare the beginnings or endings of two works, or two passages that are both turning points. An interesting exercise is to compare two different passages from different works that discuss the same object, phenomenon or theme. This can allow you to make a transition into a comparative analysis of the two authors' styles.

A commentary on a passage from a work studied in class, which has been prepared at home

For this presentation you would want to showpiece your commentary in such a way that the audience appreciates what you set out to do and how you achieved it.

Example: This presentation involves a written and possibly visual commentary on the text; the text could be marked up with colour-coding, marginalia, explanatory notes and the use of arrows, underlining and circling. Rather than repeat what you said in your commentary, you would complement it with your oral presentation, explaining and elaborating on your own written work. Answering questions after the delivery will put you on the spot, so make sure that you have de-briefed yourself thoroughly on the commentary before you present!

One of the advantages of this exercise is that it allows you to strengthen your written commentary skills and teaches you to reflect on your work. You are learning about learning as well as presenting on a subject, reflecting on the process as well as the product.

An account of the student's developing response to a work

This is a highly creative opportunity for you to take the idea of 'learning about learning' even further, not only by considering the text but the way that your appreciation has changed over time.

Example: There are numerous ways of doing this presentation. You could start by creating a type of diary or reading log that you would fill in as you read the work(s), and which would form the basis of your presentation. Alternatively you could take your reading experience and transpose it into a short sketch, piece of creative writing, internal monologue or conversation between two people (perhaps one person representing the 'early you' when you started reading the book, and the second person representing you as the more mature and informed reader).

The main element to retain is that the presentation should still allow you to show good knowledge and understanding of the work(s), while using a structured, cohesive approach and formal language. Because of this, you would need to think through the right balance to strike between personal response, creative and expressive ideas and formal analysis.

The presentation of two opposing readings of a work

There are a number of ways of looking at a text. The creative student of literature will be able to offer two readings that contradict one another, but which are still equally viable because of the quality of argument and substantiation behind each of them.

Example:
Consider the famous lines from Samuel Johnson:

> I put my hat upon my head,
> I walked into the Strand,
> And there I met another man
> Whose hat was in his hand.

One interpretation is to say that this is a parody of the simple-minded poet: the rather puerile rhyming scheme, simplistic diction and quasi-meaningless imagery are mocking the bad poet, whose writing is invariably childish and dull. A contrasting reading is to say that in fact the poem is deceptively simple – in reality it underscores a deep philosophical question: the man who puts his hat upon his head before he goes out is protecting himself from the elements and trying to separate himself from the world (the Strand in London is a symbol of the last reaches of life before the infinite ocean of death). The man who places his hat in his hand is stripping himself of that protection and opening himself up to fate and the elements. Johnson suggests that these are the only important types in the composition of humanity: those who accept and those who do not.

There is a golden opportunity to do something very dramatic here: you could oppose the two readings in the form of a Socratic dialogue, or a staged debate or argument, or through a piece of art representing the essential elements of the two opposing readings and so on. Alternatively, you could consider a more formal, sober approach.

Even if you choose not to consider this suggestion, thinking through any work in terms of opposing readings is a healthy exercise, because it opens your mind and allows you to think 'outside the box'.

 How do claims and counter-claims about a single subject help to build up knowledge and make it stronger?

A monologue or dialogue by a character at an important point in the work

If you undertake this type of presentation, you will be showing your knowledge and understanding of character by immersing yourself in the character's thoughts and feelings: you should replicate the tone, style, diction, register, but above all the mind processes of the character you have chosen, so that your portrayal is as authentic and convincing as possible.

179

The monologue should reflect upon a particularly important moment in the life of the character. This type of presentation will give you the opportunity to be extremely creative and dramatic. The question-and-answer session after the presentation would also help you explain what you wanted to demonstrate in the character via the monologue.

Reminiscences by a character from a point in later life

Similar to the presentation described above, this activity is an empathic exercise that will give you the chance to show sensitive appreciation of a character's inner thoughts and feelings. The fact that the thoughts would be reminiscences from a point later in life puts a slightly different angle on things, because you will be projecting the character to a time beyond that of the text. You need to anticipate how the character would have grown and changed between the two points in time, and how the future character still connects with the textual character.

Examples:

Some ideas could include:

- A character who has come back from death as a ghost.
- A character who has entered another work (for example, Macbeth features in a poem).
- A character's behaviour and thoughts after the end of the work.
- A character who has retired from the action of the plot and looks back at it with serene, detached wisdom.
- A character who finally confesses how he or she has felt towards someone else in the work of literature, if those feelings were not stated in the work, or those feelings were repressed or not communicated. This perspective could give you an interesting way into the relationships in a work and the inner workings of the character's mind.

An author's reaction to a particular interpretation of elements of his or her work in a given context (for example, a critical defence of the work against a charge of subversion, or immorality, before a censorship board)

Madame Bovary
In 1856 Gustave Flaubert and his editors were put on trial for the publication of his famous novel *Madame Bovary*. The work was seen to be morally offensive.

Use the full range of your imagination for the oral presentation.

The idea here is to show your sensitivity and understanding of an author's predicament by putting yourself in his or her shoes and defending the text against accusations or adverse interpretations. Naturally the type of presentation that you deliver and the dramatization that you concoct will depend to a larger extent on the work studied. Many works of literature have been published under a cloud of controversy, and court cases against works deemed immoral that are now seen as great works of literature were common in the 19th century (Gustave Flaubert, Thomas Hardy, Charles Baudelaire and D.H. Lawrence are just some prominent examples of authors who have experienced legal action).

If you choose an option like this one for your oral presentation, you will need to refer to the original work extensively to show knowledge and understanding, while appreciating literary features and themes. Be sure to think this type of presentation through carefully and to ask for advice from your teacher. It can be difficult to project your thoughts into the author, for in the study of literature we tend to look at the meaning of the text on the page, rather than assuming we know what the author meant.

The cultural setting of the work(s) and related issues

For this type of presentation, you need to be sure that you have a firm grip on the cultural setting of the works. It can be easy to fall into clichés about culture, and without careful consideration you could end up doing a presentation that is a superficial account of something that is, in reality, far more complex.

The superficial side of culture can be summed up with the famous 'five Fs': folklore, fashion, food, flags and festivities. Deeper beneath the surface you have more nuanced realities such as cosmology, notions of time, work ethic, the role of the family and so on. Consider the diagram of the 'cultural iceberg' below. Reflect on how you could look at your Part 4 works by reflecting not only on the visible sides of culture that are 'in awareness' but also those that are 'out of awareness':

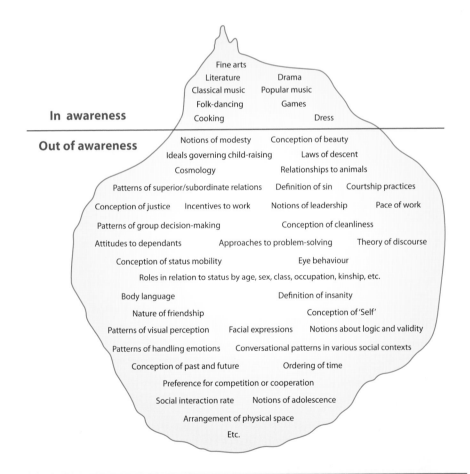

◀ Example of the depth of culture

It would be a good idea to do some careful research on the cultural setting of a work before presenting on it, so make sure that you look through some books, websites and other sources of information and give those references in your presentation.

Thematic focus

Many presentations will focus on a theme, and there are obviously many to choose from. Thematic presentations should focus on something simple that can be presented in a structured and coherent way. Make sure that you do not overload yourself with too many themes: it is probably best sticking to just one.

Using a spider diagram can be a good way of mind-mapping all of the different themes in a work. Here's an example:

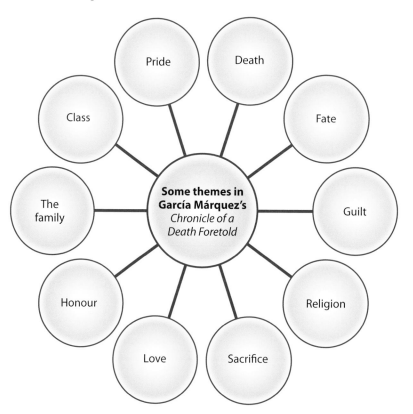

Once you have chosen a theme, break it down into more specific elements, so that you will be treating it in sufficient detail and with enough subtlety. For example, imagine you were to choose religion as your theme; you could break that down as follows:

*Religion – The Roman Catholic Church – Pagan rites of sacrifice –
Social pressure to conform to religious pressures – The façade
of church-goers pretending to believe – Hypocrisy.*

The next step would be to arrange these ideas into a pattern to illustrate the ways in which they interlock. For instance, in *Chronicle of a Death Foretold*, the overarching idea is that, on the one hand, there is a strong contrast between the societal façade of the Roman Catholic Church, which brings with it honour, face values and conformity, while on the other there is the visceral, sacrifice-based pagan urge of the group that is raw and cannot be hidden through the killing of Santiago Nasar.

In thematic presentations use plenty of examples to substantiate points, and when you think of a theme you should immediately think of a symbol, or symbols, that evoke your theme and through which the theme is represented in the work(s) studied. To give an example, going back to the list of themes suggested in *Chronicle of a Death Foretold*, you could map out symbols for each in this way:

THEMES	SYMBOLS
Death	The white linen clothes Santiago Nasar wears; the twins' knives
Fate	The medal of the Virgin that Santiago Nasar swallows as a child; the flash-forward dreams
Guilt	The smell of blood that haunts the twins
Religion	The bishop, and the paddler he arrives on; the coxcomb soup
Sacrifice	The sacrificial altar in the Vicario house
Honour	The Vicario household with the whitewashed walls; the unopened letters of Bayardo San Román

EXERCISE 6

Mind-mapping themes

Using the text you are thinking of presenting on in Part 4, work through its themes, seeing how many you can map out. Provide corresponding symbols and page numbers where the theme is mentioned or evoked.

Characterization

Presentations on characters in works of literature are common. There are a number of ways you could go about them, from a formal exposé to empathy exercises such as role play, skits, visual representations of the character and so on.

Examples:

Some of the key ideas that you could consider in a presentation on character, other than those mentioned in the fiction and drama chapters in this book, could include:

- How the character develops throughout the work.
- Key passages that exemplify the character's ideas and values.
- The relationships that the character has with others in the work. Here you could consider an entire presentation on a relationship as in 'the Macbeth/Lady Macbeth relationship' or 'the Othello/Iago relationship', but the emphasis would be less on the individual characters than on the way that they interact.
- A specific aspect of a character's personality, for example, his or her view of fate, freedom or family.
- Something that the character does repeatedly that seems to have a symbolic significance: the way he or she eats, dreams, has sex, works or uses space.
- Some key physical attribute of the character that is significant (e.g. a limp, wound, facial feature).

Whatever slant you choose, remember that character is complex and there is no end to the amount of specificity and detail you can go into to arrive at an original and thought-provoking conclusion.

In the 15th century, the French satirist Rabelais depicted one of his key characters, Gargantua, as an obese giant representing the excessively dogmatic and power-ridden ways of the Middle Ages.

Techniques and style

One of the distinctive elements of looking at technique and/or style when presenting on a work is that it forces you to consider specific literary features, rather than broader thematic content. Here are some of them:

LINGUISTIC FEATURES

Allusion: Indirect suggestion

Caesura: Dividing a line (usually of poetry with punctuation)

Chosism or Objectification: When a human or animal becomes an object

Connotation: Association or inference – when something connotes something else it *suggests* it, rather than states it emphatically

Denotation: Showing or naming something directly

Enjambment (or run-on line): When a clause runs from one line to the next without punctuation

Euphemism: Making something negative sound better, more positive (e.g. 'He passed away.')

Hyperbole: Exaggeration

Juxtaposition: When two things are set alongside one another so as to create a strong contrast

Litotes: Not saying what it is, but what it is not (e.g. 'That was not bad!')

Metonymy: When the part represents the whole (i.e. 'the crown' represents the monarchy)

Oxymoron: Two words of opposite meaning that follow one another: 'icy fire' or 'a dark light'

Personification: When a non-human subject is described as a human or when a human is described as an animal

Simile: Comparison using 'like' or 'as'

Syllepsis: A figure of speech in which a word is applied to two others in different senses, e.g. 'The runner hit the car and the limits of his endurance at the same time.'

Symbol: Something that represents something else

Synaesthesia: Giving a colour a sound, or a sound a smell, or a smell a temperature …

Sound:

  Alliteration: Repetition of consonants at the beginning of two or more successive words

  Anadiplosis: The repetition of a word at the end of one clause and the beginning of the following clause.

  Anaphora: Repetition of a word or phrase at the beginning of different clauses

  Assonance: Repetition of vowels

  Consonance: repetition of particular sounds, especially consonants

  Epizeuxis: Incremental repetition ('never, never, never …')

  Onomatopoeia: When the word sounds like the thing it is describing (e.g. 'bang')

  Stressed/unstressed syllables

STRUCTURAL FEATURES

Akoustikon: Sound effects

Anagnorisis: 'Recognition': discovery or understanding of an important event

Analepsis (flashback): When the action jumps back in time (not to be confused with memories)

Catharsis: Emotional release through artistic effects

Climax: A powerful ending

Dénouement: The conclusion

Dialogue

Dramatic irony: When the audience knows something about a character that the character does not

End-stopping: When, in poetry, a line ends with some form of punctuation

Hamartia: A tragic flaw in a character

Hubris: Wanton arrogance/ tempting fate

Irony: When things turn out differently, or are different, to what was expected or what was said

Metre: Combinations of stressed (/) and unstressed (˘) syllables give us what we call metre

  Metrical shape:
  Trochee: /˘ – 'double'
  Iamb: ˘/ – 'to be'
  Spondee: // – 'weekend'
  Anapaest: /˘˘ – 'Washington'
  Dactyl: ˘˘/ – 'Cameroon'

Mise en abyme: Infinite regress – a complex narrative system whereby the work itself is represented by a symbol within it

Monologue

Motif: A recurrent image, symbol or theme

Narrative – First person/Second person/Third person

Narrative intrusion

Narrative unreliability

Nemesis: Retribution

Opsis: What you see on stage

Paradox: Something that seems false and true at the same time

Pathos: Pity or fear

Peripeteia: Change in fortune

Pharmakos: A scapegoat

Plot, progression and pacing

Prolepsis (flash-forward): When the action jumps forward in time (not to be confused with foreshadowing)

Punctuation: Use of semi-colons, colons, commas, full-stops, dashes, exclamation marks, question marks, inverted commas and brackets

Rhyme: There are different types of rhyme, such as:

Slanting rhyme: when words almost rhyme, but not quite

Eye-rhyme: when words rhyme on paper but not when you say them out loud

Internal rhyme: if words rhyme not at the end of each line but within in a line

Rhythm: In poetry, the rhythm of a phrase is created by its use of stressed and unstressed syllables. A stressed syllable is called a beat

Number of beats per line:
Monometer – 1

Dimeter – 2
Trimeter – 3
Tetrameter – 4
Pentameter – 5
Hexameter – 6
Heptameter – 7
Octameter – 8

Setting, tone and atmosphere

Soliloquy: A long monologue that only the audience can hear. Soliloquies tend to express some fundamental theme or argument about the human condition.

Stage directions

Stanza or verse: A unit of poetry. Stanzas are named by the number of lines they contain

Number of lines per stanza:
Couplet: rhyming couplet: 2
Triplet: 3 rhyming
Tercet: 3
Quatrain: 4
Quintain or quintet: 5

Stichomythia: Rapid verbal exchange

EXERCISE 7

If you are thinking of presenting on an author's style, then you would need to spend time deciding how best to label that style. Key questions for consideration would include the following:

- How would you describe the sentence structure? Is it long and complex or terse and incisive?

- Tone is a feature of style. The tone might change throughout, but it may also be that a singular tone pervades the style – is it ironic, sarcastic, bitter, dreamy, sleepy, nostalgic, accusatory?

- The expressive quality of the writing needs to be accounted for – is the author's style surreal, realistic, allegorical, symbolical, philosophical?

Apply these three bullet points to the style of an author you are currently studying.

The author's attitude to particular elements of the works (for example, character(s), subject matter)

For this type of presentation, you would consider the overall statements made about the human condition by the author, and present on the ways that these are communicated in the work. Try to distil the attitude that the author takes to major themes, such as death, love, relationships, religion, power, justice, truth, war, appearance versus reality, freedom, hope, fear, growth, change, space and so on.

Think about the way the characters are portrayed, and what the representations say about the author's perspective on the world. Include minor characters and minority groups who might have escaped the attention of both reader and author – what does their peripheral status say about the authorial position? This type of presentation, for example, could involve

Arundhati Roy

Aleksandr Solzhenitsyn

Ken Saro-Wiwa

Some authors are famous for the strong position they have taken on political issues.

a critical examination of the portrayal of Africans in Joseph Conrad's *Heart of Darkness*, the depiction of women in George Orwell's *1984*, and the representation of men in Jean Rhys's *Wide Sargasso Sea*.

One distinction to be made would be that between the author and the narrator – do not confuse the two. The narrator's blind spots and biases might be included on purpose by the author. Think carefully before you take on this challenging topic for your presentation.

The interpretation of particular elements from different perspectives

This type of presentation allows for creative thinking. Although you look at the work from different angles, you would still need to make sure that you retain a coherent and logical analysis. In other words, try not to employ perspectives that are so eccentric that they are no longer plausible.

Example:

Take Franz Kafka's short story 'The Metamorphosis'. Grigor Samsa wakes up one morning as a giant beetle. There are numerous ways of interpreting this:

1. Grigor is sick. The beetle metaphor is there to suggest the transformative value of his sickness and how it has made him vulnerable to his surroundings.
2. Grigor has become monstrous through the societal expectations placed upon him. His work and family have made him so alien to himself that one morning when he wakes up he is unrecognizable to himself, a beetle. Beetles work very hard, so there is a particular emphasis on the idea of Grigor having worked himself into a monstrosity.
3. Grigor is no longer desired in his workplace and he is no longer wanted at home. The beetle, not a domestic animal but an insect, represents the unwanted stranger in an environment that will not make provision for him.

EXERCISE 8

Look at the Franz Kafka example above. Now choose a text that you have studied, and answer the following questions:

1 Does this work also suggest multiple themes?

2 What are these themes? Make a list of them.

3 Do you think any one theme is more important than the others? Why?

SUMMARY

Whatever style of presentation that you choose, formal or highly creative, be sure to address the assessment criteria through your presentation:

- Illustrate your ideas with salient examples from the text

- Give a rationale for your creative exercise, explaining what it is you are trying to achieve

- Reference any supporting material or factual information that you have used

- Discuss the work or works in enough detail to ensure that you are showing knowledge and understanding

- Cover themes, topics, characters or passages in such a way that you are making points and not merely observing what happens in the text

- Go through your proposed topic or at least the title with your teacher before the presentation, to make sure that you are on the right track and will meet the assessment criteria

- Avoid any hasty generalizations or clichés about the cultural setting or the work as a whole

- Avoid the intentional fallacy, whereby you assume that you know what it is that the author wants to achieve (remember that the messages from the text are those established by the reader)

Planning the presentation and tips for good presenting

Planning

The oral presentation lasts a minimum of 10 minutes and a maximum of 15 minutes. You need to plan your work within these parameters, leaving time at the end for questions. In this period you need to have covered a significant amount of material in an organized and well-expressed manner.

In the English A subject guide we are told that:

> The structure of each oral presentation depends largely on the type of activity selected for the topic. It is the responsibility of the student to select the type of presentation that most effectively enables the objectives of the topic to be realized. Whatever the activity chosen, all presentations must have a coherent structure.
> – IB English Literature A Guide

On the topics of planning and presentation:

> It is expected that students will prepare for their presentation outside class hours. When students have chosen the topic for their presentation it will be their responsibility to:

- select appropriate material for the presentation
- organize the material into a coherent structure

'Breaking it down'
Whenever you are brainstorming a topic for a presentation, try to whittle your topic down to something specific. In this picture you start with the world, but then break it down into regions and continents, and if you can do this then you can break it down more into that which you cannot see but know is there – countries, cities, neighbourhoods, households, rooms, furniture. Keep zooming in!

▼

- choose a means of presentation and delivery that is suited to the activity and topic.
  – IB English Literature A Guide

So the onus is on you to construct something that is tightly structured and pertinent, and you need to work on your presentation outside class time. There are numerous ways of going about the planning of your work and each person has a different strategy. Nonetheless, the following simple steps might be useful for you to consider, as they map out the process in a straightforward manner:

12 easy steps to planning your presentation

1. Decide if you are **working alone or with someone else**, although this decision may have been taken for you. Do not be afraid to work with someone you do not know very well or someone you feel might bring your presentation down. Teamwork can bring you together and ensure a good joint performance.

2. Start off by thinking about the text or work that you are most interested in and about which you **have something to say**. If you are being asked to present on a single text, then think about the aspect of the work that is the most compelling to you. Hopefully something will jump out at you and you will see interesting ways forward for a presentation. It's fairly pointless doing a presentation on something in which you have little interest – your lack of enthusiasm will become apparent to the audience. Above all, you want to enjoy the experience, so make sure that you spend time choosing the right topic or character.

3. Write down the topic you have chosen, look at it and decide how you can make it **more specific**. If you start with a topic or the name of a character, consider which aspect of that topic or character you could talk about. If you have simply written down a theme, then think about one aspect of the theme. For more ideas on how to be specific about a character, see the characterization section of this chapter earlier on page 183.

4. Define **where you want to take the audience**. What will your argument be? What is the knowledge destination of your work? Remember that a character, theme or technique is only a platform from which you make a point that is broader and more philosophical. You can take it further than just focusing on the character himself or herself or the way the author uses a technique. You need to be able to take it to the next level, to explain what the author is saying about the human condition.

5. Now that you have broken down your first idea even more and you have an idea where you want to take it, **run it past your teacher** to see whether he or she thinks this is a viable topic. Make sure that you ask any questions that might be worrying you, so that all is clear before you commit yourself to the presentation topic.

6. If you are working with someone else, make it quite clear **who is doing what**. Groups should demonstrate teamwork, and you will be expected to show the spirit of collegiality as you present, but you need to start off by having a firm idea of what

exactly each of you will be talking about, who will be introducing, who will give the conclusion and how you will go about the main body of your presentation. Will you decide on a presentation that has different speakers entering rapidly one after the other in a sentence-by-sentence fashion? Or will you decide to have one speaker present the first half and another the second? Perhaps there are three of you, in which case you will need to think about having three speakers lead off one another in rapid succession or three separate parts, one per speaker.

7. **Mind map** your presentation either through a diagram, flow chart, story board, summary or skeleton. Have a good idea of how the different pieces interlock. What linking devices will you use; how exactly will your presentation unfold?

8. **Run through all the literary features and textual examples** you will be using for the presentation, and make sure that they are illustrating key points. Remember that concrete illustration is needed, but don't quote more than is necessary to substantiate a point.

9. **Write out your presentation**. Do all of the extra research that might be needed and complete the audiovisual material if you are using any. Write out prompt notes – remember that it is best not to read the entire presentation off a page.

10. **Practise** delivering your presentation, timing it to make sure that your work is not too short or too long. Feel free to make amendments to your plan and/or notes.

11. **Get others to listen to your presentation** – make sure they have the assessment criteria and ask them to give you a grade using the criteria.

12. **Read through your presentation once more, this time against the assessment criteria**. Hopefully you will feel by now that you are worth the top marks!

Tips for good presenting

Beyond the ideas suggested in this chapter under the assessment criteria part of the 'Knowledge and Understanding' section of the chapter, consider the following ten tips:

1. **Know your audience.** Think about how the class and teacher will respond to your presentation. Do not ignore their presence, but try to make it a positive part of what you will do.

2. **Use index cards** or some form of reduced, synthesized material like prompt notes. These will help you avoid a situation in which you are simply reading verbatim from a script.

3. Make sure that you have gone through your presentation enough to have **memorized parts of it** so that the words come to you quickly.

4. **Listen to all subsequent questions very carefully** so that you answer them well.

5. **Avoid poor voice intonation**, in which everything is coming out in a flat, uninspired drone. Try to lift your voice at certain key points and make sure there is a lively variation in the way that you talk.

6. **Avoid a long series of rhetorical questions** – you are there to answer the questions, not ask them!

7. **Face the audience** and try to avoid standing with your back against the wall or in one static space all the time.

8. **Know where to place emphasis.** Identify the moments when you are saying something powerful or original, and make sure that those words come out a bit more slowly and with more emphasis than the others.

9. **Be yourself** and do not put on a staged, contrived performance that will irritate the audience or put them off you and what you have to say.

10. **End with something strong and memorable.**

 Knowledge grows not only through research, investigation and discovery, but also through interaction, discussion, questioning and answering.

SUMMARY

Preparing and delivering your presentation requires careful thinking and planning. Take the time to work through your presentation, thinking critically about the kinds of examples and literary features you will be using to support your argument, and be sure to get someone to listen to a timed rehearsal. Remember that good presentation skills involve dynamic use of voice, body, movement, energy, variety of presentation style, listening and eye contact.

New textualities

In Part 4 which is attached to the individual oral presentation your teacher might take the opportunity to engage you with new textualities. These are new types of writing that expand the traditional boundaries of literature and create different types of text. New textualities make us think about literature in fresh and exciting ways. Some examples of new textualities include the following:

Graphic novels

Graphic novels are an alternative type of literature, in which text and sequential images are brought together. The main difference between the graphic novel and the cartoon or magazine is that it is usually longer and of a more sophisticated standard. Some famous examples of this genre include *Blackmark* and *A Contract with God* by Gil Kane and Archie Goodwin and *The Kingdom* by Jack Katz.

Some examples of prominent graphic novels that are frequently studied as literary texts include *Maus* by Art Spiegelman, an allegorical depiction of the Second World War that

Graphic novels combine images with text, breaking down traditional boundaries between literature and art.

▼

uses mice as representations of Jews and cats to depict Germans. *Maus* was accepted as a great work of literature as soon as it came out in the 1980s, and it even won a Pulitzer Prize for literature, one of the most prestigious recognitions available. Another well-known recent graphic novel is *Persepolis: The Story of a Childhood* by Marjane Satrapi. This work has also been made into a film.

Graphic novels are an expression of the visual age we find ourselves in, where iconographic representation is used to communicate meaning more than text. If you work and present on a graphic novel, then remember that the image is part of how meaning is made and in a sense it is part of the text: you are dealing with the building up of ideas and themes through a dual, integrated voice rather than two separate channels of images and words.

The concept of the symbol and the way that symbols are used is something that shifts somewhat when you are looking at graphic novels due to the emphasis of images.

Hypertext narratives

Hypertext narratives break down more boundaries that we usually associate with literature, as here we go beyond the physical object of the book into a reading experience that takes place online. The essential idea is that instead of paging through a book that is organized in a linear, sequential way, the reader clicks on optional links that direct him or her to some other part of the story.

Hypertext, at the core of the World Wide Web, is the means to access different documents – and therefore parts of the story – by simply clicking on an icon or other linked feature. As such, the hypertext reading experience is more immediate than reading from a book.

Hypertext narratives involve the reader being able to click on different links to be directed to different parts of the narrative.

A famous example of a hypertext narrative is *253* by Geoff Ryman. The concept behind this literary creation is that the reader can click on passengers sitting in a train to find out their stories and what the relationships are between them.

Presenting on hypertext narrative would involve taking into consideration the specific relationship that is created between the reader and the text, and looking for ways to explore this, possibly through comparison between hypertext and conventional text or by giving feedback on what it was like as a reader engaging with the text this way. In the hypertext reading experience, the reader has greater power and can decide on how and when to enter and exit the narrative.

Literature and film

Comparing text and cinematographic adaptations is a fascinating exercise that can lead to a rich and interesting appreciation not only of literature, but also cinema. In your literature classes there is a chance that you will watch extracts of films or films in their entirety. The key question to keep asking yourself is what exactly the relationship is between the two. How does cinema transpose some of the content of literature through images, voice-over, special effects and music? Often the plot of a narrative is changed – sometimes substantially – to accommodate the cinematic vision of the work and this is another element to take into consideration.

There are a number of key questions that you can ask yourself when studying literature and film:

- How does the characterization change (in other words, how do characters appear in films as opposed to texts)?
- What are the challenges that face a film director in trying to transpose narrative structure into a visual medium?
- How do elements of the text transpose into visual symbols?

Core differences between literature and film

If you are presenting on literature and film then it might be a good idea to compare and contrast limited passages: a key extract that would be read to the class followed by a viewing of the corresponding scene in the film.

It is difficult to imagine a film that would ever do justice to a novel, because there is a necessary collapsing of time to fit the contents into something that usually has to be less than three hours. Much is lost therefore, and a discerning critic of literature and film will pick up on what is lost from the written work, and what effect this has on the viewing experience as opposed to the reading.

The privacy and intimacy that is established between the reader and the written text, something that we talked about in Chapter 1, can be lost when viewing a film, as this often takes place in a public space or in any case not a private one. A book can be re-read, and passages annotated and underlined, whereas a film typically flows onwards without the viewer being able to arrest time (although modern audiovisual equipment has made rewinding, fast-forwarding and jumping between scenes much more practical).

There are many famous literary texts that have been transposed into established and reputable films. Here are some examples:

When looking at the relationship between film and literature, be sure to consider how elements are transposed and changed to suit the format.

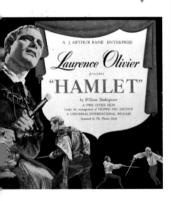

TEXT	FILM
Macbeth by William Shakespeare	*Macbeth* by Roman Polanski *Throne of Blood* by Kurosawa
The Taming of the Shrew by William Shakespeare	*The Taming of the Shrew* by Franco Zeffirelli
Hamlet by William Shakespeare	*Hamlet* by Sir Laurence Olivier *Hamlet* by Franco Zeffirelli *Hamlet* by Kenneth Branagh
The Big Sleep by Raymond Chandler	*The Big Sleep* by Howard Hawkes with the screenplay by Raymond Chandler
A Streetcar Named Desire by Tennessee Williams	*A Streetcar Named Desire* by Elia Kazan with the screenplay by Tennessee Williams
Death and the Maiden by Ariel Dorfman	*Death and the Maiden* by Roman Polanski with the screenplay by Ariel Dorfman
The Great Gatsby by F. Scott Fitzgerald	*The Great Gatsby* by Jack Clayton
One Flew Over the Cuckoo's Nest by Ken Kesey	*One Flew Over the Cuckoo's Nest* by Milos Forman
Oliver Twist by Charles Dickens	*Oliver Twist* by David Lean *Oliver Twist* by Roman Polanski
Death in Venice by Thomas Mann	*Death in Venice* by Luchino Visconti
1984 by George Orwell	*1984* by Michael Radford

In what ways does transposing a genre like the novel into film create a different way of knowing the text?

Another interesting issue to consider is how different cinematic productions of a text emphasize different elements of the work. Taking a key extract and looking at how more

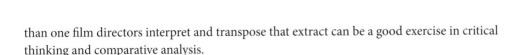

than one film directors interpret and transpose that extract can be a good exercise in critical thinking and comparative analysis.

EXERCISE 9

Take a passage from a work you are currently studying and think about how you would film it. Justify your choices in terms of what you would want to emphasize and transpose.

SUMMARY

New textualities break down the conventional boundaries of literature and invite stimulating and creative ways of engaging with the text. When considering these, you should take into account the ways that the reading experience is enhanced and/or lessened by the format of the text. When you compare film to text you should look for the transposition of elements such as symbol, mood and theme.

INSIGHTS INTO THE ORAL PRESENTATION

Now that we have come to the close of this chapter on the oral presentation, reflect on the following points that will help you approach your oral presentation with passion and confidence. Good luck!

1   The oral presentation gives you an opportunity to practise vital skills that will serve you well in your other studies, post-secondary education activities, the workplace and beyond. Try to look at this part of the course as a chance to reinforce these skills and further develop yourself as a holistic lifelong learner. What are the key skills we are looking at? They are:

- Knowing how to captivate an audience, hold their attention and sustain a dynamic relationship with them
- Knowing how to present material in an incisive, creative, substantiated way
- Knowing how to structure a presentation convincingly
- Knowing how to work in a group

2   The learning outcomes of the oral presentation should be kept in focus as you go about this part of the course. You will be:

- Acquiring knowledge and understanding of the works studied
- Presenting an individual, independent response to the works studied
- Acquiring powers of expression through oral presentation
- Learning how to interest and hold the attention of an audience

3   As is the case in any component of the subject of the diploma programme, knowing what the assessment criteria are is essential. Make sure that your teacher has distributed these to you early on in the course so you know where you are going and what you are being assessed on. Remember that the points for the assessment criteria are equally distributed (10 points each). You would do well to use them as you plan and practise your oral presentation to keep what you say and do in line with what is being evaluated.

4   Good presenting involves using your voice well, engaging with your audience in exciting but appropriately scholarly ways, using eye contact, visual supporting material, gesture and movement, so as to captivate your audience.

5 There are many different types of oral presentation for you to consider, and you might have something in mind that is not listed in this chapter. Think creatively. Think about where you want to take the audience and therefore what your argument will be, and create tight structure to keep it cogent and coherent.

6 Although an appreciation of literary features is not explicitly listed in the assessment criteria, you will need to reflect on the author's use of literary features if you are to reach into the top marks for the assessment criterion on Knowledge and Understanding. When you plan out your presentation, do not forget these, as they will help you show how the author gets his or her messages across to the reader.

7 When you think of a topic for your oral presentation, try to whittle it down as much as possible to avoid something that is too broad for an effective analysis. Try to move towards something specific enough for you to do justice to it effectively and cogently in 10–15 minutes.

THE INDIVIDUAL ORAL COMMENTARY

8

Knowledge and Understanding

The significance of the Individual Oral Commentary (IOC) in the course

The IOC is a fundamental part of the literature course. Students of literature should be able to talk about a short extract in detail for an extended period, to show their knowledge and understanding of the text and their abilities in literary analysis and the use of language. Not only is the IOC a valuable exercise in expressing and developing your oral proficiency, it helps you in your preparation for Paper 1, the written commentary. However, there is one essential difference: the IOC implies that the reader is not coming upon the text for the first time (as in Paper 1), but has studied it, discussed it in class, and can relate the passage to the entire work.

Being able to deliver a commentary is one of the higher-order thinking skills that you will develop in the course, making you a more confident and able commentator of literature. What makes the experience of the commentary interesting and unique is that you respond to a text with your full powers of imagination and insight. You craft your reaction to a piece of writing, and in doing this you establish a close relationship between text (overall work) and reader. In this way, the commentary is not about recalling remembered answers – it is a highly creative experience that demands active engagement with the text and literary analysis.

 The commentary is an valuable exercise in critical thinking. Think about the ways in which commentary is used on a daily basis. In which public situations does commentary have particular value?

There are two significant differences between the oral commentary and presentation. First, you can plan the oral presentation at home and spend as much time as you need; for the oral commentary you are only given 20 minutes' preparation time. Second, the oral commentary is an individual exercise and cannot be done in a group, as the oral presentation can. This structure means that the IOC needs to be approached in a different manner: you need to think carefully about how you can use your preparation time, how you will develop your arguments, and how you can give a cogent personal response. In short, you need to be able to work swiftly, in an organized and well-planned way and alone.

Like a dialogue between two people, in many ways the commentary is a dialogue between text and reader.

Why the skill of close reading of a single passage?

Being able to make sense of an extract of information is a vital skill for the 21st century. We are surrounded by information to the point where we could speak of an information overload. But as the Anglo-American poet and playwright T.S. Eliot said in his play *The Rock*: 'Where is the wisdom in knowledge and where is the knowledge in information?' For a piece of text to become knowledge someone needs to make sense of it – that someone is you.

● **Examiner's hints**

The poem (or part of a poem) that you will receive for HL, or the extract if you are in SL, will be something that you will have looked at in class already, so you will not be studying it for the first time. For this reason, the efforts you make in class will pay dividends in the IOC.

There are countless fields of activity in which the skill of being able to think quickly and respond to information within short stretches of time is essential.

Close reading is a useful skill that develops your sense of perception; it trains you to think on your feet and make sense of information quickly. This is one of the reasons why you are given a short preparation time and you do not know what text it is you will receive beforehand – we are dealing with skills that prepare you to handle unexpected challenges in the real world.

The commentary is a vital skill for other subjects too, particularly humanities subjects such as history and philosophy, where you are expected to make sense of extracts and rapidly present your own response. Many university courses in literature or the humanities involve some form of oral commentary.

What is the role of interpretation in building up knowledge? At which point could we say that there is over-interpretation?

As is the case with the written commentary for Paper 1, the key exercise with the IOC is **close reading**: you are being asked to look at a passage in great detail and talk about the use of language and literary features. In so doing, you should show keen observation, give relevant illustrations and make coherent arguments. These skills in themselves will strengthen your powers of concentration and creativity.

The IOC can be particularly difficult because you need to keep your textual analysis as clear as possible, stay within the confines of some discernible argument and at the same time cover the text in great detail. It is no simple affair, but there are strategies that can help you optimize your planning and processes.

SUMMARY

The IOC is a chance for you to exercise on-your-feet thinking skills, creativity, analysis of detail and a personal appreciation of a literary text. These skills can help you in a variety of unforeseen and diverse contexts.

● **Examiner's hints**

For the oral commentary you need to appreciate textual details and subtleties. When reading the text, it is always a good idea to isolate the verbs and the adjectives to see if you can discern any progression or patterns. If you notice symbols and/or metaphors, look for repetition of the same or a related idea at some other part of the text.

The assessment criteria: what is expected of you

Standard Level

Approaching the commentary: essential points

Out of the two works you study in Part 2 of the course, one will be chosen for the IOC and you will be given an extract from that work. You will not know which extract you will receive until the examination starts, but the extract will be approximately 20–30 lines long and will be accompanied by one or two guiding questions set by your teacher.

You will be given 20 minutes to prepare your oral commentary. You will not be allowed to access the work from which the text was drawn. For this reason, you will need to be well prepared and very familiar with the text, so that you can identify and place the passage in context. Once the planning is over, you will be expected to speak in an uninterrupted fashion for eight minutes (not longer and not too much under – let's say six and a half minutes minimum) and then answer questions for the remaining two minutes or so. The entire commentary, including questions, will last ten minutes.

Remember that the whole process will be recorded.

The SL assessment criteria

You are graded out of 30 points that are divided into four criteria:
- Knowledge and understanding of the extract (worth a maximum of 10 points)
- Appreciation of the writer's choices (worth a maximum of 10 points)
- Organization and presentation (worth a maximum of 5 points)
- Language (worth a maximum of 5 points)

Let's look at those criteria again in terms of the percentage that each one is worth for the total oral commentary score, which will give you an idea of where it is important to do particularly well:

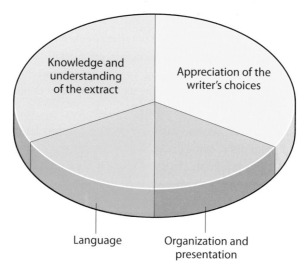

We will come back to the assessment criteria in more detail as we look at different extracts and how you could go about responding to them. At this stage it is important to reflect on the way that the marking is weighted and to keep in mind that the bulk of the marks come from your ability to show knowledge and understanding of the extract and appreciation of the writer's choices. By this we mean that you have to know and understand the texts well and comprehend the use of literary features and how these contribute to the meaning of the extract or poem.

Read through the level descriptors below to get an idea of what degree of analysis, use of language and organization is needed to score highly on the different criteria:

For the Standard Level IOC, the bulk of the marks come from your ability to show knowledge and understanding of the extract and appreciation of the writer's choices.

Individual Oral Commentary (SL)

Criterion A: Knowledge and understanding of the extract

How well is the student's knowledge and understanding of the extract demonstrated by their interpretation?

Marks	Level descriptor
0	The work does not reach a standard described by the descriptors below.
1–2	There is virtually no knowledge, demonstrated by irrelevant and/or insignificant references to the extract.

Marks	Level descriptor
3–4	There is some knowledge, demonstrated by very limited interpretation, but with some relevant references to the extract.
5–6	There is adequate knowledge and understanding, demonstrated by interpretation supported by mostly appropriate references to the extract.
7–8	There is good knowledge and understanding, demonstrated by interpretation supported by relevant and appropriate references to the extract.
9–10	There is very good knowledge and understanding, demonstrated by careful interpretation supported by well-chosen references to the extract.

Criterion B: Appreciation of the writer's choices

To what extent does the student appreciate how the writer's choices of language, structure, technique and style shape meaning?

Marks	Level descriptor
0	The work does not reach a standard described by the descriptors below.
1–2	There is virtually no reference to the ways in which language, structure, technique and style shape meaning in the extract.
3–4	There is some reference to the ways in which language, structure, technique and style shape meaning in the extract.
5–6	There is adequate reference to, and some appreciation of, the ways in which language, structure, technique and style shape meaning in the extract.
7–8	There is good appreciation of the ways in which language, structure, technique and style shape meaning in the extract.
9–10	There is very good appreciation of the ways in which language, structure, technique and style shape meaning in the extract.

Criterion C: Organization and presentation

To what extent does the student deliver a structured, well-focused commentary?

Marks	Level descriptor
0	The work does not reach a standard described by the descriptors below.
1	The commentary has virtually no structure and/or focus.
2	The commentary has limited evidence of a planned structure and is only occasionally focused.
3	The commentary shows some evidence of a planned structure and is generally focused.
4	The commentary has a clearly planned structure and is focused.
5	The commentary is very clearly structured and the focus is sustained.

Criterion D: Language

How clear, varied and accurate is the language?

How appropriate is the choice of register and style? ('Register' refers, in this context, to the student's use of elements such as vocabulary, tone, sentence structure and terminology appropriate to the commentary.)

Marks	Level descriptor
0	The work does not reach a standard described by the descriptors below.
1	The language is rarely clear and appropriate, with many errors in grammar and sentence construction and little sense of register and style.
2	The language is sometimes clear and appropriate; grammar and sentence construction are generally accurate, although errors and inconsistencies are apparent; register and style are to some extent appropriate.
3	The language is mostly clear and appropriate, with an adequate degree of accuracy in grammar and sentence construction; the register and style are mostly appropriate.
4	The language is clear and appropriate, with a good degree of accuracy in grammar and sentence construction; register and style are effective and appropriate.
5	The language is very clear and entirely appropriate, with a high degree of accuracy in grammar and sentence construction; the register and style are consistently effective and appropriate.

Higher Level
Approaching the commentary: essential points

Out of the works that you study in Part 2, you will be tested on a poem or an extract of about 20–30 lines of a poem (if it is extremely long). In addition to this extract, your teacher will ask you questions about one of the remaining Part 2 texts. Both of these exercises will last ten minutes, which makes 20 minutes of recorded commentary time in total.

You will have 20 minutes to prepare, but **only on the poem or extract of a poem**. There will be no preparation time for the second part of the oral. You will discover which text your teacher has chosen for you to discuss right after the commentary, so there is an element of further suspense!

To make it quite clear:
1. You discover which poem or extract of poetry you are to comment on.
2. You are given 20 minutes to work on your presentation.
3. You give your presentation on the text for about eight minutes (try to make it exactly eight minutes).
4. Your teacher asks you questions about your commentary and you answer these for two minutes.
5. You enter into a discussion with your teacher about one of the remaining Part 2 texts that you studied in class.

Your poem will be accompanied by one or two guiding questions.

SUMMARY

The IOC is ten minutes long. HL students then discuss a remaining Part 2 work for ten minutes. You will have 20 minutes to prepare.

The HL assessment criteria

Unlike in the Standard Level, where the 30 points are broken down into four assessment criteria, for the Higher Level there are six assessment criteria and each one is worth five points. They are:

- Knowledge and understanding of the poem
- Appreciation of the writer's choices
- Organization and presentation of the commentary
- Knowledge and understanding of the work used in the discussion
- Response to the discussion questions
- Language

The IOC is worth 15 per cent of your final English Literature grade.

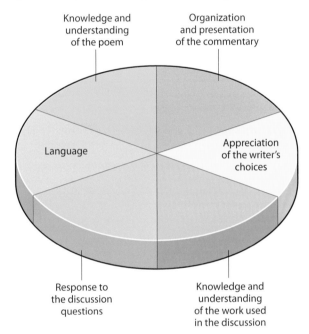

● **Examiner's hints**
Remember that there is an equal weighting of the assessment criteria for the HL IOC. You need to give a balanced account that hits all six criteria.

Read through the assessment criteria level descriptors for the HL oral commentary below. They will give you an idea of the level and pitch of performance that is expected of you to score (hopefully) among the highest marks:

Individual Oral Commentary and discussion (HL)

Criterion A: Knowledge and understanding of the poem

How well is the student's knowledge and understanding of the poem demonstrated by their interpretation?

Marks	Level descriptor
0	The work does not reach a standard described by the descriptors below.
1	There is limited knowledge and little or no understanding, with poor interpretation and virtually no relevant references to the poem.
2	There is superficial knowledge and some understanding, with limited interpretation occasionally supported by references to the poem.

Marks	Level descriptor
3	There is adequate knowledge and understanding, demonstrated by interpretation supported by appropriate references to the poem.
4	There is very good knowledge and understanding, demonstrated by careful interpretation supported by well-chosen references to the poem.
5	There is excellent knowledge and understanding, demonstrated by individual interpretation effectively supported by precise and well-chosen references to the poem.

Criterion B: Appreciation of the writer's choices

To what extent does the student appreciate how the writer's choices of language, structure, technique and style shape meaning?

Marks	Level descriptor
0	The work does not reach a standard described by the descriptors below.
1	There are few references to, and no appreciation, of the ways in which language, structure, technique and style shape meaning in the poem.
2	There is some mention, but little appreciation, of the ways in which language, structure, technique and style shape meaning in the poem.
3	There is adequate appreciation of the ways in which language, structure, technique and style shape meaning in the poem.
4	There is very good appreciation of the ways in which language, structure, technique and style shape meaning in the poem.
5	There is excellent appreciation of the ways in which language, structure, technique and style shape meaning in the poem.

Criterion C: Organization and presentation of the commentary

To what extent does the student deliver a structured, well-focused commentary?

Marks	Level descriptor
0	The work does not reach a standard described by the descriptors below.
1	The commentary shows little evidence of planning, with very limited structure and/or focus.
2	The commentary shows some structure and focus.
3	The commentary shows evidence of a planned structure and is generally focused.
4	The commentary is clearly structured and the focus is sustained.
5	The commentary is effectively structured, with a clear, purposeful and sustained focus.

Criterion D: Knowledge and understanding of the work used in the discussion

How much knowledge and understanding has the student shown of the work used in the discussion?

Marks	Level descriptor
0	The work does not reach a standard described by the descriptors below.
1	There is little knowledge or understanding of the content of the work discussed.
2	There is some knowledge and superficial understanding of the content of the work discussed.
3	There is adequate knowledge and understanding of the content and some of the implications of the work discussed.
4	There is very good knowledge and understanding of the content and most of the implications of the work discussed.
5	There is excellent knowledge and understanding of the content and the implications of the work discussed.

Criterion E: Response to the discussion questions

How effectively does the student respond to the discussion questions?

Marks	Level descriptor
0	The work does not reach a standard described by the descriptors below.
1	There is limited ability to respond meaningfully to the discussion questions.
2	Responses to the discussion questions are sometimes relevant.
3	Responses to the discussion questions are relevant and show some evidence of independent thought.
4	Well-informed responses to the discussion questions show a good degree of independent thought.
5	There are persuasive and independent responses to the discussion questions.

Criterion F: Language

How clear, varied and accurate is the language?

How appropriate is the choice of register and style? ('Register' refers, in this context, to the student's use of elements such as vocabulary, tone, sentence structure and terminology appropriate to the commentary.)

Marks	Level descriptor
0	The work does not reach a standard described by the descriptors below.
1	The language is rarely clear and appropriate, with many errors in grammar and sentence construction and little sense of register and style.
2	The language is sometimes clear and appropriate; grammar and sentence construction are generally accurate, although errors and inconsistencies are apparent; register and style are to some extent appropriate.
3	The language is mostly clear and appropriate, with an adequate degree of accuracy in grammar and sentence construction; the register and style are mostly appropriate.
4	The language is clear and appropriate, with a good degree of accuracy in grammar and sentence construction; register and style are effective and appropriate.
5	The language is very clear and entirely appropriate, with a high degree of accuracy in grammar and sentence construction; the register and style are consistently effective and appropriate.

EXERCISE 2

Consider these essential skills that are asked of you in the IOC assessment criteria. Below each one are guiding questions for you to think about as you prepare:

SL

Criterion A: Knowledge and understanding of the extract

- How well is the student's knowledge and understanding of the extract demonstrated by their interpretation?

Guiding questions: How well do you know the passage? Have you shown that you have a clear understanding of the characters, themes and meaning of the text? If it is an extract, have you explained why the passage is important?

Criterion B: Appreciation of the writer's choices

- To what extent does the student appreciate how the writer's choices of language, structure, technique and style shape meaning?

Guiding questions: How well have you shown how the different literary features in the extract or poem contribute to its meaning? Have you really appreciated the writer's choices or merely identified them?

Criterion C: Organization and presentation

- To what extent does the student deliver a structured, well-focused commentary?

Guiding questions: Does your commentary have a clear beginning, middle and end? Does your introduction contain an argument or thesis? Are you using transitional devices to move it along? Do you conclude effectively or merely peter out?

Criterion D: Language

- How clear, varied and accurate is the language?
- How appropriate is the choice of register and style? ('Register' refers, in this context, to the student's use of elements such as vocabulary, tone, sentence structure and terminology appropriate to the commentary.)

Guiding questions: Are you using formal, technical, sophisticated language to express yourself with flair, or is your commentary made up of slang, sloppy phrases and unclear statements?

HL

Criterion A: Knowledge and understanding of the poem

- How well is the student's knowledge and understanding of the poem demonstrated by their interpretation?

Guiding questions: Have you got to the core of the poem and really shown what it means at a deeper level? Have you been able to account for its subtleties and nuances or is your reading superficial and merely stating the surface meaning?

Criterion B: Appreciation of the writer's choices

- To what extent does the student appreciate how the writer's choices of language, structure, technique and style shape meaning?

Guiding questions: Have you considered typical elements of poetry such as prosody (the study of poetic metre and sound), rhyme and rhythm, graphology (the shape of the poem)? Are you merely identifying these features or showing how they contribute to the poem's meaning and how they inform your argument?

Criterion C: Organization and presentation of the commentary

- To what extent does the student deliver a structured, well-focused commentary?

Guiding questions: Does your commentary start with some sort of statement of intent and/ or argument? Does the main body progress either according to your statement of intent or, if chronological, do you connect your ideas with transitional devices? Do you conclude effectively?

Criterion D: Knowledge and understanding of the work used in the discussion

- How much knowledge and understanding has the student shown of the work used in the discussion?

Guiding questions: During the discussion on the remaining Part 2 work, are you able to show that you have understood the text well and can you relate to elements such as theme, characterization, narrative, plot?

Criterion E: Response to the discussion questions

- How effectively does the student respond to the discussion questions?

Guiding questions: Are you listening to the questions carefully and providing reflective, dynamic answers or are you merely answering with the bare minimum? Are you answers well-crafted or muddled?

Criterion F: Language

- How clear, varied and accurate is the language?
- How appropriate is the choice of register and style? ('Register' refers, in this context, to the student's use of elements such as vocabulary, tone, sentence structure and terminology appropriate to the commentary.)

Guiding questions: Are you speaking with flair and precision, technical prowess and a high literary standard or do you get by with informal, colloquial statements?

The components of the oral commentary

The text

There is a high chance that you will go into the examination hoping for one text, but you discover that you have been allocated another, perhaps one you were not expecting or did not want to receive. Not to worry! Too many times students believe that they will do better on one text rather than another, but when the actual experience of sitting down and planning the commentary is underway they realize that this is not the case and in fact they are better off discussing a text they were not expecting.

The best way to be prepared is to have gone through all of the texts that might come up in detail, getting to know them thoroughly. If you are already familiar with the texts, know how to sum up the primary significance of each and identify and analyze the prominent literary features beforehand. Then you will only have to tweak what you had planned and look for more detail and specificity.

Guiding questions

Your text will be accompanied with one or two guiding questions. You do not have to answer them and should not feel pressurized into shaping your commentary around them, especially if they do not seem to be helping the type of analysis you wish to make. This much said, it is no doubt a good idea to consider them and to try to incorporate them into

● **Examiner's hints**
Make sure that you know each of the texts well and have a rough idea of the position you will be taking on each one before the oral commentary, so that you do not have to spend too much time going over the fundamentals and re-inventing the wheel in your 20 minutes' planning time.

your commentary. After all, the guiding questions are there to help you and should be asking for a response on issues that are central to the study of the text.

Here are some examples of guiding questions. Reading through them will give you an idea of the kind of discussion you might have when you do your own IOC.

Drama

- What is revealed about the character(s) through the diction employed?
- What roles do music/sound/lighting effects have to play in this extract?
- What impact is this extract likely to have on the audience?
- For what reasons can this extract be considered a pivotal/key moment in the play?

Prose: novel and short story

- How does structure function in this extract to convey key ideas?
- How does the balance between dialogue and narrative affect your understanding of this extract?
- How are the key themes of the work explored in this extract?
- How does this extract work to change your understanding of the characters involved?

Prose other than fiction/non-fiction

- To what effect is sentence structure used in this extract?
- In what ways is the style of this extract typical of the work as a whole?
- What is the likely impact of this extract on the reader?
- How important is the logical sequence of ideas in this extract?

Poetry

- What is the relationship between the title and the poem itself?
- How does the progression of ideas contribute to the development of the theme(s)?
- How does stanza structure reflect the development of the poem's subject?
- In what ways does the final line/stanza change your understanding of the poem as a whole?

(Questions from *Language A: Literature Guide*, p.56)

HL poetry examples:

- How are sound effects employed in this poem?
- How is the character of the speaker revealed through the diction employed?
- How does this poem seek to create an emotional response in the reader?
- How does the punctuation used influence how the poem is read/heard?
- To what effect is rhythm used in this poem?
- In what ways does the tone shift throughout the poem?
- What might be considered ambiguous in this poem?

(Questions from *Language A: Literature Guide*, p.64–65)

● **Examiner's hints**
If you have been given an extract, you are not supposed to use it as an opportunity to launch into a discussion about the entire work. Remember to keep your commentary centred on the text in front of you, explaining how or why the extract is key in the work as a whole.

> **GLOBAL PERSPECTIVES**
>
> The Individual Oral Commentary anchors some of the IB Learner Profile attributes that are an important part of the International Baccalaureate experience. They are: inquirers, knowledgeable, thinkers, communicators.

Subsequent questions and discussion

The two minutes or so that you will spend answering questions after the oral commentary should be looked at positively. It is less a case of your teacher trying to catch you out, and more an opportunity for you to develop the points you made earlier. Remember, however, that this is still part of your formal commentary and will contribute to the way that you are assessed, so avoid answering the questions superficially. It may be that your teacher comes back to the guiding questions during this interaction, so make sure that you have at least considered them beforehand.

Here are some of the types of question or challenge that you might find yourself answering:
- Explain what you meant by something that was said earlier.
- Give an example of something that you said in the commentary.
- Consider a theme you did not discuss in your commentary.
- How do you interpret the author's choice of technique?
- Relate the themes or characters in the extract to the work as a whole.
- Say something general and philosophical about the poem or extract, such as why the work is important to study in the context of today's world, and what it is saying about the human condition.

Subsequent questions and discussion of literature for HL

If you are in the HL, then you will spend an extra ten minutes discussing one of the remaining Part 2 texts that you studied with your teacher. The discussion is an opportunity for you to show your knowledge, understanding, appreciation and analysis of the work. Try to give generous, rounded and detailed answers to the questions, and avoid one-worded, undeveloped and flat responses. Below are examples of the kind of responses that are good and those that are poor:

A lively, interactive discussion about a novel	A poor and undeveloped discussion on a collection of poems
Teacher: Tell me about the way that power is discussed in the novel that you studied.	Teacher: What do you feel the poet is saying about religion?
Student: Power in this work is an important theme and essentially plays itself out in two fundamental ways. First, there is the power struggle between the protagonist and the antagonist formed on the sexual politics that define their relationship. The protagonist tries to affirm himself in the community by establishing the laws in the market place, but he is seduced by the antagonist, who uses her sexuality to manipulate him into making the wrong strategic decisions [student gives examples]. Second, we have the power struggle between the village and the outside mercantile forces represented by the company that wants to buy the rainforest, which is their livelihood. This power struggle is primarily financial and can be best seen in the symbol of the tractor, which is first introduced as something positive for the community's farming but rapidly becomes an ominous signifier of destruction and industrialization	Student: That religion is bad.
	Teacher: Could you explain?
	Student: He is saying that religion is for the common people.
	Teacher: Interesting, what exactly do you mean by that?
	Student: Religion is not for the top people in society, it's for the bottom people.
	Teacher: What do you mean by bottom people?
	Student: The common people.
	Teacher: And they are?
	Student: Um, the ones who don't really like … the ones that are not on top in the way they think. It's difficult to explain.

[student gives examples]. In both cases we see a public appearance of dominance by the protagonist and the community, but behind the scenes in both cases more subtle forces are at work that underscore this appearance.

Teacher: Interesting, so it's about appearances and reality as well then.

Student: Yes, that's right, not unlike the play we studied and to a certain extent some of the poems that we discussed in our lessons. We have seen the theme of appearances and reality repeat itself. The difference in the novel that we studied is that appearances tend to be communal, but reality seems to be an individual phenomenon: it is hidden in the recesses of bedrooms, courtyards and chambers.

Teacher: Can you think of any examples?

Student: Yes, for example … [continues with a number of examples elaborating on the literary features and how they are used in the descriptions of these places and interactions].

Teacher: And how does the poet do this?

Student: By saying things about religion in his poems.

Teacher: Sorry, what I meant was which techniques does he use to communicate this to the reader, this idea of religion being the opiate of the masses?

Student: Lots of literary features in his poetry, like imagery.

Teacher: Could you give some examples?

Student: Umm …

Teacher: For instance in poem X, there's the image of the fountain in the village square …

Student: Yes.

Teacher: How does that bring across this idea of religion being a type of drug for the inhabitants?

Student: Umm … it's imagery of religion being like a drug for the people.

Teacher: What do the children of the village do with the fountain?

Student: I can't remember.

Teacher: They play in it all day long, remember?

Student: Oh yes.

Teacher: And what do you think this symbolic activity is suggesting about our approach to spirituality?

Student: That we play with it.

Teacher: Okay, any other ideas?

Student: Umm … no, that's all.

Teacher: Remember that the children muddy the water through this activity so in the end the town people cannot drink from it any more.

Student: Yes.

Teacher: So this might be saying that the source of potential life for the village is wasted by a superficial usage of it.

Student: I guess so.

EXERCISE 3

Take one of your Part 2 works and get a friend or family member to test you on it using the guiding questions listed on page 206. Make sure that your answers use examples from the text to elaborate a detailed, expository response.

Appreciation
Approaching the text in the oral commentary

As we have seen in other parts of this book, there are essentially two ways of approaching a text in the commentary: linear or thematic. Remember that the **linear approach**, also known as a line-by-line or chronological analysis, is one that follows the text as it comes. It is as if you are running your finger along the text, following it sentence by sentence and giving a running commentary as you do this.

Here is an example of a linear analysis in the main body of a commentary; it works stanza by stanza (imagine that you are speaking the text in the right-hand column):

TEXT	LINEAR COMMENTARY

'TIS the year's midnight, and it is the day's,
Lucy's, who scarce seven hours herself unmasks;
  The sun is spent, and now his flasks
    Send forth light squibs, no constant rays;
      The world's whole sap is sunk;   5
	The poet starts by establishing the time when the action is taking place. The cosmic imagery of the sun, using personification, is powerful and simple. The use of consonance ('sap is sunk') furthers the rhythm of the first stanza that overall depicts a derelict place, void of life.

The general balm th' hydroptic earth hath drunk, Whither, as to the bed's-feet, life is shrunk, Dead and interr'd; yet all these seem to laugh, Compared with me, who am their epitaph.	Here the poet reinforces images of death with the idea of a shrunken life, the symbol of the bed (sleep as a metaphor for death) and goes on to use a metaphysical conceit in describing his own grief as much worse than what is effectively the death of the entire earth.

Study me then, you who shall lovers be   10
At the next world, that is, at the next spring;
  For I am every dead thing,
    In whom Love wrought new alchemy.
      For his art did express
A quintessence even from nothingness,   15
From dull privations, and lean emptiness;
He ruin'd me, and I am re-begot
Of absence, darkness, death—things which are not.
	Here the poet speaks directly to the reader and implores him/her to study him. This interpolation creates immediacy in the relationship between the reader and the 'I' speaker. He also invokes through the third person the presence of someone who has 'ruined' him, possibly God. The atmosphere is becoming increasingly desolate and dark and by this point the poet comes across as wretched and alone.

All others, from all things, draw all that's good,
Life, soul, form, spirit, whence they being have;   20
  I, by Love's limbec, am the grave
    Of all, that's nothing. Oft a flood
      Have we two wept, and so
Drown'd the whole world, us two; oft did we grow,
To be two chaoses, when we did show   25
Care to aught else; and often absences
Withdrew our souls, and made us carcasses.
	The poet compares himself to 'all others' to compound his isolation by expressing his utter difference with the masses. The symbols and imagery of death continue to be used ('grave', 'drown'd', 'chaoses', 'carcasses'). He now evokes the presence of his lover and speaks of the emotional turmoil of their time together using the natural imagery of a flood.

But I am by her death—which word wrongs her—
Of the first nothing, the elixir grown;
  Were I a man, that I were one   30
  I needs must know; I should prefer,
    If I were any beast,
Some ends, some means; yea plants, yea stones detest,
And love; all, all some properties invest.
If I an ordinary nothing were,   35
As shadow, a light, and body must be here.
	Here we understand that the poet's lover has died. He goes on to explain how he has been born as an elixir (a type of potion) from nothing. This is a typical example of the poet's use of the metaphysical conceit, where a difficult, unlikely idea is communicated through strong and often oxymoronic imagery. Hyperbole is used to reinforce his grief and he desperately asks to be almost anything but himself in his current state of grief.

But I am none; nor will my sun renew.
You lovers, for whose sake the lesser sun
  At this time to the Goat is run
    To fetch new lust, and give it you,   40
      Enjoy your summer all,
Since she enjoys her long night's festival.
Let me prepare towards her, and let me call
This hour her vigil, and her eve, since this
Both the year's and the day's deep midnight is.   45
	Carrying on with the idea of himself compared to the many, he concludes that he can be none of these other things and therefore must remain in his self and suffer the loss of his loved one accordingly. He ends the poem with a comparison of his love that seems to transcend life and death to the 'lesser love' of those that are drawn to each other through physical attraction, symbolized by the satanic/pagan goat of lust. He ends the poem with a clear parallel between the microcosm (his grief) and the macrocosm (the winter solstice).

John Donne, 'A nocturnal upon St Lucy's Day, being the shortest day of the year'	

Metaphysical conceit

An extended metaphor or simile that links together two seemingly unrelated subject areas. Famous for this technique were the so-called 'Metaphysical Poets' of the 17th century: John Donne, Abraham Cowley, Richard Crashaw and the Earl of Rochester.

The second approach is **thematic**. This is when you extract the themes, stylistic choices, messages, ideas and developments of the text, and then use them to discuss the work using your own organized structure. The thematic approach implies a different way of performing the commentary therefore, one that requires you to re-organize the ideas and techniques in the extract or poem and present them using your own logical structure and sequence, rather than those of the poem or extract itself as it unfolds.

Here is an example of a thematic approach as it might be used in the main body. Note that the student has taken key passages and phrases from the text, colour-coded them and then used the colour-coding system to organize the different paragraphs:

TEXT	THEMATIC COMMENTARY
To be, or not to be: that is the question: Whether 'tis nobler in the mind to suffer The slings and arrows of outrageous fortune, Or to take arms against a sea of troubles, And by opposing end them? To die: to sleep; No more; and by a sleep to say we end The heart-ache and the thousand natural shocks That flesh is heir to, 'tis a consummation Devoutly to be wish'd. To die, to sleep; **To sleep: perchance to dream**: ay, there's the rub; **For in that sleep of death what dreams may come** When we have shuffled off this mortal coil, **Must give us pause: there's the respect** **That makes calamity of so long life;** For who would bear the whips and scorns of time, The oppressor's wrong, the proud man's contumely, The pangs of despised love, the law's delay, The insolence of office and the spurns That patient merit of the unworthy takes, When he himself might his quietus make With a bare bodkin? who would fardels bear, To grunt and sweat under a weary life, **But that the dread of something after death,** **The undiscover'd country from whose bourn** **No traveller returns, puzzles the will** And makes us rather bear those ills we have Than fly to others that we know not of? **Thus conscience does make cowards of us all;** And thus the native hue of resolution Is sicklied o'er with the pale cast of thought, And enterprises of great pith and moment With this regard their currents turn awry, And lose the name of action. – Soft you now! The fair Ophelia! Nymph, in thy orisons Be all my sins remember'd. – William Shakespeare, *Hamlet*	**Red** The overarching opposition in this soliloquy is that which opposes life after death to the idea of nothingness after death. Hamlet uses a number of different images to suggest this idea: the metaphor of death being sleep is used to ask the question whether we dream in that 'sleep of death', in other words whether there is a life after death. The opposition implies another dichotomy: that which asks whether life should be tolerated or commanded; whether one should be passive or active in terms of fate and death. **Blue** A strong theme in the soliloquy, backed by a plethora of different images, is that of the hardships of life. In Hamlet's speech life is not seen as something simple or pleasant, but rather a tumultuous passage of pain and hardship. We cover the spectrum of hardship from the physical (the natural shocks of the flesh, the weary life that makes one grunt and sweat), the social (oppression, pride, insolence in office, unworthiness and injustice), the emotional (love's pangs) and the time-bound (the 'whips and scorns of time'). **Green** These passages make the speaker consider philosophical questions of an immediate and highly significant order. The first of these is suicide. Hamlet evokes the idea of stabbing oneself with a 'bodkin' (dagger) and suggests earlier in the soliloquy that there is something to be desired in the idea of nothing after life, suggesting a type of death wish. **Black** However, suicide might not be the right answer to the pain of life, since it might be wrong to assume that there is no afterworld and if there is an afterlife, from a Christian perspective, suicide would involve some sort of eternal or hellish punishment for the deed. Therefore, the mind is plagued by doubt and questions that have no clear answer: the 'undiscovered country' makes one think carefully, 'gives pause' and 'puzzles the will'. **Orange** What this leaves us with is a situation in which we are too afraid to take action and we procrastinate in the key philosophical matter of suicide. Hamlet implies that this makes us cowards and he uses the imagery of sickness to communicate this idea ('sicklied o'er with the pale cast of thought').

There is no single best method for approaching the text, but you must make some meaning of the text and formulate a position (what we are calling an 'argument' in this chapter). Furthermore, you need to be coherent and not repeat yourself.

Linear analysis (otherwise known as line-by-line or chronological) can lead to simple paraphrasing (repeating what is said in the text in your own words), and needs to be applied with great care. A line-by-line analysis can cover the poem or extract in great detail, because you have left nothing to chance by following the words as you read them, but there is a chance that you repeat yourself and struggle to go beyond paraphrasing.

A thematic analysis, on the other hand, will allow you to develop a structured argument so that your points flow from one to the next. However, you run the risk of missing some of the details in the text if you use this approach, and you need to be careful about sustaining the all-important close-reading skill as you go about your oral commentary this way.

What is the role of reason in interpreting literature? In the context of literary analysis, does emotion help or hinder the processes of reasoning?

Whether you choose to give a line-by-line or thematic account of the text, you need to make sure that you cover everything in detail.

Whichever method you choose, make sure that you cover the text in detail, substantiate your points with salient examples and give a personal response.

Although there are a number of ways of approaching the text, it may be that you get stuck and need to fall back on a structure that is reliable. The following method is a useful way of summing up the basics of the oral commentary:

What, Through, Effect and Meaning

Before we begin to look at the different types of text that you could encounter in your commentary, let's discuss some of the fundamentals of the analysis of literature. The point we are about to make is actually rather important, because the following approach can be

● **Examiner's hints**
Remember that a well-organized presentation has to be coherent and cogent. Make sure that the way you present your ideas is more than a mere series of disconnected facts sewn together.

used not only for the oral commentary, but also for both the written commentary and essay writing. If you stick to this simple idea, elaborate well and in sufficient detail, plan out your argument, main body and conclusion, then it is unlikely that you will go wrong (unless you have not read the books or never attended English class!). In any case, it is a simple way of remembering what needs to be done for the oral commentary and you can prepare thoroughly during your 20 minutes' preparation time if you stick to this system.

Ready for the idea? Here goes:

WHAT ⟵⎯⎯ THROUGH ⎯⎯⟶ EFFECT and MEANING

Does it look a bit strange? Or perhaps incomplete? Well it is, but before we go into more detail, remember those four words **WHAT**, **THROUGH**, **EFFECT** and **MEANING**. Try to remember the arrow between the **WHAT** and the **EFFECT** and **MEANING** too.

These should be the questions in the back of your mind at all times, whether you are preparing to discuss a text in the oral commentary, answer questions on one of the remaining Part 2 works at HL, writing a commentary or composing an essay:

1. What is\are the text(s) saying?
2. Through which techniques?
3. What effect does this create in the reader? How does it contribute to the meaning of the work?

Now for a bit more explanation:

WHAT ...	THROUGH ...	EFFECT ...	MEANING ...
Is the poem saying?	Which techniques, type of language, structure, style and shape?	On the reader?	How does this contribute to the overall meaning?
Is the extract saying?	Which themes?	On you?	What meaning do you make of the text through this reading experience?
Is the author saying?	Which characters? Which events?	Emotionally? Sensorially?	What meaning is the author trying to present?

WHAT

For an IOC, the **WHAT** will mean what is the extract or poem saying about the human condition or the world, and what is it saying about a particular theme or idea? The text might be, superficially, about watermelons or fish or a forest, but there is a second, deeper meaning: your job is to decide what exactly this second meaning is. The **WHAT** will become your **argument**.

Care is needed here. Students often want to invent a second meaning even when there may not actually be one. The poem may just be about watermelons or a forest. You certainly need to establish the literal meaning of a work before you start talking about the abstract meaning, so be careful to take things one step at a time.

For an HL student entering into a larger discussion about one of the remaining Part 2 works studied, the **WHAT** will mean what does the novel or play, or the poems, short stories or essays, say about the question you are answering? Does the work concur with the question or does it disagree? If you are looking at a collection of short texts in your answer (for instance, poems, essays or short stories), perhaps one text agrees with the question while the other does not. If you have a question asking you to comment on what the work you have read has told you about a theme (such as death, love, religion, power, peace, freedom, entrapment, fate and so on), then your **WHAT** will, very simply, be your response to this question.

THROUGH

THROUGH is the main part of your IOC (but don't forget that it can work for other responses to the text, such as essays and written commentaries too!). Your **WHAT** needs to be translated by something and this is why the verb **THROUGH** is helpful.

In many ways **THROUGH** is dealing with Criterion B, the author's choices of language, structure, technique, style and shape. For an IOC, some of the key techniques that will always be there – whether you are in the HL doing a poem or the SL looking at an extract or poem – are the following:

The main techniques and structural devices for an IOC

- Symbols
- Tone
- Atmosphere (or mood)
- Metaphor
- Punctuation (some will know it as syntax)
- Imagery
- Narrative structure

This is not an exhaustive list, but a fall-back safety-check if your mind goes blank; there are other features to consider such as contrast, narrative perspective, pace, literal/figurative language and so on. If we put the bulleted list together in an acronym we get **STAMPIN** (think of the word stamping, but without the final 'g'). Ready to do some stampin?

Whether you are giving a line-by-line or thematic account in your commentary, this framework allows you to focus on some of the essential stylistic choices that the author has made. It may be that in the end you only focus on some of these literary features, since the others will come up in the extract or poem that are not listed here. As you work your way through the commentary, it is important to look for techniques that you might not have considered before. Each reading of a piece of literature can yield something new and interesting to the searching, creative mind.

If you are using a thematic structure to frame your commentary, then you could start your planning by thinking in terms of the points you would make. In each of these points you could look at examples of the chosen **STAMPIN** technique to say how the text makes its point and what the effect of the technique is on the reader.

It may be that there will be other techniques (such as the use of sound – known as prosody, and shape – also known as graphology) that are more appropriate for the poem or extract you are looking at. If so, do not forget to include an analysis of these techniques in your commentary.

Certain techniques are specific to the genre in question, and in the Literature course it is always good to show understanding and awareness of the literary conventions of a genre. The table below outlines just a few to consider:

Literary conventions: techniques specific to genres for consideration			
General: Metaphor, Symbol, Characterization, Tone, Structure, Atmosphere, Imagery			
Poetry	**Fiction**	**Theatre**	**Prose other than fiction**
Rhyme Rhythm Prosody (sound) Graphology (shape)	Narrative technique Plot Time structure Foreshadowing	Stage directions Akoustikon Opsis Audience	Intended audience or readership Register Rhetorical figures

EXERCISE 4

Using the above table for reference, and choosing one genre, see if you can devise your own acronym to help you remember which elements to look at in your IOC.

The language of the IOC

In the assessment criteria for both HL and SL, five points go to the type of language that you use and the way that you construct your ideas stylistically.

- How clear, varied and accurate is the language?

This descriptor for style reminds us that the language of the IOC must be clear and accurate. Knowing which terms to use and how to capture the meaning of a sentence or line with precision is a skill that can be practised and enhanced by extensive reading of quality literature, as well as through active response to teacher feedback on assignments and oral participation in the classroom. Precise, clear and accurate language will be incisive (saying something), economical (to the point and not unnecessarily wordy) and exact in the way that it phrases an idea or point.

- How appropriate is the choice of register and style? ('Register' refers, in this context, to the student's use of elements such as vocabulary, tone, sentence structure and terminology appropriate to the commentary.)

For more detail on register and what it entails, look up the section on register in Chapter 4. To be clear, the register of the IOC is formal. Your **vocabulary** should be far-reaching, literary and of a high standard, while the **tone** of your commentary should be controlled and appropriate to the task (sober and formal with moments of elevation if necessary).

The **sentence structure** of your IOC will inform the listener as to the degree of your comfort with the language and your ability to engage with higher-order thinking skills and material for study. It is usually best to opt for short sentences, and it is vital to think carefully before using any idiom, as errors in this category, whilst tolerable, can interfere with the clarity of your overall expression. **Terminology** refers to the use of the technical language you employ to describe literary features and techniques. Make sure that you are sure of the meaning of key technical terms in literary analysis, and that you use them with accuracy.

The components of the IOC

The main components of the IOC are:

- Introduction (explaing the central argument)
- Main body
- Conclusion

Let's take the famous poem 'The Tyger' by William Blake (from *Songs of Experience*, 1794):

Tyger! Tyger! burning bright
In the forests of the night,
What immortal hand or eye
Could frame thy fearful symmetry?

In what distant deeps or skies   5
Burnt the fire of thine eyes?
On what wings dare he aspire?
What the hand dare sieze the fire?

And what shoulder, & what art
Could twist the sinews of thy heart?   10
And when thy heart began to beat,
What dread hand? & what dread feet?

What the hammer? what the chain?
In what furnace was thy brain?
What the anvil? what dread grasp   15
Dare its deadly terrors clasp?

When the stars threw down their spears,
And watered heaven with their tears,
Did he smile his work to see?
Did he who made the Lamb make thee?   20

Tyger! Tyger! burning bright
In the forests of the night,
What immortal hand or eye
Dare frame thy fearful symmetry?

Now we will look at how we can analyze this poem using the three components outlined above.

Introduction

The introduction should contain three clear elements:
1. Identification of the extract or poem, e.g. 'The poem "The Tyger" by William Blake is a vivid and atmospheric account of a tiger that asks questions of how and by whom the creature was created.' This should not take you more than 30 seconds or so – a statement or two will do.
2. Statement of your argument: 'This commentary will investigate the idea that the devil is ultimately the creator of the tiger ...'
3. An indication of how your commentary is going to proceed: '... through an analysis of the use of rhetorical questions, imagery, rhythm and symbolism.'

In total, your introduction should not last more than a minute or so.

The argument

The *argument*, also called a *thesis statement* or a *statement of intent*, should be clear and concise. You are expected to remain within the logic of this argument throughout the main body of your commentary, coming back to it frequently and quoting extracts from the passage or poem that illustrate it appropriately. Finding an argument can be difficult, and to do so you will need to read through the poem or extract a few times, highlighting and annotating before you can write up a good plan.

Brainstorming an argument during the 20 minutes' preparation:

Step 1

Read through the poem and write down all of the possible themes you think the poem evokes. In considering 'The Tyger', for instance, we could come up with these themes:

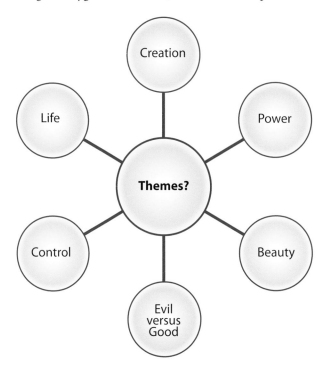

Step 2

Select the theme that expresses what the poem is saying the most accurately and the one you can say the most about. This is how you might proceed:

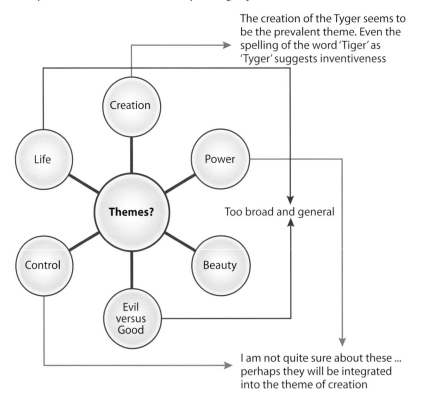

The creation of the Tyger seems to be the prevalent theme. Even the spelling of the word 'Tiger' as 'Tyger' suggests inventiveness

Too broad and general

I am not quite sure about these ... perhaps they will be integrated into the theme of creation

Step 3

Once you have chosen a theme, look through the poem or extract again, highlighting where and when you see the theme coming up. Try to synthesize all of the examples of this theme that you can find into one statement.

Step 4

See if your argument holds (in other words, now read through the poem with that argument in mind to see if you agree that this is what the poem or extract is saying).

This is what you might have come up with at this point: 'The poem "The Tyger" by William Blake is a vivid and atmospheric account of a tiger that asks questions of how and by whom the creature was created. This commentary will investigate the idea that the devil is ultimately the creator of the tiger.'

You need to think about the writer's choices and make them part of the main thrust of your commentary. This means looking for literary techniques and deciding how you can analyze them in the light of your argument. Coming back to the poem we might look to the following:

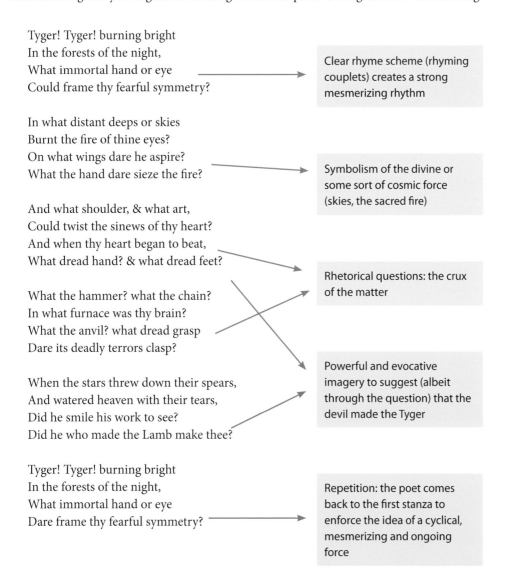

Tyger! Tyger! burning bright
In the forests of the night,
What immortal hand or eye
Could frame thy fearful symmetry?

Clear rhyme scheme (rhyming couplets) creates a strong mesmerizing rhythm

In what distant deeps or skies
Burnt the fire of thine eyes?
On what wings dare he aspire?
What the hand dare sieze the fire?

Symbolism of the divine or some sort of cosmic force (skies, the sacred fire)

And what shoulder, & what art,
Could twist the sinews of thy heart?
And when thy heart began to beat,
What dread hand? & what dread feet?

Rhetorical questions: the crux of the matter

What the hammer? what the chain?
In what furnace was thy brain?
What the anvil? what dread grasp
Dare its deadly terrors clasp?

When the stars threw down their spears,
And watered heaven with their tears,
Did he smile his work to see?
Did he who made the Lamb make thee?

Powerful and evocative imagery to suggest (albeit through the question) that the devil made the Tyger

Tyger! Tyger! burning bright
In the forests of the night,
What immortal hand or eye
Dare frame thy fearful symmetry?

Repetition: the poet comes back to the first stanza to enforce the idea of a cyclical, mesmerizing and ongoing force

This brings us back to our argument. We can take these techniques as the THROUGH part of the argument:

> The poem 'The Tyger' by William Blake is a vivid and atmospheric account of a tiger that asks questions of how and by whom the creature was created. **Through an analysis of the use of rhetorical questions, imagery, rhythm and symbolism,** this commentary will investigate the idea that the devil is ultimately the creator of the tiger.

The main body

Whereas the introduction is brief and synthetic, the main body is detailed, demonstrative (you are demonstrating your points) and well illustrated. It's important to take the points you have outlined in your introduction and to develop them fully in the course of the main body and not to merely state facts or make observations. The main body of your commentary will take up the bulk of your talk time, about ten minutes.

The relationship between the introduction and the main body should be tight. For example:

First point of the main body: how the rhetorical questions reinforce the fundamental inquiry of who made the tiger.

Second point: examples of strong imagery will be used to show how a cosmic atmosphere, a stage for the gods, is created, suggesting that some sort of transcendent force must have created the tiger.

Third point: an analysis of the way that the rhythm contributes to the meaning of the poem. The mesmerizing rhyme scheme and repetition give the reader the impression that there is an inexorable process at work, that the creation of the tiger is something that takes place in an eternal cycle of creation and destruction. This aspect could link with the second part of the commentary.

Last point: reflects on the use of symbolism in the poem, and how the pagan symbols of Promethean 'fire', 'wings' (Icarus), 'anvil' and 'furnace' (Hephaistos) and the dark forest point to a daemonic presence being responsible for the creation of the tiger. More orthodox Christian symbolism of good – 'the Lamb', 'heaven' and 'the stars' – suggests that God made the tiger.

The conclusion

The conclusion of your oral commentary should not be a simple repetition of your introduction or a re-stating of the main body, but a summation of your principal findings. You should remind the listener how your argument has been demonstrated. You might be able to synthesize the author's choices (use of literary techniques) into some sort of pattern.

It is good to end with a strong sentence about the universal significance of the text, to show some deeper understanding of its place as a great piece of literature. For example, using the example of the commentary on 'The Tyger' that we have suggested, a good conclusion might go something like this:

> In conclusion, William Blake's 'The Tyger' makes use of poetic techniques to reinforce the eternal philosophical question of the creation of evil. Whilst the rhythm and rhyme suggest, by their highly musical and cyclical pattern, that we will never find an answer to this question, the imagery and symbolism outline the two sides of the argument that such a creature could only have been created by evil on the one hand, or by a force as large as God on the other. One of the reasons that this poem has stood the test of time and is still a relevant and powerful piece of literature today is because of its infectious musicality, but also its thought-provoking subject matter.

Charting the progression of the text

Often the poem or extract that you will have to comment on will contain some sort of developmental pattern. It is important to be able to reflect on this. The poem below is followed by a commentary. While this commentary is a formal written example, it provides a general idea of the pattern you might follow in an IOC, although obviously the aim of the IOC is not to read an extensively prepared written response. Read through the poem, response and explanations in the marginalia of the commentary that show, among other things, how the commentary reflects upon the way the tension grows.

POMEGRANATES

Fat, juicy pomegranates lie in a row of orbicular perfection
Under the watchful eye of the weathered and tired hawker.
The gentle voices of the fruit sellers tick into time, clock needles
Cut about the gentle brown of nature as the wind caresses the tarpaulin.

The shadows shorten;   5
And Helios' stiff metal rays warm the feet of the children
As they scuttle about, sending small clouds of dust amidst the fruit
To settle in a fine duvet on each rounded globe of freckled brown.

The hawker wipes away that coat of earthy livery with a white cloth,
Leaving the sheen to reach out once more to the hungry eyes   10
Of the buyers that swell slowly about the fruit, their eyes growing
Wider with appetite.

He dreams of the coins that will flutter his purse with the loss of each fruit
When a voice reaches out to him, telling him to cut the fruit open
To see the juices   15
And now the wind begins to howl angrily

The sun's rays are no longer benign; the voices a chaotic, daemonic din
And the bodies press against each other to see the glimmer
Of the knife that dances in the heat
Sparkling like incandescent liquid silver   20

The hawker brings the blade high above his shoulder
And has a chance to see the smiles flicker through the crowd
Then brings it down on the fruit, searing through the skin
Leaving a deep blood red lung

The man scowls and winks, he nods his head   25
In admonishment
And the hawker wipes the gore off his blade
And states his price.

– Conrad Hughes, *The Bad Poetry Collection* (2009)

PARA 1 – Tells us what the commentary is going to do, and makes a clear argument.

The poem 'Pomegranates' by Conrad Hughes is, at first reading, a detailed and expressive description of how pomegranates are sold at the market. However, through a deeper reading and an analysis of the poem's use of symbols, tone, atmosphere, metaphor, punctuation, imagery and narrative structure, this commentary will argue that the poem is a statement about power.

PARA 2 – Makes a clear appreciation of the author's choices of literary techniques, and ends by returning to the argument.

The use of symbols in the poem is worth close investigation. The 'fat, juicy pomegranates' (line 1) are 'the brown of nature' (line 4) on the outside but 'deep blood red' (line 24) on the inside. This contrast of colours indicates that the pomegranates are symbols of strong passionate force hidden by a deceptively calm exterior of nature. The symbolic imagery extends itself into the man selling the fruit: on the outside he is 'weathered and tired' (line 2), but on the inside the reader is told that 'he dreams of the coins that will flutter into his purse with the loss of each fruit' (line 13). Like the pomegranates, the man's calm outside is contrasted with his lively interior. The effect on the reader of this symbolism and strong imagery is a feeling of something that hides its inner-nature through the disguise of the outside. By using a primary colour ('red') and associating it with 'blood' and a 'lung' (line 24), the poet is commenting on the specifically animalistic, human nature of power: it is not something abstract and indifferent but full of life and passion. The reader also notes that the pomegranates are described, symbolically as being 'under' the hawker: they are his property, his power and the crowd looks at the fruit with envy and appetite.

PARA 3 – Starts with a linking device, and charts the development of tone and atmosphere. It also makes an appreciation of the writer's choices. Returns to the argument at the end.

Similar to the explosive use of colours and contrast in the symbolism of the poem, the tone is one that alternates between the calm and the explosive. In the first ten lines of the poem the tone is serene and soothing: the 'wind caresses the tarpaulin' (line 4), the sun 'warms the feet of the children' (line 6) and the 'gentle voices of the fruit sellers' (line 3) help to create this effect. However, there is a turning point in the tone of the poem on line 15 when the man buying the pomegranates demands that it be cut open, 'to see the juices' (line 15). From this point on the tone and the atmosphere become tempestuous: the 'wind begins to howl angrily' (line 16), the sun's rays are 'no longer benign' (line 17) and what was previously the sound of gentle voices becomes 'a chaotic, daemonic din' (line 17). Not unlike the contrast between a calm outside and a passionate inside, the change in tone indicates a strong contrast, leaving the reader with a feeling of mounting antagonism and conflict. It is of interest to note that the turning point in the poem's atmosphere and tone comes at the point where the fruit buyer asks the hawker to cut the fruit open. This could be read as symbolic of someone asking another person to expose him or herself and in a sense to bring down his or her shield: indeed, the turning point is a statement that when one person asks another to relinquish some of his power, all havoc breaks loose.

PARA 4 – Begins with a linking device, then charts the poem's development of personification. The last sentence comes back to the argument.

In line with this progression, the use of metaphor in the poem moves from the calm to the living, primarily through the use of objectification in the first half of the poem and personification in the second part. To illustrate this, if one looks at the metaphors in the first 3 stanzas of the poem: the fruit are described as objects ('orbicular perfection'), the voices of the hawkers are like 'clock needles' and the sun's rays are described as 'metal'. This creates the effect of a mechanical process at work: everything works according to a pre-programmed schedule and there are no surprises. However, stanzas 4 to 7 use personification to enhance a feeling of panic and restlessness: coins 'flutter', 'a voice reaches out' to the hawker, 'the wind begins to howl angrily' and the knife 'dances'. Since the power hold of the hawker has been broken and the buyer is now putting himself in a situation of power by telling the hawker to expose his possessions, everything takes on the characteristics of animals or humans since everything is caught up in power relations which we associate with the living more than the unliving.

PARA 5 – Begins with a linking device. Explores how the use of punctuation relates to the central argument about power.

Another manner through which the passage goes from a calm atmosphere to a stormy one is communicated is through the use of punctuation. The use of full stops, commas and general punctuation in the first three stanzas allow the poem to breathe and gives the impression of an ordered universe. However, the last four stanzas of the poem are totally devoid of punctuation, using enjambment throughout. This helps to quicken the pace of the poem, adding tension to the atmosphere and it corresponds with the explosiveness of the second half when the pomegranate is cut open. To come back to the theme of power, once the power of the hawker has been challenged, the poem speeds up towards the climax of the cutting of the fruit, almost as if the power of the punctuation, which held the poem in place up until this point, has now given way to the free stream of human power that has taken over.

FINAL PARA – A good conclusion, summarizing the main points of the argument without being repetitive.

At the end of the poem the hawker has re-gained his power as he is the one to 'state his price' and it is now the buyer who 'scowls' and must pay. However, the knife, a symbol of war and violence, and the powerful image of the lung in the cut-open fruit and the gore on the blade, leave the reader with the feeling that the sacrifice made has been considerable and that someone has been mutilated. In conclusion, and keeping these last lines in mind, what Hughes is saying in this poem is that power has a destructive influence on the natural order of things. The ordained and calm atmosphere of the earlier parts of the poem is disrupted violently by the desire for power and the reaction this sparks in the crowd. The use of literary features in this poem contributes to this overall idea of the lust for power being something fundamentally destructive.

SUMMARY

A good IOC will not only reflect on the literary techniques used by the author, but chart the development and unfolding of themes, tensions and ideas in the text.

EXERCISE 5

Read through the following poem with guiding questions and consider how you would present an oral commentary on it.

To access worksheet 8.1 for example responses to this poem with examiner's comments, please visit www.pearsonbacconline.com and follow the on-screen instructions.

'The Mowed Hollow'

When yellow leaves the sky
they pipe it to the houses
to go on making red
and warm and floral and brown
but gradually people tire of it,   5
return it inside metal, and go
to be dark and breathe water colours.

Some yellow hangs on outside
forlornly tethered to posts.
Cars chase their own supply.   10

When we went down the hollow
under the stormcloud nations
the light was generalised there
from vague glass places in the trees
and the colours were moist and zinc,   15
submerged and weathered and lichen
with black aisles and white poplar blues.

The only yellow at all
was tight curls of fresh butter
as served on stainless steel   20
in a postwar cafe: cassia flowers,
soft crystal with caraway-dipped tongues,
butter mountains of cassia flowers
on green, still dewed with water.

– From Les Murray, *Conscious and Verbal* (1999)

GUIDING QUESTIONS

1 How does the progression of ideas contribute to the development of the theme(s)?

2 How does stanza structure reflect the development of the poem's subject?

EXERCISE 6

To access worksheet 8.2 to see an example of a plan relating to this exercise, please visit www.pearsonbacconline. com and follow the on-screen instructions.

The following soliloquy from Shakespeare's *Hamlet* might be familiar to you. Read through it, look at the guiding questions, and run through how you would plan out an oral commentary on the piece.

O, that this too too solid flesh would melt
Thaw and resolve itself into a dew!
Or that the Everlasting had not fix'd
His canon 'gainst self-slaughter! O God! God!
How weary, stale, flat and unprofitable,   5

Seem to me all the uses of this world!
Fie on't! ah fie! 'tis an unweeded garden,
That grows to seed; things rank and gross in nature
Possess it merely. That it should come to this!
But two months dead: nay, not so much, not two: 10

So excellent a king; that was, to this,
Hyperion to a satyr; so loving to my mother
That he might not beteem the winds of heaven
Visit her face too roughly. Heaven and earth!
Must I remember? why, she would hang on him,   15

As if increase of appetite had grown
By what it fed on: and yet, within a month–
Let me not think on't – Frailty, thy name is woman! –
A little month, or ere those shoes were old
With which she follow'd my poor father's body,   20

Like Niobe, all tears: – why she, even she –
O, God! a beast, that wants discourse of reason,
Would have mourn'd longer – married with my uncle,
My father's brother, but no more like my father
Than I to Hercules: within a month: 25

Ere yet the salt of most unrighteous tears
Had left the flushing in her galled eyes,
She married. O, most wicked speed, to post
With such dexterity to incestuous sheets!
It is not nor it cannot come to good: 30

But break, my heart; for I must hold my tongue.

GUIDING QUESTIONS

1   What is revealed about the character(s) through the diction employed?
2   For what reasons can this extract be considered a pivotal/key moment in the play?

EXERCISE 7

Look through the following extract of non-fiction from the Lebanese writer Amin Maalouf. Consider the guiding questions in planning how you would go about giving an oral commentary on it:

 To access worksheet 8.3 to see an example of a plan relating to this exercise, please visit www. pearsonbacconline.com and follow the on-screen instructions.

Sometimes, when I have finished explaining in detail why I fully claim all of my elements, someone comes up to me and whispers in a friendly way: 'You were right to say all this, but deep inside of yourself, what do you really feel you are?'

This question made me smile for a long time. Today, it no longer does. It reveals to me a dangerous and common attitude men have. When I am asked who I am 'deep inside of myself', it means there is, deep inside each one of us, one 'belonging' that matters, our profound truth, in a way, our 'essence' that is determined once and for all at our birth and never changes. As for the rest, all of the rest – the path of a free man, the beliefs he acquires, his preferences, his own sensitivity, his affinities, his life – all these things do not count […]. Whoever claims a more complex identity becomes marginalized. A young man born in France of Algerian parents is obviously part of two cultures and should be able to assume both. I said both to be clear, but the components of his personality are numerous. The language, the beliefs, the lifestyle, the relation with the family, the artistic and culinary taste, the influences – French, European, Occidental – blend in him with other influences – Arabic, Berber, African, Muslim. This could be an enriching and fertile experience if the young man feels free to live it fully, if he is encouraged to take upon himself his diversity; on the other side, his route can be traumatic if each time he claims he is French, some look at him as a traitor or a renegade, and also if each time he emphasizes his links with Algeria, its history, its culture, he feels a lack of understanding, mistrust or hostility.

– Amin Maalouf, *Deadly Identities* (1998)

GUIDING QUESTIONS

1 What is the likely impact of this extract on the reader?

2 How important is the logical sequence of ideas in this extract?

To access worksheet 8.4 for some essential points to consider when tackling this exercise, please visit www.pearsonbacconline.com and follow the on-screen instructions.

EXERCISE 8

This is the opening passage of the famous novella *Heart of Darkness* by Joseph Conrad. Read through the text, looking at the guiding questions, and decide how you would go about giving an oral commentary.

The *Nellie*, a cruising yawl, swung to her anchor without a flutter of the sails, and was at rest. The flood had made, the wind was nearly calm, and being bound down the river, the only thing for it was to come to and wait for the turn of the tide.   5

The sea-reach of the Thames stretched before us like the beginning of an interminable waterway. In the offing the sea and the sky were welded together without a joint, and in the luminous space the tanned sails of the barges drifting up with the tide seemed to   10 stand still in red clusters of canvas sharply peaked, with gleams of varnished spirit. A haze rested on the low shores that ran out to sea in vanishing flatness. The air was dark above Gravesend, and farther back still seemed condensed into a mournful gloom, brood-   15 ing motionless over the biggest, and the greatest, town on earth.

The Director of Companies was our captain and our host. We four affectionately watched his back as he stood in the bows looking to seaward. On the whole   20 river there was nothing that looked half so nautical. He resembled a pilot, which to a seaman is trust-worthiness personified. It was difficult to realize his work was not out there in the luminous estuary, but behind him, within the brooding gloom.   25

Between us there was, as I have already said some-where, the bond of the sea. Besides holding our hearts together through long periods of separation, it had the effect of making us tolerant of each other's yarns – and even convictions.   30

– Joseph Conrad, *Heart of Darkness* (1899)

GUIDING QUESTIONS

1 Discuss the imagery in this extract.

2 What is the primary significance of this passage?

To access worksheet
8.5 – an example of how
you could go about
Exercise 9 – please visit
www.pearsonbacconline.
com and follow the
on-screen instructions.

EXERCISE 9

'The Road Not Taken' by Robert Frost is a poem with a clear idea behind it. Think about the author's choices and how this idea is communicated through them. Consider the guiding questions and run through how you would plan a commentary on it.

'The Road Not Taken'

Two roads diverged in a yellow wood,
And sorry I could not travel both
And be one traveler, long I stood
And looked down one as far as I could
To where it bent in the undergrowth;   5

Then took the other, as just as fair,
And having perhaps the better claim,
Because it was grassy and wanted wear;
Though as for that the passing there
Had worn them really about the same,   10

And both that morning equally lay
In leaves no step had trodden black.
Oh, I kept the first for another day!
Yet knowing how way leads on to way,
I doubted if I should ever come back.   15

I shall be telling this with a sigh
Somewhere ages and ages hence:
Two roads diverged in a wood, and I—
I took the one less traveled by,
And that has made all the difference.   20

– Robert Frost, 'The Road Not Taken' (1916)

GUIDING QUESTIONS

1   What is the relationship between the title and the poem itself?
2   In what ways does the final line/stanza change your understanding of the poem as a whole?

INSIGHTS INTO THE INDIVIDUAL ORAL COMMENTARY

Now that we have come to the close of this chapter, let's explore some of the key skills you need as you prepare for the IOC.

1   The IOC is an exercise in close reading. This means that you need to pay exceptional attention to detail and focus on the ways that the text develops. Look for nuances, subtleties, specific details and above all make sure that you relay the meaning of the text (what it is saying about the human condition at a deeper level, rather than the subject matter as it is treated on the surface).

2   If you are in the HL then you will analyze a poem for ten minutes and then enter into a discussion on one of the remaining Part 2 texts for the next ten minutes. If you are in the SL then you will receive either a poem or an extract from one of the other Part 2 texts (the extract will be between 20 and 30 lines long) and you will be expected to speak about it for ten minutes. For both SL and HL, the ten minutes' commentary time is divided into eight minutes for your structured approach and two minutes to answer questions.

3 For HL only, when entering into a discussion on the work as the second part of your commentary, make sure that your teacher is able to evaluate the knowledge and understanding you have of the work, the originality of your position and your appreciation of the techniques and themes evoked. Make sure that you have thought about each work carefully before the examination, so that you are able to talk about any one with purpose and direction.

4 The text will be accompanied by one to two guiding questions. You do not have to answer these, but remember that they are there to help you and can be useful to incorporate into your commentary as structuring devices.

5 There are essentially two ways to approach the text for the IOC: either line-by-line (otherwise known as a chronological or linear approach) or thematic. Whether you choose one or the other you should make sure that you begin with a clear introduction and end with an equally clear conclusion. The introduction must identify the text (say briefly what it is) and contain a statement of intent where you tell the listener how you are going to go about analyzing it.

6 Make sure that you take some sort of argument or position; if you do not, then you run the risk of merely paraphrasing the text and explaining what happens. Your job is to go further and show personal response and creative analysis.

7 One of the things you are being tested on is your knowledge and understanding of the poem or extract. This does not mean that you should talk about the work as a whole and neglect the passage in front of you, but it does mean that you should show that you know the passage well and can understand its contents thoroughly.

8 A helpful way of summing up the essential aim of the commentary is through the words WHAT (what is the text saying?); THROUGH (through which literary techniques and authorial choices?); to what EFFECT (how does this affect what is being said and how does it affect me as a reader?); and MEANING (in the conclusion, for instance, you could talk about the overall philosophical significance of the text).

9 Although you need to keep your mind open and make sure that you reflect on the most prominent aspects of the text at hand, a useful mnemonic to prevent your mind going blank on the day is **STAMPIN**: Style, Tone, Atmosphere, Metaphor, Imagery and Narrative Structure. These techniques can be used to frame your commentary and you can look at the text through each of them, giving examples of effect and meaning each time.

10 To prepare well for the IOC, make sure that you go through all of the poems and/or extracts that might come up on the day and have a few ideas ready for each, including some original insights, a short summary of what the text is about and an idea of the key literary devices that are at work.

11 As concerns literary technique and linking devices, be sure to read over the appropriate sections in Chapter 7 to remind yourself of how these can be used for the IOC.

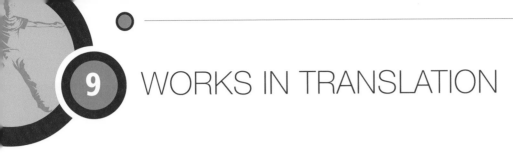

9 WORKS IN TRANSLATION

Learning Outcomes

Knowledge and Understanding
- Investigate the role of culture in literature
- Understand the essential components of the 'works in translation' section of the course
- Explore the assessment criteria for the 'works in translation' section
- Discuss the meeting of cultures in the act of reading

Appreciation
- Consider the subtleties of culture
- Explore the interactive oral presentation
- Discuss the reflective statement
- Explore the supervised writing exercise
- Examine the assessment criteria of the reflective statement and the essay
- Appreciate examples of the reflective statement and the essay

Introduction

Why study works in translation?

Literature is one of the highest forms of expression, and as such it is a diverse, creative and complex field. The study of literature is more than the technical appreciation of an art form; it involves meeting with a mind from a different time, perspective and place.

You are the student of an international course: your outlook on the world is being formed by an international experience and international learning. The study of literature is a good way to explore the human experiences and life stories that shape other people. By studying broadly and beyond national frontiers, you are engaging with the human condition in its complex web of cultural, social and geographical differences.

There is a particular emphasis on culture in this part of the course: you will be asked to respond to the issue of culture through the study of literature, taking into account your own cultural viewpoint as you do this. Consider the notion that literature is the product of a culture rather than a work of some individual imagination in isolation. The creation of literature takes place within a cultural framework, and it is difficult to disentangle literature from its cultural context.

The American psychologist Jerome Bruner explains how all cultures organize their knowledge of the world in two broad and distinctive ways: as 'logical scientific' and 'narrative' thinking. Most Western cultures tend to favour scientific, logical and sequential thinking whereas many non-Western cultures – such as African, Asian and South American cultures – tend to favour narrative, non-linear thinking. The study of literature from other cultures, particularly non-Western ones, is therefore a chance to enter into a different way of perceiving the world.

Studying works in translation ▶ opens you up to different narratives from across the world. It is a key part of your international learning.

The written assignment that you complete for the literature in translation part of the course is worth 25 per cent of your final grade.

● **Examiner's hints**

If you are in the Standard Level, you will study two works in translation, whereas Higher Level students study three. This is the only real difference between the two levels as concerns Part 1.

Knowledge and Understanding
The structure of Part 1: works in translation
The steps leading up to the essay (SL and HL)

These are the steps that you will take with your teacher to complete the written assignment:

Interactive oral

1. You will engage in an **interactive oral** on each of the Part 1 works studied. This can take many shapes and forms, but will essentially be a classroom discussion about key issues that appear in the work. It will last about 30 minutes, and it is important to get as many people as possible involved in the discussion.

2. You will be assigned to lead the conversation for at least one of these discussions and your teacher will be looking to you for leadership, drive and creativity, as well as your good ideas and an analytical approach. If you have been assigned to lead the interactive oral, then make sure that you know the topic you will be speaking on and prepare some leading questions that the rest of the class can respond to once you have initiated the discussion.

3. There are many different ways of conducting the first part of the written assignment, and your teacher will no doubt give you an idea of how she or he would like to see you go about this task. Be sure to ask relevant questions so that you are quite clear on how you go about the interactive oral.

Here are some of the types of question that you can expect as starting points for the discussion, plus some tips on how to go about them:

In what ways do time and place matter to this work?

Here you will need to think about the period in which the work was written, and how the conditions of the period have affected the writing, made it different to the present and given it something special or unusual. For example, a work written in 17th-century Europe will make reference to ideas that are no longer prevalent today, such as the Great Chain of Being, artifice and beauty as man-made rather than natural.

The Great Chain of Being

The Great Chain of Being was a Renaissance concept in which there is a natural hierarchy imposed on the world from God at the top all the way down to the tiniest insect, with human beings in the middle.

◀ Notions of beauty have changed over time, as is the case with the concept of 'artifice', which was popular in Western Europe during the early 17th century. The notion rested on principles of extremely elaborate and contrived man-made objects, as can be seen in the ornate dress style of Queen Elizabeth I.

● **Examiner's hints**
Remember that culture is extremely complex and infinitely subtle. Be sure to look at the place and time of your work with as much specificity as possible, avoiding sweeping statements about continents or entire centuries.

Place will also have an effect on the literature you study, as geography is intertwined with culture. For example, literature from South America will not necessarily be the same as literature from China due to the different religions in those places, not to mention differences in language, ethnicity and geography.

To access worksheet 9.1 to view an answer to this exercise, please visit www.pearsonbacconline.com and follow the on-screen instructions.

EXERCISE 1

Consider the different religions listed below and see if you can say in which parts of the world each one predominates:

- Baha'i faith
- Christianity: Protestantism
- Hinduism
- Judaism
- Taoism

- Buddhism
- Amish
- Islam
- Shinto
- Voodoo

- Christianity: Catholicism
- Confucianism
- Jainism
- Sikhism
- Animism

What is easy to understand and what is difficult in relation to social and cultural context and issues?

Here is an opportunity for you to develop a response that takes into account your own reading of the text. You can approach the question in more than one way, but whichever way you choose you need to think about the issues that you found difficult to penetrate: e.g. the elements of culture that were alien to you, or which troubled you or seemed obscure.

Furthermore, there may have been cultural ideas and notions in the texts that you disagreed with, and here you have a chance to explore them, taking into account your own position. For example, the foreign treatment of women, acceptance or intolerance of homosexuality, notions of sacrifice, initiation and punishment, may all be traditions that challenge you. As you read the different works in translation in Part 1, think about which concepts are at work (if any) and map them out (you can do this by writing them into the margin of your book or separately in a journal or notes), ready to explore them in more detail when you present to the group. Ultimately, however, you have to see the text in terms of its own context, rather than in terms of yours.

The meeting of two cultures is a moment of interaction that can result in harmony or tension.

EXERCISE 2

Turn to page 181 in Chapter 7 and look at the cultural iceberg, and in particular the base – those elements of culture that are 'out of awareness'. See which of the descriptions in that part of the iceberg you can talk about when looking at the works in translation you are studying. In other words, for each work, run through the iceberg to see if you can recognize the more subtle elements of culture.

To access worksheet 9.2 to see an example of a response using a literature in translation text, please visit www. pearsonbacconline.com and follow the on-screen instructions.

GLOBAL PERSPECTIVES

The study of literature can put you in challenging situations where you need to think about your principles and weigh them up against different cultural traditions, with which you may or may not agree.

What connections did you find between issues in the work and your own culture(s) and experience?

We all carry our cultures about with us: culture is beneath our skin and it influences our decisions, dreams, motivations, judgements and ideas. When you interact with a piece of literature that comes from a culture different to your own, you are not merely coming into contact with something that is different; there is an interaction between you and the text, a meeting between two cultures.

Reading literature from other cultures is like raising a mirror to oneself, as literature tells us about what it means to be human.

We sometimes speak of a culture clash when two belief systems that are incompatible come into contact with each other. One of the purposes of an international education is to enrich yourself by interacting with literature from other cultures. You do this to deepen not only your understanding of the cultures that you are learning about, but also to broaden your own cultural sensitivity.

By looking for cultural connections, you are opening your mind to elements of human behaviour that are common across cultures, the things that bring us together and make us human. As you read through the works in translation, reflect on this question:

What aspects of technique are interesting in the work?

By technique we mean literary features such as those listed in Chapter 7 (pages 184–85). You will be expected to discuss these in order to show how the author achieves his or her messages, effects and general goals. Using bookmarks or colour-marking can be a good way of keeping track of some of the principal techniques used by the author. Make sure that you do this as you read through the works in order to prepare yourself for the interactive oral, written assignment and essay.

As the reflective statement that follows is asking you to reflect directly on the interactive oral, you will need to take notes during the class discussion, whether you are the one leading the discussion or not.

Reflective statement

Shortly after the class discussion, within a timeframe set out by the teacher, you will write a short reflective statement between 300 and 400 words on the following question:

How was your understanding of cultural and contextual considerations of the work developed through the interactive oral?

You will do this for each of the presentations (so two reflective statements for two oral presentations if you are in the SL and three oral presentations and reflective statements if you are in the HL). The reflective statement will be handed in to your teacher.

The reflective statement will be marked out of 3 marks using assessment Criterion A, but this will be done externally by an examiner. Your teacher might mark this himself or herself for internal purposes. It may be that your teacher marks all of the reflective statements that you generate as opposed to just the one that you submit with the essay at the end of the process. However, only the one you select to be sent off with the essay will be marked by an IB examiner.

These are the level descriptors for the 3 marks that can be awarded for the reflective statement:

Criterion A: Fulfilling the requirements of the reflective statement

To what extent does the student show how their understanding of cultural and contextual elements was developed through the interactive oral?

[**Note:** The word limit for the reflective statement is 300–400 words. If the word limit is exceeded, 1 mark will be deducted.]

Marks	Level descriptor
0	The work does not reach a standard described by the descriptors below.
1	Reflection on the interactive oral shows superficial development of the student's understanding of cultural and contextual elements.
2	Reflection on the interactive oral shows some development of the student's understanding of cultural and contextual elements.
3	Reflection on the interactive oral shows strong development of the student's understanding of cultural and contextual elements.

Below are two examples of reflective statements, one weak, one strong:

Student Sample 1

My understanding of the culture of the Ibo was deepened through the discussion we had on religion in *Things Fall Apart* (Chinua Achebe). We debated whether Ibo religion with its emphasis on the afterworld and the spirits was based on faith or superstition and came to the conclusion that this was too superficial and artificial a way of looking at the question. A better approach would be to say that the Ibo religion is based on a cosmology that goes beyond understanding of life and death into a perpetual cycle between the living, the dead and the unborn and as such there is the feeling that the ancestors are constantly watching over the present and can be venerated, honoured or indeed shamed.

Okonkwo's visit to the Agbala shows the reader that the superstitious approach comes more from him than the religion itself as he is in a state of perpetual paranoia and power struggle. Unlike the wise chief priestess Ezeani, who reveres the ancestors and looks to them as vanguards of the present, Okonkwo despises his most immediate predecessor, his father, and in doing so breaks with the Ibo tradition. It is this transgression that causes him to become superstitious, as he no longer has the faith and confidence in the past that any honourable Ibo member of society should, and therefore he acts in increasingly compulsive and violent ways.

The class debate developed this idea in interesting ways: at first most of the class felt that the purpose of *Things Fall Apart* was to suggest that the Ibo religion is a rigid system and not as flexible and forgiving as Christianity and this was why it failed to keep the village together. However, provocative questions and statements such as 'who exactly leads the village to its downfall after all?' and 'surely Achebe is looking at culture in a more sophisticated way than this!' slowly took us to a different conclusion.

The interactive oral was a powerful and transformative experience that made us think about culture in *Things Fall Apart* more carefully and reflectively. It made us consider how culture in general cannot be considered as something that exists of its own accord without taking into account the people that embody and dramatize it.

Examiner's grading and comment

3 points: Reflection on the interactive oral shows strong development of the student's understanding of cultural and contextual elements.

This grading is based upon:

Criterion A: Fulfilling the requirements of the reflective statement

To what extent does the student show how their understanding of cultural and contextual elements was developed through the interactive oral?

Student Sample 2

In our class we studied the play *Death and the Maiden* by Ariel Dorfman. It was a good play and I really liked it. In the class discussion we talked about many things, like justice. The discussions were interesting and I feel that I really got a lot out of them.

When we discussed justice there were many interesting things that came up, for example the way that the main character wants to take justice against her former torturer. This was an interesting conversation and it made me think about culture in Chile. The culture of Chile is such that people take justice into their own hands. She wants to do this and this was something that we debated in the class.

I felt that I also learned about the role of women in South American culture through the discussion. In my culture women are free but in the South American culture they are not. Women in this culture really have to fight for their rights and it's not really fair at all. I feel this strongly coming from my cultural viewpoint.

I felt that this was developed through the discussion we had because we said many things about the main female character and gave many examples of how she is not free. For example, her husband does not listen to her and Dr Miranda, her torturer, raped her.

All in all I felt that it was a really interesting conversation that we had in the class and it definitely helped me develop my understanding of culture in *Death and the Maiden* for the reasons that I have already given. I would add that there were also contextual elements that I understood more because of the interactive oral and this was a good thing because I now feel I know the work much better.

Examiner's grading and comments

1 point: Reflection on the interactive oral shows superficial development of the student's understanding of cultural and contextual elements.

Grading based on:

Criterion A: Fulfilling the requirements of the reflective statement

To what extent does the student show how their understanding of cultural and contextual elements was developed through the interactive oral?

To access worksheet 9.5 – Suggested answer to Exercise 3 – please visit www.pearsonbacconline.com and follow the on-screen instructions.

> ### EXERCISE 3
>
> Study the student samples given above. Can you give five reasons explaining the strengths and weaknesses of each reflective statement?

> The reflective statement is a chance for you to consider your own perception of the work as a way of knowing. Consider how your specific approach to the text shapes the meaning that you derive from it. This perspective will depend on whether you can relate to the characters or not, and in which ways, the extent to which you are drawn into the style and what your response is to the ethical dilemmas and cultural variants presented in the text.

Supervised writing

In the supervised writing leg of this learning experience, you are asked to write in a limited period of time about each of the works studied, working from three prompts given to you by your teacher. You will be expected to write in continuous prose for a period of about 40–50 minutes. There is no word limit for the supervised writing exercise. This work will be handed in to the teacher at the end of the exercise.

You will be allowed to have the relevant text with you, plus any annotated notes taken in class during the teaching of the work in question. However, you will not know what the prompts are before the exercise, and you are not allowed to have access to study guides or any other secondary material.

● Examiner's hints
The supervised writing exercise is not marked by the IB and is meant to develop your work in progress as you move towards the final essay that you will submit for this part of the course.

This part of the process is designed to make you think more about the work in translation you have studied. You do not need to worry so much about the format of the supervised writing, and it does not have to be a formal essay. Your teacher will advise you more precisely on the style and format of the piece expected. The main idea is to generate a piece of writing that you will later develop into an essay.

Your teacher will give you three to four prompts. You are expected to choose one and write on it. Choosing the right prompt will be crucial. Not only do you want to generate a good piece of supervised writing, but the supervised writing is also meant to be the foundation for the essay that you will write later: it is the germ of an idea that you will develop under your teacher's supervision into a fully fledged essay.

The prompts will be fairly general questions about themes, characters or techniques in the work. You can expect them to relate to the kinds of discussions you will have had about your work in the classroom.

Here are some examples of the kinds of prompts that you could find your teacher giving you:

● Examiner's hints
Make sure that you ask your teacher to clarify any prompt that you do not understand before you start writing about it.

- Discuss which of the minor characters in this work plays the most important role.
- Which characters in the work have as a primary role the portrayal of the culture? (In other words, which characters seem to be there mainly to suggest cultural archetypes?)
- Elaborate on the use of symbols in the work studied.
- Write on the use of motif in the work.
- Discuss the role of imagery in the work you have studied.
- What is the role of tradition in the work?
- Discuss the significance of the landscape in the work.
- Explore the way that time unfolds in the work.

Essay

The last step is to choose one of the works that you have studied in Part 1 and to write an essay on it. Your essay will be between 1,200 and 1,500 words in length and will be based on a title and topic that you will have chosen, but with the guidance and supervision of your teacher. The essay will be marked externally by an IB examiner out of 22 points and, added to the 3 points that can be awarded for the reflective statement, will comprise 25 per cent of your final IB grade.

Your essay will be developed from one of the supervised writings that you write after finishing your reading of the work in translation. Your teacher will read through one draft of your work and give you feedback either in writing on a separate piece of paper or through an oral discussion.

Finding the right title for your essay will be important. Here are some examples of the types of titles you might consider for the essay, with the reflective statement prompts that initiated the process:

Essay Title: The symbolism of the colour red in Mann's *Death in Venice*
Prompt: Comment on the use of symbolism in *Death in Venice*.
Work: *Death in Venice* by Thomas Mann

Essay Title: Santiago Nasar as the sacrificial lamb in *Chronicle of a Death Foretold*
Prompt: What is the role of the main character in *Chronicle of a Death Foretold*?
Work: *Chronicle of a Death Foretold* by Gabriel García Márquez

Essay Title: The messenger as creator of suspense in *Oedipus Rex*
Prompt: How do minor characters contribute to the technical development of the work?
Work: *Oedipus Rex* by Sophocles

Essay Title: The mother as representation of the traditional Andalusian family in *Blood Wedding*
Prompt: Are there some characters whose main function is to convey cultural values?
Work: *Blood Wedding* by Federico García Lorca

Essay Title: The will to survive: the motif of bread in *One Day in the Life of Ivan Denisovich*
Prompt: Comment on the use of motif in *One Day in the Life of Ivan Denisovich*.
Work: *One Day in the Life of Ivan Denisovich* by Aleksandr Solzhenitsyn

Essay Title: Wide open space as a representation of death in *A Hero of Our Time*
Prompt: Comment on the use of space in *A Hero of Our Time*.
Work: *A Hero of Our Time* by Mikhail Lermontov

Essay Title: Moscow as a symbol of escape in *Three Sisters*
Prompt: Discuss the role of the city in *Three Sisters*.
Work: *Three Sisters* by Anton Chekhov

Essay Title: Identity and colonization through narrative structure in *Houseboy*
Prompt: How does the narrative structure of *Houseboy* develop some of its themes?
Work: *Houseboy* by Ferdinand Oyono

Essay Title: The folktale as vehicle of social cohesion in *The Tales of Amadou Koumba*
Prompt: How does the structure of *The Tales of Amadou Koumba* contribute to the values of the Senegalese culture it expresses?
Work: *The Tales of Amadou Koumba* by Birago Diop

Essay Title: The redefinition of beauty in Senghor's poetry
Prompt: How does the poet question Western values?
Work: *Selected Poems* by Léopold Senghor

In each of these cases you can see that there is a relationship between the prompt given in class for the supervised writing and the final essay. Once you have completed the supervised writing, your job is to see ways that the topic generated by the prompt can develop into a more specific treatment in the form of the essay.

Consider the following table as an explanation of this process. Of course, this process will depend on the work you are studying, but hopefully it will give you an idea:

Prompt	Potential essay topics
The use of symbols in the text …	One particular object as a symbol of something
	Symbols of death
	Symbols of freedom
	Symbols of entrapment
	Symbols of the past
	Symbols of time
	The symbolism of clothes
	The symbolism of names
	The symbolism of places
The role of the protagonist …	Scapegoat
	Tragic hero
	The leader
	The rebel
	The victim
	The dreamer
	The artist

Then from the potential topic you can shape your ideas further and design a proper essay title that will contain a sufficient level of detail. For example:

Onomastics
The study of the history and origin of names, especially personal names.

Potential essay topics	Potential essay titles
One particular object as a symbol of something	Books as symbols of free thinking in Henrik Ibsen's *Ghosts*
Symbols of death	Water as a symbol of death in Gustave Flaubert's *Madame Bovary*
Symbols of freedom	Windows as symbols of freedom in Anton Chekhov's *Three Sisters*
Symbols of entrapment	Closed spaces as symbols of imprisonment in Franz Kafka's *Metamorphosis*
Symbols of time	The husk of bread as a symbol of the passing of time in Aleksandr Solzhenitsyn's *One Day in the Life of Ivan Denisovich*
The symbolism of names	Names of religion: Onomastics in *Chronicle of a Death Foretold* by Gabriel García Márquez
Symbols of the past	Natural description as symbolic expression of the past in Nikos Kazantzakis' *Zorba the Greek*
The symbolism of clothes	Dress as an extension of values: the symbolism of clothes in Mikhail Lermontov's *A Hero of Our Time*
The symbolism of places	Eternal Recurrence: The symbolism of the non-changing place in Samuel Beckett's *Waiting for Godot*

The prompt is like a seed that grows into a tree. Consider the supervised writing as the trunk of the tree and the potential essays that you can write as the many branches that come out of that central idea.

Essay submission

Your submission of the essay and the reflective statement will be on a date set by the teacher. Your essay will be graded out of 22 and the reflective statement out of 3, but this will be done externally by IB examiners so you will not know what your score was until the very end of the course.

Before you submit your essay make sure that you have read it very carefully. It can be a good idea to have someone else (other than your teacher) look through it before you submit it. Be sure to read it against the assessment criteria and see if you can get a peer to mark it for you using the criteria.

● **Examiner's hints**
Whenever you submit a piece of work make sure that you have run through it with a fine- tooth comb for typographical errors, formatting and referencing.

The assessment criteria of the written assignment

Note: The assessment criteria of the written assignment are identical at SL and HL.

Written assignment (SL and HL)
Criterion B: Knowledge and Understanding

How effectively has the student used the topic and the essay to show knowledge and understanding of the chosen work?

Marks	Level descriptor
0	The work does not reach a standard described by the descriptors below.
1–2	The essay shows some knowledge but little understanding of the work used for the assignment.
3–4	The essay shows knowledge and understanding of, and some insight into, the work used for the assignment.
5–6	The essay shows detailed knowledge and understanding of, and perceptive insight into, the work used for the assignment.

Criterion C: Appreciation of the writer's choices

To what extent does the student appreciate how the writer's choices of language, structure, technique and style shape meaning?

Marks	Level descriptor
0	The work does not reach a standard described by the descriptors below.
1–2	There is some mention, but little appreciation, of the ways in which language, structure, technique and style shape meaning.
3–4	There is adequate appreciation of the ways in which language, structure, technique and style shape meaning.
5–6	There is excellent appreciation of the ways in which language, structure, technique and style shape meaning.

Criterion D: Organization and development

How effectively have the ideas been organized, and how well are references to the works integrated into the development of the ideas?

[**Note:** The word limit for the essay is 1,200–1,500 words. If the word limit is exceeded, 2 marks will be deducted.]

Marks	Level descriptor
0	The work does not reach a standard described by the descriptors below.
1	There is some attempt to organize ideas, but little use of examples from the works used.
2	Ideas are superficially organized and developed, with some integrated examples from the works used.
3	Ideas are adequately organized and developed, with appropriately integrated examples from the works used.
4	Ideas are effectively organized and developed, with well-integrated examples from the works used.
5	Ideas are persuasively organized and developed, with effectively integrated examples from the works used.

Criterion E: Language

How clear, varied and accurate is the language?

How appropriate is the choice of register, style and terminology? ('Register' refers, in this context, to the student's use of elements such as vocabulary, tone, sentence structure and terminology appropriate to the task.)

Marks	Level descriptor
0	The work does not reach a standard described by the descriptors below.
1	Language is rarely clear and appropriate; there are many errors in grammar, vocabulary and sentence construction, and little sense of register and style.
2	Language is sometimes clear and carefully chosen; grammar, vocabulary and sentence construction are fairly accurate, although errors and inconsistencies are apparent; the register and style are to some extent appropriate to the task.
3	Language is clear and carefully chosen, with an adequate degree of accuracy in grammar, vocabulary and sentence construction despite some lapses; register and style are mostly appropriate to the task.
4	Language is clear and carefully chosen, with a good degree of accuracy in grammar, vocabulary and sentence construction; register and style are consistently appropriate to the task.
5	Language is very clear, effective, carefully chosen and precise, with a high degree of accuracy in grammar, vocabulary and sentence construction; register and style are effective and appropriate to the task.

EXERCISE 5

Read through the following supervised writing and essay, making notes on the strong points in the essay and how it develops from the supervised writing.

Supervised Writing Sample

Prompt: Comment on the use of symbolism in *The Outsider*

The main symbol in *The Outsider* is the sun. The way that this symbol develops is complex and interesting. At first we note that there is a strong presence of heat and the dazzle of the sun in the first few pages: 'it was very hot' (Camus, 9), 'the glare of the sky reflecting off the road' makes Meursault doze off' (10).

The mortuary where Meursault's dead mother is kept is 'very bright' (12) and is bathed in 'sunshine'. The presence of the sun and the heat is intensified as the narrative unfolds further: the sun rises in the sky surprisingly quickly (20) during the procession and Meursault, who is not wearing a hat, feels the sweat streaming down his face.

The presence of the overwhelming heat and sun in the opening passage suggests that the sun is a power to be reckoned with. As it comes with the demise of the protagonist's mother it seems to represent, paradoxically, the theme of death.

The idea of the sun representing death is countered, or complemented somewhat, in the second chapter where Meursault and Marie, his girlfriend, swim together and enjoy sunbathing. Here the sun is pleasant and sensual: Meursault closes his eyes and everything is 'blue and gold' (24), Marie comments that she is 'browner' than Meursault and when it gets 'too hot' they dive into the sea. Here the reader is introduced to a new side of the sun, representing a type of freedom and simple pleasure.

The end of the first part of the novel sees the sun come to its climax. It is as if the entire first day has been one prolonged day with the sun slowly rising to its zenith. When Meursault shoots the Arab on the beach the description of the sun is very powerful and mesmerizing: 'The sea swept ashore a great breath of fire. The sky seemed to be splitting from end to end and raining down sheets of flame' (60).

This is the turning point in the novel as Meursault is knocking on the door of unhappiness and deciding his fate that will end with his execution. The sun at this point is at its most powerful. Here it seems to represent fate.

To access worksheet 9.3 to see an examiner's response to the essay, please visit www.pearsonbacconline.com and follow the on-screen instructions.

The second part of *The Outsider* consists essentially of the court case. The sun is less present in this part of the narrative, it is filtered by a 'net curtain' (66) in the lawyer's office and blinds (81) in the latter part of the trial. Interestingly, Raymond remarks that when it begins to get hot events seem to take their toll. He says: 'I knew that as soon as it began to get hot something was going to happen to me' (80).

It appears that the sun is a symbol of more than one thing in this novel, it represents death, sensuality, fate and action. The sun is filtered and lessened during the trial, which seems to suggest that the trial prevents the aforementioned things from taking place.

Essay: The Sun as a Symbol of Truth in Albert Camus' *The Outsider*

In this essay it will be argued that the sun functions as a symbol of truth in Camus' *The Outsider*. The type of truth that is represented though this symbol is one of meaninglessness. Whilst Meursault, the protagonist, responds to it in an unthinking existential manner, society, emblematized by the justice system and the conventions of mourning, filters it and thus tries to prevent the truth from being known. The essay will examine this idea by discussing the use of the symbol in different passages of *The Outsider* with reference to the use of the style of the narrative and how this develops the characterization of the protagonist.

The style of the novel and the way that it evolves tells the reader much about the significance of the sun. Indeed, as the narrative of the first part unfolds and the sun reaches its zenith in a type of ongoing day, the sentences become more and more expressive. This progression is slow and it needs to be charted carefully.

At first bald statements such as 'it was very hot' (Camus 9) and 'it was a very bright room' (page 12) mirror the famous opening line of the novel 'Mother died today' (9) and the dispassionate description of the morgue and its inhabitants. This factual style suggests, like the undeniable heat of the sun, that the death of Meursault's mother is a hard fact with little meaning attached to it. Meursault expresses little emotional reaction to the death and seems to accept it in the same matter-of-fact manner of the style in which all this is being told. The sun makes him sleepy and is described as 'beautiful' (13): Meursault is lulled by its presence but adds little comment to its potency and merely reminds the reader that it is there.

The next day, during the burial procession, the sun's intensity increases and so too does the expressivity of the narrative: the sun 'was beginning to weigh down heavily on the earth [...] with the whole landscape flooded in sunshine and shimmering in the heat' (20). At the same time Meursault's narration becomes more and more impressionistic and poetic: he speaks of the 'heat-haze' (21), blood pounding in his temples (22) and gives the reader a series of fragmented images: 'the blood-red earth tumbling onto mother's coffin, the white flesh of the roots mixed in with it, more people, voices, the village' (22). All the while the sun has become so hot that it bursts open the tarmac of the road. Meursault has become so tired that he 'cannot see or think straight anymore' hence the style of the narration has become something of a stream of consciousness.

Therefore the sun represents the uncomfortable and inexorable fact of the mother's death in the first few chapters of the novel. This fact becomes increasingly oppressive as the sun's power radiates more and more heat, causing the narrative to enter into a slightly blurred internal monologue. In this way the sun also serves as a type of barometer for Meursault's act of narrating as it mirrors the change in his mental state.

The truth of death is echoed by the truth of sensuality as the next major description of the sun comes with the time Meursault spends with Marie the next day by the sea. The poetic description of the 'whole sky' in Meursault's eyes shimmering in 'blue and gold' (24) correlates with the simple activities he engages in with Marie, swimming, lying on her stomach and laughing childishly. There is a simplicity in their interaction that represents a pure and unequivocal truth, that of the elements and the body. It is in this regard that we can look at the work as existentialist as the sheer uncommented existence of Meursault and Marie takes precedence over all else: the death of the mother, the protocol of mourning and the ethics of their relationship are swept under the carpet and instead of this there is a simple physical attraction.

The climax of the sun's meaningless truth comes with the killing of the Arab on the beach at the end of the first part. The description of the sun is very powerful and mesmerizing: 'The sea swept ashore a great breath of fire. The sky seemed to be splitting from end to end and raining down sheets of flame'(60). The sun is described as a 'dazzling spear', a 'flashing sword' and a 'red-hot iron', all connoting violence. Indeed, the use of the weaponry imagery furthers the idea that the sun is entering into Meursault, penetrating him and burning its way to his core (he describes it as 'gnawing' at him). At this high point of tension the style of the novel is at its most expressive and poetic: the reader is no longer within the tightly controlled and minimalistic voice of Meursault but deep in the throes of a type of *vox dei* that has taken control and swept up all in its fiery path. The truth of the sun is at its purest.

This is the turning point in the novel as Meursault is knocking on the door of unhappiness and deciding his fate that will end with his execution. The sun at this point, at its most commanding, represents the utter meaninglessness of the act that Meursault perpetrates as he is now pushing himself into an act that later he will not be able to explain or justify, it is simply, as he states later in the trial, because of 'the sun' (99).

The second part of the novel dedicated to the trial is quite different in the way that the style builds up and as concerns the sun as a symbol of the truth. Although the idea remains intact, the sun is less present and the theme of truth is played out in the shade of the court room. The style is, accordingly, fairly minimalistic and straightforward.

Subtle hints tell the reader that the truth is not allowed to shine in the court: the prosecutor and journalists, representing a lie to portray Meursault as a type of monster, all have 'straw fans' (86) as if to protect them from the heat of the truth. The sun is less present in this part of the narrative, it is filtered by a 'net curtain' (66) in the lawyer's office and blinds (81) in the latter part of the trial. At the same time the style of the narrative is less expressive and more matter-of-fact, merely pointing to the ruthless indictment of Meursault by the prosecution and the way that the witnesses are manipulated.

Interestingly, Meursault remarks that when it begins to get hot events seem to take their toll. He says: 'I knew that as soon as it began to get hot something was going to happen to me' (80). This indicates that the sun somehow creates action or galvanizes characters into action, and in this there is a truth albeit an existential one, based simply on things happening and the idea that in the unfolding of events there is a truthfulness that cannot be denied. However, the action that is set in place is one of absurdity as it will be the sentencing of Meursault for the wrong reasons (chiefly the way he behaved at his mother's funeral).

The emotional intensity of the narrative style increases once more as we approach the end of the novel and Meursault has the conversation about faith with the priest. It is here that he shows real frustration and decisive expression for the first time in the novel. At a crucial point in their conversation, contrasting either man's vision of truth, the priest asks what Meursault sees in the walls of the prison when he stares into them day after day. He claims that 'deep in my [his] heart I know that even the most wretched among you have looked at them [the stones of the wall] and seen a divine face emerging from the darkness'. Meursault replies 'maybe, a long time ago, I had looked for a face in them. But that face was the colour of the sun and burning with desire' (page 114).

In conclusion, this essay has shown how the symbol of the sun in The Outsider is a complex one that evolves as the narrative develops. It represents the indifferent and ultimately meaningless truth of the world. This idea is suggested by the positive corollary between the intensity of the sun and the way that events take place – the hotter and brighter the sun, the balder and stronger the absurd and meaningless events that take place. In the courtroom, a place of deceit and charades, the sun is filtered and shaded. Camus' novel presents the reader with an omnipotent natural truth that can only be shaded by humans as they try to twist its truth into meaning. Ultimately, the sun exists in spite of human will and Meursault's acceptance of it makes him an existential hero.

Word Count: 1499

Camus, Albert, *The Outsider*, (trans. Joseph Laredo) England: Penguin Classics, 1982.

Examiner's comments

Criterion B: Knowledge and Understanding

How effectively has the student used the topic and the essay to show knowledge and understanding of the chosen work?

The candidate shows excellent understanding of this difficult theme in Albert Camus' novel. The discussion of existentialism is controlled and appropriate and the insights made are most perceptive.

Criterion C: Appreciation of the writer's choices

To what extent does the student appreciate how the writer's choices of language, structure, technique and style shape meaning?

There is a continual effort to align the use of technique with meaning. The candidate writes on the use of symbolism and narrative style appositely and convincingly. There is excellent appreciation of the ways in which language, structure, technique and style shape meaning.

Criterion D: Organization and development

How effectively have the ideas been organized, and how well are references to the works integrated into the development of the ideas?

The expository treatment of the question is done well and the use of salient quotations shows good presentation skills.

Criterion E: Language

How clear, varied and accurate is the language?

How appropriate is the choice of register, style and terminology? ('Register' refers, in this context, to the student's use of elements such as vocabulary, tone, sentence structure and terminology appropriate to the task.)

The student's language is sophisticated and readable.

Appreciation

Appreciation of the subtleties of culture

Read the poem below and answer the questions that follow it:

Waiting for the Barbarians

What are we waiting for, assembled in the forum?

The barbarians are due here today.

Why isn't anything happening in the senate?
Why do the senators sit there without legislating?

Because the barbarians are coming today.   5
What laws can the senators make now?
Once the barbarians are here, they'll do the legislating.

Why did our emperor get up so early,
and why is he sitting at the city's main gate
on his throne, in state, wearing the crown?   10

Because the barbarians are coming today
and the emperor is waiting to receive their leader.
He has even prepared a scroll to give him,
replete with titles, with imposing names.

Why have our two consuls and praetors come out today   15
wearing their embroidered, their scarlet togas?
Why have they put on bracelets with so many amethysts,
and rings sparkling with magnificent emeralds?
Why are they carrying elegant canes
beautifully worked in silver and gold?   20

Because the barbarians are coming today
and things like that dazzle the barbarians.

Why don't our distinguished orators come forward as usual
to make their speeches, say what they have to say?

Because the barbarians are coming today   25
and they're bored by rhetoric and public speaking.

Why this sudden restlessness, this confusion?
(How serious people's faces have become.)
Why are the streets and squares emptying so rapidly,
everyone going home so lost in thought?   30

Because night has fallen and the barbarians have not come.
And some who have just returned from the border say
there are no barbarians any longer.

And now, what's going to happen to us without barbarians?
They were, those people, a kind of solution.   35

– Constantine Cavafy, 'Waiting for the Barbarians', trans. by Edmund Keeley
(1972)

To access worksheet 9.4 to see examples of the answers to these questions, please visit www.pearsonbacconline.com and follow the on-screen instructions.

QUESTIONS

1 What is this poem saying about cultural stereotypes?

2 Discuss the dichotomy between civilization and barbarity: how does one complement the other?

3 What would you say is the poet's attitude to the barbarians?

4 Can you relate this to anything in your own life and experiences?

Culture often involves presenting the identity of a people or nation through symbolic means, such as the African (left) and Roman shields displayed here.

EXERCISE 7

Read the extract below and answer the questions that follow it:

ACT ONE

Inside the Prozorov house. A sitting room with pillars, behind which is seen another large dining or reception room. It is midday; outside it is bright and sunny. In the dining room beyond the table is being laid for lunch. Olga in a blue dress, the official school dress for a teacher of the Girls' High School, is continually correcting exercise books as she stands or while she walks around. Masha in a black dress sits on a chair with her hat on her knees and reads a book. Irina in a white dress is standing deep in thought.

OLGA.   Father died exactly a year ago, on this very same day, on the fifth of May, on your name day, Irina. It was very cold, and snow was falling. It seemed to me as if I would not live through it, you were lying in a faint, as if you were dead. But look, a year has gone by and we can remember it lightly, you are already wearing white, and your face is full of brightness …

(The clock strikes twelve.)

And then also the clock struck in just the same way.

(*Pause.*)

I remember, when they carried father out, the band was playing, at the cemetery they fired shots in his honour. He was a general, and commanding officer of a brigade, but even so, not many came to the funeral. But of course, it was raining then. Very heavy rain, and snow.

IRINA.   Why do you insist on remembering it!

(*Behind the pillars, in the dining room, Baron Tuzenbach, Chebutykin and Solyony appear near the table.*)

OLGA.   Today it's warm, we can even have the windows open – but the birch trees are still not in leaf. Father was given command of a brigade and left Moscow with us eleven years ago. And I remember it all distinctly, at the beginning of May, just at this time, in Moscow already everything is in flower, it's warm, everything is flooded with sunlight. Eleven years have gone by, but I remember everything there, as if we left Moscow yesterday. Good God! This morning I woke up and I saw a blaze of colour, I saw the spring, and gladness bubbled up inside my heart, and I desperately wanted to be where I came from, in my native land.

CHEBUTYKIN. It's absolutely not true.

TUZENBACH.   Of course, it's nonsense.

(*Masha, deep in thought over her book, starts to whistle a tune.*)

OLGA.   Don't whistle Masha. How could you!

(*Pause.*)

Because I go to the school every day and then give lessons until the evening, that is why I continually have headaches, and the thoughts I have are those of an ageing old woman. And really and truly, while I have been working in the school, I feel as if every day my youth and my strength have been oozing away drop by drop. The only thing that grows and strengthens is one single dream …

IRINA.   To go back to Moscow. To sell the house, to finish everything here, and then, to Moscow …

OLGA.   Yes. To Moscow, as fast as possible.

(*Chebutykin and Tuzenbach laugh.*)

IRINA.   Our brother, probably, will become a professor, at any rate he won't want to live here. The only difficulty is with poor Masha.

OLGA.   Masha will come to Moscow for the whole summer, every year.

(*Masha softly whistles a tune.*)

IRINA.	With God's help it will all work out. (*Looking out of the window.*) What wonderful weather today. I don't know why everything is so bright inside me today. This morning I remembered that it was my name day, and suddenly I felt happy, and I remembered my childhood, when Mama was still alive. And what wonderful thoughts stirred inside me, wonderful thoughts.
OLGA.	Today you are all radiant, you are looking unusually beautiful. And Masha is also beautiful. Andrey would be handsome, only he has grown rather stout, and that doesn't suit him. But I've grown old, and I've grown very thin, it must be because I get angry with the girls at school. But now, today, I am free, I'm at home, and my head doesn't ache at all, and I feel myself to be younger than I was yesterday. I'm twenty eight years old, only twenty eight … Everything is fine, everything as God wishes, but it seems to me, that if I were to marry and if I were at home every day, then it would be much better.

(*Pause.*)

I would love my husband.

TUZENBACH.	(*To Solyony.*) You talk such rubbish, it's annoying to listen to you. (*Coming into the sitting room.*) I forgot to tell you. Today our new battalion commander, Vershinin, is going to visit you. (*He sits at the piano.*)
OLGA.	Well, of course, we'll be delighted.
IRINA.	Is he old?
TUZENBACH.	No, not especially. At the most, forty, or forty five. (*He plays quietly.*) Evidently, he's a fine sort of fellow. He's not stupid, that's for sure. Only he talks a lot.
IRINA.	Is he an interesting man?
TUZENBACH.	Yes, not bad, only he has a wife, a mother in law, and two daughters. And then, this is his second marriage. He visits people and everywhere he announces that he has a wife and two daughters. He'll say the same here. His wife is a sort of half-wit, with long girlish plaits, she speaks all manner of high-blown phrases, she philosophises and often attempts suicide, evidently to stir up her old man. I would have left someone like that long ago, but he endures it and only complains about her.
SOLYONY.	(*Coming from the dining room into the sitting room towards Chebutykin.*) With one hand I can lift up fifty pounds, but with two I can lift one hundred and fifty, perhaps even two hundred. From that I can conclude that two men are stronger than one not by twice as much, but three times, even more …

CHEBUTYKIN. (*Reading the newspaper as he walks in.*) For loss of hair ... two scruples of naphthalene in half a bottle of surgical spirit ... dissolve it and use the mixture every day ... (*Writes in a notebook.*) Yes my dear fellow, we'll make a note of it. (*To Solyony.*) So, let me explain to you, you get the cork pushed into the bottle, or whatever, have a glass tube running through the cork ... Then you take a small pinch of completely ordinary kvass ...

IRINA. [*To Chebutykin*] Ivan Romanich, dearest Ivan Romanich.

CHEBUTYKIN. What is it, my dearest girl, my enchantment?

IRINA. Tell me, why is it I am so happy today? It's as if my sails are all spread, above me is the wide blue heaven and large white birds are flying in it.

CHEBUTYKIN. (*Kissing both her hands, tenderly.*) My darling white bird ...

– Anton Chekhov, *Three Sisters* (1900); trans. by Gerard R. Ledger (1998)

▲
Anton Chekhov (1860–1904)

QUESTIONS

1 When do you think the action takes place and what makes you say this?

2 How would you describe gender relations in this passage?

3 Can you detect any symbolic representation of the traditional and the new in this extract?

4 What is your response to the content of the passage from the perspective of your own culture?

 To what extent can we look at works of art as expressions of culture?

 To access worksheet 9.6 – Suggested answer to Exercise 7 – please visit www.pearsonbacconline.com and follow the on-screen instructions.

EXERCISE 8

Read the passage below and answer the questions that follow it:

Days and months are travellers of eternity. So are the years that pass by. Those who steer a boat across the sea, or drive a horse over the earth till they succumb to the weight of years, spend every minute of their lives travelling. There are a great number of ancients, too, who died on the road. I myself have been tempted for a long time by the cloud-moving wind — filled with a strong desire to wander.

It was only towards the end of last autumn that I returned from rambling along the coast. I barely had time to sweep the cobwebs from my broken house on the River Sumida before the New Year, but no sooner had the spring mist begun to rise over the field than I wanted to be on the road again to cross the barrier-gate of Shirakawa in due time. The gods seem to have possessed my soul and turned it inside out, and roadside images seemed to invite me from every corner, so that it was impossible for me to stay idle at home. Even while I was getting ready, mending my torn trousers, tying a new strap to my hat, and applying moxa to my legs to strengthen them, I was already dreaming of the full moon rising over the islands of Matsushima. Finally, I sold my house, moving to the cottage of Sampû for a temporary stay. Upon the threshold of my old home, however, I wrote a linked verse of eight pieces and hung it on a wooden pillar.

Matsuo Bashō (1644–1694)

The starting piece was:
Behind this door
Now buried in deep grass,
A different generation will celebrate
The Festival of Dolls.

– Matsuo Bashō, *The Narrow Road to the Deep North and Other Travel Sketches*; trans. by Nobuyuki Yuasa (1966)

QUESTIONS

1 In what ways would you say this style is typical of what you know of Japanese writing?

2 What are the elements of culture that dominate the tone of the passage and how do they do this?

3 What does the passage tell you about the speaker's religious background?

EXERCISE 9

Read the extract from the poem 'Song of Lawino' below, and answer the following questions:

Ocol says
They want Uhuru,
His brother says
They want Uhuru and Peace,
Both of them say they fight ignorance and disease!   5

Then why do they not join hands,
Why do they split up the army
Into two hostile groups?
The spears of the young men
And their shields,   10
Why are the weapons
And the men and women
Dispersed so uselessly?

And while the pythons of sickness
Swallow the children   15
And the buffaloes of poverty
Knock the people down
And ignorance stands there
Like an elephant,

The war leaders   20
Are tightly locked in bloody feuds,
Eating each other's liver
As if the D.P. was leprosy
And the Congress yaws;
If only the parties   25
Would fight poverty
With the fury
With which they fight each other,
If diseases and ignorance

Were assaulted   30
With the deadly vengeance
With which Ocol assaults his mother's son,
The enemies would have been
Greatly reduced by now.

– Okot p'Bitek, 'Song of Lawino' (self-translated in 1966)

QUESTIONS

1 How do you relate to this style of poetry, taking your own culture into account?

2 Explain how you think this extract is typically African in its use of imagery.

3 Do you know what 'Uhuru' is? Do a web search to find out, and to enrich your understanding of history and geography by doing so.

SUMMARY

The texts that we have looked at come from different parts of the world and all carry with them certain culturally specific traits. The reflective writing that you will generate will ask you to focus on cultural matters. The descriptor, as mentioned earlier, is:

'To what extent does the student show how their understanding of cultural and contextual elements was developed through the interactive oral?'

Remember that you will be graded out of 3 points (Criterion A) for your written reflection on the work that you are writing the essay on.

INSIGHTS INTO WORKS IN TRANSLATION

Now that we have come to the end of this chapter, consider the following insights that will help you as you explore literature in translation from around the world. Remember that as you do this, you will be opening your mind to other cultures and places. Such an enriching experience makes you a citizen of the world, someone special!

1 Literature in translation needs to be looked at not only as work of literary merit, but more as a form of cultural expression. Each work is embedded in culture and each reader carries culture within himself or herself. Therefore, the reading of a book is the meeting place of two different cultures, and this is more the case when you are reading outside of your culture than inside.

2 There is a danger when discussing an entire culture that you make comments that are superficial, over-generalized or incorrect. Be careful not to jump into any easy throw-away statements on culture, and keep your ideas as subtle and nuanced as possible. Culture is a complex, interconnected phenomenon.

3 The assessment of this part of the course is on the essay of 1,200–1,500 words that you will submit. There is a specific procedure to follow when working towards the essay: the oral presentation; reflective writing; supervised writing; and then the essay. Make sure that you go through these different stages with a concentrated mind and a serious attitude, focusing on the work that you have studied in as much detail as possible. Remember that it is only the reflective statement and the final essay that will be graded externally, counting towards 25 per cent of your final IB grade for this course.

4   The essay title that you decide on will be crucial. You need to go through it carefully with your teacher to make sure that you are not embarking on something that is not going to work out well. The purpose of the supervised writing is to get you to brainstorm ideas that will then develop into the essay.

5   Make sure that you get someone other than your teacher to look through the essay before your final submission, to double-check for any mistakes that could bring your marks down.

ADVICE ON THE GROUP 1 EXTENDED ESSAY (EE)

Before you start an Extended Essay (EE) in Group 1, make sure that you:
- Explore the essentials of the EE
- Look at the structure of the EE
- Discuss and think about a potential research question with your teacher.

Introduction

This chapter will focus on the EE. The aim of the chapter is firstly to give you information on research and academic honesty, tips on how to go about researching a topic successfully and an idea of what an EE timeline should look like. As these core components are being discussed in a book about literature, there will be numerous links with the subject of literature to help you make connections.

This core component of the Diploma Programme is special and makes the IB what it is. The amount of time and dedication you put into it will determine how meaningful you make the learning voyage of the Diploma Programme. The EE reinforces key transferable skills, such as:

- Research skills
- The ability to handle extended writing
- Referencing
- Structuring written work
- Utilizing resources
- Specifying a research question
- Developing an argument
- Working under a supervisor

The EE and research: an opportunity for growth

The great stories, discoveries and laws that have marked different cultures through time have all been the product of some form of research, be it formal or informal. Without Marx's colossal *Das Kapital* the entire practice of communism might never have taken place. Without Isaac Newton's profound study *Principia Mathematica*, we would probably be living with a different sense of reality.

Many of you will become specialists in a field, and the EE could be the first serious piece of study you undertake in that direction. You might have a passion that you have never been able to pursue, something you always wanted to know. This could be your chance. It may be that you are not sure what to research, but once you have settled on something, you will find the journey to be more important than the destination.

If you are writing an EE in English, then you will be embarking on an extended piece of research in the field of literature with focus on an author or authors (attempting to take on more than one author is possible but not advised, as it makes the study less focused and much more complex) or work or group of works. It involves going into great detail, learning more about an author, reading and re-reading the books you will be studying, and reading around the books and the topic of your research.

You might have been drawn to a particular author or book during the course of your studies, or it may be that you are attracted to an author that you are not studying in your

English course. In either case, the main idea behind the research process is that you will be developing your knowledge of the author, work or group of works.

The following flow chart will give you an idea of how interest in an author could turn into an Extended Essay:

---

1. You study *Macbeth* by William Shakespeare.

2. You find that you are interested in a theme in the play, 'ambition', for instance.

3. You ask your teacher which other Shakespeare plays deal with the theme of ambition.

4. You are directed to other plays (*Antony and Cleopatra*, *Coriolanus*, *Othello*).

5. You read the plays, and decide that you want to research the way that Shakespeare treats ambition in his works.

6. You meet your teacher and talk about the project.

7. He says that it is too broad and you need to whittle it down more to make it more manageable, maybe by focusing on fewer plays.

8. You read the remaining two plays of the five great tragedies (*King Lear* and *Hamlet*).

9. You draft your research question: 'Ambition as the driver of subplots in three great Shakespearean tragedies (*King Lear*, *Macbeth* and *Othello*).'

EXERCISE 1

List at least two works or authors you find the most interesting. Reflect on how you might develop these starting points into EEs, and draft a selection of potential EE titles.

The order of your research writing

Consider this flow chart as the best way of moving towards your research question:

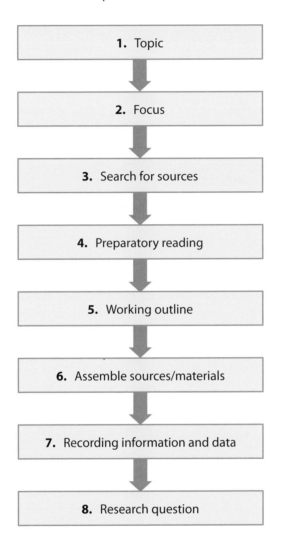

1. Topic

2. Focus

3. Search for sources

4. Preparatory reading

5. Working outline

6. Assemble sources/materials

7. Recording information and data

8. Research question

SUMMARY

Research involves the extended investigation and study of a topic that has been crafted into a viable research question. The EE provides one of the best opportunities for your academic growth and confidence, plus the chance to conduct in-depth research of a subject. It is strongly advised, however, that you lay the foundations of the EE with systematic stages of preparation, working from a general idea down to a specific research question, as shown in the flow chart above.

The research question

The research question is the heart of your essay. It is the statement (for it does not have to be in the form of a question) that will direct your research and establish its parameters. The most crucial factors to think about in designing a research question are:

- Whether the scope and amplitude of the research that you are planning is achievable (and not, for example, too broad).
- The degree to which the research statement is clear and can be clearly understood.

There are two categories of Group 1 EE: Category 1 is a literary study of an author or works from an English-speaking country; Category 2 is a comparative study of first-language literary texts from the English-speaking world and some other place.

Examples of research questions for Category 1 EEs in English

- 'What are the role and the significance of balls in *Pride and Prejudice* and *Emma*?'
- 'How is the subject of death treated in selected poems by Sylvia Plath and Ted Hughes?'
- 'How does Ngugi present historical facts in his novel, *A Grain of Wheat*?'
- 'Perceptions of nature in English poetry of the 1890s.'
- 'The theme of hopelessness in the poetry of T.S. Eliot.'

Examples of research questions for Category 2 EEs in English

- 'In what different ways do Ionesco and Beckett present freedom in their respective plays?'
- 'In what ways do the authors of *Crime and Punishment* and *The Catcher in the Rye* seek to render their protagonists sympathetic to the reader? How far do they succeed?'
- 'The image of the road in the poetry of Frost and Dante.'
- 'The motif of smoke in the poems of Mongane Serote and Charles Baudelaire.'

Academic honesty

The Extended Essay is a chance for you to appreciate and understand academic honesty. Make sure that you are clear on the criteria of academic honesty at the early stages of your research so that there are no misunderstandings.

One of the paradoxes of the digital age in which we find ourselves is that computers allow for an enhanced learning environment, but also threaten the fundamental principles of good scholarship. Students can access information with great economy and efficiency; they can cut corners and save themselves an enormous amount of clerical slog in preparing pieces of work, and they can share ideas in forums that do not need the presence of a teacher to monitor, filter and facilitate.

At the same time, the search engines that we all now rely on instead of encyclopaedias and dictionaries, and the abundance of unsolicited, potentially scurrilous information that circulates on the internet, bring substantial problems of knowledge with them. In the past the only source of information that one could use was in the form of published books, journals, magazines and newspapers. Today's young scholars have to be able to sort the true from the false amidst a mass of online material.

Today it is easy to access knowledge, but also much easier than it was before to cut and paste information.

The acknowledgement of sources in a piece of work has become a more complex ethical issue today than it was some 30 years ago. Before the advent of global access to the internet, to copy someone's work required the clearly unscrupulous act of writing down each word from a book and then deliberately pretending that it was one's own; today students can paraphrase others' work by manipulating text with a few keyboard touches, and the whole process seems more distanced and abstract.

In terms of learning, copying out text for a presentation – albeit ethically reprehensible – would still entail some basic mechanics of integration (although to copy something down is hardly the best method for assimilating information), whereas cutting and copying text can now be done without the student even reading what was copied. Such actions result in, among other things, embarrassing moments in a presentation where erudite terms will suddenly be used – obviously without proper understanding – in the midst of a delivery in an altogether different register and tenor. Similarly, a spellchecked homework assignment will be handed in on one day, but the in-class assignment the next day will be littered with spelling mistakes.

The International Baccalaureate asks Diploma Programme students to sign declarations that coursework, presentations and even oral presentations are the candidate's own work. Only one read-through of an EE by supervisors is authorized, and more checks and balances have been put into place to ensure that students are doing their own work. Any student found guilty of any form of malpractice can be disqualified from the programme. This is an extract from the IB's statement on ethical practice:

> Students will exercise academic honesty in all aspects of their work. They will acknowledge the work of others, including material taken from other sources. They will not claim as their own the work of others. They will not give their work to others to pass off as their own.
> – From 'Ethical Practice in the Diploma Programme' © International Baccalaureate Organization (2006)

Of course, an honest person does not need laws, rules and threats to know when he or she is doing the wrong thing, and the worst part of plagiarism is that a situation that is potentially laudable (referencing your work with authoritative voices is a sign of good research) turns into one that can harm the student irrevocably.

There are two basic types of malpractice that you need to be aware of:

- Collusion – this is when someone else does the work for you or with you and you do not acknowledge it.
- Plagiarism – this is when you take someone else's text or ideas and try to present it as your own.

EXERCISE 2

Below are four scenarios. Do you feel that any are cases of academic dishonesty or not? Why?

Scenario One
A student reads someone's theory on the work of a particular author, and decides that this theory would be a good topic for an EE.

Scenario Two
A student mentions an author in the Works Cited list, but has not quoted from the author in the actual EE.

Scenario Three
A student has paraphrased a passage from someone else's work, but has acknowledged the source.

Scenario Four
A student has pasted someone else's work into his essay, but then changed the wording. He has not, however, acknowledged the source.

● **Examiner's hints**
With ToK, the EE can contribute up to 3 bonus points.

The Extended Essay: basics

The essay

The upper word limit for all EEs is 4,000 words. This limit includes the introduction, the body, the conclusion and any quotations, but does not include:

- the abstract
- acknowledgements
- the contents page
- maps, charts, diagrams, annotated tables, illustrations
- bibliography/references
- appendices

The structure most used for a good EE is:

- Introduction
- Main body
- Conclusion

The **introduction** should indicate why the topic is interesting, important or worthy of study. It should place the topic in an appropriate context, and explain your particular focus. The research question should be stated clearly, and you need to outline the thesis or argument (the response to the research question).

The **main body** is the systematic development of a convincing answer to the research question. The structure and approach to this section will be shaped by the conventions of the particular subject. Some subjects may require sub-headings or separate sections for method and results, while in other subjects this would disrupt the flow and unity of the essay. For referencing sources, either parenthetical notes or numbered systems (footnotes) can be used, providing the candidate is consistent with the chosen approach throughout.

A clearly stated **conclusion**, relevant to the research question, substantiated by the evidence presented should indicate issues, unresolved questions and new questions that have emerged from the research.

The first three pages

Title Page – The title should provide a clear indication of the focus of the essay. It should be precise and doesn't have to be phrased in the form of a question.

Abstract – The abstract must not exceed 300 words. It presents a short summary of the EE. The abstract must state the research question, scope of investigation and conclusion/s. It should be written last, once you are happy with your EE.

Contents Page – Here is where the page numbering begins. An index is not required.

If there are acknowledgements, they should be between the abstract and the contents page.

Last pages

Illustrations – If they are in the form of diagrams or tables make sure that they are clearly labelled. In some subjects graphs will be integrated into the main body of the essay.

Works Cited – The style of referencing other people's work wi depend on the method your schoo uses.
e.g. The MLA method:
Coetzee, J.M. _Disgrace_. London: Vintage, 1999.
Translators and editors come after the title, this time the first name followed by the surname:
Sophocles. _The Three Theban Plays_. Trans. Robert Fagles. New York: Penguin, 1977.

Appendices – Examiners are not required to read appendices, so unless considered essential for your essay, complete lists of raw data should not be included in the EE.

SUMMARY

The first pages and last pages of the EE involve using the correct format (as decided by your school) for the table of contents and introduction on the one hand, and the Works Cited list on the other. Be sure to run through the correct procedures carefully here to avoid losing marks carelessly.

EE schedule

Study the EE schedule below. You will need to follow a similar schedule to make sure that your EE develops properly within a tenable framework. Please note that these dates work for a northern hemisphere school year that starts in September and runs until June.

DATE	ACTION
November Week 3	Introduction to the EE
December Week 2	• Select a subject and a supervisor • Complete the Consent Form #1 and return it to supervisor or coordinator
by January Week 4	Meeting 1 with EE supervisor: discuss what will be done during the spring break/reading week

by March Week 3	Meeting 2 with EE supervisor
	EE supervisor reviews/establishes:
	1. Subject-specific criteria and general criteria from the IB's 'Guide to the Extended Essay'
	2. Key points on referencing methodology
	3. The reading and research done over the spring break/reading week
	4. Refinement of area of study
	5. Reading Bibliography/list of equipment required
	6. Goals for the next meeting, including a skeleton structure of the essay
	   – Meeting with librarian about finding resources
	   – Development of a (tentative) research question

DATE	ACTION
May Week 2	Meeting 3 with supervisor (progress and planning): 1. Decide on a title 2. Evaluation of goals, set and met 3. New goals: further reading/research/analysis/experimentation 4. Outline of presentation to EE supervisor 5. Plan of action for summer break
May Week 4	Meeting 4 with EE supervisor and presentation – You will deliver a 5–10 minute presentation on your EE in front of other students, EE supervisor and librarian Your presentation must include: 1. Your aim/hypothesis 2. Sources of information/experiment details 3. Areas of concern 4. A skeleton outline or road map from title page to bibliography including chapter headings
June Week 2	Report home to parents from EE supervisor outlining progress and plan of action for summer break
Summer break	Completion of first draft (internet contact with EE supervisor over break is permitted)
September Week 1	Submit first draft to EE supervisor
September Week 3	Meeting 5 with EE supervisor
October Week 1	Report home to parents from EE supervisor highlighting progress and work to be done Optional: during this month a second draft can be submitted to EE supervisor if this is felt to be necessary
November Week 1	Meeting 6 with EE supervisor Submission of final draft, one soft copy submitted to librarian for check on plagiarism
December Week 2	Submission of final draft of EE to supervisor: 1. 3 x bound copies must be submitted to EE supervisor 2. 1 x soft copy must be submitted to the librarian
January	EE supervisor fills in supervision report, signed by the student, and submits predicted grade for the essay

NB: You should not be meeting with your supervisor for more than seven hours in total for the EE.

EXERCISE 3

Assessment

The EE will be graded by an IB examiner using the formal IB assessment criteria. Make sure that you read through your essay towards the end and just before submission of the final draft, checking that you are addressing all that is expected of you. Read through the assessment criteria now and think about how they might shape the way you go about your essay.

Assessment criteria

Criterion A: Research question (2 marks)

The research question should be clearly stated in the introduction and should be focused enough for it to be treated effectively within the prescribed word limit of 4,000 words.

Criterion B: Introduction (2 marks)

The introduction should explain – briefly – the significance of the topic and why it is worthy of investigation.

Criterion C: Investigation (4 marks)

The range of resources is appropriate but also widespread and imaginative. Relevant material has been selected with care and the investigation has been well planned.

Criterion D: Knowledge and understanding of the topic studied (4 marks)

The essay should demonstrate sound knowledge and understanding of the works studied.

Criterion E: Reasoned argument (4 marks)

The ideas of the essay need to be presented in a clear and logical manner. The argument should develop in a reasoned and convincing way in line with the research question.

Criterion F: Application of analytical and evaluative skills appropriate to the subject (4 marks)

The essay should make use of analytical and evaluative skills appropriate for English literary studies: literary criticism, textual analysis and developed, expository and demonstrative argument.

Criterion G: Use of language appropriate to the subject (4 marks)

For an essay in English Group 1 you would need to show here that you can use the academic styled language and style of literary criticism.

Criterion H: Conclusion (2 marks)

The conclusion should be stated clearly and should be effective. It should be consistent with the research question and the evidence presented throughout the essay.

Criterion I: Formal presentation (4 marks)

The formal presentation includes the title page, table of contents with page numbers and at the end of the essay an appropriate bibliography and references. Staying inside the word limit is important – failure to do so will result in zero marks on this criterion.

Criterion J: Abstract (2 marks)

The abstract is a sober summary of the essay. It must include the research question, mention of the research undertaken and the conclusion(s) reached. The abstract is not to exceed 300 words.

Criterion K: Holistic judgement (4 marks)

This is the degree of intellectual initiative that the essay shows, the insights brought about by it and the general depth and breadth.

INSIGHTS INTO THE EXTENDED ESSAY

1   The key is to make sure that you get your essay title right. The research question, which can be your title too (often the title is an abridgement of the research question) must be extremely focused. Go for something that interests you, but be open-minded about suggestions that will be made, probably telling you to get the scope of the question right. Once you have found what you want to do – and it may take some time – you should plan the structure of your essay as a type of map, channelling your ideas into chapters or sections.

2   Following deadlines is crucial. When you are in the professional world, there will not only be deadlines from your employers, but you will need to manage your own deadlines so that you complete tasks efficiently. You are not being asked to invent a new theory or make a substantive contribution to knowledge (this objective would be the goal of a PhD), but simply to undertake **independent** research on a **focused** topic.

3 Independence does not only mean following deadlines, but making sure that the work you do is your own. Good essays are pieces that make connections, that associate different ideas in an overarching argument. A good essay will draw on many sources – ones you have found in your research – and reference them in the Works Cited list at the end. Any idea that is not your own must be referenced properly; any quotation of text must be referenced accordingly.

4 Referencing is a skill that requires you to quote just the relevant information and nothing extraneous: you should likewise be able to choose quotations that are saying something, that precisely *illustrate* a point rather than lengthy, circuitous extracts. The way you reference is crucial. Make sure that you consult your supervisor to check which referencing method you use at your school.

5 If you cut and paste other people's work and do not reference the material, in any subject including the EE, you are committing plagiarism or misconduct, something that results in your being disqualified from the entire diploma. It is a serious offence and the examiners spot it very easily. Furthermore, wishing to do so means not understanding that the purpose of research is to collate other people's ideas (but in a specific, organized manner), not to steal ideas.

Chapter 11
THEORY OF KNOWLEDGE (TOK)

The Extended Essay is one of three core components of the Diploma Programme, the other two being Creativity, Action, Service (CAS) and Theory of Knowledge (ToK).

ToK is a course about thinking, a vital opportunity for you to reflect carefully on the way that knowledge is built up in different subject areas and by different means. ToK asks you to sit down and look for links across subjects, but also for factors that make them different from one another. It's a special course that makes the IB diploma programme different, and hopefully you will be able to get enough out of it to see the world as a *critical thinker*, with a renewed, philosophically inclined mind.

Thinking across frontiers

If we think back on the history of ideas, from the ancient pre-Socratic intellectuals to modern philosophers, thinking across disciplines has been a tradition. Prolific and polyvalent philosophers such as Aristotle, Plato and Leibniz could write on Science, Ethics, Art, Logic and more, while some of the famous non-Western philosophers like Lao Tzu, Confucius, Al Gazali and Avicenna asked questions that went to the core of life experience. However, with the surge in scientific advancement from the Enlightenment onwards, and the mechanization of labour during the Industrial Revolution, specialized labour started to become the norm. Today we tend to learn to meet the needs of a profession, and after school we are faced with university and professional course offerings that are more and more specific to one knowledge type.

This situation is particularly the case in educational systems in Europe and the United Kingdom, where students as young as 13 will start choosing what to study in line with university applications. Many students tailor their Diploma Programme subject packages with specific entry requirements for targeted professions firmly in mind. If you want to become a surgeon, you should study chemistry, biology and mathematics; if you want to go into engineering, you should study physics and mathematics. Even if you are in the United States or Canada, following a broad-based curriculum at the undergraduate level, sooner or later you will start to specialize and to narrow the base of expertise and knowledge in order to be competitive.

If we were to place a history textbook, a musical score, a calculator and a novel next to each other, they could very easily represent different subjects. Subjects, traditionally, have been viewed as separate entities. We go to each separate class with a distinct resource, and this is one of the clear ways of knowing that we are not studying mathematics but Spanish, and that this is not Physical Education but Design Technology and so on.

ToK is the intelligent person's course, food for thought for the critical thinker.

The Enlightenment
The Enlightenment is the period of history in Europe covering the 18th century. Otherwise known as The Age of Reason, it saw a number of philosophers such as the Great British Empiricists (John Locke, David Hume, Jeremy Bentham and Bishop George Berkeley), Gottfried Liebniz and Benedict Spinoza, use logic and science as key methods in the search for truth. The key scientific figure of the Enlightenment was Isaac Newton.

Educational systems from the 19th century to the present day have tended to privilege the idea of subjects as separate ponds or pools, making the student jump in and out of each one in a frog-like fashion, failing to see the connections between disciplines.

Thinking Caps
The Maltese psychologist Edward de Bono invented the idea of six 'thinking caps' in 1983. Each cap has a colour attributed to it and represents a certain way of solving problems (emotional, logical, objective and so on).

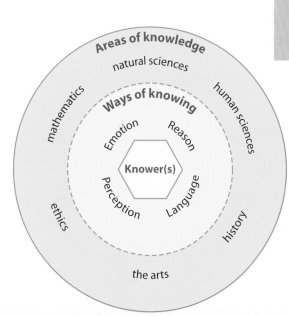

In the traditional, linear model, the student is a frog. The frog must hop from the history textbook to the calculator to the novel, or we could say that the frog must jump from one bucket into the next – briefly immersing himself in one liquid and then hopping out to get into another. As the frog leaves a subject and enters a new one, he must stop thinking one way and start thinking another way, like a sponge that is squeezed out of one liquid before it is plunged into another. In this learning-within-a-subject method of education, we put on and take off 'thinking caps' when we enter and exit each subject.

This is NOT what ToK is about!
On the contrary, ToK is the glue that binds everything together under the provocative question: 'How do I know?'

The IB student, like the ancient philosopher, is someone who looks beyond specialization and subject-specific approaches into a more integrated way of thinking. This perspective gives the student an advantage over other students, who have grown up to appreciate different subjects as givens without questioning the laws and conventions that underpin each one. The ToK student will ask questions that transcend areas of specialization. This is one of the reasons why many universities and post-secondary institutions recognize and appreciate the qualities of the IB student.

Summary
ToK is all about three central issues:
- The question 'How do I know?'
- Critical thinking
- How knowledge is built up in different subject areas

The structure of ToK
The IB Diploma Programme is very much based on the idea of the student at the centre of the learning process. It identifies four 'Ways of Knowing' and six 'Areas of Knowledge':

Ways of Knowing: Perception; Language; Reason; Emotion

Areas of Knowledge: Mathematics; Natural Sciences; Human Sciences; History; the Arts; Ethics

Assessment outline:

Internal Assessment – Oral Presentation
Assessment Criteria:

A. Identification of knowledge issue (5 points)
Did the presentation identify a relevant knowledge issue involved, implicit or embedded in a real-life situation?

B. Treatment of knowledge issues (5 points)
Did the presentation show a good understanding of knowledge issues, in the context of the real-life situation?

C. Knower's perspective (5 points)
Did the presentation, particularly in the use of arguments and examples, show an individual approach and demonstrate the significance of the topic?

D. Connections (5 points)
*   Did the presentation give a balanced account of how the topic could be approached from different perspectives?
*   Did the presentation show how the positions taken on the knowledge issues would have implications in related areas?
*   In awarding the higher achievement levels, the emphasis should be more on the quality of the consideration of connections than on the quantity of connections mentioned.

External Assessment – ToK essay on a prescribed title
Assessment Criteria:

A. Understanding knowledge issues (10 points)
*   This criterion is concerned with the extent to which the essay focuses on knowledge issues relevant to the prescribed title, and with the depth and breadth of the understanding demonstrated in the essay.
*   A relevant knowledge issue is one that directly relates to the prescribed title undertaken, or one that the essay has shown is important in relation to it.
*   Depth of understanding is often indicated by drawing distinctions within ways of knowing and areas of knowledge, or by connecting several facets of knowledge issues to these.
*   Breadth of understanding is often indicated by making comparisons between ways of knowing and areas of knowledge. [*Since not all prescribed titles lend themselves to an extensive treatment of an equal range of areas of knowledge or ways of knowing, this element in the descriptors should be applied with concern for the particularity of the title.*]
*   Does the essay demonstrate understanding of knowledge issues that are relevant to the prescribed title?
*   Does the essay demonstrate an awareness of the connections between knowledge issues, areas of knowledge and ways of knowing?

B. Knower's perspective (10 points)
*   To what extent have the knowledge issues relevant to the prescribed title been connected to the student's own experience as a learner?
*   Does the student show an awareness of his or her own perspective as a knower in relation to other perspectives, such as those that may arise, for example, from academic and philosophical traditions, culture or position in society (gender, age, and so on)?
*   Do the examples chosen show an individual approach consciously taken by the student, rather than mere repetition of standard commonplace cases or the impersonal recounting of sources?

C. Quality of analysis of knowledge issues (10 points)

- What is the quality of the inquiry into knowledge issues?
- Are the main points in the essay justified? Are the arguments coherent and compelling?
- Have counterclaims been considered?
- Are the implications and underlying assumptions of the essay's argument identified?
- This criterion is concerned only with knowledge issues that are relevant to the prescribed title. Analysis of knowledge issues that are not relevant to the prescribed title is not assessed.

D. Organization of ideas (10 points)

- Is the essay well organized and relevant to the prescribed title?
- Does the use of language assist the reader's understanding and avoid confusion? Are central terms explained or developed clearly in a way that assists comprehension?
- Note: This task is not a test of 'first language' linguistic skills. No account should be taken of minor errors unless they significantly impede communication.
- When factual information is used or presented, is it accurate and, when necessary, referenced? 'Factual information' includes generalizations.
- If sources have been used, have they been properly referenced in a way that allows them to be traced (internet references must include the date on which they were accessed)?

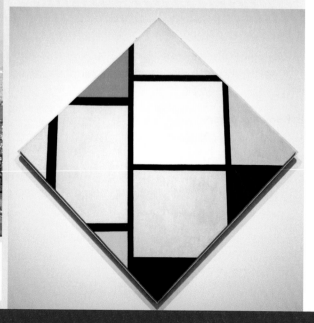

As an art form, literature is different to numerous other areas of knowledge. Unlike natural science, erected upon strong underlying rules, literature can take almost any shape and represents the infinite patterns that can come out of human expression.

ToK and literature

How do we know the world through literature?

Reflect on this question by thinking about the works of literature you have studied.

Literature is an art, not a science; it is a form of human expression that approaches truth in a unique way. A key difference between it and mathematics and the natural sciences is that there are no rules in literature, just conventions.

EXERCISE 1

Below are three ToK essay questions that students have answered in past years. Study them carefully and talk through an answer for each one, keeping the works of literature you are studying in mind:

1 'There can be no knowledge without emotion … until we have felt the force of the knowledge, it is not ours' (adapted from Arnold Bennett). Discuss this vision of the relationship between knowledge and emotion. (May 2009)

2 'We will always learn more about human life and human personality from novels than from scientific psychology' (Noam Chomsky). To what extent would you agree? (May 2008)

3 Can literature 'tell the truth' better than other Arts or Areas of Knowledge? (May 2007)

The role of emotion in literature

To appreciate literature requires a certain emotional sensitivity. To empathize with a character, understand the tone of the narrative; discern the mood of a passage, all require a sharpening of the emotions. In ToK we see how emotion functions as a way of knowing: we form decisions with emotional insight and emotions can act as enhancers but also filters to the knowledge claims we make and work through.

EXERCISE 2

Read the following extracts below and answer these questions:

The calmness of the work of art is, paradoxically, a dynamic, not a static calmness. Art gives us the motions of the human soul in all their depth and variety. But the form, the measure and rhythm, of these motions is not comparable to any single state of emotion. What we feel in art is not a simple or single emotional quality. It is the dynamic process of life itself—the continuous oscillation between poles, between joy and grief, hope and fear, exultation and despair.
– Ernst Cassirer

All good poetry is the spontaneous overflow of powerful feelings: it takes its origin from emotion recollected in tranquillity.
– William Wordsworth

Tragedy, then, is an imitation of an action that is serious, complete, and of a certain magnitude; in language embellished with each kind of artistic ornament, the several kinds being found in separate parts of the play; in the form of action, not of narrative; through pity and fear effecting the proper purgation of these emotions.

Fear and pity may be aroused by spectacular means; but they may also result from the inner structure of the piece, which is the better way, and indicates a superior poet. For the plot ought to be so constructed that, even without the aid of the eye, he who hears the tale told will thrill with horror and melt to pity at what takes place. This is the impression we should receive from hearing the story of Oedipus. But to produce this effect by the mere spectacle is a less artistic method, and dependent on extraneous aids. Those who employ spectacular means to create a sense not of the terrible but only of the monstrous, are strangers to the purpose of Tragedy; for we must not demand of Tragedy any and every kind of pleasure, but only that which is proper to it.
– Aristotle

EXERCISE 3

Questions

1 What is Ernst Cassirer saying about the type of emotion we encounter in any work of art?

2 Do you agree with the famous quotation by William Wordsworth? Why and to what extent?

3 Summarize what Aristotle is saying about the role of emotion in tragedy.

◀ Emotions play a central role in both the creation and reading of literature.

Perception and language

Humans do not merely see the world, they perceive it. To see the world you need eyes, but to *perceive* you need language. When you see something you are always seeing it *as* something with a word and concept attached to it. In other words, you cannot just 'see', but you can only interpret in and through language.

There is no 'virgin' sight. Virgin sight would be what we saw before language, perhaps as newborn babies, which we have invariably forgotten. We are taught from birth to align images with word sounds. When you see a ball, for example, you accompany the visual impression with the word 'ball', and so on. In other words, perception and language as ways of knowing are inextricably linked to each other.

If we do not apply language to images then we cannot construct ideas and communicate in the first place. An object only gains meaning once it is given linguistic meaning. For example, if you do not call a plus sign a plus sign, you may perceive it as a cross. In this way, naming something is seeing it. Linguistic determinism, the central philosophy of the Austrian philosopher Ludwig Wittgenstein (1889–1951), claims that without language there can be no thought, for thought is language. This idea is dramatized in George Orwell's famous novel *1984*.

Think closely about the role of perception and language in the works of literature you are studying.

EXERCISE 4

Questions

1 What is the relationship between perception and language in the reading of literature?

2 How can language work as a barrier to rather than an enhancement of clear communication?

Perception varies from person to person. In literature, the perception of the author and his/her characters is revealed through literary conventions such as narrative structure and thematic development.

Summary

In ToK we can look at literature as an area of knowledge, and we can also consider the issue of language as a way of knowing. Both of these factors help us appreciate literature as much more than words on a page.

Literature and art as a dream

The following extract from Friedrich Nietzsche's work *The Birth of Tragedy* evokes the idea that art is a type of transcendent dream. Once you have read through the passage, reflect on all of the ways of knowing and areas of knowledge that it evokes and how they relate to the art form of literature.

We will have achieved much for scientific study of aesthetics when we come, not merely to a logical understanding, but also to the certain and immediate apprehension of the fact that the further development of art is bound up with the duality of the *Apollonian* and the *Dionysian*, just as reproduction similarly depends upon the duality of the sexes, their continuing strife and only periodically occurring reconciliation. We take these names from the Greeks, who gave a clear voice to the profound secret teachings of their contemplative art, not in ideas, but in the powerfully clear forms of their divine world. With those two gods of art, Apollo and Dionysus, we establish our recognition that in the Greek world there exists a huge contrast, in origin and purposes, between the visual arts, the Apollonian, and the non-visual art of music, the Dionysian. These two very different drives go hand in hand, for the most part in open conflict with each other and simultaneously provoking each other all the time to new and more powerful offspring, in order to perpetuate in them the contest of that opposition, which the common word 'Art' only seems to bridge, until at last, through a marvellous metaphysical act of the Greek 'will,' they appear paired up with each other and, as this pair, finally produce Attic tragedy, as much a Dionysian as an Apollonian work of art.

In order to bring those two drives closer to us, let us think of them first as the separate artistic worlds of *dream* and of *intoxication*, physiological phenomena between which we can observe an opposition corresponding to the one between the Apollonian and the Dionysian. According to the idea of Lucretius, the marvellous divine shapes first stepped out before the mind of man in a dream. It was in a dream that the great artist saw the delightful anatomy of superhuman existence, and the Greek poet, questioned about the secrets of poetic creativity, would have also recalled his dreams and given an explanation similar to the one Hans Sachs provides in *Die Meistersinger*.

My friend, that is precisely the poet's work –
To figure out his dreams, mark them down.
Believe me, the truest illusion of mankind
Is revealed to him in dreams:
All poetic art and poeticizing
Is nothing but interpreting true dreams.

The beautiful appearance of the world of dreams, in whose creation each man is a complete artist, is the precondition of all plastic art, and also, in fact, as we shall see, an important part of poetry. We enjoy the form with an immediate understanding; every shape speaks to us; nothing is indifferent and unnecessary. For all the most intense life of this dream reality, we nevertheless have the shimmering sense of their *illusory quality*: That, at least, is my experience. For the frequency, indeed normality, of this response, I could point to many witnesses and the utterances of poets. Even the philosophical man has the presentiment that under this reality in which we live and have our being lies hidden a second, totally different reality and that thus the former is an illusion. And Schopenhauer specifically designates as

▲ Art can reach deep into the subconscious in ways that other knowledge areas cannot.

the trademark of philosophical talent the ability to recognize at certain times that human beings and all things are mere phantoms or dream pictures. Now, just as the philosopher behaves in relation to the reality of existence, so the artistically excitable man behaves in relation to the reality of dreams: he looks at them precisely and with pleasure, for from these pictures he fashions his interpretation of life; from these events he rehearses his life for himself. This is not merely a case of the agreeable and friendly images which he experiences in himself with a complete understanding; they also include what is serious, cloudy, sad, dark, sudden scruples, teasing accidents, nervous expectations, in short, the entire 'divine comedy' of life, including the Inferno – all this moves past him, not just like a shadow play – for he lives and suffers in the midst of these scenes – and yet also not without that fleeting sense of illusion. And perhaps several people remember, like me, amid the dangers and terrors of a dream, successfully cheering themselves up by shouting: 'It is a dream! I want to dream it some more!' I have also heard accounts of some people who had the ability to set out the causality of one and the same dream over three or more consecutive nights. These facts are clear evidence showing that our innermost beings, the secret underground in all of us, experiences its dreams with deep enjoyment and a sense of delightful necessity.

– From Friedrich Nietzsche, *The Birth of Tragedy* (1872)

Ethics and knowledge

Deep down inside, we know what is wrong and right. Don't we? See if you agree with the following scenario:

You are a bouncer in a nightclub and your boss tells you not to allow people from a certain national group into your club. What do you do? Your boss explains to you that what he is doing is legal. You know that he will fire you for the slightest mistake and without this job you would have difficulty feeding your family.

Whatever your decision, you have to weigh up the greater good against the lesser good. Such a question seems easy when we are not in it. Try this one, more personal:

A friend asks you to promise that you will not tell anybody or do anything once he has told you something. You agree. He then tells you that he has stolen money that belongs to someone you know needs it. You try to persuade him to give it back but with no success. The next day you find out that the person whom he stole the money from needs it to pay medical bills for her sick baby. What do you do?

Here the situation is different: you know what would be right morally, but you have promised not to tell. Much depends here on the value you put on a promise. Personal affiliations can cloud moral absolutes. Where do your notions of honour and your principles lie? Here we have to think about our values more carefully.

Many ethical debates are informed by the cultural context. For example, would you argue for or against the death penalty for particularly serious violent crimes? In Europe the death penalty is no longer used. If I asked the same question in Texas or Turkey, would I get the same answer? And who would be right and who would be wrong? Yet it is an entirely different thing to ask whether random murder is ever justified – most of us would say that this is never justified, under any circumstances.

As opposed to 'ethical relativism' (where what is right or wrong depends on the culture or context), here we have what we call absolutism (where a particular act is held as right or wrong, regardless of the culture or context). Do the ends justify the means? If the answer to this is 'sometimes', then you need to be careful about where you draw the line. At which point do the ends justify the means? If you know that hurting someone will benefit them, do you do it?

It may be that you find something at home you consider right, will be considered wrong in school. In this case, being educated means learning that others can be right, that there are two rights rather than a right and a wrong. You might also hear from someone close to you an idea that you know is morally wrong – this is where you ask 'How do I know I am right and he is wrong?'

EXERCISE 5

Questions

1 When you disagree about something with someone whom you respect, is it better to repress your feelings or to stand up to the person?

2 What if someone you love happens to be totally wrong? Do you try to correct them?

3 If everyone believes something to be right and you feel that they are wrong, what do you do about it?

Famous literary moral dilemmas can be found in the work of the Russian author Fyodor Dostoevsky.

REFLECTIVE QUESTION

What is an ethical dilemma in a work of literature that you are studying at the moment? See if you can write it down in a short sentence. What is your position on the dilemma? Do you feel that the author is wanting you to come to a particular judgement, and do you agree with that judgement?

Summary

ToK is not a course in ethics or religion, although we cover these themes; it is a course in critical thinking. What this means is that you do not take decisions complacently, but that you think about them beforehand, weighing up the arguments for and against your decision. How do I know I am right? or how do I know I am wrong? are important questions to ask as you move through school, and they are self-taught as it were.

Great literature often places characters and the reader in difficult, even insoluble ethical problems. It is partly for this reason that one has to wrestle with the text when reading literature – it is not merely a passive act, as mentioned in Chapter 1.

Different ways of knowing

The Harvard academic and author Howard Gardner outlined seven different types of intelligence. These are not the same thing as the Ways of Knowing in the ToK diagram, but by browsing through them you can think more critically about the way that you read literature and which forms of intelligence literature addresses. Here Mark K. Smith sums up the intelligences:

Linguistic intelligence involves sensitivity to spoken and written language, the ability to learn languages, and the capacity to use language to accomplish certain goals. This intelligence includes the ability to use language effectively to express oneself rhetorically or poetically; and language as a means to remember information. Writers, poets, lawyers and speakers are among those that Howard Gardner sees as having high linguistic intelligence.

Logical-mathematical intelligence consists of the capacity to analyze problems logically, carry out mathematical operations, and investigate issues scientifically. In Howard Gardner's words, it entails the ability to detect patterns, reason deductively and think logically. This intelligence is most often associated with scientific and mathematical thinking.

Musical intelligence involves skill in the performance, composition, and appreciation of musical patterns. It encompasses the capacity to recognize and compose musical pitches, tones, and rhythms. According to Howard Gardner musical intelligence runs in an almost structural parallel to linguistic intelligence.

Bodily-kinesthetic intelligence entails the potential of using one's whole body or parts of the body to solve problems. It is the ability to use mental abilities to coordinate bodily movements. Howard Gardner sees mental and physical activity as related.

Spatial intelligence involves the potential to recognize and use the patterns of wide space and more confined areas.

Interpersonal intelligence is concerned with the capacity to understand the intentions, motivations and desires of other people. It allows people to work effectively with others. Educators, salespeople, religious and political leaders and counsellors all need a well-developed interpersonal intelligence.

Intrapersonal intelligence entails the capacity to understand oneself, to appreciate one's feelings, fears and motivations. In Howard Gardner's view it involves having an effective working model of ourselves, and to be able to use such information to regulate our lives.

– Smith, Mark K. (2002, 2008) 'Howard Gardner and multiple intelligences', *The Encyclopedia of Informal Education*, http://www.infed.org/thinkers/gardner.htm

Essential points to remember

1. One of the essential elements of ToK is that it is a course about the way that knowledge is constructed in different 'areas of knowledge'. Literature is an art, and as an area of knowledge is generally more concerned with emotions and expression than laws or axioms.

2. Ethics as an area of knowledge is something that literature often explores through plot and characterization. It is worthwhile thinking about ethical dilemmas in the real world, and those in the fictional world, and considering how the two inform each other.

3. The ToK essay is written on a prescribed title and needs to be approached with an open but rigorous mind. You will be drawing links and making connections through this exercise. Familiarize yourself with the essay titles of the course early on, so that you are prepared. The ToK presentation is a chance for you to explore something you are interested in through a dynamic and interactive format. Again, familiarize yourself with what is needed well in advance.

FURTHER READING

Chapter 1

Achebe, Chinua, *Things Fall Apart* (Anchor Books, 1958)

Adichie, Chimamanda, *Purple Hibiscus* (Anchor Books, 2003)

Atwood, Margaret, *Oryx and Crake* (Anchor Books, 2003)

Brownstein, Rachel, *Becoming a Heroine* (Penguin, 1982)

Byatt, A.S. and Sodre, Ignes, *Imagining Characters* (Vintage Press, 1995)

Cao, Lan, *Monkey Bridge* (Penguin, 1997)

Chopin, Kate, *The Awakening* (Random House, 2001)

de Assis, Machado, *Dom Casmurro*, trans. by Helen Caldwell (Farrar, Straus and Giroux, 2009)

Ellison, Ralph, *The Invisible Man* (Vintage Press, 1995)

Faulkner, William, *As I Lay Dying* (Modern Library, 2000)

Findlay, Timothy, *The Wars* (Faber & Faber, 1977)

Forster, E.M., *Aspects of the Novel* (Harcourt, 1927)

Fuentes, Carlos, *The Old Gringo* (Farrar Straus Giroux, 1985)

Gordimer, Nadine, *July's People* (Penguin, 1981)

Gordimer, Nadine, *The Pickup* (Penguin, 2002)

Hurston, Zora Neale, *Their Eyes Were Watching God* (Harper and Row, 1990)

James, Henry, *The Portrait of a Lady* (Penguin Classics, 2003)

Matthee, Dalene, *Fiela's Child* (University of Chicago Press, 1986)

Ninh, Bao, *The Sorrow of War* (Riverhead Books, 1994)

Sidwa, Bapsi, *Cracking India* (Milkweed, 1991)

Wolf, Christa, *Accident* (Noonday Press, 1989)

Chapter 2

Brook, Peter, *The Empty Space* (Touchstone, 1968)

Durrenmatt, Freidrich, *The Visit* (Grove Press, 2010)

Fugard, Athol, '*Master Harold*' . . . *and the boys* (Penguin, 1982)

Hayman, Ronald, *How to Read a Play* (Grove Press, 1977)

Ibsen, Henrik, *A Doll's House* (Oxford University Press, 1981)

Willett, John, *Brecht on Theatre* (Hill and Wang, 1977)

Chapter 3

Boland, Eavan, *Outside History* (W.W. Norton, 1980)

Hobsbawn, Philip, *Metre, Rhythm and Verse Form* (Routledge, 1995)

Meyer, Michael, *Poetry: An Introduction* (St. Martin's, 2009)

Strand, Mark and Boland, Eavan, *The Making of a Poem* (W.W. Norton, 2000)

Chapter 4

Aristotle, *The Poetics*, trans. by S.H. Butcher (CreateSpace, 2011)

Camus, Albert, *Myth of Sisyphus, and Other Essays* (Vintage, 1991)

Gibbon, Edward, *The Decline and Fall of the Roman Empire* (Penguin, 2001)

Herodotus, *The Histories*, ed. by John M. Marincola (Penguin Classics, 2003)

Keller, Helen and Foner, Philip, *Helen Keller, her Socialist years: Writings and Speeches* (New York, International Publishers, 1967)

King Jr., Martin Luther, *Letter From A Birmingham Jail* (HarperCollins, 1994)

Levi, Primo, *If This is a Man*, trans. by Stuart Woolf (Folio Society, 2003)

Livy, *The History of Rome*, trans. by Valeria Warrior (Hackett Pub Co Inc, 2006)

MacArthur, Brian (ed.), *20th Century Speeches* (Penguin, 2000)

Miller, Arthur, *The Theater Essays of Arthur Miller* (Da Capo Press, 1996)

Montaigne, Michel, *The Complete Essays*, trans. by M.A. Screech (Penguin Classics, 1993)

Orwell, George, *Essays* (Everyman's Library, 2002)

Orwell, George, *Shooting an Elephant and Other Essays* (Penguin Books, 2003)

Pepys, Samuel, *The Diary of Samuel Pepys* (FQ Books, 2010)

Suetonius, *The Twelve Caesars*, ed. by James Rives (Penguin Classics, 2007)

Swift, Jonathan, *A Modest Proposal and Other Writings* (Penguin, 2009)

Thucydides, *The Peloponnesian Wars*, trans. by Steven Lattimore (Hackett Pub Co Inc, 1998)

William of Malmesbury, *Historia Novella: The Contemporary History*, ed. by Edmund King; trans. by K.R. Potter (Oxford University Press, 1999)

Chapter 5

Carey, Peter, *Oscar and Lucinda* (Vintage Books, 1988)

Duffy, Carol Ann, *The World's Wife* (Faber & Faber, 1999)

Morrison, Toni, *Beloved* (Vintage Books, 1987)

Chapter 6

Chopin, Kate, *The Awakening* (Random House, 2001)

Rhys, Jean, *Wide Sargasso Sea* (Penguin, 2006)

Roy, Arundhati, *The God of Small Things* (Random House, 2008)

Chapter 7

Coleridge, Samuel Taylor, *The Rime of the Ancient Mariner, Kubla Khan, Christabel, and the Conversation Poems* (Digireads.com, 2009)

Yeats, William Butler, *The Collected Poems of W.B. Yeats* (Scribner, 1996)

Chapter 8

Blake, William, *Songs of Innocence and Experience* (Oxford University Press, 1977)

Conrad, Joseph, *Heart of Darkness* (Oxford University Press, 2008)

Donne, John, *John Donne's Poetry*, ed. by Donald R. Dickson (Norton & Company, 2007)

Frost, Robert, *The Poetry of Robert Frost: The Collected Poems*, ed. by Edward Connery Latham (Holt Paperbacks, 2002)

Murray, Les, *Conscious and Verbal: Poems* (Farrar, Straus and Giroux, 2001)

Shakespeare, William, *The Oxford Shakespeare: The Complete Works*, ed. by Stanley Wells et al. (Oxford University Press, 2005)

Chapter 9

Bashō, Matsuo, *The Narrow Road to the Deep North and Other Travel Sketches*, Trans. by Nobuyuki Yuasa (Penguin Classics, 1967)

Cavafy, C. P., *Collected Poems*, trans. by Edmund Keeley and Philip Sherrard, ed. by George Savidis (Princeton University Press, 2009)

Chekhov, Anton, *Three Sisters*, trans. by Laurence Senelick (W.W. Norton, 2010)

p'Bitek, Okot, *Song of Lawino & Song of Ocol* (Heinemann, 1984)

Chapter 10

Austen, Jane, *Pride and Prejudice* (Oxford University Press, 2008)

Austen, Jane, *Emma* (W.W. Norton, 2011)

Dostoevsky, Fyodor, *Crime and Punishment* (Oxford University Press, 2008)

Elliot, T.S., *T. S. Eliot: Collected Poems, 1909–1962* (Harcourt Brace Jovanovich, 1991)

Ngũgĩ wa Thiong'o, *A Grain of Wheat* (Penguin, 2010)

Salinger, J.D., *The Catcher in the Rye* (Back Bay Books, 2001)

Chapter 11

Bastian, Sue et al., *Theory of Knowledge* (Pearson, 2008)

Nietzsche, Friedrich, *The Birth of Tragedy Out of the Spirit of Music*, trans. by Shaun Whiteside (Penguin Classics, 1994)

Pinker, Steven, *The Language Instinct: How the Mind Creates Language* (Harper Perennial Modern Classics, 2007)

Smith, Mark K. (2002, 2008) 'Howard Gardner and multiple intelligences', The Encyclopedia of Informal Education, http://www.infed.org/thinkers/gardner.htm

Thouless, R. H., *Straight & Crooked Thinking* (Hodder & Stoughton, 2011)

GLOSSARY

Alliteration The repetition of the beginning consonant sound in a series of two or more words in a line of poetry.

Allusion An indirect suggestion.

Anadiplosis Repetition of a word at the end of one clause and the beginning of the following clause.

Anaphora Repetition of a word or phrase at the beginning of different clauses.

Antagonist The character who gets in the way of the protagonist of a play, poem or novel and tries to foul his or her plans.

Assonance The repetition of vowel sounds within a line or series of lines in a poem.

Autobiography An account of a life written by that person.

Biography An account of someone's life written by someone else.

Cacophony A harsh and discordant mixture of sounds.

Caesura A stop in a line of poetry, often but not always indicated by punctuation such as full stops and semi-colons, or by a natural break in breathing.

Catharsis Emotional release through artistic effects.

Characterization The creation and convincing representation of fictitious characters.

Chosism /Objectification When a human or animal is treated as an object.

Climax A powerful ending to a play, poem or novel.

Comparison To show/describe/demonstrate how something is similar.

Connotation When something connotes something else it suggests or infers it, rather than states it emphatically.

Consonance The repetition of a consonant sound within a line of poetry.

Context The set of circumstances or facts (background) that surround a particular event, situation, work of fiction, etc.

Contrast To show/describe/demonstrate how something differs from something else.

Denotation Showing or naming something directly.

Dénouement The final resolution or conclusion of a dramatic or narrative plot.

Dialogue Conversation between two or more persons in a novel or play.

Diction The specific vocabulary used by a writer or speaker to express his or her point of view.

Didactic Intended or inclined to teach, preach or instruct.

Dramatic irony When the audience knows something about a character that the character himself or herself does not know.

Enjambment/Run-on line When a clause runs from one line of poetry to the next without punctuation.

Epistolary novel A novel written in the form of letters.

Epizeuxis Incremental repetition of a word or phrase.

Euphemism Making something negative sound more positive (e.g. 'He passed away.').

Euphony Agreeableness of sound; pleasing effect to the ear, especially a pleasant-sounding or harmonious combination or succession of words.

Genre A class, category or type of artistic endeavour having a particular form, content, technique, etc.

Hamartia A tragic flaw in a character.

Hubris Wanton arrogance/ tempting fate.

Hyperbole Exaggeration for rhetorical effect.

Image patterns The repetition of images, not necessarily in uninterrupted succession.

Image A word (or words) appealing to at least one of our senses, and thereby generating a response in the reader.

Irony When things turn out differently, or are different, to what was expected or what was said.

Juxtaposition When two things are set alongside one another so as to create a strong contrast.

Lexis A technical term for vocabulary. When we say 'lexical field' we are referring to the vocabulary used by an author in a given text.

Linear approach Also known as a line-by-line or chronological analysis, one that follows the text in order.

Literary criticism A school of literary criticism is an established way of approaching literature, such as Marxist or feminist criticism.

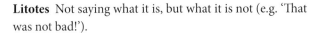

Litotes Not saying what it is, but what it is not (e.g. 'That was not bad!').

Metaphor Saying that something is something else to express emotion or ideas (e.g. 'He is a God!').

Metonymy When the part represents the whole (e.g. 'The crown' represents a monarchy).

Metre The rhythmic arrangement of stressed and unstressed syllables in verse, usually according to the number and kind of feet in a line of poetry.

Monologue A form of dramatic entertainment, comedic solo, or the like by a single speaker. It is different to a soliloquy in that the character can address the audience directly.

Motif A repeated pattern of any type within a text.

Objective Not influenced by personal feelings, interpretations or prejudice; based on facts; unbiased: an objective opinion.

Onomastics The study of the history and origin of names, especially personal names.

Onomatopoeia A device in which the word sounds like what it describes.

Opsis What you see on stage.

Oxymoron Two words of opposite meaning that follow one another (e.g. 'icy fire' or 'dark light').

Pastiche An artistic work in a style that imitates another work, artist or period.

Persona The narrator of or a character in a literary work, sometimes identified with the author.

Personification The representation of a thing or abstraction in the form of a person.

Plagiarism When you take someone else's text or ideas and try to present them as your own.

Protagonist The leading character, hero or heroine of a drama or other literary work, who drives the plot forward.

Register The style of language that is used in certain social contexts, such as formal or informal register.

Rhetoric The art of using speech effectively to persuade, influence or please.

Rhyme scheme The pattern of rhyme established by a poem, based on the sound at the end of each line.

Rhythm In poetry, the rhythm of a phrase is created by its use of stressed and unstressed syllables.

Simile Comparing something to something else using the words 'like' or 'as'.

Soliloquy An utterance or discourse by a person who is talking to himself or herself, or is disregardful of or oblivious to any hearers present (often used as a device in drama to disclose a character's innermost thoughts).

Stanza A verse in a poem.

Subjective Placing excessive emphasis on one's own moods, attitudes and opinions, or showing personal bias.

Syllepsis A figure of speech in which a word is applied to two others in different senses (e.g. 'The runner hit the car and the limits of his endurance at the same time.')

Syllogism A logically constructed argument.

Symbol Something that represents something else.

Synaesthesia Ascribing a colour a sound, a smell or a temperature.

Syntax The way that words and phrases are arranged to form phrases, clauses and sentences.

Thematic approach When you extract the themes, stylistic choices, messages, ideas and developments of the text, and use them to discuss the work using your own organized structure.

Theme A subject, idea or common element in a work of literature, which expresses an understanding of some aspect of human nature. Themes can be explicit or implicit.

Tone The writer's attitude toward his or her subject matter, such as anger, indifference or irony.

Tragicomedy A dramatic or other literary composition combining elements of both tragedy and comedy.

INDEX